BECOMING INUMMARIK

D1304691

MCGILL-QUEEN'S NATIVE AND NORTHERN SERIES
(In memory of Bruce G. Trigger)

Sarah Carter and Arthur J. Ray, Editors

Becoming Inummarik

Men's Lives in an Inuit Community

PETER COLLINGS

McGill-Queen's University Press

Montreal & Kingston · London · Ithaca

© McGill-Queen's University Press 2014

ISBN 978-0-7735-4312-6 (cloth)
ISBN 978-0-7735-4313-3 (paper)
ISBN 978-0-7735-9032-8 (ePDF)
ISBN 978-0-7735-9033-5 (ePUB)

Legal deposit first quarter 2014
Bibliothèque nationale du Québec

Printed in Canada on acid-free paper that is 100% ancient forest free
(100% post-consumer recycled), processed chlorine free

This book has been published with the help of a grant from the International
Council of Canadian Studies through its Publishing Fund.

McGill-Queen's University Press acknowledges the support of the Canada
Council for the Arts for our publishing program. We also acknowledge the
financial support of the Government of Canada through the Canada Book
Fund for our publishing activities.

Library and Archives Canada Cataloguing in Publication

Collings, Peter, 1968–, author
  Becoming inummariik: men's lives in an Inuit community / Peter Collings.

(McGill-Queen's Native and Northern series; 73)
Includes bibliographical references and index.
Issued in print and electronic formats.
ISBN 978-0-7735-4312-6 (bound). – ISBN 978-0-7735-4313-3 (pbk.).
ISBN 978-0-7735-9032-8 (ePDF). – ISBN 978-0-7735-9033-5 (ePUB)

1. Inuit – Northwest Territories – Ulukhaktok – Social conditions. 2. Inuit –
Northwest Territories – Ulukhaktok – Social life and customs. 3. Men – Northwest
Territories – Ulukhaktok – Social conditions. 4. Men – Northwest Territories –
Ulukhaktok – Social life and customs. 5. Masculinity – Social aspects – Northwest
Territories – Ulukhaktok. I. Title. II. Series: McGill-Queen's native and northern
series; 73

E99.E7C667 2014   305.38'8971207193   C2013-907272-1
                                                     C2013-907273-X

This book was typeset by Interscript in 11/14 Minion.

Contents

Acknowledgments

Twenty years' worth of field research and academic scholarship has left a trail of gratitude that I cannot hope to retrace adequately here. The process of writing this book has provided me with an opportunity to think about, and now thank, many of the people who have provided encouragement, advice, and support, not only for this project but also for my research career.

I suppose the place to start is with the most important people who influenced the course of this book. These are, most generally, the people of Ulukhaktok, who have tolerated my presence, my idiosyncrasies, and my endless and seemingly strange questions for nearly two decades. Without the support of the community, my research career would have gone absolutely nowhere. Even so, there are Ulukhaktomiut who deserve special mention, because they have provided friendship and assistance in ways that have profoundly influenced my life. Louie Nigiyok, Morris Nigiyok, Colin Okeena, Adam Kudlak, Jerry Akoakhion, Roger Memogana, Jack Kataoyak, Jack Akhiatak, Nichol Uluariuk, Albert Elias, and, especially, Harold Wright, have, over the years, demonstrated and explained the rules, provided ears to listen, dispatched plenty of good advice, and taught me important lessons. They have my endless gratitude.

On the more academic side of things, I am indebted to numerous people, though I can here single out only a few. Pat Draper, my PhD advisor, first captured my interest in the life course and human development. Her guidance, mostly, as I recall, over chips, salsa, and beer in her kitchen, helped set me on my way. I believe I learned more anthropology in that kitchen than I ever did in a classroom. George Wenzel, a colleague, collaborator, and good friend at McGill University, has for twenty years been a constant sounding board as I have worked through the material that has ended up in this book. Lance Gravlee, Alyson Young, Sharon Abramowitz, and Meredith Marten, friends and colleagues at UF, have been invaluable for keeping the writing happening, providing feedback on earlier drafts of this manuscript, and patiently listening as I worked through the problems of thinking and writing about the material presented here. Jonathan Crago, my editor at McGill-Queen's University Press, has been both enthusiastic and remarkably patient as I completed this book. His questions and suggestions have always been helpful and thought provoking, and the result is far better for his assistance and guidance. Finally, I would like to mention the continuing influence of the late Richard Condon, who was brave enough, or perhaps foolish enough, to take me to Ulukhaktok in the first place. When he earned the award that led to the 1992–93 research, he had several choices of research assistant, yet he chose me. The choice was not without some risk: he left me with the responsibility of working alone in Ulukhaktok, collecting data for his project for a full seven months. I had only completed a single year of graduate coursework, and I had no prior field research experience. Richard's untimely death in 1995 was the tremendous loss of a wonderful mentor, an excellent scholar, and a great friend.

I have been fortunate over the years to receive funding support for the fieldwork, my primary funding coming over the years from the National Science Foundation's Arctic Social Sciences Program, currently directed by Anna Kerttula. I am grateful for their support; not only did they fund Richard's work, which supported my first year in the field, they funded my dissertation research, and they supported the 2007 research that forms the foundation of this volume. While NSF has my gratitude, it is important to note additional funding sources that have enabled my research. I have been supported over the years by internal grants from both the University of Florida and Penn State University. The Canadian Embassy in Washington, DC, has also been generous in funding travel to and research in Ulukhaktok.

Finally, I must acknowledge the instrumental role my wife, Maya Shastri, has played in all of this, for reading earlier drafts of this document, for suffering some of the slings and arrows of fieldwork, but mostly for just being there, patiently supporting me during both good times and bad. In February 1997, she arrived in Ulukhaktok after four days of travel, suffering with a double ear infection. The plane touched down in deteriorating weather conditions, which quickly turned to whiteout. We lived for the remainder of that year in some of the most primitive conditions in the settlement. When we moved into the Roman Catholic Mission House, all of the pipes were broken, the water pump was not working, and the water heater bore the mysterious label "Do not plug in for 15 minutes." In retrospect, it was not a great way to introduce her to the Arctic. After a couple of days of calling in favours, however, something resembling plumbing was installed, and some semblance of normal living was achieved. A few weeks later, we discovered that the cryptic sign on the water heater really meant that the thermostat was broken. We mistakenly left the heater plugged in overnight, and the pressure release blew in the morning, turning the house into a lovely sauna for the remainder of the morning and giving us ice-glazed windows for the remainder of the winter. Following that, every week saw some similar adventure with the house. Since then Maya has tolerated my months away in the field and the evenings and weekends spent working with far more grace and tolerance than I will ever have, for which I am eternally thankful.

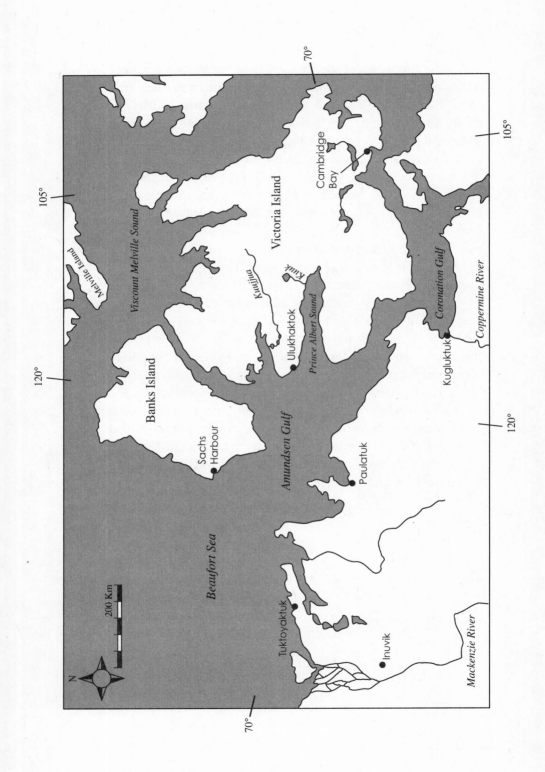

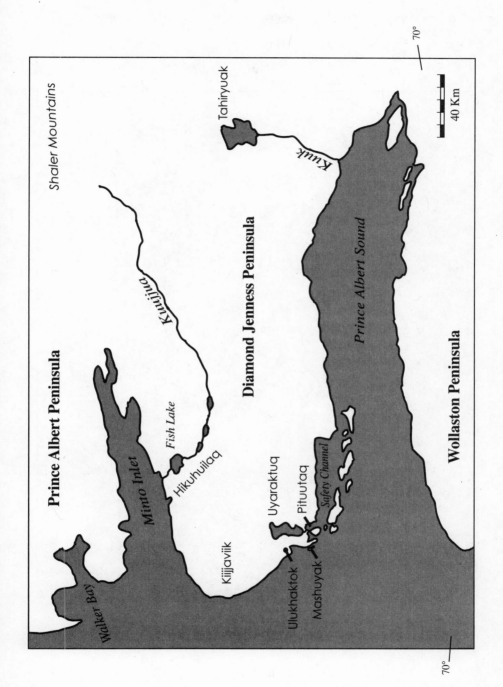

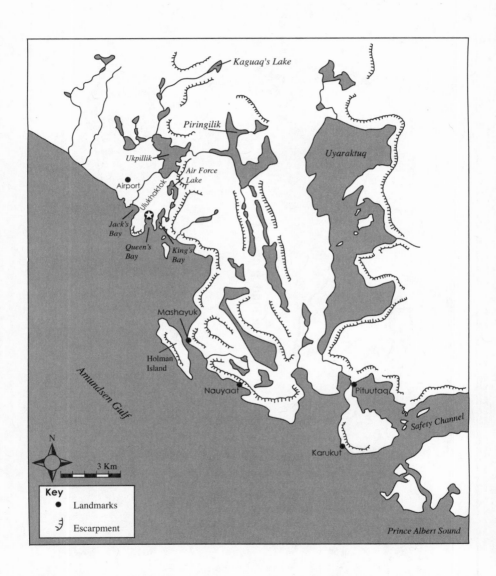

Kaguaq's Lake

Piringilik

Uyaraktuq

Ukpillik

Air Force
Lake

Airport

Ulukhaktok

Jack's
Bay

Queen's
Bay

King's
Bay

Mashayuk

Holman
Island

Nauyaaf

Pituutaq

Safety Channel

Karukut

Amundsen Gulf

N

3 Km

Key

● Landmarks

ℑ Escarpment

Prince Albert Sound

BECOMING INUMMARIK

1

Time for a Snack

The drive from the airport to town is less than three kilometres, a dusty trip along a gravel road on a dry summer day in June 2007. Despite five regularly scheduled flights each week – three from Yellowknife, two from Inuvik – and numerous charters, the arrival of a plane still draws a crowd. Ulukhaktok's population is just a little over four hundred people, but there is still a sizable group here, a combination of departing and arriving passengers and their families and friends, some airport-associated workers, and a few Inuit who are simply passing time, curious to know who is coming and going, and why.

I walk down the stairs of the plane, feeling the cool east wind in my face. The First Air agent has already backed his pickup truck to the plane. His son is beginning to pull luggage out of the hold. Two other pickups, one for the Northern Store, the other for the Co-op, wait their turn to remove their cargo: perishable groceries, equipment on order for their stores, and, in the case of the Co-op, the mail for the post office.

I make the short walk across the gravel tarmac to the terminal, a small building consisting of the ticket desk, a waiting area, two storage closets, bathrooms, and the traffic controller's office. The waiting area is half full of travellers and relatives, here to welcome theirs back to town or to see them off. Visiting southerners would find this a remarkably relaxed atmosphere, and also remarkably insecure. There are no metal detectors, nor are there constant admonitions to watch for stray luggage or to pay attention to the latest colour-coded security threat. The only hint of authority is the RCMP officer, and he is only here to pick up a courier package from the flight agent. The observer-communicator's office is wide open. Dan, who is on duty today, sits with his feet on the desk, chatting amicably with two young men who are heading out to Yellowknife.

The luggage is off the plane now, and Jonathan drives the pickup to the front of the building. Arriving passengers know the drill and make their way outside to take their bags from the truck bed. Most have rides arranged ahead of time, and they strap their bags to ATVs and hop on the back, and their drivers take off for town. A few others have arranged lifts with the Co-op or Northern workers, and they wait until the trucks are unloaded. Another possibility is the taxi, which is just pulling up with passengers for the return flight to Kugluktuk and on to Yellowknife.

All the coming and going seems a bit chaotic. Who is driving the taxi? How does the driver know who needs a ride and who does not? Yet it all works out, despite few words being exchanged. Somehow Willie knows to wait for me, even though he had no idea I would be on today's plane. I finally walk outside after some handshakes and "welcome backs," grab my bags, and head to the taxi.

Willie too shakes my hand. "I didn't know you even left town. For how long you were gone?"

"Oh, only a couple of weeks. Went down to see the family. So hard to be away, you know."

Of course he knows. Many Inuit have terrible difficulty being away from Ulukhaktok for any length of time, family connections and contact being so important to well-being. To Willie the solution is obvious. "You should just bring them all with you. You could stay longer. And people want to see your kids."

"I wish I could. But plane tickets are so expensive, eh? Especially to Yellowknife." At $3,000 a ticket from Florida, where I currently live and work, I could put a down payment on a house with what it would cost to get my family here.

This resonates with Willie, who knows that the bulk of my airfare to Ulukhaktok is the cost of flying from Yellowknife. "Oh, yeah, it's really bad. Worst Air keeps jacking up the prices. Making it hard on the people."

We load my bags into the back of the taxi – really a small bus, owned and operated by the hamlet government – and get in. Today there is only one other passenger, tall and gaunt, who has not spoken since Yellowknife. He deliberately looks at his watch, a silent reprimand, apparently, for taking too long. Willie and I ignore him. Where could he possibly want to go in a hurry? We are in Ulukhaktok in mid-June. The sun is above the horizon. The time on the clock is nearly irrelevant.

Willie starts the engine, backs out, and heads down the road to the settlement, following the billowing dust of the ATVs ahead of us.

"How's the ducks? They flying yet?" I ask.

"Oh, yeah, they're really giving her now, boy. My son got twenty-five already. He's down at Mashuyak with my father-in-law. Lots of people getting ducks now."

We talk about ducks, and about ice conditions, which are downright bad. The ice has already broken up, and hunters are going to and from Mashuyak by boat. "Seems to be happening more and more like this each year. Funny weather."

Eventually, Willie turns to ask the question related to his job, one eye on the road. "So where you going? Same place?"

"You could just drop me at Isaac's. I'm going to leave my stuff there for now." Truth is, I'm not yet sure where I will be staying. I'll have to check in at the hamlet office to find out.

"You can't stay where you were before, that duplex across from Ukaliq's? There must be no one there yet. I thought you were still there."

"Yeah, I think I can stay there, but I need to make sure. I still got the key. But Martha thought there might be a social worker coming in, so I might have to find someplace else."

"I never heard nothing about that. We already got one social worker – why do we need another? The one here doesn't do anything."

I admit I don't know as we pull into the settlement, slowing down as we drive by the housing shop and garage and turn the corner onto the main drag – for lack of a better term, as the streets seem to have no names. Before the settlement grew around it, it served as the old runway before the airport was built. Willie pulls up at the hotel, and the taciturn fellow gets off, handing Willie the $10 fare without a word.

Willie gets back in. "What's up with that guy? So unfriendly."

"I don't know. He never said anything since Yellowknife."

"Some people. I'll take you to Isaac's, then I'll give you a ride to the hamlet."

He turns back onto the main drag, and we retrace our route to Isaac's. Isaac is my closest friend in Ulukhaktok, much like an older brother. Both he and Ida are at work now, as it's only 2:30 and not yet time for coffee break, though Ida should be home soon. I drop my stuff beside the porch stairs, a computer bag, rifle case, and pack. The door is un-locked, but I'm guessing that their son Ronald might be sleeping, so I don't go in.

Willie is waiting for me. "I could walk," I say through the open win-dow. It's not far to the hamlet, and I need a walk. I've been on the plane since nine this morning.

"Get in. I'm going that way anyway." So I get in.

Willie pulls up at the hamlet building, and I pay him for the ride, pocketing the receipt. He makes for the building's side entrance that opens into the break room. He's getting a head start on coffee, though his workday is really finished. Driving the taxi is part-time, casual work, limited to meeting the planes and occasionally ferrying elders around to meetings or to the health centre. After coffee, he is likely to head home and get ready for an evening of duck hunting on the water.

The Hamlet of Ulukhaktok, like most settlements in the Canadian Arctic, is a creation of convenience by and for outside interests. It was founded during the late 1930s when the Hudson's Bay Company con-solidated its regional trading operations at the current location. As others such as Richard Condon (1994) and Peter Usher (1965) have written, the H B C was initially attracted by the deep-water harbour at King's Bay, which allowed supply ships to winter in the ice, protected from storms and drifting floes. The Roman Catholic Church also relo-cated its missionary activities here, constructing a mission house. Around the same time, Natkusiak, an Alaskan Inupiaq who had worked as a guide for the explorer Vilhjalmur Stefansson, decided to settle here with his family.

Although the Inuit in the region – then known as Copper Eskimos – continued to live a seasonally nomadic existence focused on hunting and fishing, the 1940s and 1950s were a period when they were slowly drawn into the fur trade, trading fox furs at the Hudson's Bay post. The small settlement was then known as Holman, or Holman Island, the name taken from a small island about five miles to the south. In the early days, Inuit came into the settlement only periodically, to trade for man-ufactured items, the highlights of this cycle being the Christmas and Easter celebrations. During this time, a few families began to reside more or less permanently in the settlement, constructing houses out of scrap materials. Many of these were families in difficult circumstances or struck down by illness, widows without social support, men incapaci-tated by injury.

By the 1960s, movement into the settlement increased in intensity. Inuit began to move off the land, seeking access to the manufactured housing provided by the government and searching for wage labour opportunities, a source of cash for the always-high costs of hunting and trapping equipment and imported foodstuffs like flour, tea, sugar, and tobacco. Even as they began moving into the settlement, however, most families remained committed to a seasonal round of hunting, fishing, and trapping. Many continued to spend significant parts of the year living on the land in seasonal fishing or sealing camps.

Even so, the 1960s marked a sea change in terms of Inuit social and historical processes. Residence in the settlement spurred a number of important shifts in Inuit social structure, economy, and polity that have profoundly influenced the cohort of the men, like Willie, who are the focus of this book. As Condon (1987, 1990a, 1990b) has argued, settlement brought Inuit into close contact with kin, friends, and ac-quaintances for extended periods, and this close contact, coupled with improved access to southern health care and a social safety net, re-sulted in a baby boom.

As the settlement grew over the next thirty years, the Canadian gov-ernment expanded the range and quality of services. The public hous-ing that initially attracted Inuit to the settlement first arrived in 1962, small, prefabricated units designed to keep people out of the elements and out of the makeshift scrap houses that passed for local housing. By the early 1970s, new public housing units were constructed and subsequently equipped with electricity, running water, and internal sewage tanks. Such amenities required support services, and, consequently, the kinds and number of wage-earning jobs in the settlement also grew. The need for water, sewage, and trash drivers, settlement maintenance workers, public housing workers, and support staff provided earning opportunities. A public school was built and periodically upgraded. A nursing station appeared in the early 1970s, replaced by a larger health centre in the mid-1980s, which was then expanded fifteen years later.

Today, an uninterrupted walk around the settlement can take upwards of forty-five minutes. It has grown to include two retail stores – the Holman Eskimo Co-op and the Northern Store (formerly the Hudson's Bay Company) – a hotel and restaurant (the Arctic Char Inn, managed by the Co-op), a state-of-the-art health centre with residences for two full-time nurses, a public school and associated adult education centre that provides a K–12 education and opportunities for continuing education, a community hall, a hockey arena, two community wellness centres, some one hundred public or privately owned housing units, a hamlet "town hall" building, the Ulukhaktok Community Corporation's offices, and an array of warehouses, garages, and workshops. In many respects, the activities around the settlement during the business day sound much like those in any other town in Canada, as people move back and forth between homes and jobs, service trucks move about, and kids go to and from school.

The physical expansion of the settlement is, of course, predicated upon the growth of the population. Though originally known as Copper Eskimos, and sometimes today as Copper Inuit or Inuinnait, the population of the contemporary settlement is composed of a number of different groups. The original inhabitants of the region actually belonged to one of two bands of Copper Eskimos, the Kangiryuarmiut and the Kanghiryuatjagmiut (Jenness 1922, 41), who inhabited the regions, broadly speaking, around Prince Albert Sound and Minto Inlet, respectively. These bands began trading into what is now Ulukhaktok after the HBC closed operations at Alaervik, in Prince Albert Sound, and Walker Bay, in Minto Inlet (Condon 1994). During the 1960s, as Inuinnait began to permanently settle in Holman, the two groups were joined by a smaller group of Puivlingmiut – Copper Eskimos who had lived around and traded into the Read Island H B C post, which closed in 1962 (Usher 1965, 54). While some of the Read Islanders moved to Ulukhaktok, others settled in Coppermine (now Kugluktuk).

In terms of Copper Eskimo heritage, Ulukhaktok consists of three different though intermarried bands that have all settled together in the same place with a fourth group from the west, people who trace their descent from Mackenzie Delta Eskimos and Alaskan Inupiat who began settling at Ulukhaktok. The descendants of the Mackenzie Delta Eskimos and Inupiat today call themselves Inuvialuit. Since the ratification of Inuvialuit Final Agreement in 1984, Ulukhaktok (whose residents voted to join the Inuvialuit land claim) has been called an Inuvialuit community, one that has grown from a population of about 130 in 1960 to somewhere between 410 and 440 today, depending on who is counting and what standard is being used.

The intermixing of these different groups has had cultural consequences. As but one example, the general consensus among outsiders is that the local language is endangered and possibly worse, though there is confusion – even within the settlement – about what the local language actually *is*. According to the Inuvialuit Regional Corporation, people in Ulukhaktok speak Kangiryuarmiut (Lowe 1983), itself considered a dialect of Inuvialuktun. Ulukhaktomiut, however, prefer to refer to the language as Inuinnaqtun and tend to consider it a separate language, one also spoken in Kugluktuk and Cambridge Bay, communities that voted to join the Nunavut land claim.

In any case, English is the lingua franca in the settlement. Although people do speak Inuinnaqtun in some public settings, it is far more common for Inuinnaqtun words to be employed within the context of English grammar, and for words to be anglicized as a result: "I broke my sleds and now I need to cut some new *napus*." "I went out yesterday and saw lots of *qingaliks*." "My husband is not at home. He went *audluaking* with his dad." Conversely, it is quite common to hear English constructions and usage that sound particularly strange, but upon reflection appear to be direct translations of Inuinnaqtun into English.

The ubiquitous "What you are doing?" uttered by children appears to be one of these. Others are simple turns of phrase, "tomorrow next day" used in preference to "the day after tomorrow," for example. Additionally, it is still quite common for gendered pronouns to be used willy-nilly, without regard to the sex of the referent. For the uninitiated, it can be disconcerting to ask if Joe is home and receive the response from Joe's wife, "No, she's at a meeting tonight." Inuinnaqtun lacks gendered pronouns, and even adults raised largely in an English-speaking context do not appear to pay attention to them. Even though English is the dominant language of the community, there are conventions (discussed in further detail in chapter 3) that make it somewhat different from the English of southern Canada.

SETTLING IN

As I pass through the main entrance of the hamlet building and into the large reception area, I am struck by the smell of bureaucracy and Javex bleach. I could be in any town hall in North America. Shannon, the receptionist, hangs up the phone, picks up a microphone, and calls one of the water-truck drivers. Someone needs a fill-up. She sees me and waves. Once her call is completed, she gets up and shakes my hand. "Welcome back."

"Thanks. It's good to be back. Is Lawrence around?"

Lawrence is the current (though soon to be former) senior administrative officer, the SAO for short. Many Inuit refer to the position as the SOB. Lawrence is a Qablunaaq, an outsider hired to manage the operations of the municipal government. No one seems to like him, nor, indeed, do they know anything about him. He largely keeps to himself. I have only spoken with him a few times, in conjunction with finding a place to stay while I am here.

Shannon shrugs. "He's out this afternoon. But Martha is in back. She can help you out."

I take the shortcut through the meeting chambers, walk through the break room where Willie has almost finished brewing a pot of coffee, and head down the hall to Martha's office. The second-in-command, she is the real power in the municipal government. As Shannon promised, she is happy to help me. No, the duplex is empty until August, so I can stay there until then. Yes, the rent is the same. Yes, keep the key until I leave, then just give it to Charlie before I go. I write the cheque, Martha writes a receipt, and my summer housing issue is resolved. That was easy, though I will have to come to some other arrangement for the autumn. Given the way housing is crunched in Ulukhaktok, I may have to stay in my storage shack.

When I was planning the timetable for the current research project, begun in March, I had some concerns about where I might stay. In previous years, making arrangements for housing was a generally straightforward process, though it did require a bit of a hunt to find the most suitable arrangements. Ulukhaktok seemed to be the unusual Arctic village in that housing was always available, especially for outsiders like me, even if the prices were somewhat steep and the quality was, by local standards, slightly substandard. There were always several privately owned units available for rent, and even some of the units owned by the hamlet were available.

That situation has changed in recent years, however, due to a combination of factors. One of those is changes in housing policy and rent scales that have served to drive some Inuit out of public housing, leaving them scrambling for housing in what passes for the private sector in Ulukhaktok. Several public housing units have been condemned due to age and poor condition, and a few others have been converted from residential to community use. One residence, formerly government-owned and used as housing for schoolteachers, was recently converted to a wellness centre. Another was reconditioned and now serves as a daycare.

A further factor in the current housing shortage is economic development. In the year prior to my 2007 research period, mining and exploration interests reappeared in Ulukhaktok, now the northern outpost of the Northwest Territories' diamond boom. Several companies have been in and out of the settlement since, throwing money around and promising employment opportunities galore, but in the process they occupy whatever unit they can rent and pay far beyond "market" rates.

Back in March 2007, I was fortunate enough to crash with another researcher, Tristan Pearce, a geographer working on economic development and traditional knowledge transmission among Inuit teenagers. He had secured the last empty duplex owned by the hamlet, and he graciously allowed me to kip on the floor while we were both in town. The unit itself, however, was designated as housing for "health workers." There seemed to be an agreement with the territorial health board that the hamlet could do what it wanted with the unit so long as there were no health workers in need of housing. If, however, the health centre were ever to hire health workers who required housing, they would have first rights on the duplex. I had stayed in these units in the past, several times, in fact, and had come to the conclusion that there might never be enough health workers to occupy these units. The centre itself already has two apartments for its staff nurses. There seemed to be no need for these units, though the settlement had social workers in the past. And, indeed, the other side of the duplex was already let to the social worker Willie referred to on the ride into town, a young woman in the role of "addictions counsellor."

Tristan's fieldwork ended in mid-April, but I arranged to stay on in the duplex through the first leg of my research visit, which lasted through late May. When I left, Martha and I understood that as long as no other social worker was looming on the horizon, I could continue to rent the apartment. Martha, however, has now confirmed that another social worker will be arriving in the fall, so I find myself mentally preparing for an autumn living in my shack. I'll have to spend some of the summer remodelling it to make it habitable.

There are other options, of course. I could stay with an Inuit family, but I decided to avoid that route when I was planning the logistics of this particular research trip. The current tenant relations officer, responsible for calculating public housing rents and chasing down delinquent payments, was a particularly tenacious young woman who seemed to believe strongly in the importance of following The Rules. She indicated that, were I to stay with someone in public housing, she would raise the rent to the maximum allotted because of my "salary" (or what she imagined my salary to be), which would be added to the income of the household. Somehow, workers in the hamlet offices have come to believe that researchers have an endless supply of money.

For now, though, the duplex is still mine, and I leave the hamlet building happy to know I have a place to stay. But where should I go next this afternoon? I should say hello to Isaac. The craft shop where he is working is just down the street, next door to the Northern. I can say hello and then pick up some groceries. I head in that direction, farther away from the duplex. My bags can sit in front of Isaac's for the time being. No one will touch them.

Isaac is in, working on some prints. He has been an artist in the craft shop for nearly twenty years. It is a decent living, working for the Co-op, but not a great one, as in recent years his pay has been cut dramatically. The Co-op, or, more properly, the Holman Eskimo Co-operative, was founded in 1961 at the encouragement of Father Henri Tardy, an Oblate priest who served as a missionary in Ulukhaktok until he retired in the early 1980s. Originally founded as a means for generating money through arts and crafts sales, the Co-op has since expanded into a general store, competing with the Northern Store. It is currently affiliated with Arctic Co-operatives Ltd, an association of co-ops across the North.

Isaac is rolling ink onto a woodcut, printing off the design on sheets of special paper. "Hi, Pete! *Qanuripit*?" He reaches to shake my hand.

"*Naammaktunga*! How are you?"

"Oh, I'm fine. Just finishing up here. Must be time to quit soon, go home for coffee."

"This for a collection?" I ask. I was not aware that the Co-op was putting one together.

"No, I'm doing these for myself. Ida is going out for medical in a couple of weeks. She's going to try and sell them in Yellowknife."

Isaac places the paper on the inked wood and rubs the ink thoroughly into the paper. He pulls the paper back, revealing the print. "It's good enough," he says and hangs the sheet to dry, washes his hands, and turns back to me. "Where you staying?"

"Same place. I can have it until August. My stuff is by your porch, though. I'll get it later. How's things? Any ducks?"

"I got a few, but I've been letting Sonny shoot them. He was out last night boating, got quite a few. He must be sleeping now, he was coming in at lunchtime."

I watch as Isaac cleans his tools, beginning to pack things away for the day. "Okay. What you going to do now?" I ask him.

"I don't know. I should get some grub from the store, though." Once he finishes cleaning up, we head over to the Co-op. From there we split up. Although some Inuit are dedicated to the Co-op and only shop there, most shop at both the Northern and the Co-op, searching for the best deal. Generally one has to shop at both stores, simply because by some unspoken agreement they refuse to compete directly with each other. For example, the Northern carries snowmobile parts for Bombardier machines, the Co-op for Polaris.

I make a few purchases at the Co-op, then go back to the Northern. Shopping is a slow process, partly because it's so social. Both stores are quite small, their size more on par with a southern convenience store than a grocery store. By late afternoon, they tend to be full of customers all saying hello and engaging in casual conversation. Some Inuit habitually go to the stores merely for the social interaction, with no intention of purchasing anything.

By the time I leave the Northern, my hand is sore. Although only few people seemingly knew that I left the settlement last month, once it became known I was gone, everyone began going out of their way to welcome me back. It is heartwarming and genuine. Although much of this welcoming is brief, a handshake and a hello, the formality of the greeting evident, with other Inuit it is a much longer affair, a lengthy conversation. After purchasing my groceries at the Northern, it takes me an additional ninety minutes to make the ten-minute walk back to the duplex.

Edward Kuniluk is walking by in the other direction, and we stop and talk for a while, catching up on news. "How's it going, Pete? I never see you for a long time." He offers his hand, though it's only been five weeks since I last saw him.

I take it up. "I'm doing good. But how are you? What you been up to?" When I left, Edward was out of town, working for a couple of weeks for the mining company.

"Just got back three days ago from working." The way he says it, it sounds like he's been sick. He continues, "Was doing some monitoring work up there," referring to the drilling sites about Minto Inlet, near the old Muskox mines. The site is several hundred kilometres north of town. Although Ulukhatkok claimed the lands as part of the land claims process, it has been decades since anyone hunted that far away. The mining company has been exploring for promising deposits. Though they have most of their own outside labour for the actual exploration activities, Inuit like Edward have been hired as unskilled labour in the camps or to satisfy the environmental monitoring requirements stipulated by the government and the Inuvialuit Regional Corporation. The pay is decent, but the work is temporary at best.

"You going to go back?" I ask. Edward, in addition to being a friend, is also an informant. If he is going to be gone for the summer, I won't be able to work with him then.

"Nah. Too boring, and too hard to deal with those people. Those Qablunaat, boy, they can really swear. Money's good, but it's time to go fishing. Already missing duck season. Where you staying now?" he asks, changing the subject.

I tell him I'm still in the duplex.

"That's good. Don is coming in two weeks. He's not sure he's got a place to stay."

"Is he bringing students again?" I know that Edward has occasionally done some work for Don Johnson, an archaeologist who has been doing some investigating up in Walker Bay over the past few summers. Last year he brought in a troop of undergraduates for a summer course.

Edward smiles and raises his eyebrows in agreement. "Don't know why, though. They kinda drove him nuts that one time. Going to talk to him tonight. Not sure where the students are going to stay either."

"If he needs a place, he can crash with me. You could tell him, ah?" I know the difficulties of finding housing.

The sound of an ATV slowing ends this conversation, and Joseph Qalviaq pulls alongside, driving an old Honda that looks very well used. "Welcome back," he says, first to me, then to Edward. Edward points to one of his tires, which looks low. Joseph nods. "Going to get some plugs."

I sense I'm in for a lengthy conversation. I put down my bags. Joseph, though, is more interested in Edward's report than mine. As a member of the Hunters and Trappers Committee, Joseph has a keen interest in the mining activities above Minto Inlet. "How's it going up there?"

"Not too bad," replies Edward. "Saw lots of caribou around. Had some come right close to camp. I took pictures. Sure wanted to shoot them, though."

Joseph nods. "Been a long time since I been up there. Must be almost twenty years."

As the reminiscing begins, the dark blue Housing truck pulls up. Charlie Hanayi reaches his hand out the window, a welcome back for both Edward and me. Although Edward has been home for two days, he is "backwards," sleeping most of the day and active at night. It may be late afternoon, and Charlie is thinking about the end of the work day, but Edward has just had breakfast.

Charlie turns to me. "Martha says you're going to stay in that duplex again?"

"Yeah. She says a health worker is coming in August, though." I am wondering if there's some problem Martha didn't know about.

"Well, we can't find the extra key to it." This is a true statement, but not a real problem. Charlie is really asking if I have the key.

"I have it. Martha told me to keep it when I left last month. She said to give it to you when I leave."

"Okay, that's good. See you. Stop by sometime." Charlie seems to be constantly in a hurry. He puts the truck into drive and heads down the road to the Housing shop.

Joseph also takes notice. "Can't stop, that guy. Always working." Though it occurs to me that Joseph is the same way.

Edward nods. "Some people are like that. You ever hear what happened to his boy? What did he get?"

Joseph responds, "I heard he got community service only, because it's a first offence."

I know about the case, because it was all over town when it happened last spring. Zachary, then fourteen, broke into his uncle's house and stole a bottle of booze and some money, then proceeded to get drunk and tried to break into the Co-op. I missed the court proceeding, as did Edward.

Joseph continues, "Charlie made him go down to Mashuyak for the summer. He says that Zachary can't listen, so he's hoping his grandparents can get through to him." Mashuyak is a camp down at Holman

Island where Charlie's in-laws reside for much of the summer, fishing and hunting seals – and, hopefully, getting through to some of their grandchildren.

Joseph's comment is a knowing one. He most certainly recalls his own youth and the difficulties he caused his parents, who wondered how they could get through to him. Joseph had similar issues with his oldest son too, as he readily acknowledges – though not to the same degree as with Zachary. Joseph, at least, kept himself and his oldest son out of the courts.

This book is an examination of how men "get through" – how they have transitioned from their teenage years into adulthood and middle age. In particular, the book focuses on men like Willie, Joseph, Isaac, and Edward, born during the late 1950s and 1960s, members of the first settlement cohort, the first to be raised primarily in the context of a permanent village. How have these men faced the challenges and difficulties of balancing the significant, burdensome, and conflicting demands of their own parents and grandparents, on the one hand, and the harsh realities of contemporary settlement-focused life, on the other?

Settlement cohort Inuit have been studied previously. Richard Condon (1987, 1990a, 1990b) worked with this group, focusing on the emergence of adolescence as a novel life stage, one made possible by the social changes set in motion during the 1960s. This book is partly an extension of those interests in human development and the life course. Such interests go beyond Condon's work, however; John O'Neil (1983, 1986) conducted similar studies on stress, coping, and health among the same cohort of men in a Central Arctic settlement. More recently, Lisa Wexler and colleagues (Wexler 2006; Wexler and Goodwin 2006; Wexler et al. 2008) have explored similar concerns among youth in Northwest Alaska, focusing largely on suicide prevention and mental health.

At the other end of the spectrum is research on aging and elderhood, which has tended to centre on either health issues among the elderly or the role of the elder as repository of cultural knowledge. Fienup-Riordan (1998, 2001) and McNabb (1991) have investigated the latter, paying attention to the important functions of elders in political and social movements, especially those that pertain to cultural survival. Smith and colleagues (Smith, Easton, et al. 2009a, 2009b; Smith, Saylor, et al. 2009; Smith, George, and Easton 2001) and McDonald, Ludtke, and Muus (2005, 2006) provide recent examples of work that focuses on contemporary health issues facing the elderly, especially those related to functionality, stress, and food security.

The middle ground of the life course has, however, been largely ignored. What of the period between adolescence and elderhood? When and how does an Inuk become an adult? When does an adult become an elder? This book examines the experience of these men as they leave adolescence and move through adulthood and toward elderhood, guided both by the Inuit conception of how the life course should unfold and by the constraints and opportunities presented by the social environment in which they find themselves.

As should be apparent, I have limited the scope of this inquiry by focusing solely on manhood, a relatively unexplored domain in the literature about Inuit. There is a significant body of work in the area of gender, beginning with the numerous writings specifically on and about traditional gender roles and relative status of men and women (see Balikci 1970; Friedl 1978; Guemple 1995; Billson and Mancini 2007; Saladin d'Anglure 1986, 1992, 2007). Other works have examined more contemporary issues and include investigations of women's contributions to subsistence and the public-domestic dichotomy (Bodenhorn 1990, 1993; Dahl 2003), contemporary women's roles in urban settings (Fogel-Chance 1993), and contemporary gender roles and socialization practices (Condon and Stern 1993; Stern and Condon 1995; McElroy 1975, 1978). Much more work in the domain of gender has addressed women's health and well-being, particularly in relation to alcohol and drug use and domestic violence (see Billson 1990, 2006; Billson and Mancini 2007).

This study is not meant as a comprehensive treatment or discussion of the literature on and about Inuit gender. Rather, the point is easily made: men have not often been the focus of inquiries targeting Inuit conceptions of gender. That this is so is certainly understandable, for men have been at the core of the voluminous literature on Inuit subsistence. The importance of men's activities as food producers has meant that their economic lives have been heavily scrutinized back to the earliest days of Inuit ethnography and ethnology (for some examples, see Burch 1985; Wolfe 1979; Wenzel 1987, 1989; Smith and Wright 1989; Smith 1991; Huntingdon 1992; Dahl 2003). However, the focus on men in this literature is primarily on what men *do* rather than on what men *are*, especially when it comes to the entirety of their lives beyond subsistence. A single exception to this focus on men and what they do is Hensel's (1996) *Telling Ourselves*, which examines the discourses surrounding gender and ethnicity as much as it does men's activities.

Consequently, the approach I take here is more akin to that pursued by Briggs in her examination of emotional and personal development in *Never in Anger* (1970), Brody's investigation of Inuit-Qablunaat relations in *The People's Land* (1975), or Fienup-Riordan's exploration of concepts of personhood among the Yup'ik (1986). Such works have looked more broadly at the concepts involved at the core of this study, employing narrative approaches that tackle the meaning of such concepts rather than focusing on a narrowly defined issue or role. More recent narrative approaches in this vein include Wachowich's *Saqiyuq* (1999) or Margaret Blackman's *Sadie Brower Neakok* (1989), both of which examine the meaning of women's lives through life history methodologies and narrative styles.

The secondary reason for writing this book has more to do with my interests in how anthropologists conduct fieldwork. Although a great deal has been written about fieldwork and participant observation as a research strategy (discussed in the following two chapters), and, more recently, on the conduct of what is now called participant-action research, or community-based participatory research, field research even at its most basic level is a negotiation between the researcher and the informant.

I have worked and lived in Ulukhaktok over many years, making multiple trips since 1992. I spent a year there in 1992–93, a second year in 1997, multiple months during the summers of 2001, 2002, 2004, 2005, and 2006, an additional eight months in 2007, and multiple months during the summers of 2010 and 2012. All told, the time adds up to nearly forty-eight months over a twenty year period. My primary interest has been in the subsistence economy, particularly the economic strategies of the men born during the initial settlement concentration period of 1955–70 – the settlement cohort. That I would be keen on hunting and travelling speaks to my predilections as a fieldworker, but it also speaks to my position as a researcher.

When I arrived in the field in 1992, I was twenty-four, a second-year graduate student working as a research assistant for Richard Condon, my mentor and principal advisor at the University of Arkansas. I was the same age, and certainly in the same social category, as many of the men that Condon and I were studying. I was, however, doing more than studying them. I was quickly assigned a role within the community, for I was the participant observer, hanging out with the guys, hunting and travelling with some of them, playing hockey (badly) or basketball with others. In short, I was just like many of the guys, in a cosmetic sense, the difference being that every week or so I was walking around asking them seemingly silly questions and writing down the answers. Being the same age, and focused on many of the same activities as my victims, I was in lock step with community social norms. When I returned in 1997 for a year, married and with my wife and eight-month-old daughter in tow, I was further validated as belonging securely within this age group.

And, indeed, "participant observation" in this sense carried meanings both in and out of the field, as I, too, struggled with negotiating an entrance into adulthood that was delayed by a graduate education and further constrained by an economic standard of living not unlike that of my informants. When Maya and I were in Ulukhaktok in 1997, for example, the grant that supported us for the year was roughly equal to the income of an Inuit family on social assistance. I learned firsthand the daily struggles involved in maintaining hunting equipment, paying the rent, and purchasing food from the store.

Inevitably, my research has been a window into men's lives: interviews with my informants about subsistence have nearly always drifted toward discussions about the stresses and joys of daily life, about the health and well-being of aging parents, about the disposition of children. So, although I have been academically interested in such things as hunting and economics, my interaction with my Inuit informants, and my participation in their daily lives, have necessarily resulted in substantial insight into what it means to be a man in a contemporary settlement. The ease with which Inuit men have engaged in these conversations with me has directed me, however subtly, to pay attention to these features of Inuit culture and to make them the focus of this book.

Edward Kuniluk, Isaac Kaaktuq, Charlie Hanayi, and Joseph Qalviaq are pseudonyms, as are all of the names of the Inuit mentioned in the book. It is common practice in ethnographic work to use pseudonyms. Indeed, most university institutional review boards (IRBs) effectively insist on the use of pseudonyms by requiring guarantees of anonymity for research participants. Ostensibly, the purpose is to protect informants from the possibility of material, social, or psychological harm. Whether guarantees of anonymity for participants are for the protection of informants or for the protection of the university is an open question (see Bosk and de Vries 2004; Gordon 2003; Plattner 2003; Crang and Cook 2007, 27–32). Nevertheless, I have employed pseudonyms in prior publications, and most people who work in the Arctic do the same. Some, like O'Neil (1983), have gone further and used pseudonyms for the communities in which they have worked.

For this book, however, I have gone beyond mere pseudonyms to protect informants. While a pseudonym works well in an examination of interview data or survey responses taken out of context, this book is about the ethnographic context of men's lives, and pseudonyms by themselves will not offer protections of anonymity. To be able to guarantee this anonymity – which I am required to do by the four different IRBs that have overseen my career of research – I am using composite characters. That is, I have deliberately obscured information that could identify individuals. In a number of cases, I have combined two or more individuals in a single entity. I expect and hope that Ulukhaktomiut will read this book. Simply employing pseudonyms and doing nothing else will not prevent anyone from discovering identities. Ulukhaktokmiut readers, for example, will intuitively know on one level who "Isaac" is, simply by the nature of my relationship with him and his social position within the community. On another level, however, "Isaac" is a composite who encapsulates the similar experiences and activities of several Inuit.

Changing identifying information requires some more serious measures, and it is for this reason that I have altered occupations, incomes, and other identifying information. Where warranted, I have combined individuals who share significant similarities into a single character. As with the use of pseudonyms, there is precedent for employing composite characters (Murchison 2010, 201–3) in cases where individuals may suffer harm if they are identified. Nancy Scheper Hughes, for example, employed the technique in *Saints, Scholars, and Schizophrenics* (1983) in her examination of mental illness in rural Ireland.

Using composites seems like a serious step for a work that focuses on the life course. Protecting informants is largely about protecting them from harm, and what harm is there in a book about Inuit adulthood? For some Inuit men, however, marijuana use is an important part of their lives, and some resort to selling drugs on occasion to raise money, "Edward Kuniluk" being one of these. There is the possibility – however slim – that identifying an individual engaged in such activity could have legal ramifications. However, the legality of an activity like selling marijuana or bootlegging alcohol is of far less concern than the social consequences of engaging in these activities. Many young men are more terrified of their parents' disappointment in them than they are of the RCMP, and some go to great lengths to keep their activities out of their parents' sight and knowledge. On numerous occasions I have stumbled into a drinking party, and some of the imbibers – some of them in my cohort – have asked that I not tell their parents or siblings.

I realize that perhaps concerns about anonymity are a bit silly. In a community of four hundred people, there is not much that goes on that *can* remain secret, and I suspect that most disapproving parents know exactly what their children are up to, or they go to great lengths to actively ignore their children's activities. It is, however, not my intention to out the men who may or may not be selling marijuana, bootlegging alcohol, shooting game illegally, or getting lost on the land. I make no moral judgments here about alcohol or drug use; I merely acknowledge that some men do these things, and they do them for complicated reasons that researchers have not yet figured out.

So, in summary, I am using composites partly to protect informants from the local consequences of criminal or otherwise socially discouraged behaviours like drinking or smoking up. Some readers may expect, and even prefer, a lengthy discussion of the significant effects of these problems on particular individuals and upon the community at large. I refrain from detailed commentary on alcohol and drugs, save to acknowledge that some people use these substances, and some have specific and serious problems stemming from their use. However, my purposes here are descriptive rather than proscriptive or speculative.

Why? I have worked in Ulukhaktok since 1992. Surely I must know something about these things? Indeed, I know quite a bit – more than I care to, actually – about the economics of the marijuana trade and patterns of drug use. But the focus of my study has never been about these issues, and I have never specifically investigated them.

Why not? Some of my reasons have to do with respecting integrity: there is no point in inquiring about an individual's alcohol problems when he does not wish to talk about them, and pressing the issue could do serious harm. Most Inuit, as I discuss throughout this work, place a high value on respecting privacy and integrity. On more than a single occasion I have had a Monday-evening visitor who was in the drunk tank on a Saturday night and was now facing charges. He knew that I knew about the incident, was embarrassed by it, and preferred not to talk about it except in very general and obtuse way.

Furthermore, there is an abundance of work on alcohol and drug problems in the North, and I cannot contribute to that literature in a diagnostic way. As James Waldram argues in *The Revenge of the Windigo* (2004, 134–66), the tendency of southerners is to think of aboriginal settlements as having "problems" with alcohol: "Ulukhaktok has an alcohol problem" is how such a statement might appear. The reality is that, like most things, the situation is much more complicated. *Some* people (like Edward) have difficulty with alcohol, others (like Isaac) abstain, and still others (like Joseph) drink on occasion, mostly without incident. To speculate on whether Inuit drink to cope with acculturative stress or because their genes predispose them to would be foolish, because my knowledge of alcohol use is largely ethnographic. My purposes here are to raise these issues as part of the context of Inuit life course development. On a broader level, all human lives are complicated and full of contradictions. One can decry the evils of marijuana and then proceed to sell $1,500 of the stuff. An Inuk can wax rhapsodic about respect for the land and animals knowing full well that he left two seal carcasses to rot because he was too tired to bother with them.

VISITING AROUND

It is suppertime as I make the last leg of the journey to the duplex, but I am not yet home. William Kaaktuq taps on his window as I walk by, motioning me inside. I walk up to the window, and he opens it to talk. William is Isaac's father.

"Suppertime. Come eat." He says this from his chair at the table.

I nod. "*Ii*. Let me drop my things. I'll be right back."

"You better hurry, might be no food left. My name means 'hungry,' you know." Which is true. William giggles. It is not the first time that I have heard this joke.

William's house is a matter of yards from the duplex – we can see each other's houses clearly – and it takes no time to get the contents of my shopping bags inside and into the refrigerator. I shove everything in. I'll sort out the canned goods from the produce later.

Dinner has only recently been served. The ducks in the pot are still hot when I grab a plate and help myself. The large, black, enamelled roasting pot rests on fresh cardboard on the floor. Serving is a matter of grabbing the meat fork and helping oneself. The cardboard acts as both cutting board and placemat for the meat. A large frying pan also sits on the cardboard, full of hot duck fat and fried pieces of duck skin – "Eskimo bacon" – crispy, fatty, and delicious when done just right, as Agnes does it. The ducks themselves are fresh, shot only the other day, *qingaliks*, king eider ducks. William gestures to a seat at the table, and I sit and begin eating.

William is already well into his food, as is his wife, Agnes. She peers out the window every once in a while as she eats. She is expecting more of the family to arrive.

And, indeed, they do, children and grandchildren wandering in over the next half hour. The workday is over, but the window between getting off work at five and the stores closing at six makes for a demanding

time as people squeeze in the last errands of the day. David, a grandson, walks in at half past, says hello, and grabs a plateful from the pot.
He settles on the floor and digs in. Sarah, a daughter, arrives five minutes later. She was held up at the post office, which has an unusual
amount of mail today – First Air bumped the mail from the last two
flights. Sadie, another daughter, arrives shortly after, several plastic
bags of Styrofoam boxes in her hands.

"I stopped at the hotel to get fries and gravy. I really wanted to have
fries." She sets the boxes on the table and opens them. French fries
smothered in brown gravy steam into the air, their smell competing
with that of the boiled duck. Several of the grandchildren sitting in the
T V room patter into the eating area. They have already eaten duck, like
everyone else, but they are hungry for fries, too, and eagerly help themselves. Another box contains several helpings of pie, also from the hotel, which we will consume later. Once we finish eating ducks, we move
on to the second course: bannock, a kind of fried bread, topped with
butter, jam, peanut butter, Cheez Whiz, or whatever else one can think
of, followed by tea.

Given the relatively open structure of the houses, the front of this
particular house is nearly a single room: a large room opening on either side of the entrance, with a kitchen between them in an alcove
directly across from the door. The space to the left is for the sofa and
television, the one on the right is for the kitchen table, the cardboard
for the meat, and, often, a second table for the sewing machine. The
grandchildren fade back into the T V room – a common pattern, it
seems, one of both age and culture. I have sat at more than enough
meals to realize that the adults tend to stay around the country food,
the kids around the Qablunaaq foods. The more "country" the meal,
the less likely the kids are to be in the dining area, instead subsisting on
canned soup, bannock, and processed foods. That David has chosen a
seat on the floor with the adults suggests that, though only seventeen,
he sees himself as both an adult *and* as an Inuk more interested in eating good food than store food, Qablunaat food.

The meal ends as it began, members of the family drifting in and out
of the house, an easy ebb and flow of conversation in mixed English and
Inuinnaqtun about the day's activities, news from elsewhere, the latest

happenings in town, and plans for the next few days. Sarah rises and washes the dishes, sensing that it is her turn. Agnes dries until the rack can hold the last of the dishes, which will air dry. She puts on her runners and heads out. Tonight is a sewing night at the Anglican Ladies' Auxiliary. I finish my tea, thank William for supper, and head outside too. Not to the duplex, though, not yet. I still have people to see.

I would normally take Charlie up on his offer to stop by, but I am no dummy. The weather this evening is wonderful, and I know that he wasted no time once work ended. He'll have gone out of town, taking the boat to hunt seals or driving the ATV to fish at a nearby lake. Given that the rivers are still running high but the winds are light, my money is on seal and duck hunting.

Instead, I catch Joseph outside of his house, working on his old ATV. "Where's the new one?" I ask. Joseph purchased a new ATV just before I left a few weeks ago. At the time, he said he was purchasing it so that he'd have a dedicated machine for hunting, for his use only.

"Rose has it. She went out to my parents' camp before. The kids wanted to go out there to sleep." Joseph is installing some plugs in the rear tire, the one that was low earlier this afternoon. One of the hazards of driving around town is the likelihood of running into nails and other sharp objects. The roads aren't bad, but young ATV drivers like to take shortcuts between and around houses. It annoys some homeowners, and a few retaliate by deliberately dropping nails on the ground. That's one reason why Joseph's new machine is off-limits to his kids. Tires, like most things here, are expensive.

I watch while he completes the repair and inflates the tire. "Good enough now," he says, kicking it. "Come in for tea."

We head up the stairs into the house. Joseph flips the switch on the electric kettle. "It's tap water, though. I'm out of ice water," he apologizes. Many Inuit prefer to collect drinking water from the lakes close to town, chopping ice out when they're frozen. The water provided by the hamlet is treated, and many claim it tastes funny, from the treatment or from sitting in the water tank.

Soon we are sitting at the kitchen table, drinking tea and sharing cookies. Joseph is currently out of work, having left his job as the hamlet recreation and sport coordinator. Considering his age, forty-seven, it is something of a curious decision, quitting a decent job at the hamlet. He was employed full-time in the office for twelve years, and worked part-time for years before that. "They were threatening to make me the assistant SOB," he explains. "I don't want to be the SOB. Too stressful. But I can make it okay. We have some money saved up, and Rose is making enough to keep us going for the time being."

"Did you try for the Fish and Wildlife job?" I ask, referring to an opening in the office.

"I was going to try, all right, but they gave it to Michael. But he says he may not keep it. I might try for it if Michael quits. I'm doing good with the carving, though, and I might try for some guiding this fall, too."

I also know Joseph is making decent money from the honoraria generated by his board position at Hunters and Trappers. He sits on the Inuvialuit Game Council, and he has talked about making a run for hamlet council as well.

We hear footsteps on the stairs, and Joseph's oldest son, Brandon, walks in. He is freshly cleaned, judging by the overwhelming smell of flowery shampoo that enters with him. "Hi, Dad. Hi, Pete," he says, offering me his hand.

His father is surprised to see him. "Did you just get in? I thought I heard a plane."

Brandon is employed as an environmental compliance officer, working as a liaison between Hunters and Trappers and the mining company. While Edward was working as a general labourer, Brandon was charged with ensuring that the company adheres to the environmental regulations regarding mining and exploration activity. He has been well trained to do this, but he is only twenty-three, and he is hardly the kind of person to confront a Qablunaat crew intent on violating protocol.

"Did you eat, sonny? There's *muktuk*, just came in from Inuvik. Your mum went out to Granny and Grandpa's tonight," Joseph adds, as a way of explaining why there was no cooked food for supper.

"I had a Hungry Man dinner at home. I'm good," Brandon says, but he helps himself to *piffi* (dried fish, in this case lake trout) and joins us at the table.

"How was the trip?" As Joseph sits on the H T C board, he has a vested interest in knowing how the mining company is conducting their business. Brandon relates several incidents, including a small chemical spill next to a lake.

Joseph turns serious. "Did you document it? Did you take notes?"

"I took pictures." Brandon pulls out his digital camera, showing his father the photos.

Joseph tuts. "You always have to watch these guys. They're always trying to pull a fast one on us." Joseph also knows that the company prefers to hire non-confrontational twenty-year-olds. But, unlike his son, he is more than willing to confront the company, and he will, once they are back in town.

It is 10 P M when I finally make it to Isaac's, walking into the house, kicking off my runners, and settling on the sofa next to him. Isaac has been watching television since he got home. We sit in silence for a while, watching a show called *Survivorman*, in which the protagonist gets himself into ridiculously contrived situations in the wilderness and, using his uncommon ingenuity and knowledge of the environment, manages to survive against (apparently) harsh odds. All while filming himself, of course. Isaac finds it amusing, which is why he watches it, the idiotic things that Qablunaat get up to. For Isaac, television seems to be more of a confirmation that the world "out there" is far inferior to the world in Ulukhaktok.

He nods to the kitchen. "There's tea. Ice water."

I get up and help myself. The electric kettle is hot, and I pour water from it into a heavy plastic mug, ubiquitous in Inuit households, frequently used while camping. There are teabags in a box on the counter, but I help myself to one off a pile of used bags on a saucer. Many Inuit reuse tea bags over and over, until they no longer flavour the water. I use three bags, add a little sugar, and come back to sit down. We watch the television for a while.

"How's the family?"

"Oh, they're good," I say. "Not happy that I am here, though. And hard to leave, too."

Isaac knows the issues. It is simply impossible to get my wife and three kids here while I do fieldwork. There are logistical issues involving getting the kids into and out of school, what to do about our house and cat, and so many other things we have not even considered. The biggest problem is the airfare, which I explain to Isaac, just as I explained it to Willie. To manage the fieldwork, I have arranged to be in Ulukhaktok for a schedule of roughly eight weeks on, four weeks off. The first leg seems to have worked, though Isaac and others do not hide their disappointment. Maya and Sarah, our oldest daughter, then just a baby, were with me in Ulukhaktok in 1997, and Sarah was with me during the summer of 2005. Inuit note that it would be nice to see all of them, especially Sarah, who carries an Inuinnaqtun name.

"How are things here? How come you never had supper at your dad's?" I ask. As he is Agnes and William's oldest son, I expected to see him there.

"I was out earlier with the dogs. Those pups can really run. I'm going to have a good team next winter." Isaac assumed responsibility for his father's dog team several years ago, and he has taken that responsibility very seriously, going so far as to inoculate the dogs against rabies and parvovirus, at considerable expense. He has fed and trained them well. It is much more common for dogs that are not working to be positively ignored, sometimes abused, with only a valuable bitch or bear dog given decent treatment during the off-season.

"I was out on my line, and I noticed that Matthew's dogs are in really poor shape. Three of them were standing in water. They all look cold and really underfed. I don't know when the last time he was out there. I wonder if I should say something." Matthew Aqiaruq is another hunter, one with whom Isaac seems to have an ongoing disagreement about how to properly live and hunt, though they frequently travel on the land together. It is not the first time there has been a problem with Matthew's dogs.

Survivorman ends, followed by some other equally contrived outdoors show. Isaac gets up. "Where did I put those things?" He rummages around on the television stand and eventually produces a cribbage board and a deck of cards. He flips the television off and moves to the dining table. I follow, tea in hand.

Isaac counts out the cards, finds that they are all there, and we cut for the deal. Cribbage is a common game in Ulukhaktok, played by counting points on a board. The first to reach 121 wins, with points counted by the value of the cards in the hand and by "pegging," in which the players take turns playing their cards, counting them out. The principle of scoring is to form combinations that add up to fifteen, to form runs of three or more, or to make pairs. It is a somewhat simple game, with players dealt six cards, two then discarded into the kitty, or crib, which then belongs to the dealer, counted after the hands are tallied. Though there is an element of chance involved, strategy is important. As it's a card game, it is easy to incorporate a gambling element, which Inuit sometimes do, though I never have. I grew up playing the game with my grandfather, so I am intimately familiar with it and the importance of particular card combinations. When I first arrived in Ulukhaktok in 1992, a novice field researcher, cribbage was an important icebreaker with many men my age, most of whom owned a cribbage board. It is essential equipment for travel on the land, something to do in camp, but it's important in town too, a useful pastime especially during the darkness of winter.

We finish the games, skunking each other once (a "skunk" is a victory by more than thirty points), and Isaac pushes away from the table. It is past 11 now, and the light outside is low and soft. Unusually for a June evening, traffic on the roads is light, perhaps because many of the young men are out hunting ducks. "Time for a snack." He states it matter-of-factly, and walks into the utility room.

He returns with a piece of cardboard, produces a knife from his pocket, and cuts the cardboard to the shape of the table. He turns back into the utility room, and I hear the freezer open and shut, and some additional rustling around. He lays out our snack on the cardboard: several piffis, a frozen char that we will eat as *quaq*, frozen and raw, and two slabs of white and pink *muktuk* – the skin of a beluga whale with a thin layer of fat underneath. He fetches another knife for me from the kitchen and turns on the kettle. We will have tea again when we are finished eating.

Amy, his oldest daughter, seems to have had a premonition: she walks by the window below us, holding hands with her partner, Sam. I see their heads bobbing as they pass, and I hear the crunch of their runners on the gravel. It's a warm evening in Ulukhaktok, 14°C, and no traffic kicking up dust, so Isaac has the window open. We hear them climb the stairs. Amy looks around as she kicks her shoes off.

"Quaq! And I'm so hungry, too." She is wearing a packing shirt and rocking her body gently up and down. A baby, eight months old, is tied into her shirt, nestled against her back. Amy heads for the sofa, removes the packing shirt, and the little girl slides out with a sigh, still sound asleep. Amy puts the shirt over the sleeping child, sets a pillow so she will not roll onto the floor, and comes to join us.

"Hi, Pete! Welcome back." Then, to her dad, "Where's Mum?"

Sam stands silently by and just nods. Being young, and from Kugluktuk, he is very shy around his girlfriend's father and hardly knows me at all. Isaac, at forty-six, seems to enjoy unnerving his son-in-law. He says hello in a low voice and looks at Sam over his glasses. Isaac has told me before that Sam's prospects are somewhat dim. He seems uninterested in finding a job, for example, nor has he shown much interest in hunting. I wonder if Isaac has offered to take him out on the land, but I think I already know the answer is no.

Isaac responds to his daughter's inquiry. "She's at your auntie's. She should be back soon."

The char is frozen solid, but it is relatively easy to hack off chunks with the large knife, and we take turns at the quaq, the piffi, and the muktuk. Isaac reaches for the hot sauce and pours rather a large amount over the muktuk he has cut for himself.

"This is really good with muktuk. I'm glad you showed this to me." I'm not sure that I introduced Isaac to hot sauce, as I hardly use it myself, and I certainly never thought to try it on muktuk. But I think, okay, and shrug my shoulders. I have eaten stranger combinations.

Muktuk *is* good with hot sauce. Perhaps this should not be surprising, as muktuk is not so much a taste as a texture, unless it is served stinky. Isaac's pail is full of raw muktuk. "Just came yesterday from Inuvik. Really fresh."

We cut our quaq and muktuk into small pieces, sprinkling salt on the quaq and hot sauce on the muktuk, and occasionally helping ourselves to piffi, peeling the skin from the flesh much as a child would peel old-fashioned candy buttons from the paper. Given the amount we are eating, this is not so much a snack as another meal.

Although we eat mostly in silence, the mere sharing of this meal is affirming of our social relationship. *It is good to eat traditional food together* is how I am sure Isaac would put it. I have been coming to Ulukhaktok since 1992, sometimes only for a month, sometimes longer. Sometimes I have been away for several years. For me, it is always the sharing of a meal that recalls warm and fond memories of shared experiences. As we begin to slow down on our snack, Amy asks for the salt one last time.

Isaac looks at me. "Remember that soup?" It's all he needs to say, and I nearly snort some piffi.

It was a few years ago, when I had my daughter Sarah with me for the summer. The char were running, and Isaac insisted on making a fresh one into a fish chowder. I arrived at the house a little early, expecting Sarah, then nine, to wander in at some point – she was out playing with Isaac's niece, Lucy, but knew to come to Isaac's when she was hungry.

Isaac was in the kitchen. He started by sautéing the onions, celery, and potatoes in the stock pot, using enough butter, I thought approvingly, to deep-fry a lemming. Once that was done to his satisfaction, he added salt, then water, some more salt, and a few cans of evaporated milk to make the milk base. When he added salt a third time, another generous pour from the package, I started to worry but refrained from saying anything. It would not do to criticize the cook. Isaac is older than I am, and I knew the importance of our relative ages. It was not my place to ask impertinent questions. Or so I thought.

The char added and cooked with yet more salt, we sat down to bowls of hot soup. Isaac sprinkled even more salt over his. I took a sip of the milky broth and immediately worried how I was to get down the entire bowl without becoming something like a slug victimized by a malicious child. I took a sip of my juice. Isaac did the same, much more than a sip, and refilled his glass. The pitcher was half empty. If this were to continue, we would need more juice than we had at the table. I refilled my glass too.

After four spoonfuls, Isaac finally spoke. "What's happening here? This soup is really salty." He looked at me. "How did this happen?"

"You kept adding the salt. You added it four or five times."

"I did? I don't remember. How come you never said anything?" He was laughing now, his smile wide, tears running down his cheeks.

"I thought you meant to do it that way." I was laughing too.

We are both laughing again now, remembering the soup, while Isaac tries to explain all this to Amy, an entire pot of soup ruined by what must have been half a box of salt. She giggles. Sam looks bewildered.

The muktuk goes back to the pail, the half a char back into the freezer, the piffi back to the grocery bag. The cardboard is folded up and thrown away. We have more tea before I finally call it a day, grab my bags, and make the short walk to the duplex.

Though it is well after midnight, and I have been awake since seven this morning, I am not the least bit sleepy. At least seven cups of tea (I have lost count) does that to me. One advantage of employing used teabags is less caffeine, though I have still had a decent dose. In any event, I am going to be making multiple trips to the bathroom over the next two hours. I unpack my bags, lay out my sleeping bag on the bed in the small bedroom, and put clothes into the dresser. The room is completely dark: the aluminum foil I taped over the window glass last month is still in place, a necessity for sleeping during twenty-four-hour daylight.

In the main room, I check on the kitchen supplies. When I left, there were a few glasses, a frying pan, several pots, dishware and silverware. Perhaps someone with access to the unit while I was gone took them for use in another unit. If they are still here, I will not need to pull my kitchen gear out of storage. And everything is where it should be – even some soup packets I left behind are in the cabinet – save for the complete absence of butter knives in the silverware drawer. There were six when I left. I snicker to myself and set the computer on the dining table to write some observations about the day.

As should be evident from the structure of this chapter, I have chosen to present the narrative largely through the lens of my own experience: almost everything I present in this book is an ethnographic episode in which I was either directly involved or present as an observer. The purpose here is not self-aggrandizement. Rather, the reasoning for my approach has more to do with Inuit epistemology. For Inuit, there is an important difference between knowledge acquired through direct experience and observation, and knowledge acquired from secondary sources. I am conforming as much as possible to an Inuit standard.

Adherence to such a standard for this book is, however, more nuanced than simply copying a cultural style. The choice of participant observation as a research strategy precisely replicates Inuit methods of teaching and learning. The participant observer arriving in a foreign cultural scene must, by necessity, develop what Briggs (1986) calls "metacommunicative competence," the ability to ask appropriate questions in an appropriate manner. In short, the ethnographer, by demonstrating cultural competence, reveals his or her worthiness to comprehend and respect cultural knowledge. The strategy is ultimately learner driven, in that the one seeking skills or knowledge must demonstrate both desire for and capability of further instruction. Inuit development is guided by these same principles: individuals must observe behaviour, listen to conversation, and then demonstrate both desire and capability before teachers take an interest. Learners signal their readiness, something pointed out by numerous scholars (among them Annahatak 1994; Briggs 1991; Crago 1992; Crago, Annahatak, and Ningiuruvik 1993; Fienup-Riordan 1986, 2001; Kawagley 1995; Nadasdy 2003). This style is quite unlike southern-based systems, in which teachers drive the educational experience.

A more in-depth discussion of my choice of narrative style, and the conventions I have chosen for this book, follows in chapters 1 and 3. Chapter 2 ("Things Are Really Changing around Here") more comprehensively addresses the theoretical concerns that underlie the nature of my fieldwork experience, including the life course perspective and Inuit personhood and human development. Chapter 3 ("A Congenial Dolt Learns about Inuit Culture") focuses on researcher-informant interactions, the ways in which the social position of the researcher influences fieldwork and data collection, and how these first two issues have forced some specific and difficult choices about linguistic and cultural representation.

Chapters 4 through 9 form the nexus of the book, each chapter focusing on a particular facet of men's lives. Chapter 4, "He's a Good Friend, but He's a Crook," focuses on the background of the settlement, paying attention to the material issues that Inuit confront in their daily lives. These include the difficulties of making a living, the demands of reciprocity, and the problems of being accepted socially and escaping the ill-repute that follows teenagers into adulthood.

Chapter 5, "Driving Around," discusses the problems of being young. Young men tend to spin their wheels, sometimes seemingly going nowhere, as they try to find some strategy for becoming socially and economically established in Ulukhaktok. Many young people make mistakes and misinterpret the advice of their elders.

Chapter 6, "I'm Experimenting," is about negotiating physical and social maturity. Though Inuit may be physically mature, they may not yet be socially mature. Moreover, adulthood is not an event, as southerners seem to think of it. For Inuit, maturity is rather a process, one that is not attained, in either contemporary or traditional senses, until perhaps age forty.

Chapter 7, "Expensive Women and Unbalanced Lives," explores some of the connections between men and women in the contemporary settlement. Young men find themselves living in a settlement that is increasingly feminine, managed and directed largely by women, and increasingly isolated from the land, which has become the domain of the masculine.

Chapter 8, "Sometimes I Can Feel Heavy," focuses on approaching middle age, and how men in particular deal with the dual stresses of their aging parents and their own teenagers, while struggling to make it themselves. Success requires toughness and a willingness to soldier on in the face of difficulties. Some of these men do not make it, and they fall by the wayside.

Chapter 9, "It Feels Good to Share That Much," is about becoming *inummariit*, genuine people, focusing both on the ways in which settlement cohort men reference more traditional notions of appropriate behaviour and on the increasing responsibility that these men take in the lives of their extended families as their parents age.

Chapter 10, "Real Northern Men," concludes by returning to a more theoretically engaged discussion of the Inuit life course and the ways in which the men presented here have negotiated and managed contemporary settlement life in reference to Inuit cultural values. In particular, the chapter focuses on the deeply personal nature of ethnographic fieldwork, on Inuit teaching and learning strategies as being, effectively, participant observation, and on the importance of Inuit concepts of *ihuma* (wisdom, or thinking) and *inummarik* (genuine person, and often used in the plural, *inmmariit*) as organizing principles of the Inuit life course.

Before moving on, it is worth discussing one convention I employ in the remainder of this book. In this introductory chapter, I have presented a narrative taken from my fieldwork: a day in the life of the anthropologist in June 2007. I have presented it in a linear fashion, supplemented by additional notes on community history, the main themes of this book, and the structure of the following chapters. This is, however, the last time I will provide a narrative in linear order. In the remainder of the book, I present the ethnography as a series of episodes organized by theme rather than chronology. Rarely will I provide a specific date for an episode, though a date may be embedded in the narrative where appropriate.

Some readers may find this disconcerting, but in an important sense this format replicates lessons learned during my own fieldwork experience. Rarely do one's informants step outside their lives and provide a context to help guide the anthropologist. Inuit are the last people who would do so anyway. As Jean Briggs has noted, "Why?" might be the rudest question one can ask. One is expected to observe and listen, and then volunteer or experiment with potential solutions. Rather than answering, it is far more likely that Inuit would use the anthropologist's confusion as a stepping-stone for having some fun.

My decision to reduce the visibility of the specific year during which an episode occurred – or completely omit the time frame – is likewise an important theme of this book. A major driver of social science work in the Arctic is the significant impact of rapid social change that people have experienced over the past half-century. Indeed, a number of perceived social problems – drug and alcohol abuse, domestic violence, suicide, language loss, and cultural disarray, for example – are sometimes believed to *be* the rapid social changes.

This is not to say that these problems are insignificant. Rather, to me, these issues are largely cosmetic, symptomatic of larger cultural processes that are driven by fundamental social-structural changes to Inuit societies. For men in the settlement cohort, the fundamental problem is the timing of specific historical events in their lives. The sociologist Glen Elder, for example, has demonstrated the importance of the timing of military service in men's lives (Elder and Bailey 1988), which has significant long-term effects on the adult life courses of men in specific age cohorts. Elder has likewise examined the importance of historical events in general on life course construction (Elder 1978; Elder, Liker, and Jaworski 1984), paying particular attention to the influence of the Great Depression on the life courses of cohorts that experienced it at different points in their lives (Elder 1974). For the Inuit men born into the settlement cohort, the specific historical events are the socio-economic forces that during their infancy and early childhood brought their parents off the land and, later, the collapse of the fur economy during the late 1970s and early 1980s. These two changes profoundly affected the structure of their lives and provided a set of challenges to the Inuit construction of the life course, the structure of their lives, and their interactions with their parents and children.

For me, "rapid social change" consists of two seismic shifts, demographic and economic changes that occurred in close succession, which have in turn set in motion a series of additional events with far-reaching consequences for Inuit. Before the fur market collapse of the early 1980s, requesting social assistance was embarrassing evidence that one was not self-sufficient and lacked a network of kin-based social support. In essence, taking SA was an admission that one was not a worthwhile person. After 1983, however, when the value of sealskins plummeted, SA became much less stigmatized. For those in the settlement cohort, in their teens during this time, taking SA became the norm rather than the exception. Although alcohol was present in Ulukhaktok well before 1983 (in addition to purchasing conventional alcohol, making homebrew out of yeast, rice, or cans of fruit cocktail was reasonably common), many Inuit report 1983 as the marker when many former abstainers began drinking regularly.

Consequently, my argument here is that these structural changes have likewise had a profound influence on settlement cohort men. They experienced the upheaval of change at a temporal moment during which they lacked the fully developed capabilities of their parents or grandparents. In a physical sense, the men of this cohort were only teenagers and had not yet developed the skills to successfully navigate the demands of structural change; subsistence hunting became much more difficult and expensive for young men who lacked both basic skills and experience to make it work from an economic perspective. Perhaps more importantly, these structural changes altered the timing of entrance into adulthood, creating a disjoint between the parallel processes of the Inuit life course. On the one hand, being adult – *inirniq* – is marked by completed physical development. On the other hand, it is also marked by the growth and development of ihuma and the demonstration of inummarik, becoming, in short, a genuine person, one at balance with being fully self-sufficient and autonomous yet responsive and committed to being embedded within a web of interdependency. The seismic shifts of structural change did not alter the physical process of adulthood, but they did hamper the ability of these men to become fully self-sufficient, and, hence, delayed their development in a social sense.

That the timing of historical events in individuals' lives should have ramifications for life course structures seems to suggest that temporal linearity is in fact critically important. It may seem odd to present the ethnography thematically. However, Elder's arguments for the importance of social structure in understanding life course processes and, indeed, the life course perspective in general, provide a framework for analysis. While the life course perspective highlights links between individual lives and the cultural collective, it is much less effective at generating an understanding of what it *means* to be part of a specific generation. The life course, for me, the ethnographer, and for my Inuit informants is a framework, a reference point, to which we both react. My choice in presenting the ethnography thematically is precisely about illuminating what it means to be in the settlement cohort rather than simply describing the structural factors that have formed that cohort. Central to the meaning of manhood within the context of the structural changes I have hinted at here are the concepts of ihuma and inummariit, which form the framework of human development for Inuit, and for the discussion to which I now turn.

2

Things Are Really Changing around Here

IHUMA AND INUMMARIK AS THE CORE
OF HUMAN DEVELOPMENT

It is a dark and quiet evening in October 1992. My Sorel boots crunch and squeak on the packed snow as I climb the stairs to Charlie Hanayi's apartment. I really should get some kamiks, traditional hand-sewn boots with thick, moose-hide soles and seal or caribou uppers. Sorels are very clumsy, and terrible for walking. My feet will be sore later tonight.

I knock nervously at the door, then open it myself and announce my presence. Though it is customary to just walk in, I am only three months into fieldwork, and I am not yet used to just walking confidently into someone's house. Charlie is probably the last person I should be nervous about visiting. Gregarious and friendly, he is decidedly easy to talk to and happy to have visitors, if he is home. Charlie is rarely home. He is so energetic that he is always out, it seems, at the hockey arena, at his uncle's tinkering with a machine, out for a drive on the land, or just visiting with friends and family. Richard Condon and I have done a few interviews with him already, but he has usually come to our house, by arrangement ahead of time.

I can understand why, aside from his energy, Charlie would be out most evenings, as the single bedroom apartment is quite small. Charlie's girlfriend and their infant daughter just moved in last month. They are still settling into a routine, and, being young, they have very little in the way of household stuff: the kitchen table is second, third, or possibly fourth hand, the chairs are mismatched, and the sofa too has seen better days. As a testament to their settling in – being "shacked up," in local terms – Charlie and his girlfriend still maintain their own schedules and are often apart in the evenings. To my modest surprise, Charlie is home tonight, and he invites me in.

Richard and I have been feeling some urgency to interview Charlie. He was at Fish Lake for ten days, and we have not seen him since he returned. As I sit on the sofa, it is apparent why. Charlie admits to struggling with colds, both the regular and the 40-ounce varieties, and he has not been out of the apartment for several days. He is feeling well enough to make coffee, though, so we sit down and begin talking about his trip. Fish Lake is a very large lake roughly eighty kilometres from the settlement, and it is an important part of the seasonal subsistence round. By early October, Inuit travel there to set nets through the ice, hoping to catch enough char and lake trout to get them through the winter. Richard and I went there ourselves over the Thanksgiving weekend. For many families, this long weekend is the highlight of the fall fishing season. Charlie went a little later, taking a week off from work, bookended by two weekends, to set nets for fish with his brother. During that week, he also went for a wildly optimistic and under-prepared drive to look for caribou.

Richard and I already know the results of the caribou trip from others. Charlie, his brother, and two other companions left the Fish Lake cabins and drove to the north and east, further from town. They had nothing with them save for two empty sleds, the rifles on their shoulders, a single five-gallon can of gas for four machines, and no repair equipment, stove, tent, or survival gear. It is not unusual for young men to go out "hunting" – though usually it is coded as "going for a drive" – but these young men were far from the settlement. Virtually no experienced Inuk would think to travel that far without tents, stoves, extra gasoline, and survival gear. Had they got any caribou, they might have avoided the gossip and ridicule that followed, but all they had to show for their trip was less gasoline in their engines. Luckily, they suffered no misfortune.

Shortly after news of this trip trickled back to town, Richard was privy to some of the older hunters' observations. One commented that these young men were not using their brains. Another older hunter quickly corrected him. They were using their brains, all right: the problem was that their brains were not very big, which is why they were doing stupid things like that.

Charlie knew that people in town were talking about their antics and their failure to get any caribou, but he did not let on that it bothered him. Our conversation, rather, focused on the rest of his week, which was spent checking nets. Charlie reported that he originally went to Fish Lake as a kind of vacation, a chance to get away from town, and he intended to help his brother catch fish for his parents, who could no longer travel. His brother and two companions, though, ended up volunteering to check the nets of six others over the course of the week.

For Inuit with jobs in town, net fishing at Fish Lake is limited to weekends, because it is simply too far from the settlement. But the nets must be checked regularly; otherwise the fish begin to spoil, rendering them useless for anything but dog food. By Charlie's volunteering to check others' nets, they could be kept in the water through the week. During summer fishing season, Inuit regard fish caught in nets as belonging to the net's owner, but there is an agreement that Fish Lake fish are a kind of community property. Most Inuit who set nets are fishing for multiple households – especially elders who no longer travel on the land – and these fish are widely shared. Charlie was not just helping the owners of the nets: he was performing a kind of community service.

Though checking nets might seem to be simple work, the reality is that it is quite tiring. It involves cutting through the frozen layer of ice to free the net, pulling it, tangled and heavy with fish, from under the ice, and picking the fish from it. Fish freeze quickly once they are out of the water, so the job must be done quickly. Inuit prefer that the fish freeze straight, so they can be stacked easily, like split wood. All this is done with bare hands, so it is cold work. The work does not end there. Once the net is reset under the ice, the now-frozen fish must be hauled back to the cabin or tent and secured in a box to keep them safe from wolves and foxes. Any rotten fish must be processed too, their tails cut off to alert others that they are suitable only for dog food. With eight nets to manage, it is a full day's work, with breaks only for tea and meals. At the end of the day, the combination of the work and being outside in the cold encourages a very good night's sleep. Despite the work, Charlie concluded by saying "I kinda lost track of the days. I had too much fun up there."

Charlie returned with fifty fish in his own sleds, bringing most of them to his parents, save for a dozen he gave to his uncle Albert and two he kept for himself. I left the house with one of those fish, at his insistence, which led to a significant point of discussion about the importance of giving to others. "I feel funny taking food from other people. I like eating food I get myself," Charlie said. "It seems like I get more satisfaction eating it when I caught it myself, rather than when someone goes out and gets it for me." I was quickly discovering that bringing the majority of a catch to one's parents was typical for a man Charlie's age. Charlie does not have storage space on his tiny porch, and his parents know better who in the settlement needs food. If Charlie needs or wants fish, he can just go collect one from his parents' house. In any event, he is there every day.

Charlie's tale was not unusual for the men of this cohort, certainly in 1992 and 1993 when I first worked with them. Many, if not most, twenty-somethings would have been characterized by their elders as having very small brains. Many of these men frequently went on the land without a full complement of equipment, or crashed their machines in frivolous endeavours, or became lost trying to find their way home. Most lacked critical survival knowledge and hunting skills, at least by their elders' standards. A few men in the sample – Charlie's uncle Albert was one of these – did meet with the approval of the older men, but that seemed to only cast the others in that much more relief. *If Albert Aquti can have a job and hunt so much, why can't you?* seemed to be both a message and a judgment of their priorities.

Nevertheless, it became clear during that first research year that it was not merely a matter of motivation and energy. Charlie had both, but he still struggled to get onto his feet. Though his great energy distinguished him from others, he too was balancing the difficulty of finding and keeping steady employment and the demands and costs of running a household with the desire to purchase and maintain subsistence equipment, all the while acquiring the skills to be productive on the land. For many, the hurdles seemed to be high, and a clear strategy for solving these problems was elusive. Because of economic and social conditions, becoming recognized as a hunter was very difficult. But it was also clear that an alternate path – becoming a wage worker primarily, with an identity as a hunter of reduced importance – was equally difficult, simply because so few jobs were available in the settlement.

In this light, Charlie's declaration that he went to Fish Lake for vacation, that he had fun there, and that he did not take the caribou trip very seriously, suggest that the goal of his trip was purely recreational. But Charlie had other intentions too. The week was clearly also hard work, and Charlie made a point of ruminating on the pleasure of helping others by checking their nets, and declaring that providing for others is a source of satisfaction. The mere fact that most of his food ended up elsewhere also highlighted the importance of giving as being far more important than receiving.

Although Charlie never mentioned the words – I doubt he was even aware of them at the time – his recounting of the Fish Lake trip touches on some critical concepts that underlie what he values, and why he values them. These concepts, coded in Inuinnaqtun as ihuma and inummariit, briefly introduced in the previous chapter, form the core of Charlie's perceptions of the value of going to Fish Lake for a week. Scholars frequently interpret ihuma to mean "wisdom" or "knowledge." In Ulukhaktok, the literal translation is "thinking." Ihuma is a feature of an individual that begins to develop at perhaps age four or five, when children internalize cultural patterns of behaviour. The possession of ihuma marks social adultness, though it develops independently of physical maturation or other perhaps more tangible social markers of aging. In one sense, Charlie's silly caribou trip that week demonstrated a decided lack of ihuma. In another sense, though, the week suggested an interest in developing ihuma, in "waking up" to the reality of one's existence, taking responsibility and demonstrating interest in the welfare of others, and deriving satisfaction from being a contributor.

Ihuma as a feature of human development, independent of physical or structural features of aging, is perhaps best understood in reference to work I have done on Inuit conceptions of successful aging (Collings 2001). When I explored life-course transitions during my dissertation work, several years after this visit with Charlie, Inuit were quick to focus on the importance of attitudes as key to having a good old age. That is, Inuit who were aging well were not necessarily those who were in good health and who remained physically active, or materially well off, or surrounded by a fleet of grandchildren. Rather, aging well depended upon one's reason, knowledge, and understanding of where one fit within the community. These people expressed a desire and willingness to engage their juniors and pass along their knowledge. They understood that the physical limitations of aging cannot be helped and remained balanced despite the ultimate outcome of aging, which awaits everybody. Indeed, having a proper attitude and frame of mind – ihuma, in other words – trumped economic, domestic, or physical features of human development as markers of maturity and aging.

Inummarik, usually translated as meaning "a genuine person," is the goal of human development, the outward expression that one possesses ihuma. Other scholars (Brody 1975; O'Neil 1983; Stairs 1992; Stairs and Wenzel 1992; Searles 2001; Fienup-Riordan 1986) have addressed the concept in their writing, and the general consensus is that inummarik refers to having proper attitudes and engaging in proper behaviour towards other people, animals, the land, and oneself. It references being in balance with one's surroundings.

Becoming inummarik, however, is not an event. One is never formally recognized for having achieved the status of inummarik. Rather, it is a process by which individuals, as they mature, begin to acquire the characteristics of an inummarik, to assume responsibility for their own life, and to take an interest in the welfare of others. For Inuit men, the most tangible sign of becoming inummarik is active engagement in the subsistence economy, particularly as hunters, becoming providers of food for their own family and for others. Hunting is the most public activity in which a man can engage, and it is clearly apparent who is a hunter. Equipment sits outside of the house for all to see. Travelling out of the settlement for hunting is easily observed, the main routes out of town being down the airport road toward the Fish Lake trail, which goes up onto the land, or on the water or ice out of Queen's Bay. Travellers returning to town from either route are observable for quite some time; everyone with a view of the road or the bay keeps binoculars handy to see who is coming and going. As Isaac Kaaktuq once phrased it in reference to an uncle who did not enjoy hunting, "He's missing the best part of life, that guy. Hunting is the best part of life." It was such an apt statement that "The Best Part of Life" subsequently became the title of a paper (Condon, Collings, and Wenzel 1995).

The central problem for the settlement cohort, of course, is that becoming a subsistence provider is increasingly difficult. It led Charlie to declare, at the conclusion of a hunting trip I made with him some eight months later, that there were no longer many real "northern men," which he defined as men who hunted and were not lazy. Clearly, one of the reasons that so many Inuit hunt ducks in the springtime is because the activity is materially and physically accessible, and also decidedly public. Young men measure their success in boxes of shells and corpses of ducks. Duck hunting does not require much specialized equipment, the travel hazards are minimal, and the knowledge to hunt ducks is relatively uncomplicated. Even a poor hunter – in both senses – can muster the time and effort to shoot ducks for several weeks in June, when the weather is nice. The kill itself is not necessarily meeting a nutritional need. At the end of June, freezers are stuffed full of ducks, the excessive kill of the teenagers and young men more a testament to hyper-provisioning than to satisfy actual need. Most families try to put by enough ducks to allow for one or perhaps two meals a week over the rest of the year, but many ducks remain in the freezer, uneaten, until the following May, when they are used as dog food, freeing up space for another season.

Despite the increasing hurdles to hunting, however, there are alternative mechanisms for demonstrating concern for others' welfare, for becoming a provider, and for becoming engaged in community life. During an interview, one young woman declared that people became recognized as adults once they started serving on the various committees and boards in local governance. Service on such committees, of course, includes cash payments as honoraria, which can be a powerful motivator. Inummariit, however, serve on committees not merely for the money but because of a genuine concern for the welfare of the community.

Though becoming inummarik is the goal, it remains a process, and individuals both succeed and fail at it, often at the same time. Simon Iqaluk enters a period of his life where he has less and less success as a hunter, an undiagnosed problem based on being out of balance. He simply has to keep trying to find that balance once again. As we shall see, David Kaaktuq becomes a provider for others, and does so at a young age, but he continues to have difficulty understanding the importance of what true concern for others' welfare really means. He is, it seems, only halfway there. Edward Kuniluk encounters numerous problems balancing the conflicting demands of the Canadian state. In a sense, his growth is inhibited because he has internalized the lessons of Inuit personhood and autonomy *too* well, unable to find a balance between what he wants to do, what he should do, and what he must do. Joseph Qalviaq, who truly understands what it means to be inummarik, still struggles with recognizing the boundaries of autonomy, and he offends his parents in the process.

Inummarik, then, is something for which one continually strives. It is partly for this reason that Inuit tend to be forgiving of others' failures and tolerate their idiosyncrasies. They have all been there. It is why Amos Tuktu can justly complain that William Kaaktuq is selfish and greedy, never helping anybody, yet the very next day he brings William a *natiaq* (young ringed seal) because he knows that it has been a long time since William has eaten natiaq. William might be greedy, but a provider must look to everyone's needs and recognize that people can and do change. Being inummarik, then, is as much about compassion as it is about concern for others' material well-being. Hunting, and sharing the results, clearly remains the critical path to becoming inummarik, but Inuit have shown time and again that they are flexible in adapting to changing circumstances. As Charlie Hanayi and Joseph Qalviaq both demonstrate, wage labour has become equally important in allowing men to satisfy the internal requirement to provide for others.

Consequently, my informants and friends are best understood not as cultural ideals, individuals who represent some notion of traditional idyll, or as perfectly adjusted people. They are, like the rest of us, flawed beings who nevertheless strive to be something better than they are. In the face of difficulties, Simon sums it up best: "*Ayurnarman*. It can't be helped. I just have to keep trying." Inuit recognize that one's fortunes are dependent upon external forces, that one's existence is tied to social connections and obligations to others, but one must keep going and not give up. Sometimes one succeeds. Other times one does not. But the process is made more difficult – though not impossible – for the men of this cohort precisely because they are striving within the context of shifting and uncertain economic and social circumstances. The remainder of this chapter is devoted to discussing these circumstances and the ways in which men of this cohort have adapted to them, while referencing the basic frameworks that guide their development.

THE LIFE COURSE, TIMING, AND CULTURE CHANGE

The term "settlement cohort" describes the generation of men like Charlie Hanayi, Edward Kuniluk, Isaac Kaaktuq, and Joseph Qalviaq. Although some of these men were born in a tent or *iglu*, and many spent a significant period of their childhood living in summer sealing camps or running traplines alongside their fathers, they have, for the most part, formed their identity around life in town. As such, they have grown up within two competing models of what it means to be a successful adult. The Canadian and American, or "southern," model, acquired through formal schooling, television, and a changing economy, emphasizes career planning and the accumulation of wealth as keys to a good life. The Inuit model held by the men's parents and grandparents, however, is quite different, focusing both on connections with family and on the inherent qualities engendered in living on the land. Money is a mere tool for accomplishing these goals.

In Ulukhaktok, the settlement cohort, born between 1958 and 1973, is also a baby boom generation. Richard Condon, who worked in Ulukhaktok from 1978 until his death in the field in 1995,[1] focused his research program on this generation of Inuit, paying particular attention to the changes that village life brought to them. Both Condon (1994) and Peter Usher (1965), who worked in Ulukhaktok during the 1960s, have documented the slow but steady movement of Inuit off the land and into the expanding settlement, drawn there by, as David Damas (2002) has argued, a combination of wage labour opportunities and access to government-supplied public housing. Permanent residence in the settlement also granted Inuit access to the expanding government-sponsored social safety net of support programs and medical care, which together improved nutrition and fertility. And while these forces worked to promote the possibility of children, social conditions made population growth a certainty. Young men and women were living together in a concentrated settlement rather than in dispersed hunting camps as before. The result could hardly be otherwise.

The children resulting from these unions – Charlie, Edward, Isaac, and Joseph among them – grew up in a social setting where their childhood was quite different from that of their parents. Their worldview was shaped as much by the children with whom they grew up as it was by their own parents and grandparents. The result of these changes was, according to Condon, the emergence of a new life stage – adolescence – which Condon characterized in *Inuit Youth* (1987) and subsequent articles (1990a, 1990b) as not all that unlike adolescence in southern Canadian settings.

Demographic changes were not the only alterations to Inuit lives, however. With settlement came increased opportunities for wage employment, access to a southern-based educational system, and new technologies for hunting. By the time many in the settlement cohort were at least approaching their teenage years, media diversions such as television were providing a window onto southern culture. Indeed, these kinds of changes have been well documented across the Arctic. Taken together, the result has been that these men were among the first to experience a formal education in the settlement, to learn to hunt in the context of a declining fur economy, and to come of age in a social climate in which fluency in southern culture was an absolute requirement for economic and social success.

Condon's work, however, focused on these secular changes within a narrow framework, and from a very specific direction. He was primarily interested in how external forces such as schooling, television, the collapse of the fur economy, or interaction with outsiders reconfigured Inuit lives. And, indeed, Condon documented the many (and intertwined) outcomes of these kinds of changes, focusing on alterations in family structure and relationships (1990a), conflict management strategies (1992), gender roles (Condon and Stern 1993), subsistence and identity (Condon, Collings, and Wenzel 1995), and the extension of adolescence well into young adulthood (ibid.). In addition to his placement of the causality arrow, his approach also focused on a description of these outcomes in isolation from the broader context of the community. He analyzed the lives of his informants primarily outside of the broader social context in which they occurred. When discussions of relationships with parents and grandparents emerge, they tend to focus on the conflicts between his informants' lives and their elders' expectations.

This critique is not an indictment of Condon's work but rather a reflection upon the perspective engendered by his interests in developmental psychology and the processes of culture change. I arrived in Ulukhaktok in 1992, under Condon's supervision, a graduate student conducting fieldwork for the first time. Over the intervening years, I have engaged in research with this cohort of men, becoming good friends with some of them, moving through my adulthood alongside them. When Condon passed away in 1995, some of his informants were in their early thirties, and many were younger. I have had the opportunity to observe these men as they have made the transition out of what Condon would have defined as adolescence and into adulthood. Together, we now see the headlights of middle age down the road. My interests have expanded to include observations of these men in the context of their extended families, paying attention to the connections they have with their parents, in-laws, grandparents, and their own children – some of them now young adults themselves. Rather than focus on how secular changes have fostered the emergence of a single life stage, I have built upon Condon's early work and focused on the entirety of the Inuit life course.

In the social sciences, the "life course perspective" is an approach to understanding aging within the entirety of a specific social context, and as a process that occurs across the entirety of an organism's life. In this sense, the life course is quite different from the life span. Whereas the life span (see Hagestad 1985, 1990) refers to the physiological developmental schedule that marks juvenile periods, full adulthood, and senescence, the life course is a cultural phenomenon, referring to the schedule of social changes that are marked within the context of a culturally defined sense of time. In this sense, the life course is a cultural unit, a cultural domain on par with a society's economy, social organization, or belief system (Fry 1996; Fry and Keith 1982). The life course as a cultural unit defines appropriate roles and statuses for individuals of different ages. It suggests the appropriate sequencing of social roles across a lifetime, and it provides the framework for timing transitions from one life stage to the next. It is the mechanism by which the individual is connected to the larger cultural collective. Although each culture has an ideal life course, the cultural construction of the life course provides for tremendous diversity in both managing and generating alternative life courses.[2]

The social time of the life course is thus different from either biological or chronological senses of aging. In non-industrial cultural settings – like that of the Inuit of Canada, for example – chronological and biological senses of time are frequently ignored in favour of a more cyclical, seasonal view of the passage of time. Among Yup'ik speakers in Alaska, for example, Ann Fienup-Riordan (1983) has documented the timing of ritual events and life stage transitions, noting that these life markers frequently coincide with the seasonal cycle of subsistence. Furthermore, the structure of the universe is perceived in such a way that the human social world replicates itself every few generations. As individuals pass away, their souls are reborn in the world. Babies are named after the recently deceased, and they retain the same positions within the kinship network as their namesakes. Mark Nuttall's work (1992) in Northwest Greenland documents a similar phenomenon, and these practices are likewise evident in Ulukhaktok, where an elderly woman may address a young child as "husband," and some particular behaviours may be attributed to the namesake.

In addition to its role in timing and sequencing role transitions, the life course also links individual biographies to the greater cultural collective. This linking allows for variation in how the normative life course is constructed while also recognizing the importance of the cultural, social, and historical context in which individuals age. Matilda White Riley (1986), for example, has written that cohorts must by necessity differ in their collective life experiences because of their positioning within a historical context, something that Elder and colleagues, as discussed in the previous chapter, have documented for specific cohorts in the United States.

In terms of social contexts, and closer to the subject of this book, an individual's place within social structure likewise has significant effects on his or her behaviour. Burch's *Eskimo Kinsmen* (1975), for example, discusses the role of the whaling captain (the *umialik*) as a particularly important economic and political leader in Inupiat communities. Access to the position of umialik, however, was circumstantially limited to men who were fortunate enough to be first-born children, who had an extensive kinship network from which they could draw crew members, who were fortunate enough to be born to successful and prosperous parents, and who, in addition, had the good fortune to marry an industrious woman who herself came from a respected family. Rising to the position of umialik depended as much, if not more, upon these contextual variables as it did on the individual's motivation.

In Ulukhaktok, Condon and I concluded from our 1992–93 fieldwork that our informants' participation in subsistence hunting was primarily constrained by contextual factors. These constraints included access to wage labour employment, time engaged in formal schooling (and away from subsistence activities), and the collapse of the fur markets in the early 1980s – all variables over which these Inuit had little or no control. For me, the central problem of belonging to the settlement cohort, then, is not that these men were the first to experience adolescence. Rather, it is the *timing* of the constellation of changes in Ulukhaktok that has had such a profound effect on their lives.

The changes of the 1960s, 1970s, and early 1980s may have affected settlement cohort Inuit in a specific way, as Condon demonstrated, but those changes had far-reaching consequences for older Inuit too. Health care and the social safety net improved longevity as much as it did fertility, ensuring that more and more Inuit reached old age in relatively good health. When the Inuvialuit Final Agreement (IFA) – the land claim to which Ulukhaktok belongs – was signed in 1984, the IFA (and the Inuvialuit Regional Corporation, or IRC, created by the IFA) defined "elderhood" as beginning at age fifty. This definition of elderhood was, after some discussion, based on more traditional notions of when people were judged to have passed the threshold into old age, a period of physical decline and reduced economic productivity. For many of my informants, however, fifty seems like a strange age for defining the onset of elderhood. Currently, there is some ambiguity about when one becomes an elder. Though many are quite willing to accept the financial benefits of elderhood – among them the annual payments stipulated by the IRC – most fifty-year-olds admit to feeling "funny" at being classed as an elder, equivalent to Inuit who are thirty years their senior.

In the "old days," of course, when Inuit depended solely upon a seasonal round of subsistence hunting powered by their own labour, a hard and physical life took a toll on the body. Much like a professional athlete, a hunter at age forty was well into physical decline. Access to health care has certainly improved the lives of these men, but so too have the changes in technology that Inuit now depend upon for their living. Warm, insulated houses with running water and sewage systems certainly make life easier. New technologies such as snowmobiles and ATVs have extended the economic lives of Inuit hunters well beyond age fifty, something that Condon also noted (1996) and Damas (1972) predicted, just as snowmobiles were coming into vogue in the Arctic. William Kaaktuq, for example, can now barely walk because of arthritic knees, yet a snowmobile, a boat, and an ATV provide him with the mobility to remain a productive hunter. Indeed, many Inuit men are productive hunters well into their seventies, with a few remaining active into their eighties. Harry Tamaryak, for example, is still hunting at age eighty-five, providing food for three or four households on a regular basis.

Other less obvious intersections of economic, political, or policy changes also affect Inuit lives. Changes in housing policy over the past thirty years, for example, have worked to the detriment of settlement cohort Inuit. As I have argued elsewhere (Collings 2005), a series of policy decisions by the Northwest Territories Housing Corporation (NTHC, or "Housing") has profoundly affected Inuit of different birth cohorts. Beginning from the premises that Inuit should pay for their housing according to their income, and that home ownership is something for which all Inuit should strive, policy changes have worked to the economic disadvantage of younger Inuit. Because younger Inuit tend to be working at wage-labour jobs, they have been forced either into dramatically high rents for public housing or, by moving into the "private" market, into purchasing a home by taking a mortgage and assuming the entirety of the costs for their utilities.

On the surface, this seems like a noble goal: people should be responsible for their own lives, after all. Many Inuit would themselves agree with this statement. However, the remarkably high costs of housing are disproportionately shared: older Inuit, those born before the settlement cohort, tend to have different living arrangements. Some older Inuit acquired a private unit for free, under an early privatization scheme, the Housing Assistance Program (HAP). The program ended in the early 1990s, just as many of my informants were approaching a time in their lives where they could qualify for a HAP house; instead they ended up acquiring a mortgage. Other older Inuit tend to rely on a combination of their old age pension and any traditional cash-generating strategies they continue to pursue, many of them effectively under the table. These older Inuit, for their part, tend to live in heavily subsidized public housing, usually to the tune of (in 2007) $38 per month for their rent, with heavily subsidized utility payments as well.

This reality is but one reason why many men, even those in their late thirties and early forties, depend so heavily on their aging parents for access to equipment. Isaac Kaaktuq, for example, relies on his father's boat for summer hunting trips, since he hasn't enough money to afford his own. He is saddled with house payments – payments that sometimes leave him without enough money to purchase heating fuel, let alone keep his own equipment in working condition.

Furthermore, Condon (among others) has argued that settlement cohort men found their development as hunters stunted by life in Ulukhaktok. Successful hunting requires a great deal of training at different levels in any environment, as anthropological research has shown time and again.[3] In a mixed economy like Ulukhaktok's, younger men have found it difficult to acquire important skills in a timely manner. For many of these men, time spent in school periodically interrupted their training as hunters. This zero-sum game – hunting or school? – has continued into adulthood, as the need for money to hunt necessitates a strategy for acquiring money. For the fathers of the men in the settlement cohort, that money came from fur sales and from seasonal or casual employment that did not necessarily conflict with time spent hunting. For the settlement cohort, a full-time hunting strategy is simply impossible for most, and money must come from some kind of wage work, which usually demands adherence to a thir-ty-five-hour weekly schedule that anchors them to the settlement.

Consequently, and because of these timing issues, many of the men in the settlement cohort reach their late thirties not fully competent as hunters. Some, of course, know more than others, the product of their individual experience, training, abilities, and motivation. But even the most productive hunters in this generation are effectively still learning, a point driven home a few years ago when one of the younger (at age forty-five) polar bear guides failed to get a bear that he had been track-ing for his tourist hunter. The bear crossed a recently opened lead in the ice, and the guide was unwilling to follow. His father's assessment? "He's not a good hunter yet," referring to his son's unfamiliarity and discomfort with negotiating potentially dangerous sea-ice conditions.

Others are less kind when young men fail to take an animal they are tracking, uttering things like "That's because he learned to hunt when he was thirty," and sometimes worse. My interaction with some elders has suggested that, for their part, they have little appreciation of the kinds of difficulties their children face as they try to make sense of the high costs of living, the requirements of the wage economy, and the difficulties of becoming an efficient hunter. Some men raised in the contemporary community may have the complete toolkit, but many lack the knowl-edge and experience to make the best use of it.

The other side of the coin for these younger men, of course, helping to make up for their failings as hunters, is that many have parents who are still productive. This situation can cut both ways, though, perhaps encouraging children to sit around and rely on sixty-year-old moms and dads to provide the food. What happens when mom and dad fi-nally retire?

The crux of the matter, then, is that secular changes in Ulukhaktok have effectively stretched the life course. Childhood stretched out and adolescence emerged, but the entire process of becoming and experi-encing adulthood elongated as well. Indeed, the central argument of this book is not that adolescence has emerged as a novel life stage and become prolonged into adulthood but, rather, that the nature of secu-lar changes in the settlement has prolonged the process by which men become fully competent adults, genuine people, or inummariit. How have the kinds of changes documented by academic and government-sponsored research (some discussed above) affected the lives of Inuit? More importantly, how have Inuit coped with these changes? What strategies have they pursued to "make it"? What does it *mean* to be born in the settlement cohort? How does an Inuk go about negotiating the constellation of changes that have characterized Arctic villages over the past fifty years?

To this point, this discussion of the life course has largely incorporated literature that tends to be concerned more with bounded cultural entities; Glen Elder's work, for example, focuses on the life course within the boundaries of American culture. It should be apparent, however, that addressing the Inuit life course requires by necessity an examination of Inuit within the context of connections with the Canadian state and its impact on the life course. There is a large literature that examines aboriginal-state relations,[4] though of interest here is work examining the nature of the social contract, which typically focuses on how individuals and families manage aging in the context of state societies.[5]

In the United States and Canada, for example, the state assumes a number of functions designed to provide for the well-being of individuals and families. Young families gain access to certain kinds of financial benefits through tax credits and deductions. Low-income families have access to additional benefits. The state also assumes functions that were formerly the purview of the family. Formal schooling is a mechanism by which children are socialized and educated, the goal being to create productive citizens.

The role of the state in structuring and managing the life course is not trivial. In the United States and Canada, state institutions manage and schedule the life course. The state authorizes individuals to drive, to serve in the military, to smoke cigarettes, to drink alcohol, to work, to get married. At the opposite end of the life course, the state manages old age, providing pensions, retirement benefits, and access to socialized health care. All of these thresholds, as is common in state societies, are marked by chronological age, with other developmental considerations playing a secondary role. While this form of the social contract may make some sense in a very large society, it is worth noting that not all individuals develop in precisely the same manner. Not all sixteen-year-olds *should* be licensed to drive a car, for example. Not all sixty-five-year-olds necessarily need or want to retire.

For most southerners – and here I reference both southern Canadians and Americans – the state operates in people's lives largely in the background, a part of culture that is unquestioned. Americans, for example, may debate how best to arrange and negotiate the social contract between the state and the individual, but there is no question, save on the political fringes, that the state *should* be involved in managing the life course in some way.

In Ulukhaktok, however, the state is a relatively novel phenomenon, part and parcel of the colonial enterprise in the North. It is a problematic entity for Inuit. The initial Inuit experience of the state was that its representatives, despite mostly good intentions, often behaved in ways that were harmful. Today, Inuit interaction with the state is, like most things, a complicated phenomenon. Inuit clearly recognize the state as a provider, a source of help and assistance in an economically difficult climate. The state employs a number of financial instruments that offset the high costs of living in the North. Gasoline prices, heating fuel costs, public housing, and other services related to living conditions are heavily subsidized, if not provided outright by the state, as is health care, which is nearly free for Inuit. There is also a significant social safety net. In an environment where opportunities for wage labour jobs are few and far between, the provision of social assistance is a great help for many families. Older Inuit depend at least partly upon their old-age pension for support.

That said, most of the overt, obvious, and tangible benefits, such as social assistance, tax credits and rebates, and other direct financial help provided by the state are accessible primarily to women, not men. Men who apply for public housing are given much lower priority than women. Tax credits on behalf of children are paid to women. Social assistance is also accessed by women. When men interact with the state and the state's agents, the experience seems to skew toward the negative.[6] The first experience many teenage boys have with the RCMP is usually the result of something they did wrong. Hunters interact with the RCMP and Department of Renewable Resources through the engagement of rules and regulations on what may and may not be taken, usually with an emphasis on what hunters may *not* do, lest they face sanctions.

One relevant example involves Inuit engagement with the schools. The goal of the educational system is, ultimately, to produce good Canadian citizens by providing Inuit with important and basic skills like reading, writing, and mathematics. An equally pragmatic goal is to prepare Inuit for lives as productive workers, with good wage-paying jobs. No consideration is given to the location of that job: the implicit understanding is that one is expected to sell one's labour and relocate as the job dictates.

Problematic here is that the idea of selling one's labour and relocating is not particularly appealing to Inuit, for it would require severing ties with kin, the community, and the land. There are numerous cases of young men who pursue training opportunities for careers as helicopter pilots or airplane mechanics, only to abandon them when the realization strikes that they will have to leave Ulukhaktok to pursue that line of work.

Ultimately, the influence of the state and its programs for educating and training young citizens interfere with the business of being Inuit. William Kaaktuq was quite aware this problem, noting it during an interview (also reported in Collings et al. 1998): "I don't know if my grandson will be a good hunter. He's still young, and I don't want to say yet because maybe I am lying. It would be difficult to teach him because of school and being in town most of the year. My oldest son [Isaac] was following me around the trapline when he was six and a half. I bought him a machine when he was seven. But kids have to go to school now."

The paradox here is that, even in its role as provider, the state remains a dangerous entity. In the domain of education, the problem is one that Nadasdy (2003, 43–8) sums up well. The cultural model of the southern school is that the teacher, not the student, determines when the student is ready to learn. Furthermore, the institutional setting of the school requires children to conform to a standard of behaviour. Students are expected to do what they are told, and only what they are told, which, Nadasdy argues, instils a lack of initiative on the part of the children. They then grow up expecting to be told what to do, and told what to do by non-native representatives of a foreign culture. Perhaps it is no wonder that many young people have difficulty transitioning into productive adult roles: not only are there two cultural models but they are conceptual, perhaps irreconcilable, opposites. As I discuss below, the Inuit model is quite different. For Inuit, it is individual learners who demonstrate when they are ready for instruction, both capable and ready for attention from their elders.

Many older men, for their part, advocate for a kind of primitive libertarianism and decry the ways in which the state has upset Inuit lives. In this narrative, the state has made Inuit "soft" through the perceived flood of government subsidies, comfortable living and low costs of public housing, ubiquitous televisions and computers that espouse southern rather than Inuit values, and training in an educational system that robs Inuit of the basic disposition – ingenuity, initiative, and resourcefulness – required to thrive in an Arctic environment. Over the years I have listened to numerous older people relate tales from their father or grandfather, who predicted that a time would come when Qablunaat would keep Inuit the way that Inuit keep dogs. Once Inuit are tied to the metaphorical dog line, so the story goes, the Qablunaat will abruptly depart, leaving Inuit to themselves once again, a return to pre-contact times. Things will be hard, and many Inuit will die because they are soft.

Ultimately, however, things will get better for the people who are still alive. For some older people, the evidence appears to be mounting that the time of reckoning is close at hand. A number of older men have commented that the young people lack the same capacity for work that they themselves had when they were young, that too many young people lack initiative to do anything, that they are content to sit by and wait for the government to solve their problems.

I have sat in this camp myself, experiencing first-hand some of the absurdities of the state and its regulations that make little intuitive sense in the North or are impossible to fulfil. It is equally true that the state and its agents as providers have fostered a learned helplessness among younger Inuit. The state is seen as an agent that will step in and solve one's problems, often to the point of ridiculousness. In one instance, a woman with a concern over her grandchildren's safety called the RCMP, requesting that they speak to the neighbour about cleaning up the junk machines in their yard. She perceived the rusted equipment as potentially dangerous for her grandchildren. The neighbour in question was the woman's son-in-law; neither she nor her husband could confront either their daughter or son-in-law to solve the problem. Closer to home, during 2007, I was confronted with a housing problem, which I solved by converting my storage shack into a habitable shelter. To make it work, I relied on social relationships to meet my needs for electricity, bathing, and laundry. Yet, despite a clear need for housing in the settlement, few Inuit take this kind of initiative to solve their housing problems. Young people in similar straits, faced with limited funds, rising costs of public housing rents, a lack of a stable residence, or all three, chastised me for breaking the rules or somehow cheating the system. Yet they continued to complain about the system and its perceived unfairness, seeing the solution as the state doing more than it already does to help.

INUIT CONCEPTIONS OF PERSONHOOD AND AUTONOMY

Life course perspectives can help us to understand the constellation of secular changes that Inuit in the settlement cohort face at a structural level. The life course provides a framework for understanding the barriers to adulthood and the way that the timing and scheduling of life course transitions can change over time. However, the argument I am making here is that Inuit continue to reference traditional concepts as they adapt to dynamic circumstances. The frameworks provided by the concepts of ihuma and inummariit are themselves informed by Inuit values regarding personhood and autonomy, of which there is a substantial literature.

The general theme of the work on personhood among Eskimo peoples is that Inuit and others place an extraordinarily high value on personal autonomy and individual integrity, ideals instilled at a very young age. Martha Crago and colleagues (Crago 1992; Crago, Annahatak, and Ningiuruvik 1993), for example, have examined Inuit linguistic and child socialization practices in Nunavik. Crago has noted that Inuit

instructional methods emphasize the importance of learning by observation rather than direct instruction. Children are rarely if ever encouraged to ask questions; rather, they are expected to comply with requests
and observe and comprehend the situation unfolding around them.
Inuit adults generally have little use for conversation with their young
children, the reasoning being that children have little to say that an
adult might find interesting. What could a child possibly say that an
adult does not already know? Indeed, Inuit adults determine a child's
readiness for further training when the child demonstrates readiness
for it: progress is driven by the child, not by the adult.

Two examples, I think, help to illuminate these themes. The first is
from an occasion when Joseph Qalviaq and his brother were visiting
Condon and me early in our 1992 fieldwork. The brothers were at our
house for interviews, and Joseph reported catching a fox in one of his
traps. He had not set traps in over a decade and during previous visits
had indicated that there was something of a conflict brewing with his
wife, who had no interest in processing foxes. But Joseph really wanted
to set traps, and so agreed to do them himself or ask his mother for
help. He made it clear, however, that he really wanted to do the foxes
without help. His insistence at running traps initially gave us pause: we
wondered if the reason he was setting traps was because we were, however subtly, provoking him to do so, given our focus on subsistence
involvement.

A discussion then ensued between Joseph and his brother about
running traps. During their teenage years, they lived in an outpost
camp for part of the year and would go with their father to run a trapline further down into Prince Albert Sound, a line stretching a hundred miles and more from Ulukhaktok. Both expressed admiration for
their father, who always knew where he was on the land, even in the
absolute darkness of midwinter. But Joseph also expressed embarrassment. He remembered frequent occasions of arriving at a site and not
remembering which of three traps, set close to each other, was his, and
having to ask. He was embarrassed, feeling like a small child for having
to ask, and being scolded for not knowing.

A more telling example of such training involved William Kaaktuq
and his grandson David. It was springtime, and William had a need to

get his small boat onto a sled. The idea was to drag the boat over the ice to Kiijjaviik, some forty kilometres down the coast, and leave it there to be used in July for setting nets. Although he could simply set nets closer to town, William, like many of the old men, was competitive: he wanted fresh char, and he wanted to catch them first. By setting a net at Kiijjaviik he could intercept the migrating char before they arrived at the settlement. The boat in question was a ten-footer, with a ten horse-power motor attached. Dragging the sled over the ice was both safer and more efficient than going by water.

William, however, was getting too old for the physical work of haul-ing a boat, and he also wanted to show his grandson the proper means for transporting a boat over land. So, down to the beach he and David, then twelve, went, with me tagging along as additional muscle. William sat on the AT V, directing us on the most efficient way of getting the boat onto the sled. Once we were done, he hobbled over with the line to tie the boat to the sled. After initiating the process, showing David the par-ticular knots and hitches he was using, he gave the line to him and said, "Now you do it." Having been shown how, David secured the boat. When he finished, he looked at his grandfather, who simply nodded.

Afterward David said that it was the first time he had been allowed to tie a boat down, and he expressed surprise that his grandfather did not walk around to check the knots. Later, over tea, William simply said David now knew "what to do." Ultimately, William was engaged in a kind of scaffolding, assessing his grandson's ability based on prior experience, showing the boy what needed to be done and then allow-ing him to do it. Similarly, Isaac Kaaktuq has noted that his own child-hood was spent being shown new skills, ones just at the edge his ability, enough so that he would be further motivated to develop the skill properly.

In another sense, I was also being shown, and when I spoke with William about David, I was respectful enough to not ask a direct ques-tion about the incident. The subject merely came up in conversation, and I observed that David seemed to be keen on hunting. William re-sponded enthusiastically, expressing his esteem for his grandson. David both wants to learn and is keen to demonstrate his skills as they develop.

That I did not ask directly about David is important. Both Fienup-Riordan (2001) and Morrow (1996), who have worked with Yup'ik Eskimos, have discussed the problems inherent in asking direct questions. As Briggs notes in *Never in Anger*, asking questions is viewed as a sign of boorishness, a sure indicator of lacking social skills. Only children would be so rude. Furthermore, asking is a coercive act, because it violates individual autonomy. As both Fienup-Riordan and Morrow note, one cannot flatly deny a request or refuse to answer a question, which places the individual being questioned in a difficult bind. Yup'ik, when put in such uncomfortable situations, tend to resort to the path of least resistance to end the discomfort, even if the least resistance means being evasive, giving questioners what they want to hear, or lying. Part of this behaviour is certainly due to the boundaries of the individual, but there is also a general fear of aggression among Inuit that accounts for such strategies (Briggs 1991).

In my own experience in Ulukhaktok, rarely have Inuit made direct requests of me. When Edward Kuniluk has been short on money, for example, he has never asked me directly for assistance. Instead, he has phrased his need in such a way as to leave me with an opening. A statement such as "Boy, I got no money right now, and Pampers are sure expensive. I'm not sure how I am going to get Pampers for the baby" is an invitation for me to respond either in the affirmative by offering or to decline by making an equally oblique statement. An effective way to say no might be "Yeah, I wish I had money, too, but the university hasn't transferred my paycheck yet."

Are indirect requests as effective as direct ones? In some ways, yes, but in other ways, they leave open many other possibilities, among them deflections or replacements. In Edward's case, I met one such oblique request for money with an alternative to just giving him some. "My machine is in really bad shape, and I need to get it ready for winter," I said. That statement led to Edward's offer to get the machine ready for me, and my offer in turn to pay him to do the work. Problem solved – and, more importantly, solved in a way that avoided harm to Edward's autonomy or pride. Edward got the money he needed without having to resort to the indignity of being indebted to me. In return, I solved the problem of working on a snow machine, which I generally dislike. More importantly, the subtlety of such negotiations allows for a great deal of flexibility in social interactions and problem-solving.

Respect for autonomy and integrity extends more broadly to social life and community cohesion. Inuit are generally reluctant to confront others about their behaviour or activities, even when such activities are potentially destructive and hurtful. Social correction usually comes indirectly in the form of gossip and innuendo. Direct confrontation is best left to the immediate family, who may choose to intervene in various ways. My wife, Maya, once conducted an interview with an older woman who used the interview as an opportunity to scold her daughter, Elizabeth, for her increasingly heavy alcohol use. Maya asked, "What is it like for adults in Holman today?"

Ruth K. responded, "Today the things that adults do, teens see what they are doing and follow the same pattern. As Elizabeth gets older, she will wake up and realize that things she does are wrong. It will be like waking up from sleep when Elizabeth will start realizing the things she does are bad. That she shouldn't do them. From a teen to a young adult you are in a fog. Sometimes it clears up, and the next day you are back in fog. The next stage of life is adult and you realize that what you are doing is not right. At that time in my life [moving from teen to young adult] it was like being in fog or waking from a deep sleep. You start realizing from what you've been told that what you are doing is wrong."

The daughter, Elizabeth, interpreted, and both she and Maya were bound by the constraints of the interview. Throughout the interaction Elizabeth was forced to not only hear the message in Inuinnaqtun but then had to repeat it in English for an outsider, which must have been a deeply shameful experience. It was an effective intervention on her mother's part.

The implications of the above for doing fieldwork should be reasonably obvious. Researchers make their living by making requests of others and by asking questions – in short, by lacking social graces and being rude and aggressive. Charles Briggs (1986) refers to the problem as one of meta-communicative competence. Outsiders like ethnographers or survey researchers arrive at a scene without prior knowledge of linguistic or cultural conventions, and so proceed to behave in a manner that violates local norms. In Inuit villages, barging into houses, interview battery in hand, is one such violation, but an additional problem is that the outsiders have demonstrated through their behaviour that socially they are children. Ned Searles (2000) discovered this during his work on Baffin Island, when in the early part of his fieldwork he asked numerous, seemingly innocent questions and was met with evasion, misdirection, and occasional hostility. Only after he acquired some cultural competence did he realize the significant mistakes he had made. After learning to learn by observation and then demonstrating his competence, his rapport improved and he was able to complete his work.

We outsiders compound the problems of cultural incompetence by being social children who proceed to ask deeply penetrating questions, novices seeking expert level knowledge without having demonstrated the mental capacity or trustworthiness to handle it. Alcohol and drug use, domestic assault, sexuality and STI transmission, and shamanism are only some of the sensitive and sophisticated waters into which outsiders routinely wade.

None of this is to say that Inuit do not ask or answer questions, or that they do not volunteer information, or that they do not teach others. Likewise, it does not mean that researchers cannot ask questions. The lack of directness is simply an extension of the value of autonomy and the importance of subtlety and flexibility in social interactions. When I first arrived in Ulukhaktok, I quickly discovered that telling a story was the preferred means of transmitting information. Inuit would tell stories that, on the surface, seemed like entertaining tales, but these stories also had deeper meanings, points of instruction and nuggets of wisdom to be filed away for future reference. Only upon reflection did the intent or meaning of the story become clearer to me, though I am quite sure that I missed the point of most of what was told to me. This method of instruction and interaction places the burden of teaching not upon the instructor but rather on the learner (in this case, me), something that Paul Nadasdy references in *Hunters and Bureaucrats* (2003, 96–101): the learner demonstrates his or her readiness for instruction; the teacher will not waste time on one who is neither willing nor able. If one cannot fathom a meaning behind a story, or hear a request buried within a conversation, it is not the teacher's or the requester's fault. Rather, it is an indication of the current state of the learner's development.

It is noteworthy that explorations of Inuit conceptions of personhood and autonomy are about *personhood* rather than *manhood*. While the literature on these concepts makes their meaning reasonably clear, it is not particularly helpful for providing insight into the meaning of manhood for Inuit. As I observed in the first chapter, much of the research on and about Inuit men has tended to focus on subsistence and economic activities. When gender becomes the focus of inquiry, men are typically cast as something of a problem in the contemporary setting. Recent scholarship, for example, tends to view the transition to settlement life as introducing significant gender imbalances, resulting in a number of negative outcomes.[7]

That men are viewed as being a problem created by changing circumstances is perhaps unsurprising, for manhood and masculinity have been relatively understudied in both anthropology and gender studies. Although there has always been an incidental interest in men and men's lives, the specific focus on men is a quite recent phenomenon, which has grown out of feminism and women's studies.[8] Guttmann (1997), paying particular attention to trends in anthropology, notes that studies of men and masculinity have tended to direct their inquiry in different ways ranging from examining what it is that makes men *men*, to understanding how men perform their masculinity, how men are socially male, and how men fit in the social spaces in opposition to women.

Thus, while studies of men and masculinity have increased substantially over the past twenty years, much of the scholarship of interest to anthropologists focuses on marginalized or alternative masculinities rather than the processes that underlie manhood more generally.[9] Research that does attempt to transcend the exotic or the marginal tends to lack specifics, employing national or even regional boundaries as representative of particular kinds of themes in masculinity, reminiscent of the culture area approach long abandoned in anthropology.[10]

Consequently, the broader literature on men and masculinity does not contribute either theoretically or ethnographically to understanding how Inuit construct and understand masculinity. Inuit ideas about what makes for a proper man have less to do with concerns about domination, power, or sexuality,[11] frequently the focus of the scholarship about masculinity more broadly; rather, Inuit masculinity has more to do with the importance of productivity and provisioning, concern for others, and balanced relationships with the land and with others. Indeed, the essential problem for *young* Inuit men is that in the contemporary settlement the important themes of masculinity have largely been blurred. Young men are well aware of the important themes and goals of manhood, but the ability to see a clear path to their attainment has become more difficult. As we will see in chapter 7, the settlement has effectively become the domain of women, a place largely managed and directed by women, much as, during pre-contact times, the iglu was the purview of the wife. Men who lack the ability, drive, or resources to engage with the land are in many ways emasculated, prevented from engaging in the productive activities – hunting and, by extension, providing for others – that transform one into a socially competent adult, a genuine person, or inummarik.

THINGS ARE REALLY CHANGING AROUND HERE

The Kingalik Jamboree denotes the beginning of summertime in Ulukhaktok. Jamboree is an annual celebration, a rite of intensification marked by a long weekend of feasts, dances, and games focused on the annual duck migration. In late May and continuing through late June, king eider ducks fly by the settlement in what seem like the millions. Inuit hunters take them with shotguns in large numbers, stockpiling an important food that will last until the next June. Jamboree usually occurs in mid-month, beginning with a potluck dinner followed by games, raffles, and live music, with dancing at the community hall or the school gym into the early morning hours. The following afternoon, the party recommences outside, usually at the hamlet offices, where the women light fires and cook food while others engage in games and contests of various kinds: duck plucking, seal skinning, nail driving, and bicycle racing. Inuit from other settlements fly into Ulukhaktok to take part in the celebration.

Once Jamboree ends, Canada Day is just around the corner, celebrated by another outdoor cookout, more games, and a parade. The fire truck cruises around the settlement, sirens blaring, followed by a herd of ATVs, pickup trucks, and bicycles. The parade usually has more participants than observers. In previous years, the party was held at the sandpit, a large dune on both sides of the airport road, just before the bridge over Ukpillik's River. More recently, the party has been held at Jack's Bay – the third bay after King's and Queen's bays – a shallow body of water on the west side of the three hills that form Ulukhaktok Bluff and where Ukpillik's River empties into the Beaufort Sea. A combination of gravel and sand, the beach there is good spot for launching motorboats, and, indeed, Jack's Bay tends to be clear of ice before either Queen's or King's bays. It is also a good spot for setting nets for char, and more than a few Inuit set up tents along the shore there during the summer.

Jack's Bay too is a good place for an outdoor feast. The hamlet places picnic tables on the beach, and the women, as at Jamboree time, construct fire pits and build fires out of old palettes and scraps of dimensional lumber. Games are played, contests held, hot dogs, hamburgers, and barbecued char consumed. If muktuk is available, it is boiled and served. Bannock is fried. People tend to drop in at various points during the long afternoon and early evening, stopping for a bite to eat, to visit with friends, and perhaps to participate in a game or two.

Canada Day is followed only a few weeks later by the golf tournaments. The first of these is the Gary Bristow Classic, so named for the long-time mayor of Ulukhaktok. It is a warm-up event for Inuit who want to tune up their game for the big event the following weekend. The Billy Joss Open (BJO), named for a former Hudson's Bay Company manager, is the centerpiece of high summer as Inuit from around the western Arctic fly into Ulukhaktok for three days of golf and feasting. Aficionados in Ulukhaktok claim the nine-hole course, set along the road to Ukpillik Lake about a kilometre from the settlement, is "the world's most northerly golf course in the world," as a sign proudly states. Whether this is true is open to question, but it is certainly a unique experience to play on open tundra. When the course was first designed, the putting greens were really browns: oiled sand swept smooth after a party played it. These days, the greens really are green, the artificial grass rugs standing out among the dull, rusty shades of an Arctic summer.

Golf is something of a passion for many younger Inuit, who pass their idle time during the brief summer by playing the game. During the BJO, though, golf becomes much more important, on a par with Jamboree. Another cookout is set up at the first hole, and the afternoons of the tournament are spent eating, chatting with both players and non-players, and enjoying the relatively warm temperatures.

In addition to these scheduled events, the summer is marked by numerous spontaneous celebrations. During one summer, Ulukhaktok celebrated Ocean's Day, the day after Canada Day. That particular summer, self-government was the talk of the settlement, and Ocean's Day doubled as a kind of public relations event for the Inuvialuit Regional Corporation and the federal government. Several dignitaries from both sides of the negotiations came in on a charter flight from Inuvik to provide an update on the state of negotiations and to survey the state of the communities taking part in them. The idea was to merge the municipal governments, which were funded and administered by the NWT Government in Yellowknife, and the Community Corporations, which were local governance arms of the IRC. A self-government agreement would settle the problems of overlapping jurisdictions and redundant services, with the hope of both saving money and generating true Inuit self-governance.

Of course another feast was in order. Several women set up camp-fires at Jack's Bay and cooked hot dogs and hamburger patties, barbecued fresh char, fried bannock, and made tea and coffee. Through the late afternoon and evening, many people came down to the beach to eat and socialize. Some of the young men, sensing an opportunity to show off, organized an impromptu water-skimming contest. Rumbling over the gravel, five snowmobiles made the quarter-mile trip past the last duplex and down to the beach. Water skimming is the practice of driving a snowmobile across water. Snowmobiles certainly do not float, but if they move at speed, the ribs of the track providing propulsion, they can stay on the surface of the water. Some Inuit purchase tracks for this very purpose, with longer ribs, or even "paddles" in the track, to facilitate skimming.

In Ulukhaktok, the origins of skimming were strictly utilitarian: in the spring, the snow melts off the land long before the sea ice breaks up, and to facilitate travel up and down the coast for duck hunting, Inuit move their machines onto the ice. The ice retreats from the shore as it melts, eventually necessitating "skimming" the machine over the open water and back to the land. Most hunters engage in this practice, but the point is simply to get the machine to shore, and one skims the machine twenty feet or less.

The water skimming that these young men had in mind was quite different. It was purely a display of derring-do, starting from shore, skimming over the water for as long as possible, and returning to shore. As the men took turns, the beach-goers stood and watched. The teenagers were genuinely impressed by the spectacle, oohing and aahing as the drivers turned in the water, nearly lost it, recovered, and made it back to shore. The older men were less impressed, and they fell to a discussion about the foolishness of skimming a snowmobile. Charlie Hanayi noted that the salt water would get into the engine and corrode everything underneath the hood.

Albert Aquti, arriving to catch a bite of food and check on the proceedings, nodded and added, "The sand too. Really good for polishing everything up. Going to finish their bearings right away."

We seemed to be in agreement, a group of grouchy men sneering at the stupidity of young people. These young men would likely drive their machines back to their house, park them, and discover the damage only after the first snows of the fall, after which they would realize all the work they had to do to get their machines running for the winter – work they would have to do in the cold and darkness.

"Wait 'til they sink one," Isaac noted. He must have known something, because within five minutes the skimming ceased, a sunk machine ending the show.

Jack's Bay being so shallow, Dennis Iqiahuuyuq was some forty feet from shore but in only six or seven feet of water. He misjudged his speed while turning and lost his momentum. The machine went down unceremoniously, a few bubbles and gurgles, then silence. Dennis stood on the seat, water to his waist, awaiting rescue. Though it was early July, the water was only a few degrees above freezing. No one seemed to be in too much a hurry to rescue Dennis. Eventually, a pickup truck appeared, some of the young men rowed an old boat out, and both Dennis and the machine were removed from the bay, Dennis in the boat, the machine dragged by a chain.

As all of this unfolded, Albert said, "He's going to have to take the whole engine apart now. I wonder how much he'll try and sell it for?" It was a reasonably new machine, perhaps now available at a deep discount. Albert went off to inspect it as it was loaded onto a sled, later to be dragged back to Dennis's house.

Meanwhile, on shore, events moved forward. Edward Kuniluk arrived shortly with the drums, and several of the elders began drumming and singing, sitting on the picnic benches while a few of the younger men and women danced in front of them, also singing. These first dances were in the "western" style, reminiscent of the Mackenzie Delta Inuit (now called Inuvialuit) and Alaskans, group-oriented dances in which the elders generally sit aside and drum and sing, with the others dancing in unison. The style has been popular since the late 1990s, when a dedicated troop formed and interested Ulukhaktomiut began dancing regularly at the community hall. It was one of the few venues in which old and young engaged publicly with each other, and it gained such popularity that even teenagers began asking for instruction in making and wearing their own special dancing attire.

After a few of these dances, some of the other elders produced their drums and began drumming in what people call the "old style" – the Inuinnait style of the Central Arctic, in which a single person drums, dances, and sings, occasionally joined by another. Unlike the western style, the Inuinnait style has far fewer adherents, almost all of them elders, though Edward was one of the interested, and very talented, young people to dance in this manner.

As we sat and watched, some of people began to pack up their things and clean up. The snowmobiles were long gone, as were most of the teenagers. A handful of Qablunaat sat, mesmerized by the singing, probably thinking to themselves, "Look! Culture!" – overlooking that the entire day was culture.

"I wish someone could provide a translation of what the words mean," said one of the Qablunaat dignitaries. "I wish I could know what they're singing about." Impatience in the tone conveyed a belief that the drumming was a scheduled activity designed specifically for the visitors as a cultural display. Observers thus were entitled to an interpretation.

I tried to explain that the drum dancing appeared to me to be spontaneous. "Well, you know, songs belong to people. So what Robert is singing about is really his song. He owns it. I'm not sure that an English translation would help you."

"What do you mean?"

"I'd guess that the song goes something like, *Sitting over the fishing hole, how I long for a fish! Ai-ya-ai-ya!* What do you think that might mean to us? It hardly sounds poetic. I think we could only really comprehend such a song if we knew what it was like to go hungry for a long time and then catch a fish. The songs have such personal meanings. They all refer to very specific experiences. We can only truly understand them if we have experienced the same things."

"Oh."

After the singing ended, the dignitaries hopped in the taxi for the chartered flight back to Inuvik. Most of the Inuit left too. Once the fires were out, food packed, and trash collected, I sat at on a picnic table with Isaac and a couple of the women on the cleanup crew. Everyone was some kind of cousin in one way or another, except for me. It had turned into a beautiful evening, warm and sunny, pushing 20°C, with a very light wind from the west. The possibility of self-governance was on everyone's mind, it being, after all, the reason for the charter in from Inuvik and the cookout in the first place. Still, it was not clear what "self-governance" actually entailed. It sounded good but it still meant change. I suppose that's why the subject came up very quickly.

"You've been coming here a long time now, haven't you?" The question was directed at me by Jeanette Kuptana. "When did you first start coming here?"

"Fourteen years ago this summer, 1992. It seems like a long time, but then it doesn't, you know?"

Helen Iqaluk now. "I bet you have seen some big changes around here, eh? Things have really changed since you've been coming around." She sounded somewhat sad. It was more of a statement than a question.

I intuitively knew what Helen was getting at, with *changes* really meaning *cultural changes*. In the years I have been coming to Ulukhaktok, one of the first things that has always struck me was that cultural changes were not nearly as severe as people seemed to think. I thought a moment. "What kinds of changes do you mean?"

"It's like our culture is really dying. Some of the elders are passing away. And people can be so mean to each other now."

Isaac chimed in, "It's like people can be really unfriendly. People don't help each other anymore. You walk by some people, and they can't even say hello, they don't even look at you, they're so stuck up." He made a face, his version of what a stuck-up person looks like.

Change, especially the sense that things are changing for the worse, is a common theme in the Arctic, nearly a mantra in the government and research communities, both of which have focused on documenting how people cope with rapid social change and how the negative consequences of such changes can be ameliorated. Helen and Isaac were repeating some of the literature on acculturation, the sense that Inuit culture is indeed dying, that Inuit are becoming much more like Qablunaat, losing their culture and their identity.

In some sense, these things were true. The growth of the settlement over the past forty years probably accounts for some of the apparent unfriendliness. In 1960, the entire population of the region was roughly 120 people, spread out over thousands of square kilometres. Now, depending on who's counting and how, the population is somewhere in the low to mid four hundreds, all concentrated in the same place. One of the consequences of growth has been the opportunity for relatively anonymous interaction. In Ulukhaktok, it does not take a huge effort to avoid others. In my time in the settlement, there are still a few people, shy and reclusive, whom I have only seen a handful of times and never spoken to.

And, with people concentrated in the settlement, the old mechanisms for defusing conflict, many of which involved avoidance and moving away, are no longer viable. Condon (1992) documented many of these changes years ago, suggesting that with older forms of conflict management now defunct, an outside enforcement agency, in this case the RCMP, is necessary to fill that vacuum. Damas (2002) and Rasing (1994) have highlighted similar issues in other settlements in the Canadian Arctic. People in Ulukhaktok now lock their doors when they are not home, and hunters keep their tools and equipment under lock and key, worried about their presumably less-than-honest neighbours. Even so, Ulukhaktomiut universally note that conditions elsewhere are far worse. In Kugluktuk, Ulukhaktomiut say, people break down doors to get into others' houses to steal things. In Cambridge Bay, people have to take the keys out of their snowmobiles lest others take them for a joyride.

On a broader level, though, the sense in Isaac's and Helen's statements – frequently repeated by most of my informants over the years – that Inuit culture is changing for the worse reflects a significant tradition in social science research in the Arctic. Much of this research has been engendered in the work on subsistence and economy, long an important focus in the social sciences. Initial interests in subsistence and economy in the North are best exemplified by works by Balikci on the Netsilik Eskimos (1964) and Damas, who focused on comparisons of the Netsilik, Iglulik, and Copper Eskimos (1969a, 1969b). These works, among many others, approached the study of subsistence economies from a cultural-ecological perspective, focusing on the nature of human-environment interaction, and, as Burch (1994) notes, also on the nature of foraging societies in general.

Even in the 1960s it was evident that the North was changing rapidly, and research agendas quickly expanded to examine how sedentism, new technological inputs, and fluctuating fur and wage economies forced Inuit to alter their subsistence patterns and general economic strategies. Consequently, investigations of hunting economies typically addressed one or more of three elements of subsistence. One avenue of research focused on the interplay between the subsistence and emerging wage-sector economies by assigning values to subsistence activities, ostensibly to place an objective value on subsistence (see Ames et al. 1988; Berger 1977; Borre 1990; Usher 1976; Wolfe 1979). A second avenue examined the importance of the cash economy in supporting or constraining subsistence activities (see Kruse 1991; Langdon 1991; Müller-Wille 1978; Nowak 1977; Peterson 1991; Quigley and McBride 1987; Wenzel 1986, 2000). A third avenue investigated the continued importance of subsistence hunting in rapidly changing communities where jobs were scarce and the costs of living extraordinarily high (see Burch 1985; Fall 1990; Huntingdon 1992; Kruse 1986; Smith and Wright 1989; Wenzel 1981, 1986; Wolfe and Walker 1987).

Underneath these general trends in research has been a dialectic involving two contrasting traditions of research on subsistence and economy. The first understands subsistence as a cultural form that is best described as a social economy (Peterson 1991; Wenzel, Hovelsrud-Broda, and Kishigami 2000). That is, subsistence is more than the material production and consumption of wild resources. Although it includes resources and behaviours that are visible in their outcome, and thus empirically measurable, subsistence is as closely linked to Inuit social life as it is to economic relations (Lonner 1980; Wenzel 2000; Dahl 1989).

The second tradition expresses a view of subsistence that is jointly derived from acculturation studies and neoclassical economics. This tradition focuses on commodity production, or participation in production, as the essential measure of the viability of subsistence. Based on this view, the apparent decline in subsistence participation by settlement-reared cohorts of Inuit (essentially those forty-five years or younger) is evidence of cultural changes devaluing subsistence in favour of other kinds of economic strategies (Mitchell 1996; Reimer 1993; Stern 2000). The view of subsistence as a form of economy has also changed. Subsistence from this perspective is seen as based on the production of goods for exchange or economic development (Cesa 2002; Myers 2000) rather than goods of social value (Buijs 1993).

Balikci (1989) and Riches (1990) have each argued that these two oppositional conceptual approaches – adaptation (expressed primarily through cultural ecology) and acculturation (expressed as the extent of change to or retention of traditional cultural features) – have dominated contemporary Inuit studies. Although these two opposing views have to some degree been reconciled within discussions of Inuit identity (see Wenzel 2001), this dialectic continues to be expressed in examinations of contemporary Inuit subsistence and economy, and, in a broader sense, culture.

Vallee's (1962) work on Inuit and cultural change starkly laid out the essential opposition that still persists in this literature. In Vallee's view, Inuit were transforming from being Nunamiut to being Kabloonamiut; that is, they were moving away from being traditionally adapted to the Arctic to becoming incorporated into Canadian society through domination by non-Inuit institutions. Vallee's framework may have been intended only rhetorically, but it spawned a generation of monographs on acculturation (Chance 1966; Graburn 1969; Honigmann and Honigmann 1965, 1970; Hughes 1965; Nelson 1969; Vallee 1962, 1967, among others), which is a testament to the power and utility of this approach in understanding the rapid shifts occurring in the Arctic during the settlement period.

The influence of the acculturation perspective waned during the 1970s and 1980s, but it has re-emerged recently in various ways. Mitchell (1996), for example, sees Inuit society as developing class distinctions. Reimer (1993) sees the Inuit economy as one in which subsistence is a luxury, dependent upon money as a critical input but unable to replace it. Myers and Forrest (2000) suggest that subsistence has diminished utility as anything other than a base for certain forms of economic development. Stern (2000) likewise sees subsistence as a recreational outlet. Closer to home, Condon's work specifically tackled the acculturative forces at work in Ulukhaktok.

More importantly, my own experience, informed by numerous statements like those made by Isaac and Helen, suggests that Inuit themselves have internalized the acculturation perspective. The numerous secular changes to a place like Ulukhaktok – the disappearance of the "traditional" full-time hunter and trapper, the increasing dependence upon wage labour, the emergence of social problems like increasing conflicts and alcohol and drug use – certainly lead one to the conclusion that things are, indeed, changing. At the time, and perhaps more so since, Isaac, Helen, and Jeanette were repeating a common theme. Inuit culture, it seems, really consists of only two stages: "traditional" and "modern," the problem being that modern Inuit culture, already far removed from the traditional, is moving in what is commonly perceived to be a negative direction. For those on the beach, smoking a last cigarette before heading home for the evening, their own grandparents or parents represent "tradition," a qualitatively different lifestyle and worldview completely at odds with life in today's village. Just as the Qablunaat viewed drum dancing as being "culture," while ignoring everything else about the event, Inuit did too.

That said, underneath these changes are things that remain decidedly Inuit. Over nearly twenty years I have seen significant economic changes, many of them for the worse. Each time I have returned, however, my field journals end up being full of as many positive observations as negative ones. Angus Ikayukti, who was nothing but an obnoxious and troubled teenager constantly in trouble with the RCMP, has become a steady food producer for his aging parents. Eddie Agluaq, who never learned to hunt as a child, now has the full complement of hunting equipment and, more importantly, makes extensive use of it. Joseph Qalviaq, who was struggling to simply stay off social assistance when I first met him, now is a key figure in the community corporation. Inuinnaqtun, which I rarely heard my informants speak in 1992, is now routinely used in the home, albeit differently from how their parents use it. Clearly, something is happening.

What follows is an examination of but one part of that "something," an investigation of the framework that informs and directs the lives of the men I have worked with for nearly twenty years. How do Inuit men negotiate the bewildering dichotomy between the demands of the southern world and that of their own elders? How and why are they successful?

NOTES

1 Richard Condon died in a boating accident in Siberia in 1995. He was a consultant on an NSF grant based on work in Kamchatka, and while he was in Providenya, his host, Russian anthropologist Alexander Pika, took the research crew down to a village where he worked. They went by skin boat, spent the day in Sireniki, and then started back. They never made it.

Only two bodies were ever recovered, those of a native woman, and Steve McNabb, an anthropologist then at the University of Alaska Anchorage. The events leading up to the accident were unclear. I've spoken with several people who say that the boat was so loaded down with additional passengers who wanted to go to Providenya that it overturned. A fishing-boat captain came forward to say that he saw the boat and offered to offload passengers because it was so loaded, but they refused. The official word, as I heard it, was that the boat was capsized by a gray whale.

Only a month before, I had a long talk with Rick about choosing a site for my dissertation work. Siberia was just opening up to outsiders, and we both agreed that professionally it could be very exciting and provide a huge career boost. But working in Arctic Canada had a number of advantages, among them political stability and a good health system. In the end, we decided that I should continue to work in Ulukhaktok.

2   Linda Burton's work (1990; Burton, Dilworth-Anderson, and Merriwether de-Vries 1995) with African Americans in US urban settings, for example, demonstrates how social and economic conditions in impoverished urban settings can work to restructure both the life course and family structures and to alter perceptions of social time and role transitions.

3   Surveys conducted by Gurven, Walker, and colleagues (Gurven, Kaplan, and Gutierre 2006; Walker et al. 2002) demonstrate that, in a sample of foraging societies, men do not become fully competent hunters until their mid-thirties. The examples that Gurven and Walker use, however, are from societies where there are few if any legitimate economic alternatives to foraging, unlike the case in the Canadian Arctic.

4   This work, examining both Canada and elsewhere, usually focuses on the nature of the colonial encounter. Much of this literature addresses the creation and maintenance of dependency (as examples, see Biesele 1997; Bodley 1987, 2008; Dyck 1985; Fleras and Elliot 1992; Jaimes 1992; Paine 1996; Perry 1996; White 1983). In the Canadian Arctic, more focused examples are instructive. Tester and Kulchyski's *Tammarnit (Mistakes)* (1994) and Marcus's *Relocating Eden* (1995), for example, examine the disastrous nature of Inuit relocation projects in the Arctic, most notably to Resolute and Grise Fjord. Damas's *Arctic Migrants/Arctic Villagers* (2002) documents the ways in which state policy regarding Inuit changed over the course of the contact period. Damas argues that policy changes and subsequent settlement were driven as much by Inuit as they were by the state, though Ulukhaktomiut see it differently. Inuit in Ulukhaktok, especially younger Inuit, frequently assert that the government *forced* Inuit to settle at Ulukhaktok.

5   Examples of work in this domain include examinations of structural change in families in response to institutional changes (Bumpass 1990), changes in the timing of transitions and roles in specific contexts (Burton 1996), comparisons of the social contract and aging, particularly between Japan and the

United States (Akiyama, Antonucci, and Campbell 1990; Hashimoto 1996; Hogan and Mochizuki 1988; Kamo 1988), the creation of state dependency of the elderly (Townsend 1981), or comparisons between different kinds of state contracts, usually focusing on European nations and the United States (Hungerford 2001; Popenoe 1988; Stuart and Hansen 2009). More broadly, others (Mayer and Schoepflin 1989; Mayer and Muller 1986; Street and Quadagno 1993; Kohli 1986a, 1986b) discuss the ways in which the state as an entity restructures the life course and alters family structure.

6 Shelagh Grant's *Arctic Justice* (2005) examines the impact of the RCMP and their role in early law enforcement on Baffin Island. Throughout, Grant notes the rather draconian methods employed by the RCMP in administering northern justice. Ulukhaktomiut elders remember the "old days," when lawbreakers were sent to Cambridge Bay. The reports of hard labour, poor treatment, and miserable food were enough to keep Inuit in line. To this day, RCMP officers are viewed with ambivalence tinged with fear.

7 Both Billson (2006) and Flaherty (1997), for example, discuss the increasing problems of domestic violence and sexual assault in Inuit settlements, focusing specifically on women's understandings of and responses to violence in their communities. Dawson (1995) sees the built environment as a vehicle for acculturation, one that undermines women's traditional roles and responsibilities and contributes to increasing gender asymmetry. Healey and Meadows (2007) review the literature on Inuit women's health, documenting the numerous health problems associated with settlement life, among them alcohol use, violence and assault, lack of food security, and sexually transmitted diseases. Other work (Billson and Mancini 2007; Blackman 1989; Bodenhorn 1993; Wachowich 1999) more specifically focuses on what it means to be an Inuit woman in such changing circumstances.

8 This interest grew partly out of the realization that men, like women, are explicitly gendered, socially constructed, deliberately produced, and altered across the life course (Hearn et al. 2002). Guttmann (1997), and others (Kimmel, Hearn, and Connell 2005) have documented this recent shift in the social sciences, demonstrating that anthropologists and others have largely abandoned the sex role approach formerly favoured by anthropologists such as Benedict, Malinowski, or Mead (see Benedict 1934; Malinowski 1929; Mead 1963).

9 In western, state-level societies, examples include work focusing on masculinity and criminality (see Collier 1998; Messerschmidt 1993) and homosexuality

(see Levine 1998, Nardi 2000). The anthropological literature likewise tends to focus on the marginal or exotic. Herdt's work (1987, 1994), for example, focuses largely on sexuality and ritual among the Sambia, setting up men and manhood as a largely sexual process in which men are defined in opposition to women. Guttmann (1997; Guttmann and Vigoya 2005) has pointed to particular dangers associated with this approach. He demonstrates that the concepts of *machismo* and *macho* in Latin America are largely externally created, with a recent linguistic origin rather than of an internally valid cultural theme. But, because of their otherness in comparison with American cultural understandings of manhood, they have become regarded as real phenomena.

10 Kimmel, Hearn, and Connell's 2005 *Handbook of Studies on Men and Masculinities* is particularly instructive here. The volume considers masculinities in the "Third World" (Morrell and Swart 2005), East Asia (Taga 2005), Latin America (Guttmann and Vigoya 2005), or Europe (CROME 2005; see also Hearn et al. 2002) or focuses on specific problems, such as politicizing "Muslim masculinities" (Gerami 2005). Such broad categories are perhaps useful for theoretical reasons, but their ethnographic utility is questionable (likewise noted by Guttmann and Vigoya 2005, 115).

11 Masquelier (2005) reports similar findings from her work in Niger. For Mawri men, the problem of manhood, much as for Inuit, is one of achieving social maturity, of finding a balance between contradictory conceptions of morality while at the same time struggling with changing economic landscapes that effectively delay marriage, and with it, maturity.

3

A Congenial Dolt Learns about Inuit Culture

In the previous chapter I noted that the life course perspective allows us to link the individual's experience of growing into adulthood to a larger cultural context. Although the life course approach has certain limits, it remains useful because of those links. The men in the cohort under study here are the product of a unique set of social and historical circumstances. They are the first to be born and raised within the context of a permanent settlement, yet they are intimately familiar with the rapidly eroding contact-traditional lifestyle that links with the Inuit cultural past. An exploration of Inuit socialization methods and Inuit conceptions of human development reveals that these cultural models remain both vibrant and useful frameworks for Inuit men as they negotiate transitions from one life stage to the next. These models provide signposts and references for where they should be in their life. How have Inuit conceptions of manhood and masculinity articulated with this cohort of men, who have come of age in an extraordinary time and place? The current anthropological scholarship on masculinity highlights the apparent uniqueness of Inuit manhood while providing a frame for comprehending it.

These theoretical frames set the analytic tone for the narrative that follows, and they are referenced, though sometimes obliquely, through the remainder of the book. The theoretical frame, however, is only one orientation to the narrative that follows. I have chosen to present the ethnography thematically, rather than in linear fashion, knowing full well that there are consequences to this choice, among them the potential to confuse the reader. Likewise, I have chosen to present the narrative with me squarely in the picture, sometimes even as the subject.

So it must be. I am, after all, examining a cohort of men to which I tangentially belong, being roughly the same age as or slightly younger than most of my informants. I am investigating a topic – the process of becoming a man – that concerns me deeply. I was undergoing the same process myself while at the same time learning to become an anthropologist and ethnographer. These dual (perhaps identical?) processes most certainly shaped my own experiences in Ulukhaktok, including what I was exposed to and how I processed the information presented to me. While many of my research visits with my informants were focused on data collection in the domains of subsistence and economics, the tea, coffee, snacks, and discussions around that data collection frequently centred on the events of our lives and how we manage them. I have twenty years' experience with Ulukhaktomiut, and I have lived in Ulukhaktok for something close to four years. Each time I return, I see and learn new things. Sometimes these insights inform events and episodes that are twenty years in the rear-view mirror. That increased knowledge does not make things easier; rather, it complicates the issues, adds layers of complexity, and forces me to make choices in how to present and organize the ethnographic material.

Just as my personal circumstances shape the narrative and the choices I have made, so too my position as a researcher has presented me with certain opportunities while restricting others. Inuit have had ample experience with researchers of various kinds and varieties. As a measure of protection, "researcher" is a social category into which outsiders are placed, and there are various scripts that direct social interaction with researchers and limit what they can and cannot do. Because of the time I have spent in Ulukhaktok, and because ethnographic research is somewhat dissimilar from most cross-sectional research conducted in the settlement, I have had a slightly different experience from most. Nevertheless, I am still a researcher, as I am reminded nearly every time I stroll through the settlement. A standard opening to conversation with Inuit is "How are your interviews going?"

Finally, because of the nature of my personal position, my role as a researcher, and, most importantly, the time I have spent in Ulukhaktok, my engagement of Inuit cultural representation is a bit different from that of others. There is an accepted *academic* standard and discourse regarding the representation of Inuinnaqtun, for example, just as there is an accepted social standard for representing Inuit culture. Ulukhaktok is today considered an Inuvialuit community by virtue of its location in the Inuvialuit Settlement Region, and Ulukhaktomiut are continually pressed, by various mechanisms, to adopt *Inuvialuit* as a label for who they are. At the local level, however, the issue is complicated. Inuinnaqtun as a linguistic designation is equally contested, and defined differently, depending on the context and the person discussing the issue. Again, the issue is complicated, and made more so because this book is sprinkled with Inuinnaqtun expressions and phrases. The language is clearly endangered, and English is the first choice for public interaction for anyone under fifty. Still, conversations are full of Inuinnaqtun expressions and terms, fully incorporated into English utterances and used in ways that never appear in the textbooks, grammars, or dictionaries – which are themselves suspect, for reasons I explore later in this chapter.

I begin with a timeline of my own research experience in Ulukhaktok, highlighting the social and personal spaces I occupied during fieldwork visits and the ways these experiences inform this book. I then turn to a discussion of the dynamics of doing fieldwork in Ulukhaktok, focusing on research roles, research scripts, and my negotiation of the constraints and freedoms of occupying a particular role. In closing, I discuss the representational issues of concern in this volume, and explain my choices in representing Ulukhaktomiut and Inuinnaqtun within an academic context.

WHERE I LIVED AND WHAT I LIVED FOR

I have chosen to present the core of this ethnography as a series of thematically organized episodes. This structure allows me to focus on issues common to men's lives, although it is a departure from a more familiar, linear approach, with potential hazards for the reader. This is not cross-sectional research. Joseph Qalviaq was quite a different person in 2012 than he was in 1992. When I first met him, he was struggling to make ends meet. He could find only seasonal employment, and he and his wife relied on social assistance for part of the year. He likewise struggled to satisfy his parents' expectations for how he should live his life. Twenty years later, he is a fifty-year-old grandfather, an active hunter and provider, wage earner, and community leader. When Joseph appears in the ethnography, which version of him is it?

Despite the risks, the thematic approach reflects the intense nature of ethnographic fieldwork and captures at some level the ethos of Inuit social interaction. Normal conversations take twists and turns, double back on themselves, change direction, and shift dramatically through time, depending on the whims of the conversation partners and the topics under discussion. The ethnographer's task is to make sense of the soup in which he or she is swimming. Writing field notes and journal entries is a significant part of the daily routine, a time set aside for recording the day's events, entering data, and ruminating on what the day's experiences might mean. Events may unfold in a linear fashion, but the ethnographer must find patterns, discover links between events and interactions, and, as time passes and understanding increases, discover new information previously hidden, perhaps even from Inuit themselves. It is ultimately an exciting process, though not without drawbacks. In the constant search for cultural meaning, ethnographers are prone to becoming hyper-analytic, willing to see patterns where none exist. Those three ringed seal carcasses, frozen solid and shoved into a snowbank in a precise, triangular pattern? What does it mean? It turns out it does *not* mean that someone in the house is sick and requires prayer. It was just the way the hunter shoved the seals into the snowbank.

Uncovering meaning is a process that can take years, if not decades. One particular sequence of events occurred during 1997, over a period of eight months. That year I was still young enough that I played basketball at the gym with guys in their twenties and early thirties. In late winter and spring, the gym was usually open for recreation on week nights, and a group got together to play after the school-aged kids were all supposed to be home for curfew. I tried to join in at least once a week, because I needed the exercise and there were precious few opportunities to stay in shape.

We were occasionally joined by a younger fellow, Tommy Aliuqtuq, then in his early twenties. Very few of us were any good at basketball, but Tommy played with reckless abandon, as if the game was something like hockey or American football. He was only vaguely aware of the rules, though no one called him out when he took five steps and then threw the ball at the rim, missing badly. The other players were uncomfortable around him. His eyes often had a wild, vacant glaze, indicating that he was either stoned or had some undiagnosed mental illness (or, quite possibly, both).

It turned out that he was mentally ill. In early July, he displayed psychotic behaviour several times, the last occasion ending in a confrontation with the RCMP and medical evacuation to Yellowknife. When he returned about a month later, he was much calmer, the look in his eyes one of sedation rather than mania. He seemed sleepy, and he largely withdrew from public activities like basketball.

I rarely saw him that fall – indeed, he nearly dropped out of public view – but it was not a surprise to me when I learned one morning that he had hung himself on his porch after a fight with a former girlfriend. It was a period during which there was a wave of suicides in Ulukhaktok and the neighbouring communities of Kugluktuk, Cambridge Bay, and Sachs Harbour, occurring over the course of eighteen to twenty months. Indeed, that period was so marked by suicides that when I returned to Ulukhaktok two years later for a summer visit, a common theme in my initial conversations was a relieved "We haven't had a suicide in eighteen months now." Tommy was merely the most recent, but to me it was the most comprehensible – he was crazy, after all. There was no need to resort to explanations such as "acculturative stress" to rationalize why he killed himself. Shortly after his suicide, I learned that he had stopped taking his medications some weeks before. Biomedically, it made perfect sense. He was sick, he received treatment, he did not comply, and then he killed himself.

My understanding was turned on its ear some weeks later. I was behind William Kaaktuq's house, distracting him with conversation while he was trying to work on a sled. Our talk eventually moved toward the predilection for young people to kill themselves. There had been yet another death, this time in Kugluktuk. William told me he was tired of it, young people killing themselves. He declared that he was not going to attend any more funerals, it just encouraged them. Fair enough, I thought: a few other elders I knew had made similar statements. There was silence for a few moments, but then William spoke again, and he admitted that he felt a bit guilty about it, referencing Tommy. I asked why he would feel guilty about Tommy's death. Tommy was from a completely different family. The relationship was so distant, and the age gap so great, that there was little reason for any interaction between the two beyond Tommy dropping off a gift of meat at his parents' direction.

William explained that Tommy came to him several times during the weeks before the suicide, wanting to talk about the voices he was hearing. As a former deacon in the Anglican Church, William was a logical and perhaps safe person to ask for help. According to William, Tommy was hearing the voices of his grandfather and grandmother, long since dead. They were talking to him, telling him that he could have great power if he listened and followed their instructions. William's phrasing of the interaction – "talking to" – was telling. "Talking to" young people is one of the most important things an elder can do for them, imparting wisdom and knowledge, providing a framework for understanding development, and suggesting strategies for coping with the problems of the world. When an elder is talking to you, you ignore the lesson at your own peril.

By the time William was involved, Tommy had already been to Yellowknife for treatment and was taking medication. Even so, Tommy reported that his grandparents were still talking to him, saying that he should stop taking his pills, that he could become a very strong *angatkuq* if he stopped taking them. When I asked what William's response was, he said simply that the story scared him, that he counselled Tommy to keep taking his medication, see the nurses for more help, and start going to church.

As I listened to William relate the story, I was both stunned and excited. Until that point in my experience, Inuit rarely talked to me about shamanism. When they did, shamanism was nearly always discussed in the context of a witchcraft accusation: so and so is using angatkuq against other people. Even then, these reports were made in a way that suggested that Inuit themselves did not really believe it. Indeed, those who privately accused others of using angatkuq against other people, or of being an angatkuq, included nearly all of the elders in the settlement (including William), people who were also the most devout

Christians. At the time, it seemed unlikely to me that these accusations were anything more than an expression of the tensions of living a small community.

The term *angatkuq* has multiple meanings. It is frequently used across the Arctic to refer to a particular role that outsiders often translate as "shaman." In this sense, Tommy was being called to acquire power and become an angatkuq, to become a practitioner and specialist. William, as a devout Christian, was always clear that "being an angatkuq" – being in the role of the practitioner – was certainly not Christian but rather the work of the devil, and to be resisted.

In another, more general sense, however, angatkuq also means "power," and can refer to various non-empirical abilities that individuals possess. In this sense, nearly everyone "uses angatkuq," whether consciously or unconsciously. One hunter in Ulukhaktok, for example, was widely regarded as being particularly good at net fishing. He seemed to have an unusual ability to catch more fish in his nets than anybody else. This was viewed as a special power, something that made him different from others. Inuit regard some hunters as having similarly focused abilities in relation to animals. Others may experience the power of the spirit world more directly. Charlie Hanayi, for example, related an experience from a time when he was travelling on the land in late November. He and his travelling partner ran down a pack of wolves, and Charlie shot one. His partner went on while Charlie skinned it, but in the darkness of a November afternoon and evening, they didn't find each other for several hours. It was late at night before Charlie returned to the cabin that was their base camp. He had not eaten all day, but when he got to the cabin he found he was no longer hungry. He perceived that he was covered in fur, he felt strong and powerful, and his senses were much heightened. This feeling, he said, lasted about an hour before he returned to normal and felt like himself again. His father later told him that sometimes after a hunter killed an animal, its spirit could briefly inhabit his body.

In this sense of its meaning as power, angatkuq is simply a characteristic of the universe, and it does not compromise Christian belief or practice. When one uses it frequently, though, or is actively trained in its use, one then becomes "*an* angatkuq" and risks the anti-Christian labels so frequently attached to the practitioner. Laugrand and Oosten (2010, 241) make a similar distinction between the ability of elders to interact safely with non-human entities and to protect themselves from attacks by them, while avoiding the hazards of becoming an active practitioner.

I knew none of this at the time and have acquired this limited understanding slowly and in bits and pieces since. William's revelation to me was exciting because, in addition to being a clear, emic explanation of what happened to Tommy, it signalled that I was ready for at least *some* insider information on a culturally sensitive topic. This sharing has continued over an additional fifteen years. In hindsight, William's understanding was clear: Tommy was being called to be an angatkuq, and his resistance to heeding this call (or, perhaps, his acceptance, given that he stopped taking his pills?) ultimately resulted in his death.

Just as my understanding has increased over time, my position in the community has changed. My interactions with Ulukhaktomiut have evolved, because I have aged and grown as has everyone else, and relative age is an important component of relating to others. This point was brought home one summer when I was out boating with Edward Kuniluk and we were faced with some floating ice. He asked me what we should do. "You're older," he said, in deference to me.

I laughed. He was being kind. "It's your boat. And you know better than me what to do, anyway."

Since I first arrived in Ulukhaktok, insights have built upon insights. Not only do my informants know more about themselves than they did twenty years ago but so do I. My first four months were largely spent trying to figure out who was related to whom, who lived with whom, and how I could get through my day without embarrassing myself. Much of that groundwork has served me well since, and it has made my time more efficient. Contemporary problems are more easily understood in the context of that background.

My first research trip to Ulukhaktok began in early August 1992, when I was a student of the late Rick Condon at the University of Arkansas. I had completed my first year of graduate study and was entering the field with Richard (as he is still known in Ulukhaktok) to assist him with his own research, which focused on subsistence hunting and identity among young adult men. We would be in the field together for three months, after which Rick was to leave and return to Arkansas, leaving me in Ulukhaktok until he returned the following June. It was nearly the ideal way to enter a field setting, a field school with me as the only student. Rick had worked in Ulukhaktok since 1978 and had several years' worth of time living in the settlement. He was very well liked and respected, and he shared a great deal of his information about Ulukhaktok, saving me the trouble and discomfort of making the common mistakes or errors that plague first fieldwork. I had access to his genealogy notebooks (copies of which I still have), and after the day's work Rick was a wealth of information, especially in providing insights into who was bullshitting me and who was being honest.

Peter Takuyuq, for example, looked forward eagerly to my visits that fall. Over numerous cups of coffee he provided me with all kinds of "expert" information about caribou hunting, muskox biology, fish migrations, and all things traditional. He did not realize that I already knew, through Rick, that he had never shot a caribou in his life (and perhaps had never seen a live one) and that, unlike his older brothers, he was never taught to hunt. Nevertheless, they were wonderful tales, and the information was valuable in its own way. Once Peter realized that I travelled on the land far more than he did, he stopped offering information and knowledge about hunting. We still visited regularly, though we mostly talked about hockey and basketball. We played together at the gym and frequently met on Sundays to watch basketball on television. He subsequently became a valuable informant for my master's thesis, which focused on organized sports in Ulukhaktok.

At the end of October, Rick went back to Arkansas. He had his professorial responsibilities, and a family, and simply could not stay any longer. For me, it was perfect timing: I'd had the opportunity to apprentice for three months, watching Rick interview and interact with others, and to add his expertise to my own developing knowledge and research skill set. I also had someone to talk shop with, an outlet for the inevitable frustrations that crop up just by being in a wildly different cultural environment. These days, graduate students in the field often have that structure built in through satellite connections, Skyping with their advisors whenever a problem arises. In 1992, a phone call was very expensive, and the tenuous connections and satellite delays were so challenging that it often was not worth the effort.

Still, Rick's departure at the end of October was well timed. We were living in tight quarters, and I was developing my own way of doing things. I was, after all, a graduate student, used to being up late at night and sleeping in until late morning. My sleeping pattern was encouraged by the photoperiod. By mid-October, the sky was rapidly turning toward the winter darkness, and I preferred to work into the early morning hours and sleep until mid-morning or later. Rick was (as I am now), by the necessity of having young children, a habitually early riser. I was ready to work on my own. I next saw him in June, when we overlapped very briefly: I left in early July, just before his family arrived for the summer.

It was a wonderful year, and at various points over the next few years I wondered if I would ever work in Ulukhaktok again. I returned to Arkansas, spent a year writing my master's thesis, got married, graduated, and went to Penn State to start my doctorate. When I was working with Rick, the focus of the research was on the subsistence hunting of young men – the cohort with whom Rick had worked when they were teenagers. Rick was primarily interested in identity and subsistence, in how these young men interacted with an economic sector that was viewed as threatened by rapid culture change. At Penn State, I began to think more deliberately about the position of these men vis-à-vis their own parents and grandparents, about how these relationships might encourage or hinder young men's subsistence activities, and about the interplay between individual motivation and social structure in how and why men hunt. I was also beginning to think about the nature of culture change, and what it meant for a place like Ulukhaktok to be undergoing "rapid culture change," a phrase firmly entrenched in the academic literature. Rick's influence was important here too, as he often spoke about the rapid changes occurring in the settlement and published extensively on these processes. Despite our being at different universities, we corresponded frequently, and, until his death in 1995, he encouraged me to return to the North to work on those issues.

I returned to Ulukhaktok in 1997, armed with enough grant money to spend ten months, from February through November, to work on my dissertation. The research focused on aging and human development, investigating the ways in which Inuit think about their lives as they develop, documenting how Inuit define the life course, and examining how young people envision their futures as they age.

As I planned the trip, I became anxious about how I might be received in the settlement. I had been away for nearly four years. Would people remember me? Would they care? My fears about my reception were dispelled almost immediately in the airport terminal. During the round of handshakes welcoming me back to town, several Inuit greeted me with statements such as, "Welcome back to your real home." I received bear hugs from old friends, and people took a very serious interest in the fact that my wife and infant daughter (my oldest, Sarah, was then eight months old) were with me.

It turned out – I should not have been surprised by this – that my being married and the father of a child dramatically altered my social status. I was considered a real adult, and I was incorporated into community life in a way that was much different from when I was in Ulukhaktok previously. The late-night visitations from other young single men ceased, and my social life consisted of occasional visits from other married men in the late afternoons and early evening. Afternoons in the house saw visits from women with small children – social visits to see Maya, a chance for tea, talk, and joint baby watching.

Scheduling interviews in the evenings became more challenging. Maya had sewing nights at the community hall several nights a week. During these times, I kept Sarah so that Maya could focus on what she was learning. The most significant difficulty of the year was that we were living on a stipend roughly equal to that of a couple completely dependent upon social assistance. We stayed in the Roman Catholic mission house, built in 1937 and still, it seemed, firmly in that era. It was cold and drafty, employed a "honey pot" for sewage, and the plumbing for running water (which I helped install) was temperamental. We did not lack for food, however. Mark Pihuktuq, my hunting partner during 1992 and 1993, was no longer actively hunting because of his blindness, but he regularly brought us food that he in turn had received from others. Even the wildlife officer brought us food, although he and I both knew it was, technically, illegal for him to do so.

We left in late November 1997, and for a period of years I could conduct fieldwork only during my summer breaks. I returned to State
College and completed my dissertation, and fell into a series of temporary teaching jobs at Indiana University of Pennsylvania and the
University of Nebraska. While there, I was able to secure some grant
funding to travel to Ulukhaktok during the summers of 2001 and 2002
before moving to the University of Florida, where I secured further
funding for summer field trips in 2004, 2005, and 2006. Because of my
growing family and the very high costs of travel to Ulukhaktok, these
trips were all solo, with one exception. In 2005, Sarah, then nine, accompanied me, though sometimes I think she really went on her own.
She was so quickly absorbed into the daily lives of her own age-mates
that I mostly saw her at mealtimes.

These trips allowed for me to maintain contact with old friends and
to work toward developing a larger research project, the subsistence
and aging study of 2007, when I spent another eight months in
Ulukhaktok working with the same group of men that Richard and I
studied in 1992–93. My 2007 work focused on collecting data comparable to what we collected in 1992–93, to explore economics, subsistence, and identity as it develops over the life course. Additionally, my
interests expanded to include social network analysis. The 1992–93
work was extended by network data focused on food sharing patterns
(some of the results have been published in Collings 2009a, 2009b, and
2011). In two additional follow-up trips in 2010 and 2012, the final
touches of this book were completed in a plywood cabin on the edge of
town, to the tune of CBC Radio broadcast from Inuvik.

The above is a basic timeline of when I was in the field, evidence of my
credentials as an anthropologist who presumably knows what he is
talking about. Over a period of twenty years, beginning in 1992, I have
spent the equivalent of roughly four years living in Ulukhaktok. As my
informants have aged, so have I. Like them, I have transitioned into
middle age – though Inuit are on a very different life trajectory from
mine. Many members of my cohort are now grandparents, and have
been for a decade. Even so, my own membership in this cohort was reinforced in August 2012 during a visit with Simon Iqaluk. Simon, as was

the case twenty years previously, was still unmarried and living alone, though he varied his time between Ulukhaktok and remote-site labour work, which allowed him to spend time with a long-time girlfriend – since Simon is so closely related to the entire town, there are virtually no marriageable women locally. When in town, he works for the Co-op as their inventory manager, a job he has held on and off for twenty years. Now that he's in his fifties, though, it's a bit more difficult to sling heavy boxes out of the plane and into the truck, or to stock shelves.

Simon insisted that I come over one evening to play cards, as we used to do, and I obliged, arriving shortly after suppertime. Several hours and multiple cups of coffee later, Joshua Qulliq stopped in. I had not yet seen Joshua since my return, and we exchanged greetings and handshakes. Although somewhat weathered, he looked much as he did twenty years before, and I told him so. Joshua, never one to mince words, said, "You look good, too. Except you're all white" – meaning the colour of my beard, now heavily flecked, an Arctic hare headed for winter. "You're getting old." It was a statement of fact, with neither judgment nor ridicule attached. We proceeded then to talk about the state of our backs and knees. I was happy to learn that, while my beard was going white, I was in far better physical shape than Joshua.

As further proof of my association with middle age, most younger Inuit interact with me quite differently, in a pattern of avoidance and deference common in the settlement. Given the importance of relative age in relationships, most Inuit now in their twenties, whom I recall as being babies or toddlers, are initially hesitant to speak to or with me, largely because of that age gap. The teenagers who recollect that I came to Ulukhaktok with my daughter, Sarah, in 2005, remember her quite fondly, and their recollections of me are solely as "Sarah's dad."

At the beginning of this chapter I wrote of my choice to employ a thematic rather than linear approach to the ethnography. Because so much of my own understanding of cultural process has developed over multiple years, I feel that a linear approach would be disingenuous, in that my reproduction of events in 1992 is clearly informed by what I know now. I left Ulukhaktok in 1993 with notebooks and computer files full of data but not necessarily understanding. Tommy's suicide is only one example of my difficulty, a case where a tragedy occurred that I initially understood in one way and later began to understand in another, more sophisticated and complicated way. Indeed, Tommy's suicide is a difficulty for the reader also, as there is no satisfactory explanation as to why he ultimately killed himself.

Having focused on my own social and personal position as it related to the fieldwork, I now turn to another facet of field experience that bears directly on this problem: the mechanics of being the participant observer and actually conducting research.

"DOING INTERVIEWS" AND BEING A CONGENIAL DOLT

As I noted in chapter 2, Inuit teaching methods tend to rely on indirect methods of instruction, including teaching by demonstration and by embedding knowledge within narratives presented as stories from personal experience. Both methods respect the autonomy of individual learners, who acquire knowledge and skill at their own pace. Nothing is forced upon learners who are not yet ready. It is partly for these reasons that I have constructed this book around a series of ethnographic episodes, events that have directly involved me in some way or other.

My inclusion of myself in this book as an actor – sometimes the primary one – is based on two additional observations. The first is that Inuit place a high value on the acquisition of knowledge via direct experience. During my time in Ulukhaktok, it became second nature to pay attention to how Inuit report the source of their knowledge, which is itself a kind of information. "My brother says that when the ice is this colour, it isn't safe to walk on it" is a statement emphasizing one kind of knowledge source. "Putdjugiaq got caribou, I heard about it yesterday" is another. "There's lots of fish in that place, I got lots there one time" is a third source. The source of knowledge is important, with knowledge acquired by direct experience being the most trustworthy and useful. Following these examples, the episodes that form this narrative serve as direct experiences that supplement and inform information acquired through more standard social science interview sessions, some of which are also presented here.

Again, the importance of direct experience in informing knowledge reflects the Inuit recognition that both social and physical environments are continually changing and require a degree of flexibility and openness to alternatives. Briggs (1991) has noted that Inuit are generally reluctant to condemn an individual for wayward behaviour, recognizing the possibility of change and growth – in short, being willing to revise hypotheses and collect current data. Berkes has found similar themes in ecological knowledge, especially in claims of certainty or universality of knowledge. In particular, Berkes (2008, 15) reports on the incredulity directed at a biologist who claimed expertise about caribou without having obtained that expertise in a way that resonated with Inuit – through direct experience, guided by local knowledge holders.

The structure of this book should be familiar to Inuit, especially to elders, who frequently rely on stories from their own experience when they instruct their juniors. Inuit code this style of interaction in English as "talking to young people." As I have noted earlier, talking to young people, passing on wisdom and knowledge to following generations, is an important – perhaps the most important – marker of successful aging. Younger people, including many of the men I have interacted with over two decades, have often cited the importance of their elders talking to them, noting how these interactions have been key to their own success or in negotiating sticky problems in their lives.

Whether "talking to" is effective with grandchildren is less clear. Embedding a lesson in the context of a personal narrative runs the risk of losing the attention of a generation raised in front of the television. This may be especially true with grandchildren who have much less contact with their grandparents, because of either a lack of physical proximity or a linguistic barrier. Stories from an elder's childhood may likewise seem mystifying to young people who have spent only a handful of nights in a tent, and then only during June, July, or August.

My use of this narrative style is not intended to equate my own experiences with that of Inuit elders. What I can reveal here is only the few nuts upon which this blind squirrel has stumbled. I can only speak authoritatively about what I have experienced, and what I have experienced and understood has been partly shaped by my role in Ulukhaktok and the kinds of information that Inuit have revealed to me or directed me to investigate, based on that role. I have organized this book around ethnographic episodes based upon my social position in the settlement. Non-Inuit outsiders – Qablunaat – living in Ulukhaktok are somewhat constrained by the social roles they fill in the community. These roles can be quite rigid, shaped over time by both Inuit and Qablunaat. In the case of Inuit, the accepted social roles for outsiders are a mechanism for protecting themselves from temporary visitors, destined to leave after a few years, never to return. For Qablunaat, adherence to these roles is partly about maintaining the standard of living to which they are accustomed.

One encounters *teachers*, for example, in school settings. Teachers are less frequently seen at the stores, because they, like most Qablunaat, rely for their food on a combination of bulk shipments of non-perishables delivered on the annual sea lift and fresh produce flown in from the grocery stores in Yellowknife. *Nurses* literally live in the Health Centre, but even when they are off duty and out in the community, they are still *nurses*, always on duty. The same is true of the two RCMP officers, who in the Arctic carry with them a legacy of fear and intimidation.

When Qablunaat and Inuit do interact, it is nearly always on Qablunaat terms. Transient southerners seem to go out of their way to maintain their southern standard of living, both materially and socially. Soon after my return to Ulukhaktok in 2007 (I had been away for eighteen months), I was invited to a dinner party at the home of an RCMP officer. The guest list included the social worker, both Mounties and their spouses, a nurse, a couple of teachers, and Tristan Pearce, a fellow researcher with whom I was sharing an apartment. It was a Qablunaat-only gathering.

One reason I was invited was likely simple due diligence on the part of the RCMP officers. The RCMP moves its officers to new communities every two years; to them I was a new arrival in the settlement. What was I doing in Ulukhaktok? All that was known was that I was doing "research."

The evening progressed much as I anticipated. It was immediately clear that all of the guests were in Ulukhaktok with good intentions. They were, it seemed to me, thoroughly likable people. After introductions and an exchange of pleasantries, the conversation drifted into two areas. Because everyone already knew Tristan, the first set of questions focused on me. What was it like to do research? How did one go about it? What was I studying? I obliged with a brief description of my research project and, following more questions, an explanation of my daily round of interviews, social visiting, and writing field notes. Essentially, I described participant observation, the research strategy based on trying to live as much like Inuit as possible, to understand the cultural context of Inuit lives as much as I could.

The social worker, apparently intrigued by my explanation, asked, "How do you go visiting? Do you mean that you go into people's houses?"

"Yes, I visit with people every day. People visit me too. I do research, but I am also friends with quite a few Inuit."

"How do you do that?" The social divide between Qablunaat and Inuit can be very wide. How was I to respond to her query without being offensive? In my other ear, I heard the teachers and Tristan debating the value of a southern education.

"Do you mean how do I 'go visiting?' Well, I usually walk up to the house and knock on the door to see if anyone is home. If they are, they usually say 'Come in.'"

"You just go in?"

"Yes. If people don't want visitors, they'll say so, but that's not so common. People usually offer coffee or tea, and a little something to eat. I do the same when people visit me."

The second trend of the conversation was equally predictable, a game of what I call "Local Expert." This is a competitive exercise in which Qablunaat sit around and engage in the very colonial enterprise of gossiping about the locals, vying with each other to demonstrate who has more knowledge of the community and offering ways to "fix" its perceived problems. Most fixes revolve around Inuit becoming more like Qablunaat in some way or other. It is something of a status game to know the juiciest details about so-and-so's current problems and to make pronouncements, usually negative, about individual Inuit and their "prospects." One of the teachers, for example, was quite ready to pronounce David Kaaktuq's prospects as being "dim," citing his lack of attentiveness to his schooling, and his impending fatherhood. Both

Tristan and I, who knew that David's family had quite a different assessment of his prospects, bit our tongues.

Local Expert is an uncomfortable exercise, especially since many of the pronouncements are simply incorrect, given that the participants often have minimal social contact with the subjects of the discussion. Though that hardly seems to matter. The schoolteacher had no clue that, despite his young age, David was well on the way to providing for two households with his hunting production, or that his grandparents thought very highly of his abilities and potential.

Researcher is yet another social role for Qablunaat in Ulukhaktok, one with its own set of limitations. Over the years that I have lived and worked in Ulukhaktok, the number of researchers moving through the settlement has certainly increased. A few, like me, have made long-term commitments to research in Ulukhaktok, and, over the years, they too have developed their own unique rapport with Inuit. The majority of researchers, however, are either government agents of one kind or another or academics engaging in cross-sectional research. Typically they arrive for a very brief period, quickly collect their data (or arrange for local people to collect it for them), then return south. Social science research in particular tends to focus on one of only a few different domains, and, over the years, a role for the researcher has emerged. Social research has now become scripted.

One type of social research is the survey. Survey researchers usually go house to house to collect their data: demographic information, economic data, nutritional data, or whatever might pertain to the topic of the day. Usually, the purpose of collecting these data is for informing economic development or public policy. In a three-month period in 2007 alone, three different groups came into the settlement to conduct house-to-house economic surveys. One group represented Housing. Another group represented the Board of Education (though no Inuk I talked to seemed to know which one). Another survey group was collecting data on behalf of the Inuvialuit Regional Corporation (the native land claims organization, known locally as the IRC) in Inuvik. Each organization paid Inuit quite handsomely for their time in filling out forms and answering questions. The irony was that each group appeared to be asking identical sets of questions.

"They pay pretty good, though," said Isaac, one evening after he was interviewed. "They should come around more often. They pay better than you." He was needling me.

"How long did it take to do their interview?"

"Oh, about an hour and a quarter. They paid me $50."

"And how long does my interview take? Fifteen minutes? How much am I paying you?"

"Twenty bucks." He was holding the bill in his hand, as we had just completed a session. A pause. "Oh. I guess you do pay pretty good, too."

A second kind of research is the interview, usually a semi-structured or open-response narrative that tends to focus on a specific topic of Inuit experience. This work is typically coded as "doing interviews." When I first visited Ulukhaktok in the early 1990s, most of this kind of research focused on wildlife harvesting, especially of caribou and muskoxen. At the time, both Inuit and wildlife managers perceived that there was a caribou crisis in the region. Over the previous five to ten years Inuit had been less and less successful hunting caribou above Minto Inlet, and government wildlife managers wanted to know why. The caribou issue is no longer in vogue, however, and the research questions have changed somewhat. Climate change is the latest sexy topic, the newest research bandwagon. Life histories of elders, however, never go out of style, though they typically involve cameras and recording equipment and are used not for policy but for cultural preservation purposes.

There are scripts for both survey research and interviewing. In the case of house-to-house surveys, the researcher typically hires a small number of Inuit, sometimes through the Ulukhaktok Community Corporation (the local arm of the IRC), but occasionally independently. The researcher and his or her Inuit minions split up into teams, arrive at a house, explain the research, quickly collect data, pay the agreed-upon fee, which seems to be somewhere around $50–60 per hour, and leave. Researchers rarely stay in the settlement for longer than a week or two, though I do not blame them. At over $250 a night, the Co-op Hotel is accomplished at separating researchers from their money. Whether the data they receive are valid is anyone's guess. Plenty of Inuit have told me that they routinely provide dodgy information to researchers or their Inuit assistants, and the assistants themselves are sometimes complicit in this deceit. Why should anyone in Ulukhaktok care about yet another economic survey? Why should an Inuk report sensitive personal information about what she eats or how much the household earns in a year, especially to a stranger?

Interview research has its own, somewhat different script. Inuit are approached beforehand and asked if they would acquiesce to an interview about topic x. A time is arranged, and if the interview involves an elder (as they almost always do, because the script includes the rule that "old" automatically equals "cultural expert"), an interpreter is hired.

In spring of 2007, I witnessed one of these kinds of interviews, one that exemplified the dangers confronting the outsider who tries to interview without having generated any rapport. I was at the coffee shop, having tea with a friend just before coffee break, when two government officials walked into the hotel with a couple of Inuit. The government agents were decked out in bright red parkas, sure signs of an outsider, with large Environment Canada patches emblazoned on their chest. They sat down to coffee and a chat with their Inuit companions, members of the Hunters and Trappers Organization (known locally, however, as a committee, and hence HTC for short). As they talked about their own work – environmental outreach at the school, to continue for the week – they revealed a secondary purpose of their visit: a historian in their office was working on documenting a need for a wildlife and heritage zone near a place called Parry's Rocks. In the evenings, they planned to interview elders with knowledge about Parry's Rocks. They were looking for an interpreter to assist them in their interviews.

There were five or so Inuit participants in the conversation by this point, and they looked around at each other. What was Parry's Rocks? No one quite knew for sure. I joined the conversation and asked if they were referring to Cape Parry and the Parry Peninsula, down near Paulatuk. One Inuk wondered aloud if they meant the explorer who first made it to the North Pole. I chimed in to explain that would have been Peary, who had never been anywhere near the Western Arctic as far as I knew. Parry (Sir William Edward Parry) was an English rear-admiral who explored the Arctic in the early 1800s. Several Inuit nodded at me, ignored my comment, and then went back to the conversation, quite sure that Parry and Peary must have been the same person. What the hell had I been babbling about anyway?

There was no consensus on what or where Parry's Rocks was, but arrangements were made for an interpreter, and several elders were identified as people worth talking to. I left, curious about this Parry's Rocks, hoping to be present at one of these interviews. Perhaps I would be visiting when the interviewers arrived at a house.

Though there seem to be scripts for interview or survey research, ethnography is a form of research that has no script. Participant observation, in fact, tries as much as possible to stay outside of research scripts, which are really tightly controlled environments in which Inuit and researcher reveal as little about each other as possible. As in research in general, ethnographers are in the position of being what Michael Agar (1996) calls "one-down," ceding control of most social interactions to others. Researchers believe they control the terms of the interaction, but really they cede control to Inuit in the kinds of responses they receive. Ethnographers are (mostly) comfortable in these kinds of situations, not sure what is going on, trying to figure it out, and developing strategies to cope with their lack of social power. Of course, in another sense ethnographers are simultaneously one-up too. In my case, I was largely free of the obligations generated by kinship, which can be a severe constraint on behaviour. I was also not a permanent fixture; eventually I would leave, so any social discomfort was temporary; my one-down-ness in the field setting would eventually end.

Furthermore, the participant observation associated with ethnographic research requires a great deal more time than survey research. Ethnographers cannot parachute into a settlement for two weeks and expect to learn anything. Inuit will talk to anybody, of course, but it certainly helps if they trust the questioner, and if the questioner can ask appropriate questions in appropriate ways. I have certainly seen enough newcomers in Ulukhaktok launch into an investigation of a sensitive topic, such as shamanism or traditional belief systems, and come away convinced that the old ways no longer exist, which then becomes encapsulated as evidence that Inuit culture is rapidly eroding.

Ethnography and participant observation are not without their own problems, however, and two particular ones stand out. The first is that Inuit, as I noted earlier, have a rather low opinion of questions and people who insist on asking them. Asking questions is rude and infringes on an individual's autonomy. If one is genuinely ignorant and seeking information, the appropriate strategy is to observe for a time. One learns by watching others. On the other hand, if one already knows the answer, why ask questions? To ask would be a waste of everyone's time. Over the years, as my modest cultural competence has increased, I have found there are domains about which I can no longer ask questions, lest they be thrown right back at me. That is why someone like Isaac can be such a good friend but a lousy informant. He knows me so well that any research-oriented questions are met with a wry smile and "But you know already. Why don't you tell me?" Consequently, Inuit view me as something of a congenial dolt. *He is a nice guy, all right, but he doesn't seem too bright, we always have to tell him things.* I wish I could say that I deliberately chose to be seen that way.

There are moments that highlight the difficult balancing act of being a cultural novice yet competent enough to know how to ask the right questions and receive useful information in return. During the spring of 1993, I spent nearly every weekend on the land, fishing, camping, and hunting, beginning in late March and continuing through the end of duck season. March was far too early and too cold for ice fishing, but Sam Ihumayuq and I just could not wait – we wanted fresh trout. We spent an uncomfortable night in a tent and the next day navigated home in a blizzard, nearly driving into the sewage lagoon on our way into town. However, these trips marked me as a person who enjoys travelling on the land.

One Saturday morning in mid-May, I sat outside William Kaaktuq's house, waiting for Isaac to get ready. Isaac's wife, Ida, was doing a load of laundry, insisting that we could not go camping with dirty clothes still in the hamper. I was sitting on my snowmobile, talking with William, who was also impatient and ready to go, when Amos Tuktu walked by. He was returning from the grocery store, carrying a shopping bag. He waved at me, and went inside his house a few units away

from where we were sitting. A moment later, he came out, notebook in
one hand, pencil in the other. He walked straight toward me.

"I should interview you, you know. You're always going out on the
land, not like me." He flipped open the notebook, assumed a pose, and
readied his pencil. "So. Okay, now, where are you going? How long are
you going to be out, and what are you going to catch?"

I was being rewarded for a year's worth of harassment. When I asked
for my money for the interview, he laughed. But he did not pay me.
Even then, I was still one-down.

The second sticky problem is one of compensation. Research transactions are well scripted, down to the going rate for interviews, and my
own work follows these guidelines. When I use interviews or surveys,
I pay the going rates. What about the rest of the time? The ethnographer is always on duty; every experience is fair game for documenta-
tion. How do I compensate informants for information gathered over
a game of cards, for assistance in repairing a machine, for gifts of country food? Full participation in community life depends both on a willingness to help others in need and engagement in the networks of
reciprocity that characterize Inuit social life. I am really hamstrung in
this sense. I cannot hunt anything substantial, so I cannot directly reciprocate gifts of country food. I lack a useful (in Inuit eyes) skill set. I
am only a temporary resident, so I lack significant material resources
that could be of use in exchange. Money, while expected in research
transactions, would be dangerous in a reciprocal setting. I would risk
becoming an ATM, one with no overdraft fee. Even Inuit play it close
to the vest when it comes to money.

There are mechanisms for trying to keep things close, but they do
not come anywhere near to evening up the score. When I arrived in
2007, Internet service with reasonable speeds at an affordable price had
just made its appearance, finally and irrevocably dragging Ulukhaktok
into the global information age. It was enough to encourage the purchase of second-hand computers. Although most Inuit were interested
in social networking sites like Facebook or the now-defunct Bebo,
playing video poker, or IMing their cousin across the street, a few began to explore the possibilities of eBay. That was the limit for most
Inuit, as few had credit cards that would allow for full-blown Internet

shopping. I, however, had a credit card, and it was soon put to use in the purchase of several pairs of *kamiks* – traditional style, skin-soled boots – for friends, who paid up in cash when the items were delivered. After the package arrived – six boxes, all taped together – word filtered back to me about a conversation one of the recipients had with his uncle. It was explained that I purchased them from the Internet using my credit card. The uncle's response: "Hmm. So he is good for something after all."

The very next evening I had the good fortune to witness an interview about Parry's Rocks. It came about because earlier in the day I had provided William with a length of starter rope for his gas auger. Augers are temperamental pieces of equipment, a small lawnmower engine with handles and a large drill bit for chewing through ice. They are difficult to start and even more difficult to keep running. It does not help that they spend most of their life sitting idle against the side of the house, collecting dirt during the summer and lying buried under snow the entire winter. (More than once I have been out fishing, chopping holes the old-fashioned way, with a *tuuq*, through six or seven feet of ice, building moral fibre and a good sweat, because of a buried or dysfunctional auger.) Once spring comes around, Inuit begin to think of getting the auger out and tuning it up. The first nice Friday evening in April usually sees the husband digging around in one of several snowdrifts for the damned thing, the wife standing on the porch, smoking a cigarette and no doubt thinking to herself, "I told him to get it out before the weather got good, but he can't listen." She wants to go fishing on Saturday.

William already had one auger working, but he wanted to fix his older one, which, after his repairs, needed only a starter rope. The Co-op was out, but I had some, and I offered it. William was so pleased to have a second auger working that he insisted I eat with the family that evening, fresh trout caught by Agnes and her daughter Molly. The fish was excellent, boiled in Lipton's soup mix, and we were visiting and having tea after the meal when the government researchers knocked on the door and entered the house. The older fellow, Frank, was already well known to people in Ulukhaktok, certainly to William, who had many kin ties to Inuvik and Sachs Harbour, and so he and Frank fell into conversation as tea was made. The second worker, a younger woman, recognized me from the hotel coffee shop and sat down next to me. We introduced ourselves and I asked about the interview project.

"Well, seeing as we're here, my colleague in Inuvik thought we could ask about Parry's Rocks too," she said. "We're working on setting the land aside as a heritage park."

"Do you know where Parry's Rocks is?" I asked, trying to generate a sense about the place. "I'm not sure I've heard it referred to by that name."

"I have no idea. I'm a geologist. My specialty is eskers. This is all new to me." Silence for a moment as we sipped tea. "What do you do, by the way?"

It would have been difficult for her to tell what I did. I was wearing greasy jeans, old kamiks, and a ratty, faded sweatshirt. My hands were dirty, as I had been wrestling all day with my reluctant snow machine. I hardly looked the part of an academic. "I'm an anthropologist, working on some issues with economics and subsistence," I said. We talked some more, and as I explained the project, she began to look slightly nervous, recognizing an expert witness to an interview she was not trained to conduct. For my part, I was amused at the assumption, apparently made in Inuvik, that anybody can conduct an interview, as if an interview is nothing more than reading a bunch of questions and recording the answers. It is a common mistake. I felt sorry for her.

First, however, the matter of Parry's Rocks had yet to be resolved. Neither of the Environment Canada agents had settled on where the place was, though there was still some idea that "Peary" – Robert? John? Bill? – must have visited the place during his explorations that led to the North Pole. "Parry's Rocks" must be a place where "Peary" had stayed for a time.

Slowly, I pieced together their story, and their confusion. The agents, and Inuit themselves, were confusing two people, Robert E. Peary, the Arctic explorer who journeyed in 1909 to the geographic North Pole, and Sir William Edward Parry, a British naval officer and explorer. Peary, of course, had been nowhere near Ulukhaktok, but neither had Parry. Parry had wintered on Viscount Melville Island in 1819–20. During that winter, he had explored Melville Sound and sighted and named Victoria Island and Banks Island to the west.

I recited some of this history, to the obvious alarm of most in the room. Inuit seemed shocked as I rattled off what I knew. Stunned surprise, expressions that said, "Jesus Christ, how did he know that?" – which I heard one person actually say aloud. I responded, "Well, I *am* a professor. I read a lot." It was a statement made in self-deprecation. Acquiring knowledge by reading is a decidedly suspect way of learning.

Parry's Rocks, more commonly known as Winter Harbour, is located on Melville Island, roughly eight hundred kilometres northeast of Ulukhaktok. It was difficult to see how any Inuk in Ulukhaktok could have knowledge about the site. My guess was that the interview was supposed to determine what knowledge Inuit here had about Winter Harbour, and whether there was any tradition of Inuit visiting the site to raid the cache of supplies Parry left behind, or if there were any stories about trading with Parry. There were a few stories in circulation about Captain Robert McClure's ship, H M S *Investigator*, at Mercy Bay on Banks Island, which was picked over by Inuit during the late nineteenth century. The *Investigator*'s crew, however, abandoned her in 1853. Parry's visit in 1820 might be pushing it a bit too far back in time and too far away in space.

As I explained this history and the location of Winter Harbour, William alone looked at me without surprise. "Right!" he said, "I heard about that place."

By and by, we finished our tea and the decision was made to move to the T V room. The television was switched off, and William took his seat on the sofa. I sat on the floor against the wall, closest to William. Both Environment Canada agents moved into the room, along with Trudy (the interpreter), her husband, Fred, three of William's daughters, and a few grandchildren. This was, after all, an "interview." The adult children were interested in uncovering some bit of life history that William had never talked about.

The woman who was to conduct the interview pulled out the informed consent form, explaining to William the nature of the questions and the conditions of payment of $120. The interview script begun, William looked at Trudy, who translated. He nodded, signed the form, and the interviewer dug into her bag for the tape recorder.

While she set up the machine, I leaned over to ask William, "Have you ever been to that place?" I was also wondering why the insistence on a translator. William speaks excellent (though idiosyncratic, because he is missing so many teeth) English. I have never used a translator when I have interviewed him, nor has he wanted one.

"Long ago, when I was a young man" – which would put the time into the early 1950s – "I went up that way, hunting bears with some other people," he said. "But we went the other way. We never went to that place. I don't know anything about it." He shrugged his shoulders.

That should have been the end of the interview. William at best could only tell stories about Winter Harbour that he heard from other people, not from his own experience. The fact that he admitted to not knowing anything, except perhaps how to get there, suggested that he had not even heard stories from others. If he had, he would have included "I used to hear about it" in his response. Surely he would not continue with the interview?

He did. The tape recorder was switched on, and the questions began. William assumed the typically rigid posture common to formal interviews conducted in Inuinnaqtun. Though my mastery of Inuinnaqtun is very limited, it was clear from the outset that he had no intention of trying to answer questions about Parry's Rocks. It seems that he had decided to rephrase the question to one about early explorers in general, so he spent the next thirty minutes talking about another "early explorer," Stefansson, relating stories he "used to hear about" from his father-in-law and others. Stefansson travelled through the region during the first two decades of the twentieth century. And, indeed, William afterward said that he did not want to disappoint the interviewers, so he told them something he thought they might like. The interviewers, of course, had no way of knowing this, if only because Trudy was not providing a back translation into English, merely translating the questions. She would later translate the tape back into English and send her written translation on to Inuvik.

Who knows when the researchers would discover the nature of the interview? The two Environment Canada agents were in a sense innocent, thrust into their roles as interviewers without much apparent training, or, indeed, a sense that interviewing is a skill that can be developed. But the entire episode speaks to the nature of this kind of interviewing. In the absence of an in-time translation, the interviewee maintains control of the entire interview: the questions are read, the interviewee chooses what and how to answer, and the interviewer has no opportunity to probe, follow a lead in the narrative, change the topic, or wrench it back to the topic of interest.

LANGUAGE AND CULTURAL REPRESENTATION

To this point I have focused on the ways that my social position and professional role influenced my experience as a researcher. My developmental trajectory altered my experience within Ulukhaktok, which, in turn, altered my relationships with Ulukhaktomiut. At the same time, being cast in the role of "researcher" likewise shaped what I have seen and experienced, opening some avenues for inquiry while closing others. These personal and professional constraints were further shaped and guided by time: because of the time I have spent in Ulukhaktok, and the time I have spent reflecting on that experience, I am in a somewhat different position academically. I have had to make some choices about how to represent the core ethnography, both in terms of the representation of Inuit culture, and my use of Inuinnaqtun phrases and words within the context of a largely English narrative. I alluded to some of these issues in my first chapter, but I expand more on them here because they do bear directly on this work.

I have employed the term "Ulukhaktomiut" to refer to the people of Ulukhaktok, which is entirely accurate and appropriate. Ulukhaktomiut, after all, means "people of Ulukhaktok." Even so, it is not entirely clear what it *means* to be Ulukhaktomiut. As I discussed in the opening chapter, the settlement is inhabited by different groups of people, each with different histories and former home territories. To an outsider, especially one from a large, state-level society, the thought that there might be significant differences between groups of people who collectively number less than five hundred might seem preposterous. In reality, these distinctions remain important; the relatively small sizes of each of these bands, in fact, have probably contributed to their distinctiveness, even though outsiders might not perceive it. The Kangiryuarmiut,

Kanghiryuatjagmiut, and Puivlingmiut, of course, were never entirely discrete groups because of the nature of Inuit mobility and the necessity of intermarriage, but the divisions are still recognizable, existing largely along family lines.

The land claims processes of the past forty years have further compli- cated matters. As Collignon (2006, 20–6) notes, the original inhabit- ants of the region are known as Inuinnait, though anthropologists and historians have often used the terms "Copper Eskimo" or "Copper Inuit" as a referents, which are completely foreign and based on the prevalence of locally sourced copper for making knives, fishhooks, and other tools prior to contact. I have never heard anyone in Ulukhaktok refer to themselves using either term. The Inuinnait include the people who now live in Kugluktuk, Cambridge Bay, and Bathurst Inlet. And though many Ulukhaktomiut have blood and marriage ties to these other settlements, Ulukhaktok is unique because of the significant cul- tural and economic traffic to the west, primarily through Sachs Harbour and Inuvik, initially spurred by the fox-trapping trade on Banks Island (see Usher 1971, 1972).

When Inuit across Canada began pushing for political rights and recognition during the early 1970s, Ulukhaktok was in a difficult posi- tion. Over my years of fieldwork, several elders have noted that initially there was some interest among the Inuinnait in making their own land claims to the federal government. These claims went nowhere, though, apparently because the collective population of these settlements was too small to register with the federal government. In practical terms, Ulukhaktok was then faced with a significant problem. Joining the Nunavut land claim meant that Ulukhaktok would be, as the western- most settlement in Nunavut, socially and politically marginal. Joining the Inuvialuit claim made somewhat more sense, given Ulukhaktok's relative proximity to Inuvik and the history of contact with the Mackenzie Delta region. Still, signing on with the Inuvialuit land claim was not without problems. Until 1999, nearly all of Ulukhaktok's social, political, and economic connections were through Kugluktuk and Cambridge Bay, even though the Inuvialuit Final Agreement was rati- fied in 1984. Even today, though most social services are administered from Inuvik, strong economic ties remain through Kugluktuk and on to Yellowknife, the territorial capital. Though there is scheduled air service to and from Inuvik three days a week, the planes are very small and likely to cancel or turn back due to weather. Air freight and other services continue to flow from Yellowknife, not Inuvik. Furthermore, there remain significant kinship connections between Ulukhaktok, Kugluktuk, and Cambridge Bay.

Joining the Inuvialuit claim has been a mixed bag in other senses too. In a cultural sense, Ulukhaktomiut have been subjected to a fairly steady stream of cultural pressure to identify as Inuvialuit rather than Inuit. (The term Inuinnait rarely appears in public discourse.) This pressure, it seems, is designed to foster a regional identity distinct from that of the Inuit in Nunavut. Despite this pressure to identify as Inuvialuit, there is a pervasive sense in the Inuvialuit Settlement Region that people from Ulukhaktok are comparatively backwards and easily taken advantage of, a perception with some historical depth, as Condon (1996, 108–11) has noted. Although some of this concern may simply be perception rather than reality, occasional incidents suggest continuing friction. During 2007, Ulukhaktomiut organized an economic development project that involved travelling into Minto Inlet to mine alabaster and transport it to Ulukhaktok, the purpose being to encourage carving and income generation. It was a win/win for Ulukhaktomiut – the cost of mining and transporting the stone was relatively inexpensive, and the stone would be made available to carvers for their own use. But the Inuvialuit Land Administration notified the Ulukhaktok Community Corporation that they must pay money to the ILA for rights to mine the stone, despite the fact that it was, technically, on Ulukhaktok lands. Shortly afterward, it was discovered that a mining claim had been placed on that particular site, preventing any mining without paying the owner of the claim – rumoured to be an Inuvialuk who was working in the ILA, one who had previously lived in Ulukhaktok. Ultimately, the economic development plan died, leaving some hard feelings in the process.

The political divide between Ulukhaktok and Nunavut also causes problems. The boundary with Nunavut is reasonably close to Ulukhaktok, and over the past decade there have been conflicts, particularly about bears. Hunters from Kugluktuk occasionally claim that Ulukhaktok hunters are taking "their" bears on Nunavut lands (or, in this case, sea ice). Equally problematic is the creation of separate management plans and quotas for the two communities, because the bears inconsiderately refuse to remain on one or the other side of the boundary.

Many Ulukhaktomiut perceive these issues but simply ignore them. Few people in Ulukhaktok call themselves Inuvialuit; they continue to use the term Inuit as an identifier, hinting at connections that might, anthropologically speaking, be considered more Central Eskimo. Even so, the cultural traditions of Alaska and the Mackenzie Delta have influenced the community quite strongly. When people gather for drum dancing, for example, the style is that of the Mackenzie Delta, not the central Arctic style of the historical Inuinnait.

To conclude, and to parallel points made by Collignon (2006), some external academic and political conventions for referring to people from Ulukhaktok – "Copper Eskimos," "Copper Inuit," "Central Eskimos," or "Inuvialuit" – do not necessarily resonate with Ulukhaktomiut, who seem to identify at the local rather than regional level. Although recent political and cultural developments, particularly the land claims settlements, have worked to increase regional awareness and solidarity, Ulukhaktok, because of its unique place culturally, between two political structures, remains a place where local identity has greater prominence than it might elsewhere in the Arctic.

Just as the label "Ulukhaktomiut" is problematic because of issues related to cultural and political identities, so too are the labels applied to language use. What, precisely, do Inuit in Ulukhaktok actually speak, and how should the speech of Ulukhaktomiut be represented in text? The problems are multiple. At a basic level, all textual representations of speech are compromised, given that we are attempting to represent a continuous phenomenon through the use of discrete units. But representing Inuinnaqtun is somewhat more difficult, because Inuinnaqtun lacks a literary tradition; it was first written for the purpose of spreading Christian teachings to Inuit.

As Harper (2000) observes, multiple orthographies were developed in the Central Arctic, each based on a specific time and a place and the predilections of the missionaries in question. Harper goes so far as to write that, for the Western Arctic, "each writer was very much on his own to develop his own system" (2000, 155). And despite numerous attempts over the years to standardize writing systems across the Canadian Arctic, none has yet succeeded. Currently, Inuktitut is written using a syllabic system, while Inuinnaqtun is written using a Roman system. And, although there *is* a standard orthography for representing Inuinnaqtun, devised by the Inuit Cultural Institute in 1976, Harper notes that it is unused. Nearly nothing has ever been published using the official Roman orthography (called Qaliujaaqpait), and it is usually met with resistance, if not outright hostility, in the settlements where Inuinnaqtun is spoken. People remain attached to the older orthographies developed by the missionaries.

Part of the reason for developing an orthography, at least on an academic level, is to provide a system for comparing languages. What *is* Inuinnaqtun? Is it a dialect of Inuktitut? Is it a dialect of Inuvialuktun? Is it a separate language? The Inuvialuit Regional Corporation's official position is that Inuinnaqtun *is* a dialect of Inuvialuktun – perhaps not surprising, given that there seems to be pressure for Ulukhaktomiut to identify as Inuvialuit. The Government of the Northwest Territories, for its part, lists both Inuinnaqtun and Inuvialuktun as official languages. Nunavut likewise lists Inuinnaqtun as an official language, alongside Inuktitut. Further complicating matters is the linguistic view; Dorais (2010, 32–6), for example, includes all of the variants of Eskimo language west of Hudson Bay and along the Arctic coast to be Inuktun, with three separate groups: Natsilingmiutut, Inuinnaqtun, and Siglitun (this latter usually designated as Inuvialuktun in the Inuvialuit Settlement Region).

Further complicating matters is that Inuinnaqtun, regardless of how it is classified, is an endangered language. As I observed in the previous chapter, I have, over twenty years, detected that the language is used *more* in public discourse now than when I first arrived in Ulukhaktok. However, the nature of that use is worth discussing in detail. Although the use of Inuinnaqtun has increased, the way in which it is used is quite different from what an average observer might expect. In Ulukhaktok, virtually no speaker under the age of fifty can be considered even remotely fluent in Inuinnaqtun, and many speakers over fifty are limited in their ability to speak and comprehend it. English is ubiquitous in the settlement. It is the language of public discourse, its use is reinforced by television and radio, and it is the primary language of instruction in the school.

Even so, despite the pervasive use of English and the fact that Inuinnaqtun has become seriously endangered, the language is still employed, albeit in a compromised form, in day-to-day conversation. Though far fewer than half of the population speaks Inuinnaqtun with something close to fluency, Ulukhaktomiut of all ages employ Inuinnaqtun utterances in daily conversation, code switching easily between Inuinnaqtun and English in some cases, employing Inuinnaqtun terms within an English context in others. Clearly, it is Inuinnaqtun that has adapted to English grammar. I have already noted common conventions for anglicizing such phrases: adding an *s* to form a plural, or an *ing* to make a verb in the progressive, for example.

The system for forming plurals of Inuinnaqtun words is quite different than it is for English words. For example, the plural of *hiun* (ear) either indicates dual, as in *hiutik* (two ears), or (if an individual has an unfortunate condition), three or more, as in *hiutiit* (more than two ears). Speakers of Inuinnaqtun know this intuitively, but that does not prevent the actual utterance, when used in an English context, to become "I'm going to sniff your *hiutiks*," a common practice when engaging small children, usually followed by tickling and giggling.

My approach throughout this work has been to treat the grammars, dictionaries, and "official" spellings as having become largely proscriptive. Originally designed for cultural and linguistic preservation purposes, they have also functioned to fossilize the language at a particular point in time, at the unfortunate crossroads of vibrancy and extinction. Language is a continually evolving phenomenon, and it is a natural process for languages to grow, change, and adapt to new circumstances, especially when they are in contact with one another. What I am capturing here, and representing, is Inuinnaqtun (or what is left of it) as it is used in daily, public contexts.

The choice of orthography I employ here is likewise problematic. The standard grammar and dictionary in use in Ulukhaktok is Lowe's *Basic Kangiryuarmiut Eskimo Dictionary* (1983) and *Basic Kangiryuarmiut Eskimo Grammar* (1985). There have been more recent dictionaries – the

1996 Inuinnaqtun/English dictionary published by Nunavut Arctic College, republished in 2010, is one, based on the Qaliujaaqpait. However, I use Lowe's volumes, for several reasons. Despite their age, they are standard references for Ulukhaktomiut, found in many households; in the past there were multiple copies at the school library. The orthography Lowe employs is something of a hybrid, based partly on the work of Father Maurice Metayer, in consultation with the Qaliujaaqpait. Thus it is a compromise between the ICI's standard and something that is deemed acceptable at the local level (Lowe 1983, xvii), devised specifically to facilitate teaching the language.

It should be noted, however, that even using Lowe is problematic. Because of the lack of a literary tradition in Ulukhaktok, Ulukhaktomiut themselves evidently have little sense of how particular Inuinnaqtun words *should* be spelled. Facebook is full of spelling variants that Lowe renders as *panik*, daughter, for example. Even though Lowe is as close as one might get to a standard in Ulukhaktok, most Inuit, when writing, spell Inuinnaqtun words according to their own sense of how they might be best represented. As a further commentary on the malleability and fluidity of language, it is quite common for individuals to alter the spellings of their own names over time, as suits their fancy, and as it suits subtle changes in pronunciation, which also occur. Several names, pronounced one way in 1992, are now pronounced differently, some twenty years later.

In terms of writing, then, though I am following Lowe, I am still faced with the problem of how to represent the mixed Inuinnaqtun/English utterances. How should one represent *hiutiks* (two ears) in Inuit speech? Throughout the text, I have chosen to represent an Inuinnaqtun utterance in italicized form upon its first appearance, even if that first appearance is in an anglicized form, as in *hiutiks*. Further appearances of the word will remain in regular text. I simply remind readers that, while the "s" does indicate plurality, it does so in an English context. The presence of the "s" in the terminal position of the word should easily mark the English plural in any event. Inuinnaqtun is distinct from other languages (or dialects, depending on who is making the distinction) in that it habitually replaces the "s" sound with "h."

The conventions I employ here, then, are not intended as a poke in the eye of linguists and anthropologists who have put in considerable time and effort into understanding and representing the Eskimo languages. Nor should this discussion be taken as an affront to Inuit themselves. Rather, the issues I am struggling with reflect the complexity of linguistic and cultural behaviour as it emerges in the natural habitat of daily existence. At the same time, the issues highlight one of the specific themes that runs throughout this work: one of the consequences of settlement in Ulukhaktok has been the increasing influence of the state on Inuit lives. In the previous chapter, I referenced this largely in the context of how the state manages the life course and impacts how Inuit lead their lives, but language and cultural identity make up another domain where the state and its representatives (who include the academics who arrive to study the problem of culture change) play a significant role in Inuit social life. Territorial and federal governments declare languages to be either dialects or official languages, thereby granting or withdrawing legitimacy. Other state-like structures such as the IRC attempt to standardize identity by employing an ethnic designation to legitimize a political one, insisting that, in our example, Ulukhaktok is an Inuvialuit community.

I should be clear that the communication style of Ulukhaktomiut is not something that I am replicating lightheartedly. I have heard enough outsiders poke fun at the cadence, grammar, and pronunciation of English, with utterances like "Must be it's no more good" being held up as examples of particularly poor English. By replicating these linguistic conventions here, I am not trivializing them. This is simply the way people communicate, employing a mixture of English and Inuinnaqtun words and grammatical structures in daily speech. It is an effective, nuanced, and, to my ear, pleasant system. It is how people talk to each other.

With these issues in mind, I now turn toward a discussion of the community of Ulukhaktok and the material and structural constraints that young men face as they come of age in the contemporary settlement.

4

He's a Good Friend, but He's a Crook

It is still early morning, and I am happily writing field notes on the laptop, sipping hot coffee and trying to ignore my chilly feet. I have been in Ulukhaktok for four days now after another brief trip south, and I am slowly getting used to what will be my home for the next three months. There isn't very much to see, as "home" is an 8 × 12 box with four-foot walls and a steeply pitched roof so that I can stand in the middle. My sleeping bag rests on a platform at the back, my gear stored underneath. Behind me is the "kitchen": a low table with some food and a Coleman stove on it. In front of me is another table, on which the laptop and a lamp sit. My water supply, in old five-gallon paint buckets, is on the floor by the door or under the table. Power comes from an extension cord that runs one hundred feet to William Kaaktuq's house. He has been gracious enough to let me use his electricity while I am here.

My excitement over living in the cabin has begun to wear off. It would be nice to have a proper bath. I have spent the last four days renovating, converting what was a storage shed to a living space. I am sore and tired from the work of insulating, panelling walls, and rebuilding the front door, which used to be wide enough to get my snowmobile in and out. The faint trace of engine oil still hangs in the air.

As I finish my cup, there's a knock on the door, and it opens with a jerk. Cool air rushes in as Edward Kuniluk stoops under the low door and takes a seat on an empty five-gallon pail.

"Cozy?" he asks, a big grin on his face. He does not think I can take this for long. He expects me to eventually give up and find a house in town.

"It's not too bad," I reply slowly. I would like a proper shower, but at least I am going to be sleeping really well for the next couple of months. Like most Inuit, I prefer a cold bedroom and a very heavy blanket. Isaac sums it up: it is best when you wake up and your nose is a little cold. When I woke up this morning, the temperature in the cabin was a decent 8°C, despite a thirty-five kilometre east wind and temperatures just below freezing.

Edward nods agreement. "That's the best thing about camping. Good sleeping. But you need a heater if you're going to stay here much longer. Going to get cold soon. I've got a camp heater I'll bring up for you. It's really good, you'll stay warm."

I pour Edward some coffee out of the insulated French press. He adds some sugar, and sips. We drink our coffee silently for a few minutes.

"From where you get the window?" He's referring to the one leaning against the outside of the cabin. He must have noticed it as he walked over. "You going to put it in? Going for a skylight?"

I explain that I intend to install the window in the back wall. Right now there is no natural light in the cabin, so putting the window in the south-facing wall is a good way of getting sunlight between now and the end of November when the sun will drop below the horizon. It is also a good idea to have a second exit route. Given that I am cooking on a Coleman stove, using a gas lantern for some light and heat, and will soon be using a gas heater, there is the (however remote) possibility of fire. Being able to open both a window and the door will allow for cross-ventilation as well.

Edward sips. "We should put in a *qingak*, too. You don't want to suffocate."

Most Inuit recommend a qingak, a hole in the wall to allow air to vent in and out. Most cabins have them, as everyone in town knows stories about people who have nearly suffocated by burning up the air in their cabin. Several years ago, an older couple, Patrick and Margaret, installed a new style of camp heater (some "Swedish design," Patrick called it) in their cabin down the coast. After an afternoon of spring fishing out on the land, they stopped there on their way home for tea and a snack. Pretty soon, feeling sleepy from an afternoon of fresh air, both decided to have a short nap. It was only when Patrick saw through drowsy eyes the flickering flame dying, despite a full fuel tank, that he realized what was happening. He flung open the door, the flame flared up, and he and Margaret realized how close they had come to calamity. Patrick had a qingak in the wall – it just was not large enough.

Edward continues, asking the important question. "How you going to frame it?" He again nods at the back wall.

I admit I'm not entirely sure. I am competent with power tools (and have all my digits to prove it) and have a basic knowledge of carpentry. Indeed, my skills were developed in building this very cabin over a decade ago. Still, I am not sure how to deal with the ridgepole, which is in the way. It does support the roof, after all.

Actually, I do have an idea how I will frame the window. But I know what is coming next, so I play a little dumb and pretend otherwise.

"I could help. Let me go get my tools. I'll bring the heater up for you too." Edward finishes his coffee and walks out the door. I pull my boots on and head outside too and drag the window to the leeward side of the cabin. Out of the wind, it is quite pleasant. The air is crisp, the sky clear.

The first order of business is to take the window apart. It's really two windows in a single casing: an upper fixed window, and a smaller awning window. I only need the lower one, which opens and shuts; the other one is too large for any of the walls of my cabin.

As I am tearing apart the unit, I reflect humorously on how I am "improving" my home, which has been constructed entirely out of scavenged materials. I originally built it as a warehouse from scraps taken off various job sites in town or from the crating used to ship in large items on the annual sea lift. Just about the first lesson one learns in a place like Ulukhaktok is that, materials being so expensive or rare, many things that southerners might call trash are endlessly reused or recycled. It is common for men to declare they are "going shopping" at "Canadian Tire" or "Wal-Mart," euphemisms for going to the dump to look for needed parts or materials. Edward has admitted he will often go to the dump to throw something away and come back with more than he took.

The dump has plenty of useful stuff. Albert Aquti, who drives the bucket loader and effectively manages the dump, has worked tirelessly for years to ensure that "trash" is properly sorted, old snowmobiles and ATVs all piled in one place, household trash (burned weekly) in another, building materials in yet another. He makes sure that new construction crews are educated about the proper disposal of building materials, whether they are leftover nails, house wrap, crating, or off-cuts. Correct etiquette is to leave discarded materials on the job site for Inuit to take. Anything left after that goes to the dump in a separate place, so it can all be claimed and reused. Off-cuts and small scraps typically find their way into wood stoves. Plywood and larger dimensional lumber end up as part of cabins and sheds like my own.

There are windfalls to be had from the leftovers on job sites. Because of the costs of shipping materials into and out of the settlement, anything not used, even brand new material, is not shipped back out. I still have several fifty-pound boxes of framing nails, unopened, in the cabin, as well as some unused rolls of house wrap. Inuit, of course, have done much better than I have.

My possession of a window is due to the ethic of recycling that most Inuit share. The housing foreman manages a crew of housing employees who maintain and repair the hundred or so public housing units administered by the hamlet government. Charlie Hanayi, like Albert, expends considerable effort in preserving things like empty paint buckets (now containers for my water supply) – or old windows (like the one I now possess) removed from public housing units during window-replacement upgrades. These older windows were stored at the housing shop and given out to anyone who could use them. William managed to acquire several, which he intended to install in his cabins.

How did I end up with one? When I arrived a week ago and set up shop behind William's house, I made a pre-emptive strike of goodwill by purchasing a new fishing net for him. William is seventy-three this year and nearly crippled by arthritis in his knees. His lungs have been ravaged by bouts with tuberculosis and pneumonia. His son Isaac figures that William is finished as a hunter, but I know that one thing that William can still do, and do well, is fish with nets. He did not have one.

In a conversation several days previously, William told me his "good net" had been stolen. He had a good idea who did the stealing, too – his next-door neighbour, Paul Tigliktuq. "He's a good friend, but he's a crook," William phrased it, while Agnes, his wife, rolled her eyes. She is not sure it was really stolen. William explained that Isaac brought the net back in the spring – Isaac had gone to Fish Lake, some eighty kilometres distant, to get some nets for summer fishing, and brought back all of them, including William's "good one," which was left in his boat and subsequently stolen. Now William has no good net for ice fishing at Fish Lake this fall.

The day after our conversation, I sat down with his daughter and went through the Northern catalogue, found the proper net, and ordered it. It was $350 through the catalogue, quite expensive as nets go, but William is old. If he just sits around, he is going to wither and die, and right now he is short on money for a new net. William has done much for me over the years, including keeping an eye on my cabin when I am away. I was also thanking him in advance for letting me run a power cord to his house so that I can have electricity in my cabin. I did not tell him I bought a net for him, nor did I have to. His daughter called from the Northern to tell him before I even left the store.

William, however, in the way of reciprocity, now feels like he owes me something. And he *hates* feeling like he owes somebody. The very next day, three days ago, he promised that I could stay in the Anglican mission house. He thought the house was empty.

The Anglican mission is a large structure, a three-bedroom house with a monstrous kitchen, living room, and office. I have stayed there in previous years, and it was reasonably comfortable as far as houses go. Earlier in the year, it was occupied by the "minister," as everyone called her, though she was not ordained. As far as I knew, Ulukhaktok had not had an ordained minister for about ten years. Since then, there had been sporadic visitations by various missionaries, really laypeople, who typically stayed in Ulukhaktok for very brief periods.

William thought that the minister was gone and not coming back. Unfortunately for him, he was wrong: she did come back a few weeks later. William is a deacon in the church, and he and the minister do not get along. There are several church elders in the settlement, old men used to running the show without outside assistance, and they seem to resent the appearance of missionaries. The more immediate problem, though, is that with the minister returning, he is not sure how he can satisfy his imagined debt to me. The window is an attempt to even the score. William and I have been engaged in this kind of reciprocity for much of the past year, me providing the occasional piece of equipment, a tool, or material, and William in exchange yielding in kind.

Edward, in his own way, is engaged in the same kind of reciprocity. Two days previously, he effectively asked me for a "loan" of $100 to get through the week because he was out of money and groceries, and he has children to feed. I say that he "asked," but in reality he declared a need for money and never asked me outright. We both knew that the "loan" would not be repaid, at least not in cash; I met his indirect request by arranging to pay him to change the track on my snowmobile and get it ready for winter. Despite that arrangement, he still feels indebted, so he is helping me. He sees an opportunity to settle our score and open up an avenue for further reciprocity on my part. Ideally, these kinds of cycles never really end. There are really only two guidelines: generosity is important, and it is better to do the giving than the receiving. To be called stingy is one of the worst insults imaginable.

Edward really needs the money. Now in his late thirties, he essentially grew up on the land. He had his own snowmobile when he was twelve and spent much of his childhood not in town but running traplines and hunting seals and caribou. The value of a formal education was never clear to his parents (or, indeed, to him), and in any event, men like Edward find many of the wage-labour options in the community abhorrent. There is a reason the office jobs mostly go to women. Men prefer to work with their hands, to see the results of their work at the end of the day. This includes putting meat in the freezer, getting a broken snowmobile to run, or installing a new furnace in public housing. Pushing paper or stocking shelves does not seem to provide the same satisfaction.

Edward has his demons, too, that add to his problems with money. His parents, both heavy drinkers during his youth, were abusive, and Edward has anger management issues of his own. His problems with alcohol are well documented. Like many in his generation, he has spent time in "Camp Yellowknife" for assault. He is well aware of these problems and stays away from the booze as much as he can. But he does have relapses, both with alcohol and marijuana, which he also uses.

Higaaq is less of a problem for his temper, but it takes money that could be used for more immediate household needs. Edward and his wife are currently off both, however. Nevertheless, he has a reputation for being unreliable, and this gets in the way of his finding and keeping a steady job, despite his competence as a carpenter and, to a lesser degree, as a mechanic.

Edward's latest crisis has to do with his rent. Over the summer I heard rumours about his impending eviction, but Edward confirmed it the other day when we arranged the exchange of money for repairs. He is several thousand dollars in arrears on his house.

For men like Edward, who live by going from one casual job to another, and who depend heavily on guiding sports hunters in the spring and fall, there are lean times during the year when money is scarce. Edward worked as a guide for polar bear hunters last spring, acting as a helper on four different hunts over a seven-week period, earning about $14,000 for his labour. Over the summer, he worked as a general labourer on the construction of two new housing units and also did some work for the mining company that is exploring above Minto Inlet.

It was a puzzle to me why he was so far in arrears on his house. After all, he made enough money to purchase a snowmobile. It was a used machine, but as it had belonged to a teacher, it might as well have been new. Edward spent late spring and summer hunting and fishing to produce quite a bit of food, not only for his own family but also for his mother, brother, and two sisters.

An inquiry at the hamlet revealed the source of the trouble. The hamlet administers public housing, and the office is charged with assessing rents on units based on an arcane formula that considers the age, size, and condition of the house or apartment. These factors establish a baseline "market value" of the unit. For most single-family units, the market rate on a six-hundred square foot house is over $2,000 per month. Residents then apply for and receive a subsidy based on the declared income of the renter. Theoretically, it should be simple: the hamlet inputs the data on the income, and out comes the rent for the month.

Currently, the hamlet manages about one hundred public housing units, some of them single-family homes, some apartments in duplexes or four-plexes. The units vary in size, age, and condition, though half of the units are over twenty-five years old. The local housing board assigns applicants to units based on another magic formula that uses input variables like family size and perceived need for housing. In any given month, families are swapping houses as units open, family sizes change, and Inuit fall behind in their rent payments.

There are two problems with this method, and both have caught Edward in his current bind. The first is that the system is set up based on the assumption that Inuit are regular wage earners – that is, that a person like Edward has a steady income each and every month. In reality, people like Edward can go three or four months with no income whatsoever, depending on social assistance to keep their families going. During those times, their rent is set at a minimum payment, currently $38 per month. Such was the case for Edward, until last April, when he made $12,000 guiding. Because of that, his rent was assessed at $2,100 (the maximum) for that month, instead of the $38 the rate of the previous month. The trouble, of course, is that there wasn't enough of that $12,000 to go around. He needed new equipment so he could hunt – hence the $5,500 for the snowmobile, in addition to gas to keep it going. His kids needed new clothes. He has debts at the Northern and Co-op that had accumulated over the previous months. By the time he received notice of his rent change, the $12,000 was long gone.

The second problem is one of paperwork. Edward, like many Inuit, would rather not be bothered with paperwork. A common strategy for dealing with it is to ignore it until the problem goes away. Under current policy, it is Edward's responsibility *each month* to apply, and then reapply, for the subsidy on his house. Should he fail to apply, he receives no subsidy, and so pays the full "market rate" rent on the unit, $2,100.

None of this makes sense to me. Edward will be lucky to earn a total of $10,000 over the next ten months. He is not guiding hunters, for one. For another, he is barely literate, as is his wife, and neither can stand bureaucracy. For people like Edward, who live by their own rhythm, their activity patterns are far different than the 9-to-5 nature of the office workers. Edward compounded his problems with Housing by missing multiple mitigation meetings, which were scheduled at 9:30 AM. During the summer, he, like many Inuit who do not work full-time jobs, was what Inuit call "backwards," sleeping through the day and active at night.

In other times, Edward might not have had this problem with his rent, but the former housing liaison officer quit her job a year ago. Part of the reason that she left was precisely because she did not like being the one to deliver the bad news to a tenant about to be evicted – to, as she called it, "boss people around." She also did not care for the recent change in policy that called for stricter income tracking, yet more paperwork, and constantly hounding of tenants for rent payments. The new officer was both younger and much more tenacious about following The Rules. On more than one encounter with her, I heard complaints about tenants being a problem because they couldn't "get with the program" or "be responsible." That she is Edward's cousin adds to the insult.

Should Edward be responsible for paying the rent on his house? Of course he should. I am also well aware that he and his wife also earn a modest income from periodically selling marijuana. Much of their earned income literally ends up in smoke. Still, it easy to see how such a foreign state system – bureaucracy, rules, forms, paperwork, and arcane formulas, all devised in Yellowknife or Ottawa – is so at odds with actual social and economic conditions on the ground.

Edward has been threatened with eviction if he doesn't pay the $5,000 he owes to Housing. He has been served notice, and though he doesn't say anything about it to me, everyone knows about it. And, everyone has an opinion, though people seem interested not out of malice but because Edward's problems are something to talk about. In another three months, someone else will be in trouble with Housing and threatened with eviction. For Edward, the money doesn't really mean much, except that $5,000 is a lot of money, and it does not quite register with him the way it would, say, with me, or with any other money-oriented southerner. It seems like the money is simply part of a yearly "Now I have some and now I don't" cycle.

The casing comes apart relatively easily as these things run through my mind, and it only takes an hour to cut a hole in the back wall, nail in a couple of cripples and a header, and install the window up high, right above the level of the sleeping platform. Edward does an expert job, and from the inside I squirt insulating foam into the cracks and add some molding around the casing. We clean up the tools and break for more coffee. The weather has warmed up a bit, to 5°C, so we sit in the doorway, sheltered from the wind, and sip our drinks.

BOATING WITH SIMON IQALUK

On a similar September morning, fifteen years earlier, Simon Iqaluk asks if I want to go hunting with him, and I accept. I have been in Ulukhaktok for less than a month, so to be asked to go out on the land with someone, rather than having to impose my presence on someone else, is a big deal at this point in my field experience, brief as it is.

"What are we going to do?"

"My dad wants me to go down to Mashuyak to check on the camp and close it up. We'll go down there, then we can go hunt seals down in the islands."

It sounds exciting. I get ready. Though it is very early in September, there is already plenty of snow on the land, a harbinger of the coming autumn, which will be extraordinarily snowy. Otherwise, the weather is perfect for this time of year.

I head down to the beach with Simon, and we meet his father, Harry Tamaryak, by his boat. It lies next to an imposing freighter dory, built out of steel plate and thirty-eight feet long, and among a pile of older boats, many of them looking far from seaworthy.

Harry is loading supplies into his eighteen-foot aluminum boat, locally referred to as a speedboat. Harry sees us, nods hello to me, and gets down on his hands and knees to reach underneath an old wood and canvas freighter canoe, twenty-two feet long, with a flat stern on which an outboard motor can be mounted. These were once the workhorses of the community, but they have since fallen out of favour, replaced years ago by the speedboats. The canoes are much better at hauling loads, and they are much more stable in the water than an aluminum speedboat. However, the canoes seem to require more care. Their canvas skin is easily torn on rocks and drifting debris, such a common occurrence that travellers used to carry extra butter or lard with them to temporarily patch the tears. (In the event of a leak, one shoves a blob of fat into the hole. The cold water solidifies the mass and seals the leak.) Additionally, the gravel on the beaches eventually wears through the skin. The canoes are also heavy, especially after hours in the water. The biggest reason that they have fallen out of favour, however, seems to be that they are slower than speedboats.

When it comes down to it, Ulukhaktok as a settlement site is not well placed for subsistence purposes. Its location is due to the presence of King's Bay, a well-protected, deep-water harbour, a very attractive feature for the Roman Catholic missionaries and for the Hudson's Bay Company, which first established a post here back in the late 1930s. Both organizations required a safe location to anchor their supply vessels in the event of an early freeze-up. The King's Bay site was also roughly halfway between Walker Bay, across Minto Inlet, and Alaervik, down in Prince Albert Sound. The HBC maintained posts at both sites during the 1930s; the RC mission also tried to maintain sites at both of these locations, serving the bands of Inuit who roamed in each of these territories. To save money, the HBC simply closed both and relocated to Ulukhaktok, hence serving two different bands of Inuit in the process.

But Ulukhaktok, being between two hunting grounds, is far from both of them. Safety Channel, some twenty to twenty-five kilometres by boat to the south, at the opening of Prince Albert Sound, is the closest of the "traditional" grounds for Inuit who live in Ulukhaktok. Caribou hunting during the summertime has for many years required lengthy boating trips down into Prince Albert Sound. A round trip to Kuuk and back, for example, is well over 320 kilometres. In a freighter canoe pushed by a thirty-horsepower motor, that is a long trip. Ulukhaktomiut have tended to favour speed over cost, choosing speedboats and bigger motors. The gasoline is expensive, but the journey is much faster.

It is difficult to fault this decision to select speed. The trip into Prince Albert Sound is a risky one in terms of both weather and hunting success. Both are intertwined. Wind and storms can increase the danger of a boating trip multiple times over. A speedboat reduces time on the water in adverse conditions or, ideally, makes the best use of a brief window of good weather. Wind also pushes floating ice; what starts out as a productive trip can turn into a disaster if winds change and ice is pushed into the sound or up on the beach, trapping hunters.

Such conditions can delay a return. The primary purpose of summer caribou hunting is to produce food to be stockpiled for the family for the remainder of the year. With little storage capability in August, Inuit stuck on the land by weather must resort to drying their meat, a process that can be hampered by warm temperatures and damp conditions. With the limited capacity of the boats, there is also the problem of supplies. A prolonged stay on the land can turn a trip from an expedition hunt designed to stockpile food to a break-even camping trip in which the travellers have eaten what they caught. While they will not starve, many would consider such a trip – several weeks on the land, returning to the settlement with no surplus food – a failure. The speedboat seems designed to try to solve the problems of long-distance expedition hunting.

Harry turns the canoe partly onto one gunwale and rummages around underneath a tarp. Soon he emerges and reveals what he has been looking for: a 12-gauge shotgun, a .22 magnum, and a .22-250. Apparently, he stores these underneath the canoe, protected only by the hull and an old blue, poly-whatever tarp. He leans these against the speedboat, takes up the .22-250, and opens the bolt. A shell is already in the chamber – Harry keeps 'em loaded. He closes the bolt, and raises the telescope to his eye, scanning the water. Some eighty metres out in the middle of the bay is a seagull, blissfully ignorant of what is about to happen.

The gull flies off in a spray of feathers and water, the report of the shot still in our ears. I am not sure if Harry missed deliberately, but he is apparently satisfied. He laughs softly to himself. "Heh. You could have this one. It's good enough." He gives me the rifle. Simon picks a box of shells out of a canvas bag, and hands them to me. I place shells and gun in the boat – the chamber is now empty. We put the other two guns in the boat as well, and shove out into the water.

Harry calls to us from the shore as we drift, stowing our gear. "There's some shotgun shells down in the cabin. You could use those." Simon only has one shell for the shotgun with him.

This incident occurred before the "new" firearms legislation went into effect in Canada – full implementation is still some years away – but it was clear that Inuit were rather cavalier with their firearms. Even in 1992, guns were supposed to be kept under lock and key for safe storage, ideally to prevent such things as children getting hold of a loaded firearm and accidentally killing themselves or somebody else. The RCMP officer was making an effort to check for shoddy storage and request that hunters take better care when storing their rifles. To its credit, the RCMP was using an educational rather than punitive approach. To my knowledge, however, not one person in Ulukhaktok had any kind of secure storage for firearms, nor did anyone have trigger locks. Most people stored firearms on the porch, in the shack, or in the house, many securing them (as I did) by storing the bolt and ammunition elsewhere in the house from the gun.

In the time since, promotion of secure storage seems to have worked, though it is unclear if education or the new laws encouraged this. Locking up guns may have been due more to the increasing reality of theft. Nevertheless, the new firearms legislation required secure storage. The legislation also required the registration of all firearms, disposal of unwanted guns through the RCMP directly, and new licences to purchase or sell firearms. By 1997, an FAC (Firearms Acquisition Certificate) was required for the purchase of guns, though ammunition could be purchased by anyone, it seemed. By 1999, the licensing had changed to a "Possession Only" licence or a "Possession and Acquisition" licence (PAL), both of which could only be acquired by completing an approved firearms safety course and passing a written and oral examination. Inuit could apply for the PAL under an exemption designed for subsistence hunters – though even this was fraught with difficulty because the definition of subsistence was, predictably, rather rigid, and unsuitable for the Arctic. The original definition of a subsistence hunter required so many days living out in the bush. This requirement simply did not work in the Arctic, where the primary limit is the productivity of the land. It makes more sense to live in the settlement and make long trips, rather than live in the bush, where travel is more difficult: trees, lakes, marshy ground, deep snow all conspire to make bush travel slow and difficult. In the Arctic, long-distance travel is reasonably easy (though physically challenging), but the problem is one of productivity.

For Inuit hunters, another issue with the FAC/PAL was the simple hurdle of bureaucracy: people had to fill out the paperwork and apply for the things, and many Inuit, especially younger Inuit, never bothered to do so. The general hostility towards paperwork and regulations is deeply entrenched in Ulukhaktok. Inuit also seemed convinced that the current firearms regulations, like so many other regulations before them, encompassing many different domains of Inuit life, would eventually just go away. Finally, and perhaps foolishly, younger Inuit continued to depend upon their parents, who already purchased much of their ammunition anyway and also regularly bought firearms for them as needed. Simon was but one example. The guns were all Harry's, as was the ammunition and, indeed, the boat.

We drift for a few more minutes while Simon hooks up the gas can to the motor. The engine fires up on the first try, and he makes to head out of the bay, opening the throttle as soon as the bow comes around. Harry, I have already been told, liked to go fast, and so does his son. We brace ourselves against the gunwales, leaning forward as the boat lifts out of the water and planes. We remain standing, the better to see around us, the wind whipping our hair. As we leave Queen's Bay and make for the little islands outside of King's Bay, Simon begins focusing his attention on the water. The wind is light and from the west, as it so frequently will be this fall. I assume we are looking for seals, but Simon is also on the lookout for late-season birds – qingaliks swimming on the water, not yet gone for Siberia. We soon see a small bunch bobbing in the light chop. Simon turns the boat and makes straight for them as fast as he can go, coming up upon them as they slowly spring from the water. Unlike dabbling ducks, eiders are divers, heavier birds that require some time to become airborne.

Simon grabs the shotgun at his feet, takes aim, and fires his one shell. He does this while keeping his knee on the steering wheel. The ducks are flying now, and both they and we are moving at high speed. They are just a little out of range, but Simon hits one. We retrieve it from the water, wounded but still alive. "Only one? I was trying to get more than that with my one shot all right." He grabs the duck by its neck and spins it around in a circle, killing it. He drops it into a plastic tub.

We pull into Mashuyak a short time later, moving through the little narrow that separates Victoria Island from Holman Island, just across the way. Holman Island is perhaps five kilometres end to end, but it is high, its west side a line of forbidding cliffs of broken basalt, smashed by ice and west winds but protecting Mashuyak on the east side of the island. Though there are a few cabins on Holman Island, most of the camps are on the gently sloping gravel beach on the "mainland" of Victoria Island. Simon pulls the boat up behind the gravel spit, right to his dad's camp. Though there is an inch of snow on the hills behind and on Holman Island, the gravel beach itself is free of snow.

The cabin is rather large as cabins go, a hodgepodge of scavenged plywood, dimensional lumber, and some tarps. It's a summer camp, so there is no need for a plywood roof. The canvas and poly-whatever tarps allow light into the interior, obviating the need for a window. The structure looks as if it has been expanded several times over the years. Harry has added space, renovated, and repaired as the number of summer residents has grown over the years. He and his wife, with plenty of grandchildren and great-grandchildren in tow, have spent the majority of their summers here, usually staying from the onset of duck season in early June through break-up in July, coming back to town only in late August. Simon is here to begin the process of closing up the camp for the year.

Gas cans, plywood boxes, and old chairs are scattered around outside. Several empty gas drums closer to the beach serve as trash cans of a sort, but they also function as the supports for drying racks. Several dozen Arctic char are hanging from 2 × 2 poles, in various states of being dried into piffi. On large poles at either end of the racks, some seven feet in the air, are dead gulls, wings splayed and nailed crucifixion-style to the poles. Scare-gulls. After several days unattended, the piffis appear unmolested.

We cart a few bags to the cabin and pull in Harry's nets, which have caught two char. We throw the char into the plastic bin in the boat and stow the net in the bow. After twenty minutes of turning the cabin upside down in search of the promised shotgun shells, Simon shrugs and gives up. Either Harry is misremembering, or the shells have been misplaced. More likely, another of Harry's children has taken them and not yet informed Harry. "We'll just have to shoot ducks with rifles now," says Simon, neither angry nor disappointed at this development.

We return to the boat and shove off. Simon turns us to the south, and we pass Mashuyak, move beyond Holman Island, and head for "around the corner" as Simon puts it. "We'll go down to the islands and hunt seals and rabbits."

We motor along a bit slower than on the way to Mashuyak, probably because he is now much more serious about hunting. He points out some of the landmarks. At the last cabins, he gestures to a river that comes down from the land. "You could go up there and get into the land that way. It's a funny lake, must be a spring under it, the ice is always broken in winter, and the river overflows, too, even in winter. When this is all ice, water could come out on top of the ice and then freeze. You have to be careful you don't go through and get wet."

A little while later he says, "This is Nauyaat," referring to cliffs along the shore. Like Holman Island, they face west and the waters of the Beaufort Sea. Strong west winds and storms have pounded these rocks over the years.

"Seagulls?" I ask, inquiring about the meaning of the Inuinnaqtun word for them. Simon nods.

After a month in Ulukhaktok, I know a few Inuinnaqtun words, but I am finding it frustratingly difficult to acquire any of the language beyond single words. People like Simon – my age – rarely speak Inuinnaqtun in public settings, and many of my age-mates express with some embarrassment that they have little control over the language. While their parents may speak to them in Inuinnaqtun, they reply in English or not at all. I have also been finding that even asking older people to teach me some of the language is an exercise in frustration.

Ulukhaktok is really three, perhaps four, different groups of Inuit, the three groups that were originally called Copper Eskimos (Inuinnait in their own dialect) and a fourth, now called Inuvialuit, people originally from the Mackenzie Delta. Two of these groups were involved in the original move from Minto and Prince Albert Sound: the Minto Inlet people, the Kanghiryuatjagmiut, and the Prince Albert Sound people, the Kangiryuarmiut, were two of the bands that originally settled in Ulukhaktok. Another group, the "Read Islanders," lived around and traded primarily at the Hudson's Bay Company post on Read Island. When the HBC closed the Read Island Post, roughly halfway between Ulukhaktok and Kugluktuk, some of the Inuit there moved to Ulukhaktok.

I often think of these groups as discrete bands, though identifying which individuals belong to which group can be difficult. There was plenty of mixing between the groups even before contact, through both intermarriage and migration, with numerous kinship links between Ulukhaktok and Cambridge Bay, on the southeastern side of Victoria Island (some eight hundred kilometres away), and Kukgluktuk, on the mainland.

The Inuvialuit are yet another group that has married or migrated into the settlement. Indeed, the first Inuit settler in Ulukhaktok was Natkusiak, "Billy Banksland," an Alaskan Inupiaq who settled here in the late 1930s after a career guiding the explorer Vilhjalmur Stefansson. Others have come and gone since, and there are likewise numerous kinship links between Ulukhaktok and Inuvik in the Mackenzie Delta. Other Inuit in Ulukhaktok have kin ties with Sachs Harbour on neighbouring Banks Island, a settlement founded in the 1930s in response to the fox-trapping boom there of the 1920s and 1930s.

Thus, the settlement is linguistically a bit of a jumble, and contemporary identity politics have not helped matters. Ulukhaktomiut voted some years ago to join the Inuvialuit land claim. In 1984, the Inuvialuit Final Agreement was ratified, creating the Inuvialuit Regional Corporation (IRC) and a number of regional community corporations in the settlements that act as the local arms of the IRC. The other Copper Eskimo settlements, Cambridge Bay and Kugluktuk, opted to join the Nunavut land claim, which in 1999 resulted in the creation of the new territory of Nunavut.

When I first arrived in Ulukhaktok, I hardly ever heard the word "Inuvialuit" used to describe people in the community. But a steady diet of IRC-sponsored literature over the years has promoted the position that people in Ulukhaktok are Inuvialuit, a designation that, like many terms people use to describe themselves, means "people." Yet people in Ulukhaktok, like those in Kugluktuk, tend to refer to themselves as Inuinnait (which also means "people," though in the local language), and there seems to be some confusion about what one is supposed to be. "I thought we were all Inuit? Whatever happened to that?" Charlie Hanayi phrased it some years ago. After nearly twenty years, I am still confused by the politics involved.

Even to a novice's ear, Inuvialuktun is decidedly different from Inuinnaqtun. Entire words are pronounced differently, and the presence of sounds that are absent in Inuinnaqtun betray one's origins. Locally, Mashuyak should be pronounced "mahuyak," and some Inuit still prefer this "correct" pronunciation, because Inuinnaqtun lacks the "s" sound. But even the local Inuinnaqtun is problematic, with subtle variations used by people of different origins, each with their own linguistic idiosyncrasies. With so few truly fluent speakers left, it is sometimes difficult to tell idiolect from dialect.

I confronted this reality almost immediately when I asked William Kaaktuq to teach me a few phrases, the beginnings of what I hoped was to be an understanding of the language and some minimal fluency. William did so happily, and I carefully memorized the words and utterances he taught me. Pleased with my performance, I immediately tried out my new knowledge on Paul Tigliktuq, when I went to visit not long after.

"*Qanuritpit*?" I asked him. *How are you?*

Paul laughed. "*Naammaktunga!*" *I am fine.* His next utterance was completely incomprehensible, totally different from what I expected him to say, based on what William had told me. I thought it meant "*And how are you*?" and responded as I thought I should.

Paul's high-pitched, machine-gun giggle stopped him from speaking. When he recovered his breath, he said, "You talk funny. Like those people from Minto. You sound like William." He laughed some more. And that was the end of the conversation.

Upon reflection, of course I *would* sound like William. He is missing quite a few teeth, which is bound to affect his speech. In my desire to be as precise as possible, I was inadvertently replicating his linguistic idiosyncrasies.

At the same time, though, I began to understand why some of my age-mates were reluctant to speak Inuinnaqtun in public. Rather than encouraging me to speak *more* Inuinnaqtun, Paul instantly shut me down, reminding me that, no matter what I did, I would never be able to speak properly, that I would always sound "funny" in the eyes of these older men. I could imagine how much worse it would be for a young Inuk, learning some Inuinnaqtun at home but taught at school almost exclusively in English and expected to conduct his or her public affairs in English. Is it any wonder that young people refrain from using Inuinnaqtun in public discourse if the end result is derision? Many of my age-mates probably speak Inuinnaqtun with an English accent. *You talk funny. You sound like one of those people.*

Such issues are not restricted to language use. Young men who, for no fault of their own, never learned to hunt as children or teenagers are ridiculed for making simple mistakes while travelling, like running out of gas ten kilometres from town and having to walk home, or miscalculating conditions and becoming lost while returning from Fish Lake. It is as if such things never happened to these older men when they were themselves young, though these things did happen to them. Every hunter over age fifty has at least once walked home after breaking down. Indeed, there is sometimes a sense that the older men, especially, view themselves as occupying a moral high ground in regard to their own cultural identity. They were hunters, damn it – they know what it's like to go without food, to walk home after a breakdown, to be tough. Not like kids these days, who go to school, do not hunt much, lead soft lives cushioned by the social safety net and wage labour jobs. Men like William or Tigliktuq seem to misunderstand that times are indeed different, that men my age simply cannot have lived the same experience as their parents. Social and economic conditions have made the contact-traditional lifestyle impossible.

Nevertheless, there remains a sense that the current generation of Inuit elders, many over age seventy, is the last "traditional" generation of Inuit, the last bearers of the culture, even though they themselves led remarkably different lives from their parents, whose lives may have predated European contact and the cash economy. There has been a kind of internal colonialism in this matter. In 2005, I had a lengthy conversation with James Annuttuq, sitting outside the wildlife officer's office, James smoking a cigarette while we drank coffee. Margaret Agluituq had recently passed away. She was a remarkable woman who died somewhere in her mid-nineties, though many of her descendants insisted that she was well over a hundred years old.

"Our elders are passing on. Soon there won't be any left, and our culture will go with it," James said, staring sadly into his coffee cup.

"But James, you're an elder now, aren't you?" I said. "Aren't you a bearer of the culture? Can't you talk to your children and grandchildren, and pass along what you know?"

James just continued to gaze into his cup. It has been one of the most frustrating facets of working in a place like Ulukhaktok that even Inuit themselves seem to believe in a traditional-modern dichotomy, in which "Inuit culture" can only be an idealized traditional culture, a fossilized abstraction that precludes the inclusion of mechanized foraging equipment, a passion for hockey and country music, or the incorporation of wage labour into Inuit social life.

Simon and I move slowly past Nauyaat, or at least it seems that way. "When I was little, we used to collect eggs from there," he says. "My dad would tie a rope to me and hang me down, holding my legs, to get eggs from the nests. Been a long time since we've done that, though. Not many people collect gull eggs anymore. They're big. Really *mamaq*."

We cross an opening, the mouth of a large bay on our left, either north or east of us, I am not sure. Simon says we are going "around the corner." He points into the bay. "Inside there is Pituutaq, a little piece of land between two bays. Lots of people camped in there long ago, but not so much now. Some people say there are little people camped around there. Maybe we'll go there after.

"Here's Karukut. This is where the water can get really rough, boy, coming right in from the west. And there's funny currents here too, you have to be careful. One time I was coming back with Dad from caribou hunting, and the weather was so rough, the waves were so high, that between them you couldn't see Karukut, then you could, then it would vanish again. Really scary." As at Nauyaat, the cliffs are high around this place. It's scary thinking of such swells, even in the calm seas we have today.

Simon is telling me these things, and I am not sure whether his focus is on the story itself, reliving important memories, or if he is educating me, telling these stories for my benefit. *Be careful of standing water on the ice in this place. Be careful of currents and weather around this place. If you want gull eggs, this is the place to go.* I suspect he is engaging in a little bit of both, a young adult already reminiscing while passing on his knowledge.

We pull into Safety Channel, heading toward a maze of islands across the opening into the channel proper. Simon finds a sheltered beach on one of the islands. We pull the boat up and tie it to a large rock, then walk inland, rifles on our shoulders, I with the .22-250, Simon with the .22 magnum. Our eyes are peeled for the distinctive white of an Arctic hare against the dull browns and greens of the land. Unlike around Ulukhaktok, there is no snow on the ground here.

"I never hunted rabbits here before, but I bet there's lots of them around now. See?" Simon points across the little valley. "You go get that one. It will run, but it will stop right in the rocks. Sneak up to it and you can get it. I'll go this way." He walks in the opposite direction.

I take the bunny in two shots, doing just as Simon tells me. The hare hopped out of sight into the rocks, but I found it sitting against a south-west facing rock, picking up what little heat the sun provided. Simon is also shooting, and I follow the report of his rifle – six shots in all. When I find him, he is retrieving his second bunny. "My scope was out. I never checked it before we left. Good now." He holds up the rabbits.

We have been out for some three hours, and we are getting hungry. Perhaps it is dinnertime. Neither of us has a watch. Simon produces a can of Klik from his bag. Klik appears to be a Spam substitute, of somewhat lower quality if such a thing is possible. Hunger is the best sauce, however, and we snack on it, supplementing it with a piffi, as we get the boat ready to go, adding our rabbits to the plastic tub. We will not go hungry, but we are here to produce food, not eat it.

We push off, heading back into the calm of the channel. Simon idles the motor and we putter slowly along. He pulls his rifle close and suggests I do the same. In the lee of the wind, the water is nearly flat calm, though the boat is bobbing gently in the slight swells from the sound. After a few moments, he hisses and raises his rifle. I look just in time to see it before he fires: the head of the animal is barely out of the water, looking around. Simon puts the rifle down and hits the throttle nearly all in the same motion, heading for the spot where he shot.

He got it, and the seal is still bobbing in the water, only slowly sinking. It is a medium-sized ringed seal, dead instantly. Simon puts the gaff hook into it. "Grab a flipper, we'll pull it in."

I reach down and grab one of the flippers. The water is cold, and the animal feels heavy, though it cannot weigh more than 45 kilograms. "On three," Simon counts, and we bob the animal in the water a couple of times before we haul it in.

We are a little exuberant and end up pulling the entire animal into the boat, which is not what Simon intended. "Ooooh, what a mess!" Blood is still flowing from the wound in the seal's head, but what is worse is that its bowels are voiding over the bilge.

We rest the carcass on the gunwale, the nearly black blood from the wound dripping into the water. Simon bails the mess out of the bilge with an old plastic cup.

"Let's look for more." He is pleased despite the mishap. "Your turn."

I am not so sure about it being "my turn." Before coming to Ulukhaktok, I had only limited experience with a "real" gun. And in Ulukhaktok I have only had a month practising with a .22, shooting at rabbits, only somewhat successfully. Now I'm to shoot a seal, from a boat? Is it even legal for me to do so? I suspect not, but I am hardly one to decline; Simon is both inviting and testing me. Am I a colonial, just another Qablunaaq living *in* Ulukhaktok, but not *with* Inuit?

We see it as we approach the shore of a different island: a younger seal sitting in the water, apparently not at all concerned about us. It must not know about people yet. It is about to find out. "Go ahead," Simon says.

I put the scope on the seal's head, which now appears even smaller despite the magnification of the scope. I am instantly aware a number of problems. The first is that, though I have ignored it to this point, the boat is bobbing all over the place, up and down and side to side. It is difficult enough to shoot standing on solid ground, and here I am, a rank amateur, trying to shoot a target while both target and shooter are moving in seemingly random directions. And that head is so small, even at 75 metres and through a telescope. There's not much room for error.

The seal is now wary, looking over at us, but still it does not dive. Deciding that sooner is better than later, I fire as soon as I think I have the crosshairs on the animal. It feels like an eternity, but my hesitation must have been only a few seconds.

"Whoa. That was really close, you almost got it!" Simon is encouraging. "You only missed by a really little bit." He holds out his thumb and index finger, showing me how close the shot was. I have no idea where the bullet went. I suspect Simon is being generous.

We never see the seal again. It seems to have learned very quickly about boats, for it stays under the water for some time, and likely comes up for air at a distance, out of our sight. Missing on the first try is not necessarily a sign of failure, because it is difficult to hunt seals in open water. The strategy used in open water hunting is to spot the seal, shoot at it and force to dive under the water, then drive as quickly as possible to the spot where it was. One reason for doing so is the possibility that the animal has been killed. Seals in summer have lower fat stores and are not buoyant. They sink, so the hurry is to get the gaff hook on them. If that fails, the sinking hook is used, a treble hook on a heavy lead, thrown into the water to snag the animal before it sinks too far. In the waters where we are now, using the sinking hook is not terribly problematic. The waters here are clear and somewhat shallow, so one can see the animal as it descends, and even retrieve it off the bottom if necessary. In other locations, however, deep and murky water requires incredible skill with the sinking hook. Such was the case up in the waters around Minto Inlet; Inuit have told me that William Kaaktuq, for example, never missed a sinking seal. Having hunted there for much of his adult life, he could judge the angle and speed at which a seal would sink in the water and throw the hook in such a way as to intercept it.

In the event of a missed shot, the hunter scans the water from the boat, waiting for the animal to surface again, shooting at it quickly. The idea is not so much to kill the animal as to harass it, preventing it from taking a good breath before it is forced to dive again. Eventually it becomes so tired that it surfaces closer and closer to the boat, allowing for a better shot. It seems hardly an efficient method and requires a great deal of gasoline, unless the hunter is an exceptionally good shot – which, Simon tells me, is the case with most of the elders. They have had years of practice, and many do not really need a telescope, or even iron sights, when they shoot.

Simon is hoping to get "my" seal by driving and harassing it, but in the maze of islands we have no luck. After a fruitless search and a glance at the slowly darkening skies, we turn the boat and make our way home, but not before stopping at Pituutaq, where Simon shoots two more rabbits and manages to take another qingalik, this one with the rifle. He is pleased with the catch we take back to Ulukhaktok: a seal, five rabbits, two eider ducks, two fresh char, and several dozen piffis, a very successful trip.

We pull the boat onshore in Queen's Bay eight hours after departing, both of us feeling a bit chilly and very hungry. It is nearly dark. We've only eaten a shared can of Klik and some piffi. We unload the boat, each taking an end of the plastic bin full of food. We leave the seal on the beach.

"We'll leave it here for a couple of days before I cut it up," says Simon. "They taste better after they've aged. Let's go and eat. Mum's got food at the house." So we do, leaving the bin on the porch and sitting down to a meal of boiled seal, mipku, and fish stew.

VISITORS

Whenever I return to Ulukhaktok after a long absence, I am privileged by a steady stream of visitors, old friends dropping by to catch up on news, welcome me back, and see how I and my family are doing. This kind of visiting is customary in Ulukhaktok, an extension of the handshake and small conversation offered to any who have been away from the settlement for any length of time, whether on the land or out in another settlement. Rick Condon used say he felt like the mayor, everyone stopping to shake his hand as he walked down the street. The visits from those closest to me are simply a more substantive version of this tradition.

This time, however, I am unprepared for such a degree of visitation. Over the course of 2007, I have been in and out of Ulukhaktok on numerous occasions, balancing the fieldwork with my own family life. My last trip south was only for a month, hardly calling for such a stream of visitors. Indeed, many Inuit were seemingly unaware that I had left, judging by the reaction when I got off the plane. *Where were you? I didn't know you'd gone out. Now I know why I hadn't seen you in a couple of weeks.*

After the second visit, though, I begin to realize why I am suddenly seeing more visitors again, people who normally do not visit me. Putdjugiaq has come by for tea. So has Matthew Aqiaruq. Trudy and Fred Ukaliq stopped by the other day. They are all coming out of curiosity. What is the Qablunaaq doing with that old shack? For the cabin has sat here quietly behind William's house for well over a decade, long enough that it has faded into the background, hiding in plain sight. Until I began my renovation several days ago, transforming the shack from a warehouse to a dwelling, most Inuit, I think, were unaware that I even *had* a cabin.

So, sheer curiosity in the why and how I am living is part of the reason for increased interest. For one thing, my cabin is different. Whereas most cabins in town tend to have higher walls and nearly flat roofs, mine has a peaked roof and lower walls. When I built it, my reasoning was that an 8 × 12 with a 6-in-12 roof made the most efficient use of 4 × 8 plywood sheets and eight-foot 2 × 4s, which were for me in limited supply. But most Inuit suspect I am a bit thick in the head, always asking questions that for Inuit have seemingly obvious answers. I generally do things differently.

Paul Tigliktuq, William's neighbour, the good friend and crook, was one of the first to take a serious interest in what I was up to. I am behind Paul's house also, so he has a pretty good idea when I am out and about. We have always been friendly, but we have become friendlier since last winter. I have spent the entire year in the neighbourhood anyway. The duplex I rented from the hamlet earlier in the year is just across the way, clearly visible. We were even then within shouting distance of each other. Paul, who smokes prodigiously, is continuously outside having a puff, for he does not smoke in the house. We have had numerous and friendly conversations while he smokes, though that has always been the extent of our interaction. In his eyes, I was just another Qablunaaq. Paul's view of me seemed to change last winter, after Isaac's sports hunter got a bear and I was invited to eat with the family.

While the sports hunter shot the bear, everyone knows that it was really Isaac who got the bear. He tracked it, stalked it, and loosed his dogs on it. The tourist merely pulled the trigger. Bear hunting remains an important activity for Ulukhaktomiut for both cultural and economic reasons. Economically, bear hunting is a big deal because a tourist hunter spends some $30,000 on the operation, with half to two-thirds of that money remaining in town. Most bear hunts are organized by the Hunters and Trappers Organization (the HTC), which contracts with an outfitter in Yellowknife. The outfitter books hunts and arranges travel, while HTC runs the show in the settlement. HTC hires the guides as independent contractors. The guide receives $8,000, the helper $3,500. Some tourist hunters pay for additional support, "spotters" who drive around on their snowmobiles looking for tracks. They might make another $3,000. The HTC takes a chunk of the remainder, split with the outfitter in Yellowknife. The tourist hunter then has two weeks to shoot a bear. The hunt must be conducted on dogsled, though snowmobiles can be used to haul equipment and supplies to base camps on the ice. Once two weeks are up, the hunt is over, bear or no.

Culturally, bear hunting is even more important. In spring of 2007 there were only four working dog teams in town, and so only four guides. Two of these guides were "old-timers" – Paul was one, though he often spoke of giving it up, citing the hassles of feeding and training dogs. The aggravation of dealing with tourist hunters is worse. They are generally a pain to manage and occasionally dangerous. One was so nervous about shooting a cornered bear that he managed to shoot Paul's bear dog with the first shot instead. The other guide, Mark Anguhuqtuq, shows no signs of slowing down, however. There are others, older men who have kept dogs in the past but who for one reason or another do not have full teams.

The other two with working teams are Isaac Kaaktuq and Albert Aquti, younger men in their late forties who have inherited their dogs from their fathers. Isaac took over his dad's dogs, built up his team and trained them, and he has been guiding for three years. Isaac had three hunters during spring of 2007, and when his first hunter got his bear, the town was abuzz with excitement. *It is good to see the next generation carrying on our traditions* was the most common comment I heard, something that was repeated when Albert's hunter got a bear a few days later.

Once Isaac's hunter got his bear, the animal was field dressed and butchered, then returned to the settlement. The skin was then handed over to Agnes, Isaac's mother, who with her kin properly cleaned and prepared it for shipment out of town with the hunter. Most of the meat remains with the guide, who usually gives sizable chunks to the helpers and spotters if they want any, and then, by custom, distributes smaller parcels to other households in town, often in token amounts. In Isaac's case, he distributed the meat to his helpers and several of his elderly relatives, but he gave most of it to his parents, who did the bulk of the distribution.

The evening after Isaac came back to town, I stopped to visit just after dinnertime. I had not seen him since he returned from his hunt, and I was eager for his version of events. Although Ida and the kids had eaten, Isaac had not, which I found odd. The phone rang.

Isaac answered, "Yes. Okay. No, he's here. Yes."

Isaac looked at me. "It's time to eat. My mum says you should come too. She was looking for you, but you weren't home."

"Why? What's going on?"

"We're having bear feet."

"How come no one else is coming?"

"Ah. Ida is allergic to bear meat." I guessed this was a cover. *Does not like bear feet*, really, though this is likely true of more than a few Inuit.

We put on our shoes and dashed across to the house. Everyone else was already there, eight others at the table or on the floor, plates in hand, either sitting and starting to eat or pulling steaming chunks of meat out of the pot: Isaac's parents, William and Agnes, Paul and his wife, Ada, the next-door neighbours, Putdjugiaq and his wife, Lucy, who is Agnes's sister, and the Ukaliqs, who have a nephew/niece relationship with William.

There is not much to say about eating bear feet, except that what would be the equivalent of metatarsals on a human foot were the size of turkey drumsticks. The meat was good, if oily and fatty. The bigger problem, I discovered, was speed. Standard procedure when eating boiled meat is to first take it from the pot and, when it is finished, to grab a small bowl and dip out the broth, the *imiraq*, and drink it like soup. Inuit generally are fast eaters. I am a slow eater, and I was interested in bear feet as an exercise in dissection as much as in eating, so I ended up with a bowl that was largely liquid bear fat. I was ignorant of the contents until my first sip. It was at that point I realized that everyone in the room was watching me. I could see them all watching me surreptitiously as I looked over the rim of the bowl, oil dripping into my beard. They were trying not to be obvious about it, but everyone knew I had a bowl full of bear fat.

At nearly forty, I was the youngest in the room, and, indeed, the entire house. William's house at mealtimes is usually full of children, grandchildren, and great-grandchildren, some eating in front of the TV, others coming and going in, grabbing food as necessary. Not tonight. Bear feet are not for everyone, it seems. They are a delicacy that many younger people seem to go out of their way to avoid. I was not sure why. The feet were quite tasty. Bear feet are not nearly as difficult for me to eat as the constellation of stinky foods: fish heads, duck guts, or seal flippers, all served rotten. Those are the truly acquired tastes.

The imiraq was warm but not hot. I chugged it. I shudder to think how many calories are in two cups of bear fat; I was hot, sweating, for hours afterward. In Paul's eyes, though, I apparently passed the test. The next day he was butchering the bear that his hunter took four days earlier. An axe in one hand, a cigarette hanging off his lower lip as he worked, he was cutting up the spine, hacking it into chunks for his dogs.

He stopped and looked up as I walked by. "Ai. You like bear meat, I know. Makes you strong. Have some." His cigarette bounced up and down on his lip as he spoke. He reached over and picked up the haunch, a twinkle in his eye.

"Only a little bit." I was leaving in a few weeks, and I was only one person, after all.

I thought he would use the axe to hack off a chunk of meat, but instead Paul gave me the entire haunch. It must have weighed fifteen kilograms, though much of the weight was bone. "That's too much. I can't eat that much."

"But I know you like it. Make you a strong Inuk yet." He laughed his distinctive machine-gun laugh that sets everyone around him laughing too. I took the haunch home, eating some, but passing half of it on to another, who appreciated the gift.

Paul keeps an eye on me now, curious about the tools I am using as I repair/renovate my new home, and curious as to how I will accomplish my task. He has taken an interest in my handsaws. For small work, I prefer Japanese-style pull-saws, which I have shipped in by mail order. Paul has never seen them before, and so is curious, especially given the speed with which they cut through plywood. Most Inuit would simply use the circular saw to cut plywood and frame a wall, but for such a small job I couldn't see spending the money on a good circular saw. I am not losing much time this way, there is no risk in losing a digit, and the handsaws have other uses too. I can carry them in a sled, for example, and use them to cut or repair a broken *napu*. Also, these are not only unusual-looking handsaws but of much higher quality than the junk that the Northern ships in and calls a handsaw.

So, Paul Tigliktuq watches me while I work. He is keeping an eye on my gear too, I notice out of the corner of my eye. Because I am working on the inside of the cabin, my sleeping gear is outside. Perhaps William is right about him. I had better keep an eye on my stuff. I can already see he has his eye on my foamy, a piece of green carpet foam that people use as a sleeping mat, usually for camping but also for bedding in the house. Mine is a double.

"How much you want for that?" he asks.

"Why? I'm not really planning on selling it. I'm sleeping on it."

"I really like this one, and my son needs one for next week, he's going out camping and doesn't have a foamy." His son Jack is going to take out some kids for a youth camp, an opportunity for some of the younger teenagers to be out on the land. They will be out for a week or so.

Paul is offering to pay for it, but he knows that I really do not want money, and I know that he really does not want to pay. Indeed, the approach he is taking, offering to pay, is really a cover for a request. I have encountered this elsewhere, usually regarding food: *Does anyone have any caribou to sell? I'd like to buy some.* The thought of a fellow Inuk having to buy caribou from somebody is just too weird for Inuit, and the utterance usually has its desired effect. If anyone has caribou, they volunteer to bring some by, with the added statement *You don't have to buy caribou, I have some you could have.* In Paul's case, the problem seems to be that he has plenty of money to purchase a foamy, but right now there are no mats at either the Co-op or the Northern, though some will be flown in sometime in the next two weeks. He needs one now.

"You got any caribou skins?" I ask. I can buy another foamy when the new ones come in, and I do not need a double anyway. It is left over from 1997, when my wife and I were here together. Skins, however, would be much harder for me to acquire. I cannot hunt caribou myself, and caribou skins are wonderful to sleep on. They are very warm, very soft, and extraordinarily comfortable – the only downside being that the hair gets all over everything. I already have a muskox skin, acquired from Paul's son Jack when we went hunting together last spring. Jack only wanted the meat and did not want to be bothered with scraping a skin.

Paul thinks for a moment: is this a good deal for him? "Yes, I have some. I'll give you two good ones for the foamy." Perhaps he thinks it's just as easy to get two more caribou skins.

A deal. He brings me the skins, and I give him the foamy.

"You better watch that William, though. You leave your stuff out like this, he might grab it. Nice guy, but he's a crook."

That was several days ago. Paul has since taken a keen interest in what I've been doing lately: building the outhouse, a very small shelter for the honey pot.

Although the town itself has managed to convert all of its houses to flushing toilets and enclosed sewage tanks, there are still a few privately owned units that continue to use honey pots for human waste. Any Inuk with a cabin or frame tent on the land also uses a honey pot, essentially a metal can with a toilet seat cover on it, and lined with a heavy plastic bag. Two bags, one inside the other, are better. When the bag fills, it is tied up and left outside, to be picked up and taken out to the sewage lagoon for disposal. In Arctic regions, this isn't nearly so bad as it might sound, as a honey bag freezes quickly. Only in summer is the honey bag a problem. Leaky bags attract flies and generally smell bad.

For the rest of the settlement, an internal sewage tank collects all wastewater – both grey water from sinks and washing machines and sewage from toilets. All of this is stored in a heated tank, usually located under the house. The tank is emptied, usually twice a week, by the sewage truck. The only difference between the tank system and septic systems elsewhere is that residents rush to the sinks when the sewage truck begins sucking out the tanks. That's because the suction also empties out the traps in the plumbing, allowing sewer gases to vent back into the house. Filling the traps immediately keeps the smell to a minimum.

The two sewage trucks are busy each weekday, moving between houses, emptying tanks, and, when the truck's tank is full, driving out to the sewage lagoon. The lagoon is roughly five kilometres from the settlement, on the other side of the airport, in a flat, low-lying area. It is not an ideal solution to the problem of waste management. The lagoon has been slowly filling up over the years, and there have been times when sewage has leaked out and filtered into the local drainages. Two rivers that flow down from the land have been contaminated by occasional overflow or seepage, and residents are sometimes told to avoid taking water from these rivers.

Water is likewise pumped into internal tanks in the house, delivered via tank truck from the pumping station at Air Force Lake. The water is treated at the pump house, and Inuit universally complain about the taste of the chlorine. That funny taste, however, may also be due to the plastic storage tanks. Housing periodically cleans the tanks, because algae build up in them over time. Housing hires temp workers to drain each tank and scrub out the insides with bleach, a process that requires the worker to crawl inside the tank to complete the task. Occasionally, the workers forget their brushes and make do with whatever is on hand. William lost a summer jacket once, disappeared right out of the house, only to be discovered several weeks later floating in the recently cleaned water tank. "Boy, that jacket was ever clean," he said – it was probably used as a scrub brush.

Given the permafrost, it is simply not cost-effective to run heated pipes to each house in the settlement. Water tanks are filled twice and sometimes three times a week, and the drivers are continually busy. Water demand in recent years has reached such levels that one truck driver is always on call in the evenings for "call-outs." Residents pay an additional fee (most of which goes to the driver) for an extra fill-up, in addition to the cost of the water itself.

Because of the perceived bad taste of tank water, though, many Inuit prefer to supplement their water supply by going to collect water themselves. The preferred method for much of the year is to chop ice out of one of the local lakes – Air Force Lake, Ukpillik, or Father's Lake, which is across King's Bay. It is a simple enough process, accomplished by using a *tuuq*. The tuuq is a large chisel, made from the leaf spring of a truck and attached to a long pole. One simply finds a deep crack in the ice and chops roughly parallel to the crack until a large chunk fractures out. Inuit often comment on the importance of having ice water for tea. In summer, people resort to filling five gallon buckets directly from the lakes, which is what I am doing now for my water, relying on friends to use their AT Vs to fill my buckets.

Driving for the hamlet, as a sewage truck driver, water truck driver, or trash truck driver, is a steady and very well paying job. The work is monotonous, but the pay is exceedingly good, and it is also accompanied by annual bonuses, "vacation travel allowances" that are paid each spring.

As far as municipal services go, though, I am living independently of hamlet services. I will take the honey-pot bag out myself. I am producing so little trash that I can haul that too. I have arranged for water. I will pay for my electricity by contributing to William's bill to cover the costs of what little I use.

I am not the only one living in this manner. There are a number of other cabins like mine, sitting behind some or another house, with an extension cord running from a house to their shack. Most houses in town have a shack or cabin behind them, although these are generally storage shacks or workshops. But some are living spaces. The residents of these cabins are there for different reasons, but the most common one is that there is simply no housing available. There is no room with kin, their relatives' houses are full. Some must stay in a shack because they have been evicted from public housing; they cannot rent their own unit, nor can they reside with another. Consequently, for most of these residents, the only available place to stay is a shack, really just an outside bedroom with a heater or stove, where one can stay while waiting for a public house to become available. As the weather turns colder, however, most do find room in a regular house.

It used to be that Ulukhaktok had a glut of housing, with plenty of units available for rent, so that even single men had no difficulty securing housing. Over the past decade, however, the demand for public housing has increased as the number of available units has decreased, and this, coupled with the removal of many subsidies on rents and utilities, has resulted in a shortage of available public housing and a shortage of private housing, too. For Inuit with jobs, this crunch has been a big problem. Inuit with high-paying jobs would prefer to rent private housing, because those rents are now far less expensive than for public housing. But even those units are occupied, whereas once they stood empty.

William and Agnes knock on my door and come in and sit down. I have been here for over a week. They are both very interested in the cabin, especially the design. William is famous for building flat roofs. Which leak. We have tea, and William talks at length about how pleasant cabin living can be. He is eyeing the sleeping platform I built four feet off the floor, the height of the side walls, leaving ample storage space underneath, with enough room to get around in the space to organize things.

Agnes, always reluctant to speak in English, utters something to William, who translates. "She says she really likes it. If you want to sell it, she could buy it."

For elders like William, Putdjugiaq, and Tigliktuq, there are distinct advantages to living in cabins, good sleeping being only one of them. All of these older visitors, in fact, spent much of their adult lives living in such settings. Although the settlement itself dates from the late 1930s, it really was not until the 1960s that Inuit moved permanently into town, a process, at least in Ulukhaktok, driven by a combination of individual health issues, the attraction of wage labour, and a supply of subsidized housing. Even after "settlement," however, many of these elders, and their children, continued to live out on the land in tents, frame tents, or cabins for a large part of the year. For young men like Edward and Simon, spring and summer were spent in camps, hunting seals. During their childhoods, sealskins were worth quite a bit of money, enough to fund a seasonal round's worth of subsistence activities.

Families would come back to town to await freeze-up. After freeze-up, the men and any teenagers old enough to travel would spend the winter running traplines for foxes.

By 1980, however, the economy had begun to change, and in 1983 the end came when the European Economic Community enacted a boy-cott on the importation of sealskins, responding to increasing pressure from animal rights groups. Nearly overnight, the economy collapsed. Families that once spent their summers hunting seals from camps on the land started spending their summers in the settlement, increas-ingly dependent upon social assistance. Children and teenagers, on the cusp of becoming productive hunters, found their own development stunted from a sudden lack of practice. As one resident described it, "1983 was the year that a lot of people here tried alcohol for the first time." From that point, the "traditional" lifestyle, based on living on the land, hunting and trapping, and minimal engagement with wage la-bour, was no longer a viable career strategy for men like Simon or Edward. The old people could make a go of it, relying on subsidies, their own experience and knowledge, and supplemental income through casual wage labour, fur sales, arts and crafts sales, and fees for guiding tourist hunters. But younger people found it extraordinarily difficult, especially as the formal educational system and southern mass media competed for their attention.

William looks up from his tea. He and Agnes do drink coffee, but usually only in the morning. Like most elders, tea is their preferred drink. William is looking around at the ceiling and the back window, quietly humming parts of an old hymn. Social visiting does not require constant conversation, and it is not unusual for a visit to be conducted entirely in silence. Qablunaat generally find a lack of constant conver-sation uncomfortable.

Suddenly, however, William's eyes narrow, and he breaks the silence. "From where you get that caribou skin?" There is an edge to his voice.

"I traded for it with Tigliktuq. He needed a foamy, so I gave it to him for a couple of caribou skins. They're really nice. I like sleeping on them. Why?"

"I'm telling you he's a crook. See!" He points at the skin. Only part of the skin, perhaps a quarter, is visible under my sleeping bag. I am not sure what the problem is. William stands and steps over to the platform, lifting the skin to look at the bottom. "I knew it! He's been stealing these from Fish Lake. They were missing out of my cabin. I should take these back. You should be giving them back to me."

He sits down. He is neither ranting nor fuming, but he is clearly angry. Great. Now I am caught between two old men, each of whom thinks the other is a thief. How am I going to get out of this one? I cannot afford to have William angry with me, but I am not sure how I am implicated in a crime if I was ignorant of the circumstances. In truth, I am not even sure how William could know they were "his" skins. To me, every caribou skin looks pretty well like any other. How would William prove they were his? Unlike equipment and large tools, which Inuit engrave with their initials to identify them, no one marks caribou skins with their names.

Agnes apparently feels the same way. She puts an arm on his, and he settles down. After a few minutes of silence, he finally speaks. "You could keep those skins. I could get more. But I'm going to talk to Paul about stealing my stuff. He's probably got my good net too. That guy never changes."

"Thanks for tea," Agnes says as they scramble out of the cabin and head back to their house.

A FEW BEERS WITH THOMAS KAYUQTUQ

"You ought to fix up the house against the kids." Edward refills his mug from the coffee pot. He is here to request some more money, enough to tide him over until he gets his paycheck. He has just landed a temporary job with a construction crew, working on the interiors of two new duplexes under construction. He has managed to avoid eviction from his house, mostly because Housing will not evict anyone with nowhere else to go once the weather turns. And the weather has turned. We are well into late October, there is snow on the ground, and temperatures have been hovering near –20 °C for the past week.

I am trying to figure out how to say no to the request I am sure is coming. I have nothing more he really can do for me here, and I would rather avoid being a bank, handing out money for charity. I only have another month before I head south for the holidays and the beginning of a new semester.

Edward continues. "They will really like the sloped roof, great for sliding. They can get up there from the outhouse now, you know."

Though the kids have over the years mostly ignored the cabin, the outhouse does change things a little. William has looked after the shack for years, and there has not yet been a problem with kids vandalizing it or trying to break in. Once I leave, it will simply fade back into the landscape, an old shack sitting amidst a pile of junk, as it has always been. Edward is right, however. Now that there is an easy way for kids to climb onto the roof, I will need to work something out. Before now, my worry had been older kids – teenagers – interested in breaking into the cabin, not children sliding on it.

It is really more the principle of the thing. Before 2007, anyone trying to break into the cabin would have been confronted by an old snowmobile and lumber and plywood, all packed in like a Tetris puzzle. The "good stuff" – tents, stoves, and clothing – was stacked at the back. I have ensured that getting in requires a significant effort, even from me. I cover the door with plywood secured with screws that require different drivers. The door itself is screwed into the frame, secured in the same manner. Even getting to those hurdles, however, is hard, the entire front of the cabin blocked off with old pallets and a dead snowmobile. Finally, I trust William. He keeps a good eye on things, since his own storage shacks are close by. I have never really worried about teenagers.

Children, however, might be more trouble in the long run, bouncing on the roof as they slide down the steep pitch. I'm not sure the rafters could handle much of that. Edward's two youngest kids have already been over here, talking in excited tones about how much fun sliding will be, teasing me. They seem to see themselves as Bugs Bunny. I refuse to become Elmer Fudd.

"You should put nails up along the edges. That will keep them off." Edward knows about this cold war between the destructive tendencies of wayward children and the efforts of adults trying to protect their possessions. Edward has protected his shack behind his house in the same way. The nails that stick up are a good deterrent. There is the potential for immediate pain, and perhaps a tetanus shot, though I suspect that a tear in the snow pants is far worse. At the same time, children are provided so much leeway that I am likely to be blamed when a kid climbs on the roof, tears a new parka, and ends up with a cut on the arm. Even though everyone knows that the kids shouldn't be on the roof, it will still be my fault if they get hurt. Edward has reported recriminations from an angry mother whose child ran afoul of the nails in his roof. He simply shrugs his shoulders when I ask about this potential problem. "That kid doesn't climb on roofs anymore. Learned his lesson, didn't he?"

Nails provide a significant, and perhaps the only, deterrent. Yelling does not work. Children and teenagers are seemingly unsupervised during much of their day, really from the time they can begin to take care of themselves. Children eat when they are hungry, sleep when they are tired, and pursue activities as their interest dictates. To outsiders, it appears as if they are simply running wild, both in the house and outside, and, perhaps, that their parents do not care for them. This is untrue. Many parents are quite aware where their children are and what they are up to, either because they are directly observing them or because they are being provided with frequent updates by observers. Unfortunately, the updates tend to be provided in the form of "They're just playing out," rather than "They are jumping up and down on Edward's shack."

And so, a few days later I set about installing my Kid Deterrent System, using nails and a few screws, driving them into a 1 × 4, which I then will drive into the edge of the roof. It will be obvious to anyone what I am up to. But, as usual, I am barely starting on the work when a passerby stops to chat. I have not even pulled out the hammer and nails from my toolbox when the ATV drives up and Thomas Kayuqtuq removes his helmet. It looks like it will be a quick visit, however, as the engine is still running.

"You should come by later. I just got a box in on the plane today. We're going to have a few, just relax for a bit. You'll come?"

"Sure. Where are you staying now?" I have not seen Thomas for over a week. I knew he was moving, but I was not sure where.

"Mum and Dad's. We couldn't find anyplace else yet. It's kinda small, but it's good enough. Only for a few weeks though."

I agree to stop by after supper, but say that I am not sure when. I try to stay away from drinking parties and would normally find an excuse to not go. I am not unilaterally opposed to alcohol. Drinking with Inuit can be a pleasant experience, but I try to keep to small gatherings that are limited to those who know me very well. Drinking parties rarely end at "a few"; it is customary to simply finish the entirety of the liquor supply. Not all Inuit drink, and very few drink often. Indeed, individuals can go months, an entire year, without drinking, and then go to a drinking party and get very, very drunk. The drinking party is in many ways a therapeutic device, a social setting in which it is acceptable to express emotions that are otherwise suppressed, whether those emotions be anger, sadness, happiness, or affection. Behaviour that occurs under the influence of alcohol is viewed through a different lens than that which occurs while one is sober. A sexual assault under the influence of alcohol is not nearly as offensive as one that occurs while the perpetrator is sober, for example.

The problem is that one is never quite sure which direction a drinking party will go. Most parties I go to tend to evolve into pleasant evenings of expressing gratitude, affection, and solidarity with kin. However, I could very easily end up as a generic Qablunaaq challenged to a fight by a belligerent drunk. Better to stay away, if possible. I do not know who else will be at the party.

I might not be able to ignore this invitation, however. Thomas owes me, and this is yet another way of trying to pay me back. I like Thomas and have a fair bit of respect for him. He is a young fellow, only twenty-seven, and he has managed to pull himself through the fog of adolescence into some semblance of a normal adulthood. Like most young men, he's had his fair share of trouble in the community. As a teenager, he was charged with a break-in at one of the local stores and a break-in at the school. He was also caught dealing marijuana a few years ago. He did a stint of a few months at the correctional centre in Yellowknife for the break-ins.

For Thomas, making a living on the land is next to impossible. Younger than Edward or Simon (he was born in 1980), he received some exposure to the land as a child, but not nearly enough to prepare him as even a part-time hunter. His father might have taken him as a kid on a day trip to hunt muskox, they may have vacationed for a week down in Prince Albert Sound during August to hunt caribou, or he might have taken a day trip in spring to jig for fish now and then. Trapping foxes or hunting seals is beyond Thomas, these activities having been suppressed since his childhood. But jigging for trout, summer caribou hunts, and day muskox trips do not generate much in the way of cash. And money generators like guiding for sports hunts are out for him too. He lacks the skills to effectively do these things for himself, let alone for tourists, and he is at the end of a long line of older men wanting to be assigned as guides for tourists hoping to shoot a trophy muskox.

The same is true for the jobs in town. The truck drivers are all so well established that the positions are largely entitlements, a tight cabal of soon-to-be middle-aged men who have been driving for upwards of a decade. These men, part of the baby boom generation, are very comfortable in their decidedly undemanding jobs, happy to collect their paycheques. Some of the drivers are, in fact, suspected of deliberately underperforming, to encourage more call-outs for water and sewage so they can earn overtime pay. What chance does Thomas have? It is a long, hard slog to try to capture any kind of decent employment here.

But to me Thomas is impressive because he has done some thinking outside of the box. Having been caught selling drugs and having spent time in prison for the break-ins, he decided to pursue a different line of work. Through persistence and patience, he managed to line up a series of temporary jobs through Housing, working for several years as a summer intern, and then acquiring some basic carpentry skills by working for his uncle, an independent building contractor. Thomas has since gone out on his own, forming his own business, and over the past two years he has made a decent living by hiring out to clean and renovate public or private housing in need of such work. He recently completed painting two of the empty hamlet duplexes, pocketing a tidy sum.

I was so impressed by his determination, work ethic, and planning that earlier in the summer I loaned him money to help him purchase tools and supplies for the business. It contradicted my own policy about handing out money, but in his case I felt it was worth the investment. Thomas was, after all, trying; many of his age-mates, like Dennis

Iqiahuuyuq, were content to sit around and complain. Now, flush with the cash from a completed job, Thomas was having a little party, and inviting me, an expression of gratitude.

His business is young, and it may yet fail, but over the past eighteen months he has earned enough money that Housing raised his rent to "market rates" – which was enough to convince him to move into what passes for the private housing market. For the past eight months, he has bounced between his parents, in-laws, and private homes vacated by owners who will be out of the settlement for any length of time. "I couldn't keep up with their rent payments, man, they were so high," Thomas says. "There wasn't enough left for food." He could not easily go back to public housing, as he was several thousand dollars in arrears on his unit. He would have to repay that before he could be eligible for another unit. By comparison, Dennis might be pursuing a more sensible economic strategy: not working, but in no danger of falling several thousand dollars in debt on his house, either.

Despite his early business success, Thomas still finds it difficult to get along socially, and he occasionally comes to see me to talk. I am not a relative, so I am safe to talk to, a kind of therapist, I suppose. Thomas's problems are not unusual. Because he appears to have a steady income, he finds relatives hanging on him, asking him for money, expecting that he should be giving them money out of his business profits. When he does not share his money, he is accused of being stingy.

Furthermore, because he was once caught selling drugs, for many Inuit he will always be considered a drug dealer, even though he has not sold drugs for more than four years now. "The money was really good, I tell you. I could make $6,000 in one night just selling to people in town. You'd be surprised how many people smoke up. But the cops were really onto me. Some people got really jealous and tried to rat me out, and I don't want to go to jail. It's not worth it."

Ratting out is a problem for dealers, though the RCMP has not been particularly vigilant in trying to catch them. It used to be that drug dealing was a one-time event rather than a career opportunity. Inuit would make a trip to Yellowknife and strike a deal with a more serious dealer there, becoming mercantile capitalists by reselling in Ulukhaktok at a much higher rate. The RCMP would occasionally catch a dealer, but it was mostly through the dealer's own ineptitude. A court date followed, and the offender would typically be slapped on the wrist. Thomas was one of these, caught when a potential client felt cheated by the amount or quality of the marijuana sold and then called the RCMP to complain. Complaints are a common occurrence, though they usually come long after the dealer has liquidated his or her supply.

In recent years, the arrangement has become more complicated. One young fellow, for example, has entered into an arrangement as a kind of middleman. Other Inuit who have acquired drugs in Yellowknife or Inuvik effectively contract with Robert to sell drugs for them, Robert taking a cut of the profits. Dealers seem to consider it a safe arrangement. Clients do not rat on Robert, knowing they would lose a reliable and steady source for drugs. The suppliers do not rat on him either, because they are happy for Robert to assume the risk of selling by being the front man. It is quite an open arrangement. Everyone knows what Robert is up to, and many Inuit refer to his house as the "Pharmacy" or the "Drug Store." The RCMP is either unable or unwilling to do anything about this. More than one officer has told me that RCMP efforts at suppressing drug crime are more focused on Yellowknife and shutting down the dealers who transport drugs from points south.

Though he no longer deals, Thomas still smokes regularly. He is quite open about why, stating that having a blast is important for dealing with the stresses of living in town. His relationship with his girlfriend is a bit rocky. They have been shacked up for two years, but old girlfriends occasionally "stalk" him, he says. Sharon is constantly with him, guarding her man, and that alone generates some stress, Thomas feeling a bit hurt that she does not trust him. Living on top of family members in a small house is equally stressful. Thomas has recently discovered that Sharon is again pregnant, and he is not quite sure if he is happy to have a second child yet.

After a few minutes Thomas leaves, and I complete a single strip of nails before I call it quits. The wind has come up, and I find an excuse to avoid suffering. I have a whole month to do the roof. I head to the Northern for a few supplies before it closes, then return to the cabin for a quick supper of boiled char. At 7:30 I make my way out for the evening. The wind is a little stronger now and looks to be picking up into yet another storm. I decide to make a circuit of town before it gets too bad.

I am lost in thought, listening to the wind ruffle my hood, when I hear Thomas yelling from the porch. I am not sure if I forgot about the invitation or lost track of where I was as I walked around the settlement. Had I been paying attention, I might have not walked by. In truth, I hardly hear him through the burgeoning storm. He is sitting on the porch out of the wind, door open and light on. "Hey, Pete, you just about walked by the house. Did you forget where you were going?"

I walk up. "What's going on?" I look around the porch. There are two old chairs here. On the plywood shelf behind him are a couple of muskox horns, a Dremel tool, and some sandpaper. A half-finished carving, two muskox horns carved into the shape of sandhill cranes, sits next to them. An ashtray sits on the floor, next to a can of propane. Two butter knives, tarnished at the ends, sit in the ashtray. The smell of marijuana is in the air.

"I just finished my last hoot, or I would offer you some." He coughs a little as he says it. He was hot knifing, heating the ends of the knives with the torch, and burning a piece of marijuana between the blades, inhaling the smoke. It is the most common way of smoking up here, so much so that butter knives are in short supply. (When I stayed in the duplex last spring with Tristan, I immediately noticed that, while there were plenty of forks and spoons in the silverware drawer, there were no knives. Whoever had last cleaned the apartment had run off with them.)

"Come on in. I'll get you a cold one. I got plenty of beer left."

It turns out that it is not really a full-blown drinking party. Thomas ordered a flat of beer – twenty-four cans – and a large bottle of vodka for his parents. Vodka seems to be the preferred alcohol of choice these days. In 2005, rum was the favoured liquor, rum and Coke being quite popular. In 1992, it was rye whisky, cut with water and lake ice. Tonight, Thomas's parents are drinking the local version of vodka and orange, using Tang as orange juice substitute. All alcohol is expensive in Ulukhaktok. It must be purchased in either Yellowknife or Inuvik, at a government-run liquor store, as Thomas has done. The order is then flown in via air freight on the plane. Because the freight is paid by weight, liquor is preferred over beer, beer being heavier and containing less alcohol.

Because of the high cost of purchase and shipment, the alcohol that people purchase tends to be the least expensive and lowest quality available – Screech. That Thomas has purchased beer, which he does occasionally, says something about him and how different he is from his parents. For Thomas, the beer is not about heading into oblivion; it is merely about feeling good, just as he promised.

We drink our beers and make small talk about the weather, but mostly we stand in silence, leaning against the kitchen counter and watching the scene in the living room, a window into his parents' view of what a drinking party should be. Abraham, Thomas's father, is slumped in his chair. The booze has only been in the house for three hours, but Abraham is already passed out. Elizabeth, I can tell, is not so far away from unconsciousness either, sitting on the sofa humming to herself while Timothy, her brother-in-law, tunes his fiddle. Timothy has been drinking nearly as long as the other two, so the tuning is not going very well. I think he and Abraham were planning to make music this evening, but the booze has done its work. Thomas's sister Jane is here too, as is his girlfriend, Sharon. Sharon is not drinking and looks sour. Jane, though, is happy, turning the stereo up when a good song comes on and turning it down when it is over. She is not nearly as plastered as her parents. From counting the cans, I surmise she and Thomas are only three beers down and currently on their fourth.

I barely finish mine when Elizabeth wanders in from the living room to refill the pitcher of Tang and fetch some ice. She looks at our empty cans. "You shouldn't be drinking beer, you should be having good stuff." She returns to the living room for the bottle of vodka. It is half empty. Grabbing a couple of plastic drinking glasses, she fills them with lake ice, vodka, and Tang – though I notice as she fills me up that I am getting much less vodka than anyone else.

"Have a shot!" She takes a sip of her own drink.

Thomas has had at least an hour's head start on me, so he's better lubricated and high to boot. After a few gulps of vodka and Tang, he grabs my ear a little more seriously. We are beyond small talk, and he clearly has something he wants to say. He is right in my face, so close that flecks of spit hit me as he talks. He probably thinks he is speaking quietly so that the others can't overhear, but he is almost yelling. I finally solve the problem of getting the weather with the news by sitting and stretching my legs in front of me. Thomas tries to kneel close to me, but he's uncomfortable on one knee and finally retreats to a chair, pulling it close to me. Elizabeth is on my other side, sipping at her vodka.

It is a relief at first that Thomas is giving me his standard litany of problems, though he is less coherent than usual and not always making sense. He complains about the high cost of living, the high rents, the poor quality of housing, the grievances others have about his perceived success – the same things he always talks to me about. It is not an unpleasant conversation, though loud. After the vodka and Tang settles in, however, he shifts to a more accusatory mode.

Like all Inuit, he is keenly aware that I am the outsider. Eventually I will leave and go back to my life down South. And, like most Inuit, he assumes that life in the South is much easier, though he knows little of the realities of mortgage payments, car payments, retirement funds, college funds, or insurance costs. I try to explain that getting by on an assistant professor's salary is hardly a life on Easy Street, and that perhaps we share some commonalities. It does not stop him. He is trying to make a point that, were I to live here long term with my wife and children, I would find it just as difficult as he does, which may or may not be true. "What would you do if you had to live here like us, eh? You'd find it hard, too, wouldn't you? What would you do, huh?"

Sharon stands at the other end of the table and says softly, perhaps to no one in particular, "I'm going to get Sonny from Mum's." She puts on her parka and walks out.

Jane says, "Thomas, this is so depressing. You know what we need? We need a cheers!"

Thomas ignores her. He stares at me, waiting for a response.

"You're right, my *panik*! Cheers!" Elizabeth says, and she and Jane take a sip of their drinks.

I struggle for an appropriate response to Thomas and his gaze, falling back on a time-honoured Inuit one. "*Nauna*. I don't know."

"See, you don't know! You have no idea what it's like to live here!"

There is no way to make a reasoned argument. I can only shrug.

Meanwhile, Elizabeth on my other side is trying to initiate a conversation about the hazards and hardships of residential school, not being allowed to speak Inuinnaqtun, being forced to eat strange foods, and being kept away from home for years at a time. I think this soliloquy is supposed to be a justification for why she drinks so much, but I am not sure. Thomas keeps grabbing my shoulder to turn me towards him, like a little kid demanding attention. Elizabeth keeps poking me on the other shoulder. I wonder if Thomas is going to want to get in a fight soon. I begin to calculate how I will handle that. I am twice his size.

I also wonder, as I am poked and grabbed and pulled in two directions, if Thomas and his mother have ever had their respective conversations with each other. Thomas clearly feels no one understands his problems. Does his mother feel anyone understands hers? There seems to be a disconnect.

Jane, meanwhile, has turned down the stereo. "Thomas, what the hell are you talking about?" Elizabeth shuffles back into the other room to listen to Timothy torture his fiddle some more. Thomas repeats to his sister what he has been telling me, emphasizing the parts about it how it is so expensive to live in Ulukhaktok, how it costs so much to rent a house, and how some people have it easy. He looks at me smugly. Apparently I have it easy.

Jane asks me, "Is it true you're living in that cabin behind Tigliktuq's?"

"Yes, it's true."

Thomas piles on. "Yeah, this guy here, he's living in that cabin by Sharon's parents." Which is true. Her parents are just across the way from Tigliktuq's. She is probably there now. I am wishing I could be too.

Jane ignores Thomas. "You're crazy. Why are you living there?"

"There isn't any housing in town I could live in. I've got no choice. But it's comfortable. It is insulated, so it's very warm. Doesn't take much to heat it."

"You're still crazy. It's too weird." She flips her hair back. How could anyone live in such conditions?

"People live in cabins all the time," I tell her. "The only thing I don't have is a shower or a laundry."

She gives me a look as if I'm mentally subnormal. "People live in cabins in *summer*, duh! They don't live in them right now. Only crazy people would live in a cabin in winter!"

I know I am not going to win that argument, not now, not with her. But then the exchange changes again. Thomas is not done. "And, get this, Jane, he's not paying any rent! He's not paying any taxes on the land!" He now has a look of glee in his eyes. I'm not sure if he is proud that I am a rebel or if he is accusing me of something horrible.

Jane's eyes open wide. "Wow, you're a criminal! What about land-lease? How long has the cabin been there? Ten years?" Jane works in the community corporation office, so she knows a bit about these things. She is getting excited. "You're cheating, not paying for the land!"

"Yeah, that's $600 a year for land-lease, and $66 in taxes. You owe the hamlet $6,066!" Thomas is doing the math on his fingers. I don't correct him on what I might or might not owe.

Both of them are happy now. Perhaps they think I am okay now. Like most Inuit in public housing, I am, at least symbolically, "behind on payments." Or, like them, I am pitted against the system, an acceptable person because I have not manipulated it for some kind of deal available only to Qablunaat. *Nauna.*

In any event, the shack is on William's lot, so there is nothing to lease. I have asked the hamlet before about my location, and there has never been a complaint, nor has there been a request to move the structure.

To my relief, Thomas abruptly stops the conversation. "I need a smoke." He gets up and goes to the porch, extricating a packet of cigarettes from his jacket. I join him while he smokes, briefly worried because he lights his cigarette with the propane torch.

The night is young. There are fourteen more cans of beer.

After a drinking party, the participants seem somewhat sheepish. Although I tend to see Thomas often, usually on his way to and from his in-laws, I do not see him for a couple of days. Perhaps he feels embarrassed for having accused me of cheating, or whatever it was that he accused me of doing. We only had one more beer before we called it quits for the night – hardly a smashing party.

A week later, I am back outside finishing installing the screws on my deterrent system. I have used a combination of metal wood screws and nails. As I am working, Sharon, Thomas, and their son drive down the road to Sharon's parents' house. It is Sunday and must be around noon. The sun is just about below the horizon. Soon it will vanish, not to return until next January. Thomas waves as their machine goes by. I wave back and return to the work. It is snowing lightly and a bit chilly working without gloves, and I would just as soon finish this now.

A few moments later, I hear footsteps in the snow. It is Thomas. "Hey, Pete, how's it going?"

"Oh, not too bad. I'm just putting in some nails to keep kids off."

"Yeah, the kids will wreck things right away. It's good that you're doing that."

"I'm not sure about these screws, though. Maybe I should have used drywall screws instead."

"Oh yeah, those drywall screws, they hurt like a bitch." Then he realizes what he is saying: he knows this from experience. Once he sees that I know how he knows, he smiles.

"My mum says come for dinner. We're having muskox, the one I shot the other day. We're heading over in a few minutes, just dropping Junior off with Sharon's parents."

Thomas drives away, and I pack up my tools, wash up, and make my way to dinner.

5

Driving Around

I am out visiting, walking around the settlement, engaged in my nightly routine of interviewing and social visiting. There are twenty-two men in the study sample, so I need to keep at it if I am to interview each one every two weeks. I am a bit behind on the work. Some of my informants are difficult to corner for an interview. They keep themselves busy, or they are simply difficult to find. I also have developed my own friendships with Inuit who are not in the study sample, and so I sometimes lose opportunities for interviews by visiting elsewhere. Jonathan Aullaq, however, is an easy target. He is nearly always home in the early evening, and, true to form, his snowmobile is sitting in front of the house.

Jonathan at twenty-two is technically an adult: he and his girlfriend, Emily, have been shacked up for nearly four years and have two small children. They also have their own house, a unit that they rent from Housing. A house, a partner, and children all seem to add up to adulthood, at least in southern eyes. But, despite these appearances, Jonathan is to my mind in more of an extended adolescence.

Neither Jonathan nor Emily has a job at the moment, and it is unclear whether they are even looking. It is not as if there are any available jobs in the settlement. Their primary source of income is social assistance, "SA," which provides some money to meet basic needs. SA also fixes their monthly rent to Housing at $32 per month, with no charge for utilities: heating fuel, electricity, water, sewage, and trash are all at no cost. Even so, the money is not nearly enough for an entire month.

They do own a telephone. It is plugged into the wall and sits decoratively on the coffee table. However, they could not keep up with the bills, and their service was cut off months ago. Their household goods and furniture all seem to be second, third, or even fourth hand, passed down through their kin networks. The television was once Emily's brother's. The colours are odd, rather yellowy-green, as if the picture tube is slowly failing. There are tears in the sofa, metal springs poking through in places. Two of the wooden legs have broken off, so it rests on old phone books and blocks of wood to keep it level. The coffee table is equally damaged, the particle board underneath the plastic exposed in places.

I walk up the stairs and into the house, having mastered the art of knocking on the door and opening it at the same time. "Hello? Anybody home?" It is customary to remain in the entrance, halfway in but ready to go back out unless invited. If Jonathan does not want a visitor, he can avoid me by remaining in a back room, or by feigning sleep on the sofa. However, he tells me to come in. He knows it's me. I have already been told several times that I have a very heavy step that resonates through the house when I come up the stairs.

Jonathan is sitting slack-jawed, a bowl of stale potato chips and an empty can of pop in front of him on the coffee table. He is watching Television Northern Canada (TVNC) at the moment but is waiting for the hockey game. The Oilers play tonight at eight.

At this time, late 1992, Ulukhaktok receives five television channels. The hamlet has arranged, for a cost, to receive broadcast television via satellite, which it then rebroadcasts on a low-power transmitter. The lineup is limited. TVNC and CBC North are publicly available channels. CBC North is a slightly modified version of the CBC. TVNC is a native-run and native-managed station that focuses on northern news and Aboriginal programming. The other three stations are commercial and include ITV broadcasting out of Edmonton, CTV out of Vancouver, and WDIV from Detroit, Michigan. Although ITV and CTV are Canadian stations, a good portion of their programming originates in the United States.

I wondered at this selection of stations until Simon Iqaluk set me straight. The CBC and TVNC are essentially provided in all the settlements, but the hamlet had to pay additional money to include the commercial stations. The three on offer in Ulukhaktok happened to be channels that owned the rights to broadcast their local hockey teams: the Canucks in Vancouver, the Oilers in Edmonton, and the Red Wings in Detroit. Cable and satellite subscription service is still five years away, though a few households (two schoolteachers and two Inuit) have large satellite dishes in front of their houses.

Television is a curious window on southern Canadian and American culture, especially through the Detroit station. WDIV is an afternoon of soap operas and lowbrow talk shows ("Up next! Men who father children with their transgendered sisters-in-law!"), followed by the local news. The news, as presented by WDIV, is an hour-long litany of arson, murder, political corruption, and labour strife in the recession-ravaged city. For Inuit, the programming seems to reinforce what they already know. The world outside is scary, and there is no better place to live than Ulukhaktok – though the increasing proliferation of Natashas, Alexandras, and Sophies among Inuit children points to the influence of the soap operas on Inuit life.

Jonathan's posture, the pile of travelling clothes on the floor, and his wind-burned face all tell me that he has been out driving around. Given that he has no windshield on his machine, the warm house is probably making him very sleepy. I walk past him and sit at the other end of the sofa. "How's it going?"

"Oh, not too bad. Going to watch the Oilers tonight. They're on soon." Right now, though, he's watching an old Netsilik film. Despite the attraction of hockey or the news out of Detroit, the television is also another kind of window. The "last channel" button on the remote, for example, is almost always set to TVNC (or, more recently, the Aboriginal Peoples' Television Network, which replaced TVNC some years ago). Over the years the different Northern Store managers have all reported that the most popular video rentals are animal films, which Inuit find mesmerizing, though for different reasons than most southerners do. Meerkats are indeed adorable, but Inuit seem to be more fascinated by their behaviour than their apparent cuteness.

Jonathan rises from the sofa and ambles to the kitchen, an alcove rather than a separate room, a few feet away. He puts a pot on the stove. It appears to be hot already.

So it begins. I do not really want coffee, and I cringe at the thought of drinking Jonathan's. I have many more stops tonight. Simon wants to show me his progress in recording hockey scores, I have several other men that I want to interview tonight, and Isaac Kaaktuq will be expecting me later, my last visit of the evening. By 1 AM, I will have visited five different households and been loaded up with different varieties of caffeine that will keep me awake into the wee hours.

I should not struggle with this so much. It is mid-October, and the daylight is fading fast. In another month the sun will drop below the horizon, not to return until late January. Like many people Jonathan's age, I am already backwards, sleeping through much of the day and active into the early morning. The pattern works for me. Once I get home, I can offload the caffeine while writing up the day's field notes. And, for me, it is a regular pattern: in bed at four, awake at eleven or noon, an afternoon of errands and visits to the stores, and an evening of interviewing. For many young Inuit, however, there seems to be no rhythm at all, especially around the solstice. Some stay awake for days, then crash. Some completely lose track of the time. They lie down to sleep and wake up not knowing whether the 6:32 on the clock is morning or evening, or even what day it is.

I accept the coffee. I have not yet learned how to decline, and I do not want to offend Jonathan, who has already said that he receives few visitors. His coffee is, as he calls it, "cowboy coffee," the grounds boiled in a pot. I have no idea how old it is, but it is served with sugar and "cream," really evaporated milk, also of uncertain vintage, judging by the yellow crust around the rim of the can. Most Inuit offer non-dairy "whitener" with coffee, which seems more expensive but is preferred because many Inuit are lactose intolerant. Milk, half-and-half, or real cream are never offered (or rarely purchased), simply because, having been flown in, they are far too expensive.

I add sugar and milk to my mug, noting the remains of Jonathan's dinner. A Shake'n Bake pork chop and some french fries sit on a baking sheet: store food. I make a mental note of it for later.

As it happens, though, the pork chop was from the previous dinner, not this evening's. "I only got back about an hour ago," Jonathan says.

"Let's see. I got up around three, and went to hotel for fries and gravy. Then I went out for a drive." He is anticipating an interview, even though I have not yet asked for one.

"You went out?" I already knew as much. "Where did you go?"

"I was just driving around. Went to Kanguaq's Lake and then down the coast for a while. I almost flipped the machine. I think I damaged a ski, but I'm not sure. It was steering funny on the way home. I'll check it later."

"How did you damage the ski?"

"I was chasing a fox. I sure wanted to run it over, but I hit a rock. The snow is really soft, I couldn't even see it."

Jonathan's machine should probably break down more than it does. It is an amalgamation of several different snowmobiles, all put together with what appears to be duct tape and bailing wire. He does not own a rifle or a shotgun, nor does he have his own sleds. He could acquire these easily, of course, particularly from his parents. He could probably borrow their snowmobile too. But he seems to lack interest in doing anything beyond driving fast and trying to run over foxes.

"I haven't had supper yet. I was going to go to my parents after. Emily is at her dad's, I think."

I pick coffee grounds out of my teeth and think about the pattern I am seeing, one shared by many in Jonathan's cohort. Young, unemployed, and on SA, Emily and Jonathan keep very little food in their own house beyond snacks and junk – cookies, chips, pop, "juice" (really powdered Kool-Aid or something similar) – and a few canned goods. The SA money is not nearly enough to provide for a month's worth of decent, healthy meals purchased from the stores. The power of the SA money is further limited by the nature of the stores themselves, which seem to be set up to keep people in the red. Jonathan and Emily have accounts at each store, established so they can charge purchases when they are short on cash. Each month they pay some of their debt down, but they are nevertheless slowly and steadily falling behind. To keep going, they depend heavily on their parents for assistance.

For most young Inuit, whether dependent on SA or no, at least one meal a day is typically taken at the parents' house, and often separately. Emily has gone to her family, and Jonathan will soon go to his. The meal offered is usually country food supplemented by store food. When Jonathan goes to his parents' home later this evening, he will likely help himself to whatever is left over in the pot. It might be boiled muskox, or maybe char, given the time of year. That might be followed by dried meat – mipku or piffi, and then bannock or bread with butter and jam, and maybe some canned soup if there's not enough left over in the pot.

Such a meal may be at either lunch or dinner, and it is an important cornerstone of the diet for young people while also serving to keep the extended family together. Indeed, though it is early in my fieldwork, it is increasingly clear that nearly all the men in the sample are engaged in this kind of pattern. What keeps Jonathan and Emily going the remainder of the day is the assistance that follows them home. Emily is likely to leave her parents' house with two or more shopping bags. One bag will contain enough raw meat for a meal, or perhaps a snack of dried meats. Another bag will contain store food, perhaps some cans of evaporated milk, some coffee, a Ziploc bag with sugar, or a jar of jam. If Emily is low on diapers, her mother might send some of those along too.

We sit quietly for a few minutes. The hockey game is about to start, and Jonathan is attentive to the pre-game introductions. Only after the game begins does he speak again. It turns out that he has secured a job, only yesterday. He tells me he will be the Economic Development Officer, a new position created by the Inuvialuit Regional Corporation. He isn't sure yet what the job duties actually are – he thinks they might involve reviewing grants by Inuit starting their own businesses – but he will be working out of the community corporation offices. Better yet, the job is part-time, with his hours from one to five in the afternoon. So, he has a job, he gets paid (though he is unclear on the rate), and he can still sleep in.

Compared to his age mates in the settlement, Jonathan is "educated," so he is considered something of a natural for this position. He is the youngest in his family. He has two older sisters and three older brothers, and it seems as if he was somewhat lost in the chaos of a large family. He finished his schooling in Ulukhaktok and then went off to Yellowknife to attend high school at Sir John Franklin. In my later conversations with his mother, in fact, she intimated that she and her husband targeted him for an education. Jonathan's eyesight was poor, and there was some thought that he could get a wage-labour job and help the family with his income.

"Sir John" was the territorial high school, a residential institution at which Indians and Inuit from the settlements were housed on campus in Akaitcho Hall and educated alongside the residents of Yellowknife. From the accounts of Inuit who have talked to me about it, the place was horrific, a series of daily conflicts with Indians and Qablunaat. None of the three groups got along well, much less liked each other. The teachers and staff, I have been told, were perceived as racist while enforcing a set of rules that appeared capricious, nonsensical, or down-right mystifying. For Inuit raised in the villages, where they were large-ly left to their own devices, having to live by strict rules must have been extraordinarily difficult. Even worse, the outcome of all of this was an education with at best a questionable relevance to village life.

Jonathan made it through grade eleven before dropping out and re-turning home, but the damage had been done. He possesses few if any land skills, having spent most of his teenage years in Yellowknife. I have been told that he has never seen a live caribou, much less shot at one.

Once the game is well underway, I ask if we can do an interview. We have done several before, so Jonathan knows the questions that are coming. I pick more coffee grounds out of my teeth, noting under *Did you go hunting anywhere in the past two weeks?* that Jonathan went driving around (which he considers hunting) three times and got one rabbit. He gave it to his parents. When I ask about food he received from others, he declares a bag of fish from his in-laws and some ground muskox meat from his mother. I also note that he has found work. The interview takes very little time, perhaps ten minutes. Most of the infor-mation I require has emerged during the coffee and conversation lead-ing to the actual interview.

Have you eaten anywhere in the past two weeks? Where did you eat, and what did you have? I know the answer to this question already. As I have discovered the general pattern of eating for young people, the question sounds increasingly stupid to my ears. Jonathan must think it is pretty dumb too, come to think of it. But he knows the routine, so he varies his answers from the previous interview.

"Let's see. I guess I ate at my parents about every other night. We mostly eat land food over there. I took the kids with me once. My brothers and sisters are usually there too. Sometimes I'm there for lunch." It is like asking Jonathan how many fingers he has, as if the answer might change from week to week.

We complete the interview, and I hand him $10 for his time. We sit for a little longer, discussing some developments in the hockey game but mostly sitting in silence. Aside from the game and his adventure driving around, there really is not much more to talk about. The first period ends, and I get up to leave. "I guess I should go walk around for a while. Thanks for the coffee, and for the interview."

"Sure, come by anytime. Thanks for coming." As I exit, Jonathan begins to stir from the sofa. The first period over, he can get over to his parents for a late supper and watch the rest of the game there.

THE PARADE

It is late August, and I am sitting outside, talking to Amos Tuktu as he works. We are behind his house, and Amos is attempting to weld together a metal frame. His ultimate goal: to manufacture a trailer for his AT V. A little trailer is just the thing for hauling stuff around town, he says. Amos just got the welder. He knows a little about welding from his years working for Housing, though he is hardly more than a novice. Our mutual friend Stephen has been instructing him, providing insights on identifying different kinds of steel and the different rods one uses for each.

"Stephen says that there are two or three kinds of welders: real welders, stickers, and gobbers. Stephen says he's just a gobber." He says this as he pulls the welding mask back and examines his work. It is a mass of molten cauliflower attached to two pieces of metal tubing. He has blown a hole in one side. "Me, it's like I'm not even a gobber yet." He laughs.

We have been out here for perhaps and hour or so, me watching and talking with Amos while he works at cutting the tubing to length for the trailer. He is recycling the metal frames used for crating snowmobiles. The sea lift was in last week, and both the Northern and the Co-op each took delivery of a large number of machines. There are rumours that the government is going to make cash payments to Inuit who attended residential schooling in the Territories, a sum of $10,000 plus an additional $3,000 for each year in school. The payments are designed to settle the alarming number of claims of abuse at the hands of the teachers and staff at the boarding schools run by the churches years ago. It is less clear whether students who attended Sir John Franklin and were inmates at Akaitcho Hall are also included. No one is quite sure what the actual terms of the settlement are.

Nevertheless, it seems as if everyone in the community expects a large cash payment in the next few months. The store managers seem to think so. They also seem to think they will make a major killing selling new equipment for cash, a real bonus for their bottom line. Usually Inuit purchase machines from the stores by making a down payment, enough to "get it out of the store," enough for the store to break even in the (apparently) common event that the buyer does not pay off the rest of the machine. With all that cash on hand, though, the stores could make a huge profit.

Amos, for his part, scored the short-term job assembling the machines for the Northern Store. Amos opened the crates, installed the skis and windshields, and prepared them for sale. While he works on the trailer, he provides a narrative of the experience, which took only a couple of days of work for him but paid well. Amos used to work for Housing as a maintainer, but he left that position five years ago to pursue, as he calls it, "other opportunities." His wife works full-time at the school, so she brings in a steady income, which allows him to try to live more like a "real hunter," though he also says that he grew tired of dealing with other people, both residents and co-workers.

"That crating is pretty good, protects the equipment real good, though sometimes there's a little damage," he observes as he bangs on the hot metal. I know the crating is useful stuff, as I am sitting on some of it. Amos was paid for his work in cash, but he also asked for and received the crating, which the Northern manager was just going to haul out to the dump. We agree that the manager seems to be a rather dim bulb before Amos changes the subject. "The Co-op manager had one come in with a cracked hood on it. I saw it, not even a big crack, just a little one, but he convinced the board to just write off the machine, and then he bought it for practically nothing."

"I heard that the last Co-op manager did the same thing."

Amos raises his eyebrows in agreement. Co-op managers have a dodgy reputation in town. The last four all left hastily under clouds of suspicion. The local Co-op is rumoured to be some $80,000 in the red, all supposedly owed to the national organization. Previous managers are likewise rumoured to be the cause, embezzling money and using it for their own business interests, which, according to some people, include drug dealing, purchasing carvings on behalf of the Co-op but keeping the sales proceeds for themselves, stealing the mail, and making sweetheart deals with suppliers. Nothing has been proven, let alone investigated, but there is a conventional wisdom that has developed over the last fifteen years: do not trust the store managers under any circumstances.

The silence of the evening is broken by the sound of an ATV going by, a quick *vroom* followed by billowing dust from the gravel road. The driver is going far too fast for town, which, theoretically, has a speed limit.

"Must be nine o'clock." Amos checks his watch and goes back to work. It is another pattern of settlement life. Before 6 PM there is a steady stream of traffic – ATVs or snowmobiles, depending on the season – as people head home from jobs or to the stores for some last-minute shopping. For the next three hours, though, the settlement is eerily quiet; almost no one is driving anywhere. At nine, however, the roads suddenly fill with machines, nearly all of them operated by teenagers or young adults. Why nine? Amos muses that it has to do with food.

"It's Qablunaaq food. Lots of these kids don't eat very good, they eat too much Qablunaaq food. It's like it never really fills you up good, but it sure does make you dopey. Maybe all these kids are in a coma or something."

I nod, because I think he is onto something. Most of the teenagers do not seem to eat much in the way of country food if they can help it. Duck and caribou are popular, but they seem to prefer beef jerky, Hungry Man dinners, pizza, and fried chicken. These are all highly processed, typically high-carbohydrate foods that, I think, send them into a kind of pre-diabetic stupor following dinner. The effects are likely exacerbated by sleep deprivation. I have noticed this for years, even among many adults, which is why I rarely go visiting before 8 or 8:30

in the evening anymore, unless it is to see somebody like Amos, who rarely, as Inuit say, "feels really lazy" after supper. Any earlier, I find that I will enter a house to discover the occupants, adults included, snoozing on the sofa or sitting passively in front of the television, eyes glazed, the result of eating a heavy meal combined with the exhaustion of staggering through the workday. The coffee from coffee break at three has long worn off, the after-dinner tea has not yet kicked in. It is only by 8 or 8:30 that people are beginning to stir again.

This behaviour seems to affect Inuit of all ages save for elders, perhaps because the old people eat Shake 'n Bake pork chops or frozen pizza much less frequently. The ATV traffic at nine, however, is more restricted than earlier in the day. It seems to be mostly teenagers, just driving around, with an occasional mother packing a baby, trying to lull the child to sleep. The traffic is something like a parade that will continue for another three hours. Both slow and fast drivers move in an endless loop around the roads of the settlement – along Queen's Bay by the waterfront, around the loop by the airport road and Housing shop, down the main street past the hamlet offices and the Northern, then down around "Easy Money," the newer houses on the spit of land between King's Bay and Queen's Bay, so-named because many of the houses are privately owned. Then, another loop, perhaps including a trip up around the school for variety. For even more variety, there might be a trip out to the airport, where one can really open the throttle, or perhaps a climb up the first or second hills overlooking the town. The young men, prone to showing off, perform tricks, popping wheelies, doing doughnuts in the road with both ATVs and snowmobiles, driving as fast as they can down the airport road. In the summertime, the evening parade kicks up so much dust that an observer from the top of Ulukhaktok Bluff (the "third hill") can see a dome of haze over the settlement.

The parade continues until midnight, the curfew for machines. After that, anyone operating a vehicle must be either going out on the land or coming in from a trip. Otherwise, vehicles must be parked, and people must walk, except for elders, who have an exemption.

This ordinance, however, is more of a general guideline. During the summer, the bylaw officers are really only on duty between midnight and 1 A M, and they tend to be rather lax in their enforcement. They are part-timers, young fellows charged with enforcing the speed limits, chasing loose dogs and kids out after curfew, and keeping machines off the roads after hours. The R C M P occasionally calls them in for assistance. Mostly, however, they just drive around, but they do so in a truck rather than on an AT V.

The position is one of authority, and men who have held it note that it can be socially uncomfortable. The position requires confrontation, and it is made worse because relatives expect breaks, and every confrontation seems to generate a grudge. I witnessed one just the other night. I was out walking and saw Donald Maraaqtuq working on his AT V. As I did with Amos this evening, I stopped to say hello and chat while Donald worked. The bylaw drove by as we were talking, and I waved at Andrew Kudlak. I hardly ever talk to Andrew – indeed, I hardly know him – but we are friendly and wave at each other. As I spend my evenings walking around, we see each other quite a lot.

Donald just glared at him. "That fucking bastard. He wrote up my daughter the other night. Cited her for driving after curfew." His voice dripped malice.

"*Was* she driving after curfew?" I knew that she was, because I saw the whole episode from the window where I was visiting. His daughter is one of the worst offenders both for driving too fast and driving after curfew. More than a few Inuit had complained about her.

"She was just going home, and she was out of town, on the land. But he wrote her up anyways."

She was doing no such thing, of course, but this is what they all say, claiming that driving to and from the airport is going out on the land, or engaging in some other form of sophistry. Faced with such hostility, the bylaw officers eventually tire of the confrontations and acrimony and quit. It is a thankless job, but far worse during the school year, when children also have a curfew.

Ten o'clock is the curfew for children under sixteen. The bylaw runs the siren at the fire hall at 9:45 P M and makes his way to the gym and the arena to shoo kids home. The kids, however, want to stay and watch the older teenagers and young adults play, and in any event they are not that interested in heading home just yet. Some continue their own game, "Hidin' from the Bylaw," in which they spy out where the bylaw truck is at any given moment, hiding when it finally does drive by, hoping to remain out of sight. The more daring run across the road and into the shadows, close enough for the bylaw to see them but not close enough to recognize them and write them up.

The odds are stacked against the bylaw officer. There are plenty of houses, workshops, and storage shacks to hide behind and around, and the truck's headlights are visible from nearly anywhere in the settlement. On occasion, a second bylaw will move around on foot, sneaking up on the kids to catch them. For the most part, though, the bylaw just drives around until 11, when he goes in for coffee, and then returns to drive around between midnight and 1 AM By eleven, the fun of "Hidin' from the Bylaw" has worn off, and most kids are cold, hungry, or tired. They go in of their own accord, happy to have exasperated the bylaw yet again.

BUGS BUNNIES

One of the first orders of business upon arrival in Ulukhaktok is a visit to the Fish and Wildlife office. The primary purpose is one of legitimacy. If I am going to study subsistence hunting, I might as well engage in it myself, and it gives me an excuse to be on the land.

However, because I am outsider – a US citizen, no less – my hunting and fishing rights are limited. Ulukhaktomiut have a general hunting licence that effectively grants access to all species at all times of the year, within some set boundaries. I am entitled to only two licences, one for small game and the other for fish. Even then there are restrictions. While small game includes marmots, rabbits, woodchuck, groundhogs, porcupines, and squirrels, only the Arctic hare is found in Ulukhaktok. Though my fishing licence grants me access to many species, only two – Arctic char and lake trout – are available locally (though in large numbers), but with serious catch limits. Luckily, some species, like Arctic cod (which is quite tasty), are not restricted at all. I could theoretically get a license to shoot migratory birds, but the season on ducks and geese is limited to the autumn, precisely when the birds are not here.

Acquiring the licence is an easy process, though I sometimes have to help the officer fill out the form. The position has since its inception been staffed by a local Inuk, and I am probably the only US resident they will issue a small game licence to during their tenure. My impression is that it is best that a local resident staff this position. A local officer acts as a liaison between the bureaucrats in Inuvik and Yellowknife and the community, and he does have some leeway in choosing how and when to confront hunters who violate regulations. At the same time, continually having to confront one's relatives about violations is also stressful, similar to the problems the bylaw officers face, which is partly why the job changes hands every few years.

After some small conversation, I then make way over to the Community Corporation, tracking the current whereabouts of the Hunters and Trappers' secretary, who may or may not be in. My purpose here is to obtain permission to travel on Inuvialuit lands. This permit is a simple form where I provide my name and address and a brief description of where I intend to go. In return, the H T C asks that I record where I fish and what I take.

All of this is relatively straightforward if people are in their offices. The Fish and Wildlife officer may be out on a job-related errand, the secretary likewise. At both offices, however, I get a nearly identical conversation that invariably begins with, "So, you're going to hunt Bugs Bunnies, eh?"

The question is uttered partially in jest and occasionally in derision. "Bugs Bunnies," the joking reference to Arctic hares, are among the lowest game animals in the status hierarchy. Many Inuit consider them starvation food, and many younger Inuit avoid eating them. They are plenty of work for very little meat. It does not help that many of the bunnies close to Ulukhaktok have a reputation for feeding at the dump or the sewage lagoon.

The irony of acquiring my small game licence is that one of my first hares was not produced via firearm. My first autumn in Ulukhaktok was marked by an extraordinary amount of snowfall, the most any Inuk in the settlement could remember. There was snow on the land by mid-August of that year, and during the first half of September it snowed nearly every day. For hunters, some early snow is very welcome, as autumn travel is often an adventure involving rocks, gravel, and ice, all of which can be hazards to both snow machine and driver. Snow cover makes everything easier. And, while Inuit were initially happy at the thought of being able to get on the land before freeze-up, everyone quickly realized there was such a thing as too much snow. Soft and light snow was followed by wet, heavy snow, all of it coming in on a west wind. Such conditions made it difficult to pull sleds and drive snowmobiles, which frequently bogged down in the stuff. The conditions taxed engines and tracks, drank gasoline, and allowed drivers to seemingly find every rock hidden underneath the blanket of white.

An additional problem revealed itself – ice in the gas lines. Gas line antifreeze was flying off the shelves, and snow seemed to be getting into snowmobiles' every corner and crevice. Hunters of all ages and experience were complaining about it. A week previously, I had run into a problem: the engine would not idle properly. On top of that, I snapped my starter cord on a trip with Edward Kuniluk hunting muskoxen. Edward and I discovered both problems while we were out on the land, so it made for an interesting experience, trying to start my machine whenever we stopped for a break or, ultimately, to shoot and butcher the muskox.

And so, on this particular afternoon, Simon Iqaluk was helping me repair the starter. I had not asked for his help, he simply showed up. He was visiting his uncle next door and saw me staring into the engine with a box of tools at my feet. This is, in fact, a sure-fire way to attract attention: just go outside and start to work, or even pretend to work. Soon a crowd of young men and children will appear, wondering what the Qablunaaq is up to now. This is true for Inuit as well. Eventually, people will come by and ask what's going on. Sometimes, bystanders will help, other times they will watch, but most of the time they will simply just talk. It is a wonder that any mechanic actually achieves a repair, given all the distractions.

Simon's offer of help, though, was genuine and enthusiastic. He enjoys working on machines – almost, I think, more than he enjoys driving them. He is older than I am by a couple of years, and thoroughly at home in the world of high technology and wage labour. Though he grew up mostly on the land, and, it seems, hardly went to school, he does not hunt nearly as much as his parents would like him to, and he limits his activities to those that can be undertaken close to town. We quickly became friends, going fishing together in the first week I was in town. It was a walking trip to one of the local lakes, which immediately marks Simon as unusual, as almost no one walks anywhere anymore. We later went seal hunting by boat and formed a friendship.

Simon also informed me early on of his grand plans for the upcoming hockey season, and in so doing he displayed what, at the time, seemed to me to be an uncanny mechanical ability. He was, he told me in hushed tones, going to record the scores of each and every NHL hockey game for the 1992–93 season, pre-season through the playoffs. Indeed, we spent an entire evening poring over the league schedule, Simon marking down which games were expected to appear on the locally available TV channels. We constructed a matrix for recording scores and team records, and the star players for each match. To get into the mood (because the season was still more than a month away), Simon produced a videotape of highlights from the previous hockey season.

To Simon's dismay, the video player seemed to have difficulty tracking the tape properly. Rather than give up, though, he calmly went to the porch and returned with a set of screwdrivers. He removed the cover, inserted the tape, and began adjusting several different screws inside the player. Twenty minutes later, it sat on top of the television, wires and cables spilling out but nevertheless chugging happily away as it showed the Pittsburgh Penguins celebrating their recent championship.

"How did you do that?" I wondered if Simon had some technical training in his background that I did not yet know about.

He kept his eyes on the screen. "Oh, I saw my uncle fix a machine like this once." He shrugged as if this were a common occurrence – which, I later thought, it probably was. There is no electronics repair shop in Ulukhaktok. Like most things, if you want something fixed, you have to learn to do it yourself or go without.

So Simon, to my good fortune, is on the case of my snowmobile. I know I can execute this repair, it is not difficult, but we are outside in –20°C temperatures and some light snow. I am sure Simon can finish this more quickly than I could. We have decided to simply change the entire starter rather than try to replace just the cord. Since I have an identical starter scavenged from a machine that no longer runs, it makes sense to just swap them out. Later on, I will replace the cord on the broken one, and then I'll have a back-up in case the replacement fails. Simon also wants to tune the carburetors, as he thinks part of the idling problem lies there, in addition to the ice in the gas line.

We hardly set to work when another curious visitor appears on the scene. It is Isaac, who is here to check up on me. His house is only a stone's throw from mine, and he can see my yard from his window. He has, I think, two concerns. The first issue is to make sure I do not mess up. Isaac has demonstrated a genuine concern for my well-being and wants to ensure that I do not make the problem worse by performing shoddy work. A shoddy job is even worse than no repair at all. A broken machine does not go anywhere, but what about one that is *about* to break down? The environment does not easily forgive mistakes, and he is sure that I lack the experience or ability to improvise a repair on the land. He is right, of course.

Isaac is also concerned about the disposition of his tools, which he has lent to me. When Isaac handed me his spare set the day before, he did so with a warning. Tools have an unfortunate habit of disappearing, vanishing under the guise of a loan. Sometimes people borrow tools for legitimate reasons and with honourable intentions of returning them. This lasts only so long as the tools remain in their possession, however. It is quite common for a relative, especially an older one, to simply help himself to a box of tools, borrowed or not. Soon they are lost downstream, never to be seen again. Actually, they might be seen again, but they will go unrecognized. There are only a few brands of tools in circulation in the settlement, available via the Co-op, Northern, or (via mail order) Canadian Tire, so everyone has essentially the same sets. Isaac is making sure his tools do not go downstream, to wash up in someone else's toolbox.

We finish the starter and tune the carbs, and Simon suggests that while we are here we change the gas tank too. It is full of ice. I agree to this, but only after dinner. I am reciprocating by feeding Simon, and now Isaac. We are going to have muskox ribs, from the young animal that Edward shot the previous week and that I helped butcher. I threw them into the oven long before we set down to work on the machine. They have been in for several hours now, roasting at low heat.

The ribs are delicious. Although muskoxen are exceedingly common in the pot today, in 1992 it was still somewhat unusual for Inuit to hunt them, as the population was protected for so long. Muskoxen on Victoria Island were nearly wiped out, and for decades there was a ban on hunting them. At the time, many claimed they did not care for muskoxen. After that meal, though, I could not understand why.

Once we've had tea, we get back to the gas tank, a surprisingly quick replacement. The engine starts on the first try, and it idles properly too. The snow has moved off, the evening sky now crystal clear. Even through the streetlight that illuminates our work I can see the stars twinkling overhead. It is such a nice evening, Simon declares, that we should go and hunt rabbits.

I am intrigued. "How do you hunt them in the dark? Do you freeze them with your headlight and then shoot them?" I am trying to think of the most efficient way to kill rabbits at night.

"Nope. Run them over!" Simon utters this with unmistakable enthusiasm, a gleam in his eye I last saw when he formed grand plans for the hockey season. Isaac just stares into the engine, his face a blank mask. I agree to go with Simon. I am, after all, the anthropologist, and I am documenting hunting. This seems to qualify.

We finish up, and Isaac packs away his tools. They are all there. I look at him, one eyebrow raised. "You coming?" Even before asking, I know he is not interested, but I am not sure why.

"No. I've got to work on my machine now." I know this is not true. He worked on his machine two days ago and declared it perfectly fit for travel. "See you later."

Simon, meantime, has run off to his house to get ready, so I go and change into some travelling clothes – wind pants, my heavy parka, travelling mitts, and kamiks. I drive the short distance to Simon's and find that he is all ready to go. He is just topping off the tank. I shut down my engine, and watch him close up the can and put it underneath the house.

He lights a cigarette. "Lots of people hunting bunnies in town now, so we're going to go out a little bit to get ours. Down the coast some." He hops on his machine, fires it up with a single pull, and takes off down the road. I follow. We drive out past the hockey arena, down the hill, and then out across the flat toward the golf course, turning in long, slow arcs across the snow, away from the ridge, then back, looking for a hare to chase.

As we climb up toward Air Force Lake, we see one, and I see why paralyzing them with headlights has no appeal to Simon. These bunnies know about snowmobiles. This one runs right into the rocks on the hill for safety, and we are forced to let it go as it vanishes. Neither of us has a rifle. We make our way down to Ukpillik. Ukpillik is a large lake, three or four kilometres across, and we head straight to the other side, gliding across the glare ice, which allows for no turns. Our skis simply slide right over the ice, so we adjust our course periodically on the narrow bands of windblown snow that lie on the ice, slight ridges running from west to east, in the direction of the prevailing winds.

We come off the lake on the northwest side, climb the bank, and make our way back onto the land, finally crossing the Fish Lake trail at a high spot out past the airport. Simon stops his machine, and I follow suit. Having long finished his cigarette, he lights another.

"I really like hunting on nights like this. There isn't as much wind as there is in town, and the Northern Lights are really out, too." We both look up at them, brilliant green, dancing and shimmering, looking near enough to touch. Simon is right about being out here. We are only a couple of kilometres from my house, but the settlement is obscured by a large hill. Behind it we can see a dull orange glow from the street-lights. Straight overhead, though, the sky is absolutely clear.

Simon finishes his smoke. "I really hope we see a fox, too. I want to chase a fox. And you haven't seen one yet."

I tell him that Jonathan chased a fox a few nights ago and damaged his ski on a rock.

"That's because lots of guys make a big mistake when they chase foxes. They're really smart animals. They're really fast, and they like to jump behind a snowdrift and then change directions when you can't see them. You can really break your machine that way. You have to tire them out first, then run them over."

We make off for the northwest, down to the coast, heading for the last of the cabins along the shore. The land through here is reasonably flat, pocked with small ponds, and the snow is soft and deep. We're still driving in long arcs, looking for bunnies, when I hear Simon's engine roar and he takes off. I turn to follow, squeezing my own throttle, and I see that he is moving not in a straight line but in irregular, herky-jerky turns. He has a bunny in the headlights, trying to line it up so he can run it over. I am having difficulty keeping up, and it occurs to me that he has a much more powerful engine than I do. I do my best to keep a direct line to the pair, my headlight trained on the bunny as much as possible.

After a few more twists and turns, Simon again squeezes the throttle. The animal vanishes under the roar of his machine. I keep my headlight trained on the spot. It would not do to kill it but lose it in the darkness. To my surprise, the bunny rises from the snow, and shakes itself off. Simon hasn't killed it. In fact, it looks to be in perfectly good health, judging by the speed at which it runs off, fuelled by terror of my snowmobile in hot pursuit.

It is difficult to keep a headlight on a scared rabbit, which does not run for speed so much as it continually changes direction. My snowmobile, unlike Simon's, is not made for precision turns, let alone speed, and I have no experience with this sort of thing. My machine is a long track, designed for hauling and touring, not for racing.

No matter. Simon soon catches up, zooming in from the side to nail the bunny. It has mere seconds to emerge from the snow before I run it over too, feeling the slight bump as the weight of the snowmobile pushes it back into the snow. Would that be enough to kill it? I turn around, and the rabbit is off again, moving a bit slower now, but still looking healthy, and still terrified. It must be getting tired. Simon chases it. I muse upon the unforeseen problems of too much soft snow as I make a beeline for Simon.

Simon hits it again, much more quickly this time, and, while it gets up again and tries to run away, it no longer looks healthy. It is probably exhausted. My turn, and I manage to hit it with both ski (a hard thump as I catch it between the ski and a rock) and track. I bring the snowmobile around slowly this time, and pull up next to Simon. He has already turned his machine off and is reaching for a cigarette. I keep my engine running, the light trained on the corpse.

I look down at the body. The skin is ripped away from the left back leg, which looks broken. I look at Simon, who takes another pull from his cigarette. We look up again at the Aurora, still shimmering brightly. "You could have that one," he says, after yet another puff.

"Why? You saw it first, and you ran it over more times." Three to two, by my count.

"But you got it last. Besides, I've been eating lots of rabbits at my parents lately. I'm a little tired of them." He picks up the bunny and puts it into the utility rack on the back end of my snowmobile, securing it with a bungee cord. "Let's go look for some more."

We drive for a while longer, making our way to the cabins before finally coming back along the raised beaches by the shore. We do not see any more rabbits, but Simon doesn't seem upset. "At least we never got skunked," he says right before we go back to town, he to his house, I to mine.

The entire trip has taken surprisingly little time. We have only been gone for 75 minutes, and it is a little past 9 PM when I walk back into my house. Figuring I ought to butcher my bunny before too long, I bring it inside and lay it on a piece of old cardboard on the table. I find my sharpest knife, and start skinning it.

Immediately I understand why hares are rather low on the status hierarchy. They are, simply put, a pain to skin. It would help, I suppose, if the animal not been run over a half dozen times, with what now appear to be multiple broken bones. Even so, the skin tears easily, and soon bits of skin and fur are stuck to my hands and clothing. Even worse, little black bugs are jumping off the animal onto the table. What the heck are those things? Are they going to infest the house?

As luck would have it, I hear a knock on the door.

"Come in!" I shout. I do not want to drip blood on the carpet.

Roy Kudlak walks in. An older fellow, one of the last to come in off the land in the late 1960s, he works for the hamlet now, though he is still quite an active hunter. "I was on a call-out and saw you come into town. Wanted to see what you were up to. Ah – hunting Bugs Bunnies." He looks down at the animal, halfway skinned, then looks at my hands. "I'll make tea." He heads over and turns on the kettle.

I clumsily work on the skin and he sits and watches for a few minutes, occasionally offering advice, an amused smile on his face. Mostly, he reminisces.

"I hate those damn things. One year at Walker Bay we had to live on rabbits for two months, we got stuck by bad weather. It's like we were always hungry, even when we had lots of rabbits. I'll never eat them again." Walker Bay, up across Minto Inlet, was once inhabited by multiple families, many of whom used to hunt and trap north of Minto and into Prince of Wales Strait. Roy's family was one of the last to come in.

"What are these black bugs? They're all over the place." Perhaps he can tell me something about them.

Roy nods sagely. "Rabbits are full of them. They don't do anything except get everywhere. Most people leave it out for a while before they skin it. Once the rabbit gets cold, the bugs jump off and freeze. That one is a mess, though. You run it over?"

I explain that Simon took me out to run over rabbits.

Roy nods again. "My nephew. Some young people like to do that. I'm not sure why." It is unclear whether he is simply stating a fact or if he disapproves.

I get the last of the skin off and gut the animal, but, as Roy advises, I do so into the sink. As he foresaw, the animal suffered from significant internal bleeding before it died. The guts are a mess. I clean out the body cavity and put the mangled carcass into the fridge. I'll finish butchering it tomorrow.

Later that evening, I am back at Isaac's for tea, a game of cribbage, and Sports Night, ITV's nightly sports news broadcast from Edmonton. Darren Dutchyshen is a major celebrity among the young men.

"How was your drive?" Isaac is curious, but I can tell he does not approve. I tell him about the trip, and about the mangled rabbit now sitting in my refrigerator.

"How come you didn't come?" I ask. "I thought you might like a drive."

"Too hard on the machine to run over rabbits like that. Not worth the trouble."

I can see his point. All that turning, braking, gunning the engine, not to mention the rocks underneath the snow, could all damage different parts of the machine. I suppose that for a teenager those things have a certain attraction, especially if someone else is paying for the snowmobile.

"Rabbits don't taste very good if you run them over, either." Another good point. But then, I was no longer sure how many young men actually ate what they ran over. It seemed that, like Simon, they gave the animals away, usually to their parents. Probably they didn't want to deal with the mess of butchering them.

"It's also illegal. You're not supposed to run over things." This also was true, though that had not stopped Isaac from trying for a fox a few weeks ago. Foxes are much more difficult to run over, and Isaac did not get his. Simon said that foxes will run and jump down behind a snowdrift, then change direction just when you can't see them. And foxes are more agile. Then again, fox pelts are worth money, so I suppose there is more of an incentive to try to get them. Traps, however, seem easier.

A week has passed, and Edward Kuniluk has dropped by for a visit. He has brought with him a Northern bag with a chunk of muskox meat, frozen. It's enough for several meals for me. "It's some of the last from that one we shot. I'm going to have to go out again soon. But you should have some more before it is all gone. My brother's been bugging me again."

"What is he bothering you about?"

"That there's no food in my box. He's always coming down to help himself. He came down last night, found only really old bits in the box. He complains when it is like that." Edward has several brothers, but he is referring to his older brother, who does not hunt at all save for foraging trips to his younger brother's larder.

"So how come he didn't take this?" I point at the bag on the table.

"Oh, that? I have another box under the house. I keep the best pieces in there. He doesn't know about that box. Don't tell him."

I grab the cribbage board from the coffee table and bring it to the kitchen table. It is a slow night in town, a rare Monday evening with no meetings and no hockey games at the arena. I shuffle the deck, we cut, and I end up with the first deal.

"I started to set some traps the other night, just down the coast a ways." Edward is referring to the same places Simon and I drove to look for bunnies.

"You're going to run a trapline this year?" I have not known Edward to be a trapper. He ran one when he was a kid, I know, but he has not set traps for years. He will be the third member of the sample running traps this year.

"I don't know. I put out four traps. I got three foxes on Saturday, but they were really dirty, the fur is no good. So I brought them back in. I might put them out later this month." It is still early for foxes, even though the season has opened. The fur gets better as the weather gets colder.

We play our hands, pegging and counting the cards. Edward's turn to shuffle. He collects the cards while continuing his story. "I took my girl with me, and we saw some rabbits out there, too, near Kuneyuna's camp. Two of them ran right away, but the other just stood there. My girl wanted to watch it for a while, but it never moved. I gunned the engine at it and just stood there. It had a broken leg."

"What did you do?"

"That one I ran over, it was really suffering. Somebody probably ran it over and either let it go or lost it. Some young people do that, but they shouldn't do that, all right. I got another one later, shot it while it was stuck in the headlight."

Edward surely knew that I had been out with Simon, he probably crossed our own tracks multiple times. It seems to me that he is directing the story specifically at me: do not run over rabbits. I take it as an admonition, intended or no.

I am sitting at the kitchen table with Sam Ihumayuq. We are having tea on a stormy evening. I am conducting an interview. Sam has been both a friend and informant, a hunting and fishing partner on occasion, and a kind of perfect "marginal man," thoughtful and introspective. Sam has spent his life between Ulukhaktok, Sachs Harbour, and Inuvik. Though his own parents and grandparents were born and raised on Victoria Island, Sam went with his parents to run foxes at Sachs Harbour when he was young. He was educated in Inuvik and Aklavik at the boarding schools. He has spent a good chunk of his adult life in Inuvik, having married a woman from the Mackenzie Delta, and he has a fleet of relatives there still. He's older now, his youngest fifteen, though he and his wife have adopted their granddaughter, now three, their eldest daughter's child.

"So, Sam, tell me about the people who you would call *nutaraq*. For how long would you call them that? What is it like to be that age? What do they think about?" We have already established the parameters. *Nutaraq* is the general gloss meaning "child." Sam is defining this life stage as incorporating those as old as fifteen or sixteen, after which, to his mind, they become "young people," with their physical bodies still developing.

He sips his tea and leans into the table. His voice is soft and low, very gentle for such a powerful man. "Well, I guess I am wondering if your questions refer to these days or to when I was a young boy."

I am trying to let the conversation be as open as possible, to let Sam dictate the course of the narrative. I do not want to lead the witness, or allow him to tell me what he thinks I want to hear. "Both," I reply. "We could start with what it's like to be a nutaraq today."

He thinks again for a moment. "To be a nutaraq these days, I think because children are seeing so many things, they seem to want more of whatever – clothing, modern clothing, up-to-date clothing, modern things, and keeping up with the modern world. And I think they're thinking about, well, what they see on TV and in the community. They're not seeing hunting like long ago, so they're seeing work, and jobs, and they're hearing and seeing a lot of things that are negative. So, I think they're probably having too much on their minds right now. Whereas when I was growing up, we didn't have the house full of like you see here now, with computers and radios and things like now." He points to the sofa in the corner, the guitar hanging on the wall, and the electronic keyboard.

He continues. "Our house in them days was just basic, full of hunting equipment and bedding and cooking gear. It was just based on survival. So we didn't see or hear other things as much. But our mind in those days was only to be a good hunter and look after our dog team good, and those were really important to us as a nutaraq when I was growing up. Because other nutakaat growing up beside you were doing those things, and you wanted to keep up with them. It helped that way to do things, you know, the right way I guess, and to learn things about becoming a hunter and provider. But nowadays it's very different."

"How is it different? Are there good things about being a nutaraq?"

"Well, being young and energetic is good, you know, and there is education today, and everything is provided for you. Health, modern sports equipment and facilities. These are some of the good things to be a nutaraq these days."

It occurs to me that some of these things might not necessarily be good things. Sports and education would seem to take away from hunting, for example. "What about when you were young?"

Sam's eyes light up ever so subtly. "Learning things. Season changes used to really stand out in my memory because springtime is warmer, and there is lots of sunlight and you can go out fishing and travelling and staying on the land longer. Those were the good things about being young, because you are tireless and you could sleep whenever you wanted to. Those were good times then. Like when your dad was out hunting and trapping for days sometimes, and maybe longer – a week, ten days, before coming home. Those were good to see, like when he was coming home with the dog team and a full load of caribou or whatever, or foxes. Those meant lots in those days."

"Were there bad things about being a nutaraq?"

"Well, long ago, I can't really say anything, or any bad things about the traditional lifestyle, but the bad things about those days were when I was going to residential school and was separated from my family and their love and their care from day to day, so those were bad times for me. Even though we were looked after most of the time, we didn't have someone to cry to and get love and care, and being very homesick, it took a lot from us, I suppose. Nowadays the things about being a nutaraq that are bad is in the area of social problems, I think. There are social problems related to alcohol and drugs that are very visible in all communities to varying degrees. And kids and teenagers are seeing that, and it's not a good thing and it's very hard to convince the young kids … I have kids, and their minds are mixed up. It's hard to bring them up. They're seeing videos which show lots of violence, and as a young nutaraq they're seeing things that they might believe it's real life. I remember thinking that when I was young I saw movies as a kid at residential school and I saw lots of old movies, cowboy and Indian movies, and I thought that was real life. I used to look up to those Indians, those very proud people."

Sam and I have been over some of this ground before in casual conversation. Sam was a victim of residential schooling. As a young boy, he was shipped to Aklavik, to the residential school there, and so for some years was raised and educated in an institution rather than with his family. He has had plenty of problems of his own with alcohol, though he and his wife have been mostly sober for at least twenty years. Although he has moved down the path of sobriety, he has never, at least in front of me, spoken negatively about people who continue to drink or who have serious trouble with alcohol. My sense is that he sees alcohol as something that is exceedingly difficult to resist, an evil attraction that many simply cannot refuse. For Sam, drinking is not necessarily a moral failure.

This sense that forces can lure a person is, indeed, a common explanation for behaviour, often expressed as being caused by external pressure. Drinking is largely a social event: one simply drinks with others, rarely alone, and there is strong pressure to participate and "keep up." This is not only true with alcohol, but in many kinds of social endeavours where one imposes one's will on another, whether it be with having another drink or having another piece of cake. "Oh, you're really making me have more cake" is one way of phrasing a response to a hostess who is strongly suggesting that a guest have seconds or thirds.

On the other hand, using drugs seems to be viewed a moral failure. Marijuana is the drug of choice for the younger set in Ulukhaktok, though in recent years Inuit who have gone to Inuvik or Yellowknife have spoken about trying cocaine and heroin. Methamphetamines appear to be a more serious and growing problem for some young people who move between Ulukhaktok and Yellowknife or Inuvik. For Sam, and, indeed, for most Inuit born before 1960, however, "drugs" is a euphemism for marijuana and quite separate from alcohol. Marijuana is widely believed to cause both mental illness and birth defects, and behaviour motivated by drugs is viewed as a moral failing, very unlike alcohol, which seems to be viewed as an acceptable, though unfortunate, coping mechanism.

Perhaps I can convince Sam to expand a little on this topic. "What about people who are in their teenage years – you called them *nukatpihaat* – what is life like for them?"

"It's primarily much the same as the nutaraq, except that they are even more impacted negatively because they are all into alcohol and drugs, and they have a lot of problems with girlfriends, boyfriends, and when they take drugs and alcohol, those problems get really big. And that might be one of the reasons that suicide might be so high in the North. I think they're very insecure at this age."

"Was it like that when you were a teenager? Were you insecure at that age?"

"Well, again, in my traditional upbringing I didn't have much of a problem, except that I had to learn to be tough and take the cold and the darkness. If you could accept those things, then you could learn to survive. But where I experienced where it wasn't good for me was when I was going to school in different places like Aklavik and Yellowknife and Inuvik. I wanted to keep up with other people and be like other people in school, and I tried to keep up by taking alcohol and tobacco and cigarettes. Those were the tough parts, wanting a lot of things that other people had, but not having enough money to get what you wanted. When I was a young person, I saw a lot of people using alcohol, and a lot of violence, like in Inuvik where there was a lot of influence of the modern world, and development, and all kinds of people from all over the world, actually. And it was not easy to not go to the bar or to a party with them after work to drink. That was a lot of times the only thing to do, so we had to tag along. It was the only thing to do. It was a lot of fun at first, but it took a lot of money to live that way."

He thinks for a moment. He raises his cup, but it's empty – time for a refill. While he pours more tea for us – unlike many Inuit, Sam brews a full pot of tea, in a glass coffee pot – I say, "You are an elder now. Can you do anything for young people? Is there any way to keep them off of drugs and alcohol?"

Sam is, indeed, now an elder, at least in a kind of legal sense. According to the Inuvialuit Regional Corporation, one becomes an elder at fifty. It is a somewhat contested marker, with some Inuit noting that many fifty-year-olds still behave like teenagers, and others noting that in the contemporary settlement, with more Inuit living longer, fifty hardly seems old in the same way that it used to.

"Well, it seems like elders like myself are very concerned for the younger generation." Sam gives me a sly look. He knows I am poking a little fun at him. We have talked about this before, and he is uncomfortable being classed as an elder, mostly because he still feels young and lively.

He continues, excluding himself from that category. "In a lot of ways they're very concerned about the younger generation and sort of feel helpless to help them because, in a lot of ways, younger people do not want to listen to them. Because we grew up and the elders always traditionally had been the ones to give advice, and they had been very strong in giving their advice. Very stern, what I remember is all the elders were very stern. But I think that's lacking these days."

KIIJJAVIIK

It is late July, and Isaac Kaaktuq, George Putdjugiaq, and I are bumping along the trail, heading toward Kiijjaviik. July is a dry time of year. May and June are awful for travel on the land, the melting snow and ice swelling the streams and rivers that flow off the land into Amundsen Gulf, making plenty of mud in the process. Trying to go anywhere by ATV is unwise if not impossible. By July, however, the land has dried up. The streams and rivers are fordable again, and much of the mud has turned back into hard, cement-like dirt.

Kiijjaviik is a narrow spit jutting out into Amundsen Gulf, just shy of forty kilometres from the settlement, the first point in a somewhat featureless coastline. It is a reasonably easy drive from Ulukhaktok. Just before the airport, we turn onto the gravel track that leads along the shore. We drive past a series of cabins and frame tents built up among the raised beaches. Over the years, the size, sophistication, and number of cabins have grown. Little territories have been carved out on the rocky beaches: Kuneyuna's camp, Okheena's camp, Nigiyok's camp. Children, now grown and married, with their own children, have built cabins next door to their parents.

These days the cabins are mostly for weekend use, the occasional evening out, or sometimes for parties. Originally they were employed as fishing camps, and Inuit would move out here for a month or more, setting nets for char, hunting seals, and only occasionally coming back to the settlement for supplies. Today, they are more like vacation homes. Few set nets out here anymore, and most Inuit, especially the younger ones, claim that they come out to the cabins to "get away from town" for a while. Ironically, it is just as noisy on the weekends at the cabins as in town, with a steady stream of ATV traffic and all of the people one wants to get away from having the exact same idea.

Hanigayuq's River is at the end of the cabins. Once we ford the stream, finally low enough to cross, and head through the mud flats on the other side, we are into a largely flat, gently sloping landscape, a mix of low, marshy areas interrupted by slightly higher, dry areas covered in gravel and dirt. Rocks abound, and we find a large one on which we leave our helmets. They are required in town, but we feel daring out on the land. Not really – we are all reasonably slow drivers. Isaac and George both have bad backs and cannot stand the pounding that comes with going fast. We are in no hurry; the sun is above the horizon, after all, and will stay that way for another month. Still, we move along at good speed, and I have a difficult time keeping up. I am a slow driver, even by the standards of the older and the cautious.

We are headed to Kiijjaviik to set nets. George thinks the char are ready to start running, descending from their winter homes in the lakes to feed in the ocean for the summer. They run up and down the coast, first moving "down" from Minto Inlet toward Prince Albert Sound, then, in August, going back "up" into Minto Inlet. Where are they going, precisely? Isaac just shrugs: "They could go anywhere." Recently a char was captured that had been tagged far away in Iqaluit, in the Eastern Arctic.

We want the very beginning of the run, which George says has the biggest fish, very fat and good for freezing and eating as quaq, frozen and raw. The smaller ones caught at this time of year are gutted and split, and hung to dry as piffi. Given that the spring fishing through the lake ice generally yields only lake trout, most households are very low on char now. Hence, Isaac and George have a strong motivation to be the first to get some.

It is only forty kilometres, but for us it is a nearly two-hour trip to get here. My back is sore and my thumb is numb from working the ATV's throttle. My arms will be very sore tomorrow. We pull up onto the gravel spit and unload. There are two cabins here, both now belonging to H T C, which uses them to run an "elders camp" later in the summer. It is a chance for some of the elders to camp with children and teenagers and provide instruction about more traditional kinds of land skills that young Inuit should acquire.

We will use one of the cabins to store our grub and stay out of the wind. The other one, a larger cabin with a window large enough for a bear to go through, is a mess. We know the window was big enough for a bear because a bear went through it, smashing the Plexiglas to get inside and wreck the interior. George speculates that the last camper here, probably in the fall, left some open food and trash inside, which attracted the bear. George and Isaac exchange looks. They know who did it. "Some people are really lazy" is all Isaac will say.

An old rowboat, a ten-footer, is drawn up onto the beach. It belongs to Isaac's father, who left it here at the end of last summer. The motor is back in town, and part of the reason Isaac is here is to assess whether this boat can be dragged back to town on a sled. To Isaac's mind, it would take far too long to bring the motor – a 10-horsepower – here and drive the boat back on the water. But since we are here, we push the boat into the water and set the net. We have tied one end of it to a large rock on the beach, and we start to paddle out, feeding the net into the water as we go. George is in the cabin, making tea and cleaning up the mess.

Before we get too far, a thought occurs to me. "Don't we need a rock for this end?" I ask Isaac, and point at the net in the boat. Because I am the neophyte, I am trying to think through how things are supposed to be done.

"Oh, yeah. Right. I always forget that part." He chuckles, remembering that the same thing happened to us the previous summer. We paddle in and grab a good-sized rock from the beach.

We pay the net out slowly. There are still some big chunks of ice in the water, and the bottom is quite rocky. We want to avoid snagging the net on the bottom. Eventually, the task is complete, and it's time for tea and a snack. We have all afternoon and evening if we want it.

Indeed, we spend the afternoon on the beach, drinking tea and eating piffi, pilot biscuits, sardines, and Klik, and throwing rocks into the water. George says that in the old days they would throw rocks into the water upstream from the net. The plunk of the rock in the water scares the char into the net. The char, says George, are funny. They swim into the shore from deeper water, go along the shore for only a little ways, then go back out into deeper water. The trick, he says, is to know the best places where they come into shore before they go back out. Kiijjaviik is one of those places, though Ulukhaktok is good, too. All the bays around the settlement, and the little islands close by, are good spots for fishing with nets. But the char will come here first, on their way to Ulukhaktok. George is hoping some will travel to Ulukhaktok on the back of an ATV.

Several hours later, many rocks thrown and much tea drunk, we have fish: a good number and many large ones. Isaac and George open the plastic tubs both have brought with them, load them with fish, and tie the tubs to their ATVs. The fish are cold from the water and will stay that way all the way home. It is only 10°C today, after all.

The ride home would be uneventful but for Isaac's ATV. George's machine is brand new, and I am riding a borrowed ATV in excellent shape. Isaac's ATV, however, does not inspire confidence. It's on its third engine, the frame has been welded back together in several places, and the tires are a disaster. The ratio of tire plugs to original tire is high. The bearings need replacement. Isaac is the only one of us who has a teenager in the house.

There is nothing particularly unusual about a welded machine, spare engines, and replacement bearings on an ATV in this environment. Those kinds of problems are, however, associated with older machines. Isaac's is only two years old, but it has aged ahead of its time. While land travel can account for some of the damage, most of it, to my mind, is due to his son. Ronald, now sixteen, has taken to driving around as part of the evening parade, damaging the bearings by doing doughnuts, aging the frame and suspension by climbing Ulukhaktok Bluff repeatedly, and stressing the engine with sudden acceleration and deceleration along the airport road. Ronald seems to miss the meaning of "You shouldn't drive too fast, son. It is not good for the machine."

For most Inuit, such an utterance is a directive, much in the same way that Edward's "People shouldn't run over rabbits" statement to me is a directive. *Don't run over rabbits. Don't drive the machine like a mad-man.* But this is seemingly lost on Ronald, raised on television and hip-hop, with a need to go fast. Isaac seems unable to get through to him, unsure why his patently obvious (to Isaac) admonitions are ignored.

We are nearly halfway home when I notice that Isaac's rear wheel is wobbly. I speed up to get a closer look, and realize that the wheel is about to fall off. Coming alongside him, bumping on the rough ground, I yell at him to stop, which he does. George, oblivious, crests the next hill and drops out of sight. He will be back in a few minutes, once he's realized he has dropped us.

Isaac gets off his AT V. "What's going on?"

"You're going to lose your wheel."

Isaac looks down at the wheel and points to the ragged metal along the rim. We both kneel down for a closer look. "Yessir, it sure looks that way," he says.

The rim is obviously the wrong size and kind for this machine. In a way, it is exasperating: why not just get the proper rims for the machine? In another way, though, it is admirable, finding a way to make do with what one has on hand. We're going to have to do that now.

I am curious. As long as it is not my machine, I secretly long for breakdowns on the land, if only to see how Inuit solve the problem. What kind of new and interesting repair can Isaac devise? One of the most important land skills one can have is the ability to repair a machine to get home. It is the biggest difference between Qablunaat and Inuit that I can think of. Whereas a Qablunaaq like myself places a high value on keeping a machine in tip-top shape – preventative mainte-nance – an Inuk like Isaac places a much higher value on the ability to get a broken machine home under its own power. It does not seem to matter what kind of condition a snowmobile is in when it leaves town, only that one travels with enough material to get the machine home when there is trouble. There will be trouble, regardless of the condition of the equipment. In fact newer machines are much more likely to break down on the land, as they are increasingly constructed of "cut-ting edge" materials designed to make the equipment lighter and faster but not necessarily more durable. After all, AT V and snowmobile manufacturers are not designing for the High Arctic, nor for the kinds of working loads Inuit routinely place upon them.

We tip the ATV on its side so we can examine the problem more closely. George drives up and shuts his machine off. It is very quiet here, save for the sound of the breeze ruffling our windbreakers and a few longspurs chirping some distance from us.

George looks at the wheel. "Gee," is all he says, long and drawn out. Isaac nods. George is disappointed, not in Isaac for his choice of wheels but in such clearly faulty material. How dare the rims rip like that?

The holes through which the bolts are mounted are torn. The incorrectly sized rim apparently had too much play. Over time and many doughnuts in the road, the bolts began to tear into the rim. Two of the four nuts have worked loose and are long gone, and the other two do not look like they will last much longer. I'm thinking that we are looking at leaving the machine here, heading to town for a new rim, and then coming back to replace the broken one. All we have are the emergency toolkits that come with the ATVs.

Isaac thinks a minute. Then he rummages through his tool bag and emerges with a number of washers, all different sizes, that will fit over the mounting bolt. He carefully places washers on the rim, and slowly tightens them down, as tightly as he can. He does this twice, then a third time, taking one nut from the other rear wheel. Each rim now has three bolts holding it onto the axle. "That oughta do her."

The entire process has taken forty-five minutes. We pack up and head out, stopping every ten or fifteen minutes to tighten the bolts, which continue to work loose.

As repairs go, it is not terribly impressive. I have seen better work out of Isaac, including fixing a pair of seized-up pistons while out on the land with nothing but a can of WD-40, two screwdrivers, and a set of wrenches, all in a thirty-kilometre wind at −25°C. To me, the really impressive bit is that Isaac takes his ATV on the land at all.

A few days later I am watching Isaac and David Kaaktuq work on William's ATV. The machine is on its side, and Isaac and David are looking at one of the rear wheels. A pile of tools and parts sits on an old cable spool used as a table; more tools and parts can be seen inside the storage shed behind them. David is Isaac's nephew, his sister's son, adopted by William and Agnes and raised mostly in their household. Nearly the same age as Ronald, David is quite different from his cousin. An equally reckless driver, he is absolutely committed to hunting and fishing in a way that Ronald has hardly ever shown. I rarely see David driving around in the evenings, for example. If the weather is nice, he seems to be devising ways to go out on the land.

Agnes, Isaac's mother, is on the other side of that shed, butchering a seal. David was out boating earlier in the day and shot it out by the little islands. Several freshly split trout are hanging from the drying rack alongside the char Isaac got in his nets at Kiijjaviik the other day.

Isaac is fidgeting with something in the wheel, so I step closer to see what the problem is. He seems to be having difficulty putting the wheel back onto the axle. It is getting toward late afternoon, but for us it is just after breakfast, as we are both backwards. I was at Isaac's last night, playing cribbage until well past three.

"Good morning, sleepy." He grins and gets back to work. David stands alongside, watching and ready to help.

The two of them are spending yet another day on this machine, really a collection of parts and pieces from two older machines, known previously as "the green Honda" and "the red Honda." Yesterday, they installed the engine, and they were puzzling over the front chassis. The engine from one machine was a 2×4, but the frame they were using was from the 4×4. I left them debating whether they needed to remove the linkage in the front. I assume they resolved that issue, because David took the machine out last night to go fishing, and he returned with the half-dozen trout that are now drying a few feet away from us.

Like most mechanics here, Isaac and David are largely self-taught, though David, age seventeen, has had the benefit of the small-engine repair classes that the school offers as part of the curriculum. He is in and out of school as his interest dictates. Lately, he has not had much interest. The transient Qablunaat have caught my ear about this multiple times, lecturing me about how David is not going make anything of his life if he does not complete his education. These discussions have not gone well, and I usually manage to offend the teacher in question when I suggest that for David, an education has a limited utility. He certainly has shown no interest in an office job. Though he is young, and reckless in the way all young men seem to be, he has also shown clear signs of becoming a provider. Indeed, he is here with his uncle because he wants to get the machine running, to get out of town to hunt and fish. He has no equipment of his own, so he depends on his grandparents, who think so highly of him that he has nearly free rein with their equipment. William has declared that David does nearly all of the hunting for the household. "I'm just the driver now," William says.

Being self-taught has its ups and downs, however. Isaac and David both repair their equipment based on prior experience with the machine. When they confront something novel, it usually takes them some time to puzzle out precisely how things work. This is usually accomplished by simply taking the entire thing apart and putting it back together again, experimenting with how things look like they should go together. Sometimes, however, young men like David become tinkerers, imagining problems that do not exist and then executing needless repairs. Occasionally, they make a problem when no problem exists.

Edward Kuniluk, in fact, was like this when I first met him, an inveterate tinkerer. Shortly after our first muskox hunting trip, he purchased a fancy new machine, a liquid-cooled snowmobile with a powerful engine. The machine was designed for racing more than anything else, and it looked like it would have limited utility on the land. Most old-timers preferred fan-cooled engines for travelling on the land, because the liquid-cooled machines of the time had problems with overheating while pulling heavy loads. They depended upon heat being dispersed through heat exchangers that ran along the footrests of the machine. The idea, I think, was that the heat would not only disperse out of the engine but would also warm the driver's feet. Pulling a heavy load, however, seemed to tax the engines, requiring frequent stops to pile snow on the heat exchangers to facilitate cooling. They also made rubber boots a must, because kamiks, far superior for warmth and comfort, would become soaked. To keep a fan-cooled engine cool, one simply could remove the hood.

Nevertheless, Edward was pleased when he made the purchase, until he imagined four months later that he had a leak in the coolant system. He was sure there was a leak, because the machine kept overheating when he was pulling a load. Over the course of three weeks, he took the engine apart looking for a leak, refilled the coolant, and tried a number of other tricks, all with no luck. He then stumbled on a bit of advice from a friend: black pepper.

"The pepper is small enough that it will stop a tiny leak," he told me at the time. Still, the engine kept overheating. He kept adding more pepper.

At the end of June, he had enough and sold the machine to the hamlet foreman, Albert Aquti. "That machine was just a lemon, can't stay cool. Got a deal from Albert, though, almost half of what I paid for it."

I went to see Albert and found him to be very happy with his purchase. "Got it for half the price of a new one, and it is in great shape. Not sure why Edward wanted to sell it, though. He said he thought he engine ran hot. But there's nothing wrong with it."

"Did you check it out?"

"I overhauled the engine and drained the coolant, everything. It was full of lots of these black specks. But otherwise it is fine."

Isaac explains the problem with the linkage, and how they managed to get the engine to shift properly, with David adding a few details. "We were just checking the bearing on this wheel. It sounded a little funny."

Isaac drops the machine back onto all four wheels, starts it up, and drives over the hill for a little spin. He's trying to listen to the wheel bearings.

"I hope that wheel stays on," David says to me. Isaac put the wheel on the axle, but our conversation distracted him so he forgot to secure the bolts. David smiles, holding out the bolts, and we start laughing. We soon hear a thunk and a scraping sound from just over the little hill. A few minutes later, Isaac is back, a huge grin on his face.

"This machine is trying to trick me. I was going along, yessir, and then I hear a funny sound, look back, and my wheel is going on down the hill, trying to escape." He laughs.

"It's good then?" David asks his uncle. "I could have it?"

Isaac nods, says, "Don't drive so fast. You have to take care of this machine, lots of people use it."

David tightens down the nuts on the wheel, starts the engine, and tears off down the road, spitting gravel. He wants to go fishing. Isaac sighs. "That kid. He's going to wreck it right away. Really hard on machines, that one. He's got no ears." He grabs a piffi from the drying rack, a nice char, halfway dry, half wet – the best kind, to my mind – and we head inside for tea and a snack with his parents.

Isaac doesn't stay annoyed long. The rest of the evening he periodically breaks out in fits of giggles, remembering the wheel that made a break for Queen's Bay and freedom.

Two days later, I am walking past William's place, and Isaac and David are again working on the same ATV. I walk over to say hello and immediately feel the chill in the air. Isaac curtly says hello and heads to the house for a part. I ask David what's up, and he launches into the story. He seems to think I will be a sympathetic ear.

Apparently, after leaving us, David went out fishing with two of his friends, to try some of the local lakes for trout. They did not get far, only to around Kanguaq's Lake, about eight or ten kilometres from the settlement, when the wheel fell off. It was the same wheel that tried to trick Isaac, the same wheel that Isaac suspected of having a bad bearing. This time, though, the cotter pin that held the wheel to the axle had fallen out, and then the nut fell out, and shortly after that, the wheel followed suit. According to David, there was no chance of finding either the nut or the cotter pin. David instead improvised a repair. He placed the wheel on, stuck a nail on the axle through the hole for the cotter pin, wrapped a string around it to hold both it and the wheel in place, and declared everything was "good enough." The problem was that instead of coming home, David continued on, driving to Ekahavik and back on the broken wheel. In his estimation, he had travelled an additional thirty or forty kilometres on the repaired wheel. By the time he got home, however, the wheel bearing was a mangled mess of metal and plastic.

Isaac wasn't happy about having to put yet more hours into the machine. William had directed Isaac to supervise the rebuilding of the ATV in the first place. Isaac may be self-taught, but he is competent, he is meticulous when he works on an engine, and he has experience that

David lacks. David can improvise a temporary repair, but William and Isaac are both hoping that, by watching Isaac work, David will acquire some important skills.

David, however, simply cannot understand why Isaac is upset – as he clearly is, by the tone of his voice, low and icy with a hint of exasperation. David, however, did come home with more fish, and he wonders how anyone could be angry at that.

Isaac comes out of the house, several old bearings in hand. "You gotta be careful. This machine is only good enough for in town, you shouldn't be taking it out on the land." They appear to be continuing a conversation begun long before I arrived.

"Gee." It is almost a tut, the vowel moving toward the back of the throat, an expression of anger at being insulted. David has taken Isaac's statement at face value, and obviously disagrees. "Yours is a bigger piece of junk than this one, and you keep taking that one out on the land."

What Isaac is really trying to say is that the problem is David, who is, to be blunt, a wrecker. The directive sails clear over the youngster's head. I hear both sides of the story over the next hour, the two so frustrated with each other that, even though they are both "working" on the same machine, they are never within earshot of each other.

"That kid ..." Isaac mutters under his breath, and then complains about how David drives, how he cannot listen, how he never thinks about all the others who use that ATV. And Isaac is correct on that score. The ATV is the only one William has, and with three adult daughters, a spouse, and multiple grandchildren, the machine is in constant use when it is running.

Isaac walks off into the shed to look for a part, and David materializes from the house with a new tool. "Don't know what's wrong with him. He's so grumpy." Observations about his uncle follow: he is always grouchy, he is so anal, and he is always being bossy.

I begin to see the fundamental problem. Isaac is engaged in this repair only partly to demonstrate some techniques for repairing equipment to his nephew. The more important lesson he is trying to impart is that it takes more than coming home with food to be a real hunter. Although David is providing food for his grandparents, he is still thinking only of himself. He may have produced fish for his grandparents, but by damaging the machine in such a manner, he has deprived them of their only transportation while making much more work for himself and for Isaac. From Isaac's perspective, being a provider in not about food alone. It is about providing for others' well-being. David has yet to grasp this important lesson. There is also a good chance that Isaac is likewise upset because he is having difficulty getting through to David, just as he is having difficulty getting through to his own son. He is talking to these younger people, but why are they not listening?

Despite this tag team of repairs, they cannot find the proper bearing for the wheel. Every part they have is slightly different. Eventually, however, the repair attracts another bystander. Angus Ikayukti arrives on his Honda to see what's going on. A shade younger than Isaac, Angus is a distant cousin and friend of the family, a person that Isaac and William both respect because of his hunting skills. He has a reputation for being very good at geese. Eventually there is an exchange between Angus and David, who has just come out of the house. Even though Angus has had enough time to finish a cigarette, Isaac and David have continued their active avoidance of each other, enough so that Angus raises an eyebrow at me. I shrug.

"Dad wants to know how much you want to let go of that other Honda," David says, apparently referring to a dead frame Angus owns, with plenty of salvageable parts but a broken engine. "They want to buy it from you for parts."

Angus doesn't respond immediately, instead pulling out another cigarette. There is silence while Isaac rummages around in a box of parts and David idly wipes the axle with a rag.

Angus finally speaks. "There's a bearing on that old machine, you could just have it." He finishes his smoke, starts up his ATV, and motions to David to get on. They drive off.

About thirty minutes later, they're back. David hops off the machine, hands the bearing to Isaac, and they install the bearing and wheel together. Angus sits on his machine, watching the process through yet another cigarette.

Once the job is finished, David turns to Angus. "Anytime you need parts, just come and take them." He waves towards the table and shed. Angus says thanks and drives off.

The acquisition of the wheel bearing is a fairly common kind of exchange, an indirect way of asking for something, under the guise of "I would like to buy that from you." Sometimes such a statement is taken at face value, and there is a market for old machines sold for the value of their parts. However, more often "I would like to buy that from you" is simply a coded way of asking someone like Angus if he has the needed part. There are other methods of asking indirectly: "Boy, I really need a bearing for this wheel but there's none at the Co-op" accomplishes the same thing. And Angus and William, though separated by decades in age, have been involved in these kinds of exchanges for years.

A week later, I see David at the store, looking wind-burned, buying a soda, a package of beef jerky, and some kind of ATV part. "How's it going?" It is the ubiquitous greeting in Ulukhaktok.

"Really good. Just got back from Kiijjaviik. Forty minutes! A new record!" He is excited. A twelve-year-old boy in line behind David looks up at him, eyes wide with adoration.

Uh-oh. That's not a bad road, as I know, having driven it myself. But while it is not rough at my speeds, it is far too rough for a forty-minute trip. I imagine Isaac's head exploding.

"You went on William's machine? The one you and Isaac were working on last week?"

An eyebrow flash. "Yup. Broke a shock on the way back, but I could fix that tomorrow." He holds up the replacement he is about to purchase. "But, boy, these are really expensive. Glad I can charge it to Dad."

6

I'm Experimenting

FISH LAKE

Once September arrives, Ulukhaktomiut start thinking about Fish Lake. Both a time and a place, Fish Lake has long been an important part of the seasonal round, a time when the Arctic char return from the ocean into the larger lakes to spawn. Char are the most valued fish in the local diet, taken at different times of the year as opportunity permits. In July, and again in August, Inuit set nets in the local bays, catching char as they move up and down the coast. Young people will fish for them with rod and reel. In the spring, Inuit jig through the thick lake ice, mostly catching lake trout but always hoping for char. Fish Lake time is especially important, the most important part of the year for catching these prized fish.

Inuit look forward to Fish Lake, whether or not they actually intend to travel there. One of the reasons for the heightened importance of Fish Lake is that the char are migrating and so can be caught in nets in large numbers. An added advantage is that temperatures have dropped below freezing, which alleviates the problem of storage. Summer fish are typically dried to make piffi, with only the best specimens laid flat to freeze in the porch freezer. Fish caught in autumn freeze quickly, and they stay frozen, stacked in a plywood box, secured from foxes or loose dogs. Fall fishing is also important because of the strong desire for *ivitaaruq* – spawning char, "red bellies," so named because of the colour of their skin. These fish are richer in fat and taste better, according to Inuit, and make excellent quaq, eaten frozen and raw. There is

certainly nothing better than a meal of quaq, followed by tea and bannock, for warming up after a day on the land.

Fish Lake is the last (or first) lake along the Kuujjua, a large river that
originates in the Shaler Mountains to the east and north, runs for well
over 150 kilometres, and drains into Minto Inlet. Roughly eighty kilometres from Ulukhaktok, Fish Lake carries an important historical
significance that predates the settlement. Fish Lake was well into the
territory of the Kanghiryuatjagmiut, who lived in the lands around
Minto Inlet, Walker Bay, and Prince of Wales Strait. Some of the current generation of elders grew up in the area, and a few just now on the
cusp of elderhood were born there. There are indications of prehistoric
occupation in the area, and early historic settlements at the mouth of
the Kuujjua.

A significant human presence is still in evidence at Fish Lake, in the
form of cabins, frame tents, and storage boxes. Some of the frame tents
barely qualify as shelters, just plywood sheets hastily tacked around an
old tent, a canvas tarp stretched over to make a roof. Other structures
are essentially plywood tents, 6 × 8 dwellings with low roofs, a small
window, and a gravel floor, heated by the ubiquitous Coleman camp
stove. Then there are the more professional cabins: 12 × 16, with eight
foot high insulated walls, an oil stove for heat, windows for natural
light, and an enclosed porch for secure storage and the honey pot.
These cabins were likely constructed in Ulukhaktok, dragged to Fish
Lake on sleds behind a snowmobile, and assembled on site. They are
very comfortable.

Until the early 1990s, Fish Lake was a much more important place
for Ulukhaktomiut hunters than it is today. In addition to fall fishing,
the lake was a staging area for caribou hunting to the north and east, a
way-stop for hunters going further into the land during the fall and
winter months. Declines in the caribou population during the late
1980s, however, made such lengthy trips unproductive and increasingly expensive, and Inuit switched their hunting strategies from caribou to muskoxen, which were readily available locally. In 1993, a formal
ban was placed on hunting caribou from the Minto herd, as it is known
locally, even though Inuit had already stopped hunting them. The ban
remains in effect, although Ulukhaktomiut are unsure what is actually

banned or under whose jurisdiction enforcement falls. Even the Fish and Wildlife officers seem confused about the regulations.

A small number of Inuit, however, continue to use Fish Lake as a staging area, but for caribou hunting trips *east* of Ulukhaktok. The absence of caribou north of Kuujjua and Minto Inlet has made summer caribou hunting around Prince Albert Sound much more important, and Inuit have devised ways to try to maximize the number of animals they take, including trying to hunt those caribou into the autumn. Prince Albert Sound caribou are thought to be from a different herd than the Minto one, wintering closer to Cambridge Bay on the other side of the island. One strategy for extending hunting opportunities for these caribou is to travel to the end of Prince Albert Sound over the sea ice by snowmobile, though there is significant risk in this. The sea ice is usually not safe for snowmobile travel until mid-November, by which time the caribou may be gone. A second strategy is to try an overland route by travelling up the Kuujjua, negotiating several gaps in the bluffs and cliffs that form the overland barrier between Ulukhaktok and Prince Albert Sound. Once "up on top" of the plateau, it is a gentle ride down to the shores of the sound.

But that route is much longer, and for the hunters who use it, Fish Lake becomes an important staging area, a place to store gasoline and other supplies. Even so, using Fish Lake as part of the overland route to Prince Albert Sound is risky. It is a rough road for snowmobiles, and very expensive. Snowmobiles are not efficient in terms of gas mileage, and hunters say that they must plan ahead during the summer, caching gas along the route for refuelling. In recent years, some younger Inuit have taken to using ATVs for this trip, trading the limited hauling capacity of the ATV, which can only pull small sleds, for better gas mileage and a smoother ride. They cache caribou meat in Prince Albert Sound, returning for it once the sea ice is in and safe for travel.

Another factor in the decline of Fish Lake's material and cultural importance to Ulukhaktok is the fish themselves. In addition to char, Inuit also net lake trout and, in lesser numbers, whitefish, unusual this far north but valued for both variety and taste. Char are still the clear favourite, however, and Fish Lake has been heavily fished over the past few decades. By the early 1990s, declines in the numbers of spawning char, and in char in general (for the fish do not spawn each year), generated significant concern for both Fisheries and Oceans (known locally as DFO, headquartered in Inuvik) and the Hunters and Trappers Committee (HTC) in Ulukhaktok. Following monitoring of the problem for several years, Fish Lake was closed in the mid-1990s, and then reopened on a limited basis, with a quota on the numbers of fish taken. In 1997, the quota was thirty-five fish per household, although it was unclear whether the quota was for thirty-five fish in total, or thirty-five char, or if ivitaaruq were themselves banned from being taken. Additional confusion was generated by concerns about household size. Is a household one house? Or is a household the number of houses a single hunter supports? There seemed to be some agreement that an individual fisherman could take thirty-five per household; that is, an Inuk could be setting nets not only for the residents of his own house but also for those in other houses, specifically older Inuit who could no longer travel on the land or hunt and fish for themselves.

As with the caribou regulations, individual Inuit seemed to have only a vague notion of what the rules were. Furthermore, more than a few Inuit disagreed with the conclusions of the DFO/HTC study of the problem, arguing that char "go anywhere," and that low numbers in Fish Lake essentially meant nothing because char could spawn in any lake they wanted to, and there were many, many lakes that Inuit did not fish. A char taken that summer, with a tag from Iqaluit (on Baffin Island, far to the east) was usually cited as proof that Inuit knowledge about char was superior to that of the biologists. Consequently, the most common explanation for why there were so few char in Fish Lake was that the water levels in the river had been unusually low. The fish had therefore decided to try other rivers.

The desire for Inuit to continue fishing Fish Lake seemed to be based on ease rather than lack of alternatives. Most noted that there were plenty of other places to catch char – any lake that drained directly to the ocean would have char in it. Fish Lake, however, the largest, closest lake to the settlement, has historically produced more fish and is the easiest to travel to in the autumn. There are cabins and tents there, so people keep using it.

It is certainly for all of these reasons that I am at Fish Lake during October 1997 with William and Agnes Kaaktuq and their grandson David. I am here – Maya and Sarah stayed in Ulukhaktok – to help "work on" William's cabin, though we are really taking it apart and moving it across the river, to a raised gravel bar where all of the other cabins now sit. The cabin has been here for many years, but William says that during the spring and summer it is on wet, marshy ground. He also says that since he no longer travels here in the summer – thus explaining his tolerance of a cabin on wet ground – he doesn't need to worry about being on the wrong side of the river when he is here. The gravel bar is on the north side of the river, and inaccessible during the summer, though some Inuit leave old canoes on the south side so they can get across.

William's cabin is one of the older structures at Fish Lake, a large, Frankenstein-like shack built in multiple stages, nailed together haphazardly, with a flat roof. William likes flat roofs. He says they use less material, there is no complicated math for laying out rafters, and they go up quickly. William is not a particularly good carpenter. It is not that he is not capable of quality work: he simply has other priorities. His cabins are designed with the single purpose of providing basic shelter so he can go hunting. Taking the time to create a quality structure detracts from time he could be hunting. Is he constantly repairing his cabins? Does he tend to burn more fuel heating his cabin? Yes, on both counts. But fuel has not been a scarce resource until recently, and he can do his repairs during his down time, between eating and sleeping, and on those days when the weather is not suitable for hunting.

William's objective is to make the cabin smaller and so easier heat. Fuel might not be a scarce resource, but money is, and he realizes that he is slowing down. His own children are grown, and they rarely travel to Fish Lake with him. He no longer needs a large cabin. I am here because I have not travelled here for over five years, and Fish Lake is a beautiful place. I also think that I can "pay my way" by helping to move the cabin. William and Agnes are healthy and active, but they are in their early sixties, and David is only seven. I am nothing if not young and free labour.

After two days the cabin is down, and we have managed to move most pieces across the river to the new site. We pulled nails out of all of the boards and plywood, reusing as much material as we can, even the nails. William picked through the 2 × 4s and 2 × 6s for the best pieces to use for the floor, and we have constructed the floor joists and laid out the plywood for the floor itself. Walls will soon go up. We are doing this work in between setting and checking nets, the real purpose of this trip. William was so keen to get here on Thursday not just because of the time involved in rebuilding his cabin but also because he wanted to get a good spot in the river, to fish without competing with other fishermen. He already has quite few fish piled up on plywood staging, frozen solid. William is using a liberal definition of the catch limits, so he is counting only char toward the limit of thirty-five per household. He says that he is fishing for three or four other households, too – two elders who no longer travel, and two of his adult children and their children.

Is he really fishing for these other households? He will store the fish for his children in his own freezer, after all. But he is not lying. He says he is fishing for four other households, but the fish he catches here will go well beyond those households. He will check on most of the elders who no longer travel and provide all of them with fish. Other households will also receive fish, for he shares widely.

It is Saturday morning of Thanksgiving weekend, and we are expecting more travellers from Ulukhaktok later today. The gentle, low hiss of the gas is the only sound beyond the scratching of my pencil on the notepad. I have been up for a while, writing notes in my journal and running the stove to heat the little cabin George Putdjugiaq was kind enough to allow me to stay in while I am up here. It is well stocked with tea, sugar, jam, pilot biscuits, and several pots, dishes and mugs. In turn, I will leave a few items of my own behind for the next visitors. I am also expecting company today. George's son-in-law, Amos Tuktu, will be staying here too.

My asking George to use his cabin was largely a formality. Most Inuit simply use a cabin as needed and notify the owner after the fact. Indeed, many owners leave their cabins unlocked in the event that a traveller is faced with an emergency and needs shelter or food. However, over the past twenty years, this kind of generosity is becoming less common, and some Inuit now lock their cabins because of increasing incidents of theft and vandalism. This is especially a problem closer to town, where many summer cabins are stretched along the shore northwest of the settlement. Over the summer Mark Pihuktuq was plagued by frequent thefts, the gas cans he left at his camp emptied. Rather than lock up, he spiked a gas can with heating fuel, quickly identifying the culprit (a freeloading teenager), and prevented further thefts without the need to involve the RCMP.

Thefts are increasingly problematic at Fish Lake and Prince Albert Sound too. Hunters report caches of gasoline being raided by unscrupulous travellers, equipment taken, and cabins damaged. Not only are these inconveniences, they are potentially deadly for anyone in dire need.

The silence of the morning is broken by the steadily increasing hum of a snowmobile, William returning from an early morning drive. Given that sun is only now, at 10 AM, peeking above the distant bluffs across the lake, William has been up since well before dawn. I quickly finish my tea and oatmeal and walk to his cabin for a second breakfast. It is not his cabin, of course, which still lacks a roof and walls. He is borrowing another, much as I am doing. William tells me over more tea that there are lots of wolves around. Although an abundance of tracks in the vicinity proves him right – we find plenty around the cabins this morning – he did not see any on his drive. We finish our tea and head down to the river, all of thirty yards away, to check his nets. We load twenty-three fish into a small sled and haul them up to the cabin, where we put them in a box to keep them safe from hungry wolves.

As noon approaches, we hear the whine of snowmobiles; William knows who these travellers are by the distinctive sound each machine makes. The long Thanksgiving weekend makes this a popular time to come to the lake, allowing those with employment obligations in the community extra time to travel and fish. Fish Lake is one of the most important times of the year for Inuit from Ulukhaktok, but it is also one of the last chances to escape town for a few days before the darkness and cold discourage many from travelling more than a few kilometres.

The new arrivals are a mix of older couples and single adult men, and there are not as many as in past years. Previously, Fish Lake was a community event, one of the few subsistence activities that involved entire families, some of them staying for a week or longer. One reason for low numbers this year is the limits on fish. For many younger people, it makes more economic sense to let a father or father-in-law travel to Fish Lake and stay there until quotas for all of the members of the extended family are filled. Another reason is the weather. Though the lakes are all frozen, the land within thirty kilometres of Ulukhaktok is free of snow. It is a bumpy ride on a snowmobile. A few have come on ATVs, trading a smoother ride for potentially greater difficulty in starting the machine.

People waste no time once they arrive. Some gear is immediately unloaded at the cabins – food boxes, tents, stoves – but this is done only to get at the important equipment for nets: the *tuuq*, a large chisel made from the leaf spring of a truck, attached to a long wooden handle, and the *kuvyiqtuq*. Actually, I'm not really sure what this second tool is called, since the word actually refers to setting a net. When I asked William what it was called, he simply shrugged. So I suppose it's a "net setting thing," a wooden device with a pivoting arm that, with small tugs on the line, travels under the ice and allows one to set the net. The device is pulled out of a newly opened hole, the line is tied to the net, and the net is pulled under the ice, tied off on blocks of ice set on the surface of the river. Checking the net is a matter of pulling the net out of the water, leaving a length of line tied to the other end so it can be easily reset.

The first priority is to get nets into the water. Only then do people return to the cabins to set up camp and make tea. By the time the last travellers arrive, about 2 PM, there are twenty-one people, a good mix of older and younger hunters, some of the older men travelling with their wives, all of the younger men travelling with age-mates. Jonathan Aullaq and Eddie Agluaq are two of the younger men, also friends of mine. Though among the first to arrive, they do not immediately get a net into the water like the others, preferring instead to set up their canvas tent and get all their gear inside. They take quite a bit of time setting up. Their tent is at some distance from the main camping area.

Jonathan and Eddie typify the young men at Fish Lake this weekend, but on a broader level they typify the average young adult Inuit male in Ulukhaktok. Jonathan is twenty-eight and has been shacked up for almost a decade. He has three daughters, the eldest almost ten years old. He has worked as one of the hamlet's water truck drivers for about four years, starting first as a back-up driver and then stepping in full time when there was an opening about a year ago. Still, he hunts infrequently. He has many kin connections in the community through both his wife and his own family (he is one of six children), but neither his parents nor his wife's parents are now living. This is his first trip to Fish Lake in nine years.

Eddie is three years younger than Jonathan; the two are cousins and good friends. Eddie has never held a full-time job but is currently employed on a casual basis as the back-up sewage driver for the hamlet. He is currently shacked up with his girlfriend, and they have a baby almost a year old. They live with Eddie's elderly parents. Eddie has never been much of a hunter or even shown much interest in hunting and travelling; he is the youngest of seven siblings. Like many young males, he has had some trouble with the law, but unlike most Ulukhaktok males, has spent some time in prison in Yellowknife for domestic assault.

I walk over to say hello and stick my head into the tent. They look alarmed, but ease up when they see it is me. I did not think they were going to come to Fish Lake this year. Eddie said earlier in the week that his machine was not running, and he thought he would not make it. Jonathan's machine needs a new track, and it is even worse shape than Eddie's. Both say that they are here to catch some fish for the upcoming winter. Jonathan says his wife has been bugging him all summer about going to Fish Lake. Eddie says he is here because his parents really like fresh fish, but, due to their advanced age and poor health, they can no longer travel in the fall and winter. Indeed, I suspect that Eddie's parents really put them both up to it: Jonathan is using his uncle's machine. Of course, they also say that that they are here for vacation too, as a way of getting on the land to relax and be away from town and the "old ladies" for a weekend. Both have been said to "have trouble" with their spouses on a somewhat regular basis.

I figured they were interested in taking it easy the moment I opened the tent – simply from the smell and the two tarnished butter knives on the Coleman stove, still warm from hot-knifing. They have brought a rather large bag of marijuana with them and have not wasted any time on the relaxing part of the trip. "Thought you were my auntie. You gave us a scare all right. She'd tell us off if she knew we were smoking up," says Eddie.

With that, they get ready to set a net. They do not mind that I tag along: Jonathan says they would welcome the help, and I quickly see why. It is painfully obvious even before we get the nets, the kuvyiqtuq, and the tuuq that they do not really know what they are doing. I am much more proficient at setting a net under the ice than they are, and their being high has nothing to do with it. I would hardly call myself proficient either – most Inuit will let me watch, but many seem to think I am a danger to myself with sharp objects like a tuuq. After a brief discussion about location, they decide to set their nets apart from everyone else, roughly one hundred metres downriver in a bend. They say the main channel of the river is clogged with nets and they don't want to make anybody mad. I suspect that they choose their site because they don't want anyone else to see them mess up.

I help them get the net in the water, which takes quite a bit longer than it should. I decline their offer of a celebratory smoke and instead head back to say hello to Amos Tuktu, my new cabin-mate, and to talk to some of the other arrivals. Amos chuckles when I tell him what Jonathan and Eddie are up to. Amos is only slightly more proficient than Jonathan and Eddie when it comes to net fishing, but he is with his older brother, who knows what he is doing. "Those guys. Figures they would do something like that. They're going to get hell if Mary catches them, though. She hates that stuff. And you shouldn't get high on the land anyways. You come out here to dry out a little bit, and get your head right again. That's what the old people say when they have trouble with booze, anyway."

By the evening, Jonathan and Eddie have two fish in their nets. William, by contrast, has already caught 135, including twenty that afternoon. And, indeed, by Sunday morning, William has decided he has enough fish – below his declared limit of 175 char – and grants one of his own age-mates the rights to take fish from his nets. In their tent on Saturday evening, Jonathan and Eddie complain between puffs of *higaaq* that everyone else is hogging the good spots in the river. They moan that they weren't left with a good spot to fish, but their complaints alternate with admissions that they do not really know where else they could fish.

Eddie lightens the mood. "It doesn't matter, because I'm experimenting anyway." He giggles. The real truth of the matter is that some of the elders are not having much luck either, which is one of the reasons that William has loaned his nets. Since he was here first, he naturally took the best spot in the river.

I go to see William for dinner, knowing that he and Agnes are having – what else? – fresh fish. Agnes's brother Frank and his wife, Mary (Jonathan and Eddie's auntie), are also having supper, and we have a fine meal of quaq, bannock, butter, jam, pilot biscuits, and Klik. Supper is accompanied by an excess of joking and laughing, with most of the jokes centred on my predilection for eating quaq with my knife. William has taken the opportunity to broadcast this perceived idiosyncrasy by HF radio across the Western Arctic. We all find this terribly funny, as no one else in the cabin is using a fork either, and any observer might wonder if the old people in the cabin were themselves smoking up. When the laughter subsides and our ribs stop hurting, I ask William if there are other good places to fish on this side of Fish Lake. He immediately suggests five places along the lakeshore, all within a mile of the cabins, while admitting that there are probably a few other places that no one remembers. Two of them are even better than the river for catching char, he adds.

"Why don't you fish in those places if they are better?" I ask.

"I'm old and I'm lazy. I don't feel like to be out in the cold for so long. So I fish in the river. It's good enough."

"So why aren't the young people catching anything? How come Jonathan and Eddie can't catch anything in that part of the river?"

"There's no fish in that part of the river. But young people, they don't know anything. Anyone could tell them that they can't catch anything there."

"Why don't you tell them?" I respond.

"I could tell them, but they have to ask." William smiles.

The next morning, Sunday, I am up and cleaning around my cabin when I see Jonathan and Eddie getting ready to go down to their nets. I walk over. Mary, who is loading a sled with a second net and getting

ready to go across the lake to set it, also walks over. She suggests that
the spot where they are fishing is not very good, and maybe they would
like to try a spot along the lakeshore, pointing to several of the places
that William suggested at dinner. She points out a place from where we
stand and says that she and her husband used to fish there when they
were younger. It's a spawning bed, and so there is a great opportunity
to get ivitaaruq.

Jonathan says, "Yeah, we were kinda thinking we should move the
net. I think today we are going to go under the cliffs across the lake.
We'd like to try for some whitefish."

Mary says there are some good spots there and people were getting
whitefish yesterday. She and Frank are heading over soon to try.
Jonathan and Eddie go down and pull their net. Unlike the elders, they
have only brought a single net with them. It makes sense to have multiple nets, as one is more likely to catch lake trout and whitefish under
the cliffs, and the quota at Fish Lake apparently applies only to char. I
tag along.

It's a long drive to the cliffs, because Fish Lake is not frozen in the
middle yet. We have to drive along the shore, and Fish Lake is miles
across. As we reach a spot where we should start thinking about setting
a net, under the cliffs on the south side of the lake, we see Harry
Tamaryak and his grandson, Dennis Iqiahuuyuq. Harry is old, seventy-
five now, and he has bad knees. Dennis is only thirteen, and this is his
first trip to Fish Lake. Clearly he has been sent partly to help Harry and
partly to learn from him. Dennis is the youngest of five children. He is
also nervous around his grandfather and seems in awe of him.

We stop to help. Harry is still untangling his net, talking to himself,
and he does not pause when we stop and turn off our machines. He
directs us to cut a hole in the ice and to start feeding a line underneath,
which we do. Once the net is untangled, he then directs us to set it using the kuvyiqtuq. While Jonathan is trying to feed the kuvyiqtuq along
with little tugs on the line, the rest of us watching its slow crawl underneath the ice, Harry walks over to Jonathan's sled, pulls out Jonathan's
net and declares that this is such a good spot to fish that Jonathan and
Eddie should set their nets here too. Jonathan and Eddie do not have

much choice, for Harry has already made the decision and is cutting the hole himself. "It's good," he says. "You'll get lots of fish here."

As we finish setting the first net, Dennis asks if they can go jigging for fish. Harry grunts assent, and Jonathan and Eddie and I decide to go jigging with them. We drive along the shore to the spot where Kuujjua feeds into Fish Lake, and head further upriver. Harry is not interested in jigging for fish when he has a net in the water, but his grandson enjoys it, even though the fish do not typically bite at lures in the autumn. Harry uses the opportunity to look for wolf and muskox tracks. He sits on his machine while we jig, and tells stories and points out important features of the landscape. It occurs to me that this is the first meaningful interaction between Jonathan, Eddie, and any of the elders at Fish Lake.

Indeed, at the cabins there was no social visiting between younger and older people. On several occasions, Jonathan and Eddie's uncle Frank poked his head into their tent to invite them to eat, which Jonathan and Eddie declined, claiming that they had already eaten. For Jonathan and Eddie, the significance of the exchange was not the invitation to eat, but rather that Frank almost caught them smoking up.

Harry is clearly using this time with the four of us youngsters for instruction. We do not catch many fish by jigging, but when we return to check the nets, they are reasonably full. In fact, Jonathan and Eddie keep their nets in overnight, and by the time they pack up tomorrow afternoon, they will have nearly fifty fish, a good mix of char, lake trout, and a few whitefish.

Later in the afternoon, back at the camps, there is excitement. Jonathan, Eddie, Dennis, and I return to camp on our snowmobiles (Dennis hitches a ride on a sled), but Harry goes off for a drive, rifle slung over his shoulder. We've been back for about an hour when we hear the whine of Harry's machine from a different direction, to the north of us, coming over a low ridge. In front of him are a dozen muskoxen, fleeing in terror from the noise of his snowmobile, running directly toward our camp. People down on the ice stop to watch the animals run in a slow arc onto the river and around the cabins and tents before finally stopping to catch their breath. Harry hops off his machine, selects one of the smaller animals, and shoots it, only fifty metres from his cabin. As the other animals totter off, Harry hitches a line to the carcass and drags it to his cabin door. Recognizing an opportunity, I walk over to help him skin the animal, knowing he will give me some of the meat in return, something to take back to town for Maya and our daughter. Harry has no real need for help, but he cannot refuse my offer. Indeed, it is a common and accepted strategy to offer help as a way of indirectly asking for meat. His grandson Dennis stands off to the side, as does younger David Kaaktuq, who has come over to look. David looks excited, but Dennis looks nervous. I wonder if this is the first time he has seen someone shoot a muskox. Harry tells him to get a knife and help, but Dennis does not move.

As we skin the animal, Harry says he saw the fresh tracks close to where we were fishing. He followed them for a short way and eventually found the herd. This small group broke away, and Harry made an effort to run them to camp. "Less work to shoot one right here," he says, adding that fish get boring after a while. I think to myself that Harry was also showing off a bit, too, and not only for me, Dennis, David, or the other younger men. The older men are highly competitive themselves, engaging in subtle games of one-upmanship – who can catch the most fish, who can get the first caribou of the season, the first ducks. Who can get to Fish Lake first, and get home first. Harry and Ungayuk, two of the oldest men at the camp this weekend, are also two of the craziest drivers, racing each other here. In fact Ungayuk crashed and hurt his back on his way here, and he's been on a steady diet of Ibuprofen for the past two days.

This competitiveness is unspoken but palpable, and seemingly shared by men of all ages. When a hunting trip turns toward home, there seems to be a subtle calculation. When are travellers a "safe" distance from the settlement, so that a partner with a breakdown is not in danger? Once that point is reach, partners become competitors, and it becomes a race to see who can get home first. I have rarely participated in such endeavours as a competitor, always on a slower and less powerful machine – but I also enjoy having my limbs attached and my spine uncompressed.

As we work on the carcass, a young muskox comes back over the hill, wandering toward the river, quite close to Harry's cabin. It lost the rest of the herd and cannot find its way back. It is bleating for its mother, according to Harry. "Dennis, shoot that one," he says. "It's no good now." Dennis just watches. The animal wanders closer to the river, right at the point where the lake begins to empty.

"Dennis, you got to shoot that one before it gets to the river." Urgency in his voice, Harry looks at me but nods at the river. "Ice is thin there, always. You have to be careful or you'll go through. It's not too deep, but it is wet." I keep it in mind, though I am not sure when I will need to use that knowledge.

Harry finally sighs and gets the rifle out of the sled. He shoots the young muskox before it reaches the thin ice and then drags that one to his cabin, too. Nearly everyone is eating fresh muskox that night, and with the abundance of meat, I end up taking home a rear quarter for myself. I also take home some of William's fish for him. William is staying for a few more days to finish the roof of his cabin. I think I've convinced him to at least put some slope on the roof, but I'm not sure.

Monday dawns with light snow and promise of more to come. Holiday over, I am headed back to Ulukhaktok, following many of Saturday's travellers. Some of the older couples are staying – William, Harry, and his grandson Dennis, Ungayuk, and a couple of others. But the weekend is over, and even those Inuit who are not beholden to wage labour jobs are heading back to town. Because I do not know the route well, it is a good idea that I go back with a large pack. Once I get within about twenty-five kilometres of Ulukhaktok, I know the land reasonably well, but out here I am completely lost. As expected, the drive is beautiful, white snow against the stark bluffs to the south and east, along a trail that winds around and through small valleys and over frozen lakes.

Despite the beauty of the ride, however, it is not all fun. The snow cover is still thin, and bouncing over an occasional unseen rock is not enjoyable. My companions – Amos, Jonathan, and Eddie among them, are driving a bit faster than I would like, though a few others, Frank and Mary among them, are staying with me, in no hurry to get back to town. For the young men, speed to and from Fish Lake is a kind of measuring stick of manliness. How long did it take you to get home? A few men claim to make the trip in forty-five minutes, or an hour at most. I will be lucky to do it in three or four hours.

And, as luck would have it, I am about fifty kilometres from town, ten or so kilometres from our tea stop at Akaluataq's Lake, when I hit a rock hidden in a drift of powdery snow. The ski crunches, the machine bounces, and my skis stop responding to the turn of the handlebars. I get off and inspect the damage.

I know how to fix this one! Sometimes I am lost in a breakdown, but this one I know! A tie rod, a narrow metal rod connected to the steering column by a ball joint, has snapped, and the ski is hanging freely. This is such a common breakdown that *everyone* is prepared for it. Smart hunters always travel with tools and spare parts, and one of those parts is often a length of hockey stick. Some even plan ahead for a steering problem by tying a length of hockey stick between the pull handles of the skis before a tie rod gives way. If one tie rod breaks, the other is still intact, and the hockey stick forces the other ski to remain parallel.

But something is wrong. Both skis are wobbling freely. Amos, coming back to check on me, checks out the damage, and we both look into the engine. "Damn French engineering," he mutters. "That's why I quit buying Ski-doos." This Bombardier model has only one tie rod, connected to one ski inside the body, the other tie rod effectively serving as an internal hockey stick. I now have no steering.

Amos shrugs. "I don't know how to fix that one. You'd need to weld it. You could leave the machine here and I'll tow your sled back to town. You can ride on the sleds and come back for the machine sometime."

It is a kind offer, but I am forced to decline. The machine is otherwise in good shape, and my time in Ulukhaktok is coming to a close. Maya and I and our daughter are leaving in a little more than a month. When am I going to find time to get all the way up here to tow this machine home? It is a bit far to retrieve a broken machine. We have already passed the remains of a few ancient snowmobiles that broke down on the land, permanently left behind by Inuit who thought they might come back for their machine "sometime."

I tinker for a few minutes and manage to fix the skis in a straight position. I find that if I lean hard to my left or right, I can steer in gentle, long curves, though I occasionally have to get off and point the machine in the direction I want to go. Perhaps I can get home this way.

I make it to Akaluataq's Lake just as the rest of the crew is packing up their sleds and finishing their tea. For the younger men, it is now time to race home – who can get there first without dumping their sled contents all over the land? I have no hope of keeping up, and no plans to anyway. The weather is worsening, snow coming in big, wet, fluffy flakes, and the wind is picking up. Not quite whiteout, but not much fun either. And steering is tiring. Frank and Mary are hauling my sleds for me, and, like Amos, have offered me a lift too, but they understand my motives. William is Frank's brother-in-law. He knows that William would be happy to "look after" my machine after I leave Ulukhaktok, and that William would use the liberal definition of "look after" to include "borrowing" parts I am not currently using, like the engine, skis, bearings, and track. William drives the same model machine as I do.

I manage to get within twenty-five kilometres of the settlement before I am forced to give up by a combination of exhaustion and bare ground. Still, I am closer to town, I know where I am, and all I need is a borrowed machine to retrieve it. I finally accept a ride from Frank, who kindly and patiently kept his speed slow to look after me. We are the last to return to Ulukhaktok, a full ninety minutes after the others: Jonathan, Amos, and Eddie were among the first arrivals. Amos has already showered, changed, and eaten by the time I turn up, just before a sunset obscured by clouds and blowing snow. I learn all about their trip, because he sees me come in on the sled and comes by to ask me the whereabouts of the machine. "It's good that you tried to get it closer. That William, he'd be happy to take care of it for you while you're gone. Goes through machines, that guy."

That night I head over to Isaac's for tea. He wants a report about Fish Lake and about how his dad is doing with the fishing. We play cribbage. I am washed and fed, feeling warm and sleepy inside the house and tired out from the afternoon's trip. After five days on the land, all the houses feel too warm. But, despite my sleepiness, I am crushing Isaac at cribbage, as usual. I have long suspected that he deliberately tries to lose at crib, but damned if I can figure out how. He is not breaking up obviously good hands, and he is not avoiding good pegging opportunities. But I frequently win, even when I am deliberately trying to lose without Isaac catching on.

Isaac has long been my closest friend in Ulukhaktok, akin to an older brother. He and Rick Condon were also close, and I fell into a similar relationship. Isaac has always looked after me when I have been in the settlement. He has made sure I have enough food, helped me when I needed to make repairs on equipment, provided advice as necessary. I can call him *angayuq* (older brother), and he responds. I see him nearly every day, and if several days go by without a visit, I hear about it. *Gee, haven't seen you in awhile. Wondered what you were up to.* Inuit guilt-tripping. On my evening visiting rounds, there is nearly always a stop at Isaac's for tea, a snack, and a couple of games of crib. Sometimes we go for days without actually talking to each other beyond "What's new in town?" followed by "Not much," "Have tea" several minutes later, and the calls of cribbage ("seven," "fifteen for two," "twenty-four for three") as we peg and count our hands.

Being incorporated into a kin structure in this way has its pitfalls. As a kind of older brother, he has a claim on me, usually in the form of borrowing tools if I have them, using my phone for long-distance calls, and other kinds of assistance. Not that I mind. He has done far more for me than I will ever be able to reciprocate, and he has never pulled rank the way a real older brother might. Some men in town live with older siblings who are like that, making constant claims on goods and equipment. Edward Kunilik and his freeloading older brother come to mind. Isaac has older sisters who seem to stop by each evening with a need for coffee, sugar, or flour. Those visits appear to increase after I arrive in town, for I always bring coffee for Isaac, flavoured coffee purchased in Yellowknife and unavailable in either of the two stores. Isaac hides it right away so that when his sisters come, all they see is the Northern coffee.

Isaac asks about the machine.

"It's just the other side of Atuaqtaavik, I think about twenty-five kilometres from here."

"That's not too far. We could go up and get it this weekend if the weather is good. You could borrow one of my dad's machines. He's coming back Friday. Just talked to him on the radio. When are you leaving?"

"Another month. Not too long now. Not sure we're ready to leave yet."

MASHUYAK

A few nights later I am sitting at a table with John Takuyuq and his wife, Margaret. We're having tea, and John is showing me some ulus – the ubiquitous semi-lunar women's knives – he has made for Maya. Some months ago Maya struck up a friendship with Margaret at the women's sewing nights, and last month we finally convinced John to let me interview him. Famously shy, John has been retired as a hunter for many years, arthritis in his joints preventing him from working much with his hands, the pain in his knees making it difficult to walk, and a failing heart making his children reluctant to let him go out on the land alone, as he prefers. But John still occasionally makes things for family members and others, and Maya had asked about some ulus. She learned to use them at the women's sewing nights and wanted one for herself. John offered to make her a set.

In typically Inuit fashion, materials designed by southerners for one task are put to use for quite another. For John and others, the cheaply made handsaws for sale at the Northern are highly desired, not because they are handsaws but because the steel is high carbon and holds an edge well, and the saws are inexpensive. Anyone who wants a saw for actually cutting wood uses a power tool. John explains that from one saw blade he can cut five ulus – a large one and medium-sized one for use in the kitchen, and three smaller ones for use in sewing. The tang is brass, harvested from a truck engine. The handles are carved from the boss of a muskox horn. They're beautifully made. We have tea and then continue an interview begun the previous week.

Like many Inuit born before 1950, John's first language was Inuinnaqtun, the local dialect spoken by Inuinnait, once called Copper Eskimos. But John knows the western dialects equally well and, though he was shy and reluctant to speak it, he knows English well too. For this interview, we talk in a combination of English and Inuinnaqtun, with Margaret providing the translation. Normally, I would have brought an interpreter, one of two younger women known to be fluent in both English and Inuinnaqtun and also experienced as translators. But John is uncomfortable with both these women and prefers to talk in English and, when he can't find a suitable word in English, to use Margaret.

When we left off last time, we had finished defining life stages. The next step is to illuminate what those stages are like. In particular, I'm interested in pursuing what makes one an adult. How does someone know he is no longer *inuhaat* and is now *inirniq*? I open by asking this very question.

"Things are different now," John tells me, "but *inuuhuktuq* is a young man, one who is just getting himself going, starting out with a young family, and learning to provide for himself. When I was starting out, I had a sled, a tent, and a rifle, and I felt like a rich man, but I was still inuhaat. You would be a good example of someone who is inuhaat – you're just starting, with a young family, getting out on your own, just getting going."

"But I'm twenty-nine."

"Exactly. You're just starting out."

"So I'm not inirniq, an adult?"

"Yes, you're that too. Inirniq means 'fully developed body.' You are both at the same time. I remember when I was that age, one time I was travelling with my dogs, alone, checking my trapline. In those days I stayed at night in an iglu – it was more comfortable than a tent, kept me out of the wind. The dogs were tied up on the line. In the middle of the night I was awakened by the dogs all barking outside, and I could hear one of them on the top of the iglu. I was too tired to go outside, so I just yelled and yelled at them to be quiet. That dog eventually went off the roof, and the other dogs became quiet again. So I went back to sleep.

"When I woke up in the morning, all the dogs were tied up, and there were bear tracks everywhere. It was a bear on my roof, trying to get in." He chuckled.

John's words resonate with what other elders have said directly about adulthood, highlighting an important idea about the concept of adulthood and how things have changed. That July, I had a similar exchange with Mark Pihuktuq that set me on this trail. During the summer he and his wife moved out of town into his camp, a frame tent five kilometres down the coast, where he set nets in the ocean for char. I made the walk out there for the afternoon and evening, mixing bird-watching with a visit and interview with Mark.

Mark was having difficulty getting around. For the five years I'd known him, he had a bad hip and feet that were damaged years ago during a blizzard. He was also legally blind in one eye from a childhood injury. None of this prevented him from hunting; he was tireless on the land, even in old age.

Like most of my interviews with elders, this one with Mark was partly his life history and partly answers to my questions. We sat inside his frame tent, a 12 × 14 structure with plywood walls and a heavy canvas tarp stretched over an eight-foot ridgepole. The floor was the gravel of the beach.

The sun shone through the canvas, which gently flapped in the breeze. I continued our conversation over tea and piffi. "So, when you came back from Aklavik [where Mark had been in the hospital for some time], you were inirniq then?"

"I was inirniq. And inuuhuktuq. A young man. Even twenty years old, even a little more, you call them inuuhuktuq, because they're young men, young people, you know, inuhaat. You know, you, you're not old, someone's going to call you inuhaat. If they see you here, if somebody is asking me about you, and never see you before, if I'm talking to that guy, that's guy's going to ask me how old you are, and I'm going to tell him you're inuhaat. You're inuuhuktuq anyway, that's you, you know. You're still getting going, still learning things. How old are you anyway?"

"I'm twenty-nine. So I'm a young man, eh? Is inuhaat the same as inirniq?" I am thinking I should be inirniq. I am an adult in my own culture, after all.

Mark looks at me, perhaps wondering if I'm as smart as he thought. "Inuhaat is same as inuuhuktuq."

"Okay, but what about inirniq?"

"It's a little bit different. Inirniq is, you know, like me, you know, I'm inirniq. So are you. When you get married, when you get old, a little bit old, you know, it's you're married, your body never grow up anymore, you never go down, you never change: then you're inirniq."

Both Mark and John were referencing older meanings of these words. Today the terms have become codified as "teenager" (inuhaaq), "teenage boy" (inuuhuktuq), and "teenage girl" (arnaruhiq), stages assumed to be over when one turns nineteen or twenty, though my younger informants were themselves unsure when their "teenagerhood" ended. Indeed, most informants reported these Inuinnaq terms as variants of "teenager," beginning at thirteen and ending around twenty, something that most informants said "just happens, I guess."

Inuuhuktuq and inuhaat (the plural for teenager; the singular is inuhaaq) both literally refer to a process. Lowe (1983) lists the suffix -*haaq* as meaning "just" or "recently," suggesting that the terms are descriptive of processes rather than static states. That is, the terms that now mean "teenager" literally mean "becoming a person," a variation of other terms used and reported in other dialects. Elders like Mark and John use these terms in this manner – that a man who is inuuhuktuq is not a teenager but what English speakers might call a young adult, based on social characteristics. Inuhaat, in this sense, are physically mature but socially still young people, still "getting going."

On a broader level, the more traditional meanings of these words identify a central theme of Inuit identity and personhood: the notion of what has elsewhere been described as the inummarik, the "genuine person," a person who acts, thinks, and behaves in ways that typify traditional Inuit values, however those might be defined. While it may be seen as a state of being, it is the end stage of a process that one undergoes and demonstrates. It is not marked by a particular event.

And, indeed, though some important changes in an individual's life are marked by events, these by themselves do not automatically signify the transition to a new life stage. Shooting the first seal and first caribou were, and are, important events in a boy's life. A man's first bear has long been regarded as a marker of physical maturity, especially so in the contemporary settlement, where only the most active and experienced hunters specifically target bears. These are milestones, and important, but a real marker of transition to acceptance as a real person seems to be more of a process than event.

Mark's and John's remarks echo those of other elders, and I am immediately reminded of an extended conversation with Amos Tuktu earlier that June.

On a warm and pleasant evening, I am walking around the settlement, stopping and visiting anyone who might be in town. Some young men are out on the land, hoping to intercept the last of the migrating eider ducks flying low above the ice, heading south and into Prince Albert Sound to their nesting sites. Other young men are out at the golf course, playing "skins" – all the players put money into a pot, with the lowest score on the hole winning the money. Amos is one of the few men around, puttering with some of his gear but not really looking like he is going anywhere. Normally, he would be playing golf.

"I'm out of money, so I can't play," he tells me. "I have to go down to Mashuyak and pick up my machine. I was going to go with my brother, but he backed out to play golf. So I guess I'm just going to borrow his machine to get mine."

"What happened to it?"

"Blew a piston halfway home the other day. It's just sitting on the ice."

I know there is some urgency about this. It's been an unusual year in that the fast ice is still quite stable and shows no signs of breaking up. There has been little wind this spring, and the temperatures have remained cool. Current conditions do not predict the future, however. The previous year the ice broke up in May, and Inuit were hunting ducks by boat.

Amos knows he needs to get moving to retrieve his machine. A strong east wind could break up the ice quickly and push it out to sea, taking his snowmobile with it. A crack could open under the machine, and it could fall through. Such events are not unusual: several lakes close to town currently store machines and equipment at the bottom. Freezer Lake was so named because years ago a propane-powered freezer was left on the ice and fell through.

"How are you going to get the machine onto the sled?" I ask, knowing how heavy a snowmobile can be. "Do you need help?"

Really, I am asking if I can tag along. Amos is no stranger to machine breakdowns, and he admits that his repair skills are limited. As the youngest of four brothers, he often relies on his older siblings and his father for help and advice. He accepts my offer. I run home, only a few houses away, and get into my travelling clothes. Although it is warm in the settlement, slightly above freezing at 11 P M, on the ice it is much colder. I pull on my wind pants, parka, and travelling mitts, grab the emergency bag, a small stove, food, nylon tent, and sleeping bag, and head down to the ice.

The middle of the night is the ideal time to be on the ice in June. The sun is low on the northern horizon, the wind is generally calm, and the temperatures are at their coldest for the day. With daily highs above freezing, and the sun high and bright in the sky, daytime travel is difficult. The ice is softer, and wet, meltwater pooling on the surface. In the cooler temperatures, it is easier to travel on the sea ice, and generally one stays dry. As a measure of changing conditions, there is no snow anywhere in the settlement except for a few rapidly shrinking drifts. For three weeks now people have been leaving their snowmobiles parked on the ice as close to shore as they can. Eventually they will take their machines off, usually when the ice is separated from shore by a significant space of open water. They get a fast running start with the machine and skim over the water to the land. When this is done correctly, driver and machine stay dry. Done poorly, someone must find a pickup truck to retrieve the machine from waist-deep water.

My snowmobile is on the ice, as is Amos's brother's, and we start them up and head out of Queen's Bay, toward Mashuyak. While we are out, Amos is going to make the trip down to his cabin. Duck season is effectively over, and he wants to retrieve some of his camping gear. If he does not get it now, he might not get the chance for another two months or more.

Although it is only ten kilometres in a direct line, as soon as we leave Queen's Bay we are forced to find a route around some large ponds of standing water before we can head to the little islands. We will have to go through some water eventually, but these meltwater ponds are too deep, and we do not want water in our engines. We both have sheets of plywood tied to our skis to keep water from splattering the engine and us, but they will not help for these. We intend to move along the shore rather than go straight to Mashuyak. Amos knows from earlier reports that there are several large cracks forming, and he wants to play it safe. He admits he is not very comfortable travelling on the ice, and he does not like to take chances. Even if we go close to the shore, we will have to jump some large cracks that have opened up.

We arrive at the little pass between the two little islands, and Amos stops the machine. "I think we'd better go around. I don't think this ice is safe." He points between the two islands. "See? The ice is all dark right there. My brother says that when the ice is like that, it's not safe for a machine. There's a current here, that's why."

So we move along the shore of the last island, going further out of our way, but then cut across to the other side. We can see Amos's machine now, sitting on the ice. We pull up to it. "I'll just leave the sled here for now, and we can pick it up on the way home," he says. "I could just put my stuff in your sled."

A short time later we are pulling up at the cabins at Mashuyak. There are several cabins here, as this is a very popular spot for duck hunting. Mashuyak is a narrow passage of water between Holman Island and Victoria Island, visible from the settlement. Only a week ago, the place was lively and active. Eider ducks were flying by in tremendous numbers, and Inuit were camped here, shooting them with shotguns. For young men, and teenagers especially, duck season is a big event. Eider ducks migrate in large numbers, and they are highly prized. And Mashuyak is close to town, so even hunters without transportation can easily get a ride to and from the settlement, and even the least skilled hunter can manage to shoot some ducks. For many young people, this is also a chance to be on display. It is one thing to hunt but quite another to be seen hunting. At Mashuyak, there are plenty of people here to see one engaging in an activity that signals an adherence to Inuit values.

And, indeed, among the younger men there is a kind of status associated with different measures of success. Conversations between young men during and immediately after duck season typically involve numbers, a small number (ten, or twelve, or even twenty) followed by a larger one (seventy-six, eight-four, a hundred). The second refers to the actual number of ducks taken, the first to the number of boxes of shells fired. It is apparent from higher first numbers and lower second numbers that many of these hunters are not good shots, a combination of inexperience, youthful exuberance, and, perhaps, the simple joy of making noise. The ducks have been migrating down the coast for several weeks, and they have been under fire for quite a few kilometres. Last week, while many of the young men were here, Maya and I were camping some fifteen kilometres to the north, where Isaac and William and a few other families were shooting ducks.

So, although the ducks usually fly low to the ice, by the time they get to Mashuyak they are much higher in the air and sometimes out of shotgun range. That doesn't stop people from firing, however, and a common sound at the Mashuyak camps is the gentle patter of shot as it falls on the roof of the cabin or tent. The older men and women are much more efficient. Rather than fire rapidly into a bunch of flying ducks, they wait, and wait a little longer, firing at the precise moment when the shot pattern will strike the maximum number of ducks. William and Harry, for example, commonly take three or four with one shot.

For many of the younger men, especially the teenagers, taking multiple birds with one shot seems supernatural. One year at Mashuyak, Harry Tamaryak was asked by an older teenager how he managed it. Harry carefully and seriously responded to the young man: "When you pull the trigger to fire, make sure that you jerk the barrel, because it spreads out the shot, so you get more." The young man departed, apparently determined to try it, Harry chuckling as the poor fellow walked away.

The tale demonstrates an essential difference between the older hunters and the younger men. Men like Jonathan, Eddie, and Amos have simply not had the time, practice, or pressure to become expert with their firearms. An endless supply of shells, provided by parents or grandparents, removes any sense that each shot must count, that ammunition is precious and must be conserved – certainly the case in decades past. And many of the younger men learned on pump-action or semi-automatic shotguns rather than singles or doubles. With a single or double, there is only time for a few shots before the birds are gone.

Furthermore, there are fewer and fewer opportunities for the younger men to learn how to become expert. Inuit training in hunting depends on observation rather than direct instruction, and there are fewer opportunities to observe. Many of the older men, especially those with teenaged children, no longer actively hunt ducks. With several teenaged grandchildren vying with each other for ducks, older men see no need to lift their own shotguns. Their freezer will be full of the efforts of their grandchildren, more than enough for the following year, and encroaching on space better used for the char that will be running in a month.

Mashuyak is now very quiet. A few camps will remain in use through break-up – Harry and his wife will stay here for much of the summer, using the opportunity to stay away from town, to hunt seals, and, once the ice is clear, set nets for char. Their son-in-law, Mark Anguhuqtuq, will do the same. But both families are in town this evening, purchasing and loading the last of the supplies they'll need for what might be a month-long stay here. Once the ice begins to break up, the only way back to town is on foot. Steep cliffs come right down to the water between here and Ulukhaktok, and there is no overland route navigable by an ATV.

Amos and I pull up to the shore and turn off the machines. It is suddenly very quiet, the only sound the slow movement of ice and water, the very slight breeze, and the sounds our clothing makes as we move around. Although we are here to "clean out" the cabin, we are in no hurry, and we are not emptying the entire thing either. It is a typical cabin, 8 × 12, constructed of plywood and 2 × 4s, though unlike most, it is skilfully put together. Amos has been trained in basic carpentry and knows what he is doing when it comes to construction.

Amos is twenty-eight, and, like Jonathan and Eddie, his situation is typical for Inuit men his age. He dropped out of school once he completed grade 8, but he realized, after some years on social assistance, that he had no hope of securing decent employment in town unless he improved his education. He enrolled in the adult education classes offered in Ulukhaktok through the Arctic College and managed to gain a grade 10 equivalency. Arctic College is administered out of Inuvik and exists as a double-wide trailer adjacent to the school, managed by a white southerner. Amos's objective was to do just enough to qualify for a job with the Housing Corporation as a housing maintainer. He was originally hired on as an apprentice in the early 1990s and has spent his time between working for wages in Ulukhaktok and attending six-week training sessions in Fort Smith, a town in the southern NWT. Each of these training sessions focuses on a different skill set he needs: carpentry, plumbing, electrical, heating systems. He has one more session to go, and he is flying out in two weeks. Hence his urgency at getting down to close the cabin for the summer.

Despite the decent salary – in 1997 he is earning $40,000 a year – Amos still finds it a financial strain. When he is at training sessions, he is not paid, so his wife and four children struggle to make ends meet. He also has to deal with his and his wife's parents questioning his priorities. Both constantly remind Amos that he should hunt more, that he should not be thinking so much about work and should instead be thinking about fishing and hunting. He did manage to take an occasional muskox, and he spent considerable time fishing during the spring. But his work obligations keep him in town during the week, limiting his opportunities for hunting to the weekends.

One reason he continues to use his current snowmobile s because he simply can't afford another. In 1993, he and his wife made the choice to leave public housing and purchase their own house. They did so because the Housing Corporation had reworked the rent scale on public housing, and he was paying a very high rent on his unit. A new housing program, Access, promised to lower his monthly payments from $1,600 to $800, with the added bonus that he would own the house. It sounded great, and Amos saved a fair bit on money by doing some of the work on the house himself, including almost all the interior finish work. But then he discovered the pesky problem of utilities. In public housing, he paid very little for electricity and nothing for water, sewage, or heating fuel. Now during the winter he'll easily spend $400 a month on heating fuel, and electric bills can be a further $200. Together with water, sewage, and trash, that's almost what he would pay on the house to NTHC. Utilities and Housing payments together eat 45 per cent of his monthly salary, leaving the rest for food, which is barely enough, given the high costs of groceries at the Northern and Co-op. His father earns roughly the same income through trapping, guiding sports hunters, and collecting his old age pension, but lives in public housing for minimal cost and pays little or nothing in the way of utilities.

Amos doesn't complain about his situation as we sit and drink tea in the doorway of the cabin. The cabin is only three years old, built from the leftovers of his Access Program house, and well equipped with a stove, gas heater, and cooking utensils. The view back toward Ulukhaktok and the prominent bluff that provides the settlement with its name is striking. The sun is low on the horizon. Amos is thinking about equipment. The snowmobile is four years old, really just about finished. In addition to the pistons, he's worried about the track (an $800 replacement), and he is not sure it will make it through another winter. With the house payments and the payments to the Co-op for his ATV, purchased last year, he cannot afford a new machine. But he won't need the snowmobile until next October, at Fish Lake time, so he is not going to think about it yet. I ask him how he manages.

"My generation, it's like being in the middle, and we've just got to ride it out. Like, when I was a kid, there wasn't really too much to worry about. I liked to be with friends, do things with them, biking around, sliding around, playing out. You didn't have nothing to worry about, plain and simple, except for your own safety. Even school – you didn't worry about school."

"What about today?"

"Life for kids today is more like what the rest of the world is going through. We're going through, what's it called, colonialism? 'Cause when I was a kid, this community was just getting started, and we mostly lived like we did long ago, and we were just starting to get into it. And right now my kids are living like the rest of the world is living like, so it's a big difference. We're all living the colonial life now. They're going to school so they can become doctors or mechanics or whatever."

"But you're in the middle?"

"I think so. My generation kind of has to do both. Some guys just never got it, still don't get it. It's different now. I hope to continue raising my kids, continue working, keep on going. Someday in the future I'm going to get a boat, so then I'll have everything. That's going to be the biggest thing. I'll have a Honda, a Ski-doo, and the boat and kicker. That will be the biggest thing."

Amos pauses. "Except that damn Ski-doo is broken now."

We laugh, look at our empty tea mugs, and set about cleaning out the cabin, loading some food, some of the dishes, pots, pans, and the sleeping bags into my sled.

BECOMING A PERSON

A central theme emerging from the interviews, and from life in Ulukhaktok, is that there is a tension between being physically old enough to be recognized as an adult – inirniq, a fully developed body – and being recognized as a real person. Over the years, this tension has emerged in various ways and in various settings. It ranges from parents admonishing their children to play less hockey and hunt more (because one could get hurt "doing nothing" while playing hockey) to declarations that some parents simply spoil their children so that they never grow up.

And, certainly, Jonathan and Eddie's experience at Fish Lake – too much higaaq, too few fish – suggests a kind of dissonance between the two stages. Perhaps Jonathan and Eddie, and maybe even Amos, are indicative of a significant cultural change to the structure of the life course. The experience of formal education and the transmission of southern cultural values, the lack of any realistic possibility for a career based on wage labour employment, and the inability of many young men to acquire rudimentary skills as hunters and trappers all point to young adulthood, the period from age twenty to thirty-five, as a kind of prolonged adolescence, a period in which young men "experiment" with different combinations of cash generation and subsistence, struggle with the demands and lures of each, and find their way to adulthood, albeit much later than their own parents and grandparents did.

John's interview, however, suggests something quite different is going on, something more difficult to tease out in the context of a settlement in which nearly everyone speaks English, increasingly as a first language, and in which the milestones are changing. One woman suggested to me that one became an adult when one started "serving on committees," which seems silly at first glance but fits. Sitting on a committee, such as the Hunters and Trappers Committee, is a social responsibility. Being involved in governance is a demonstration of one's social maturity, willingness to serve, and dedication to community.

Despite these changes in language and shifting milestones, and the appearance of contemporary young adulthood as a kind of prolonged adolescence, the statements made by Mark, John, and even Amos suggest there is a trajectory for becoming fully socially adult, one that plays out over several decades. Amos certainly seemed to think that he would be set up with the entire toolkit, ready to fully participate as a hunter and wage earner, by the time he was in his late thirties.

Charlie Hanayi is an excellent example of one such trajectory. When I first met him in 1992, he was a twenty-four-year-old bachelor. He had been employed part-time at the Northern Store for several years and had recently been promoted to a full-time position as the store's assistant manager – the highest position available at the Northern for an Inuk. Nevertheless, despite the promotion, the pay was still poor, and Charlie estimated that he would earn only $20,000 for the year. At the time he was focused almost entirely on his job, although the money he made from it was invested in several ways. Some of the money went into equipment – over a twelve-month period he bought four snowmobiles from people in town, and he also purchased a boat and kicker. He spent additional money on hockey equipment and was an avid player at the arena. His remaining money was spent on marijuana, which he enjoyed periodically.

At the time Charlie was not using the equipment for hunting. The snow machines he purchased were all in various stages of decrepitude, and he was quite open about his reasons for purchasing them. He bought them to repair them (and so spent a good chunk of his income on the purchase of snowmobile parts) with the thought of possibly re-selling them at a profit. In reality, these machines ended up being borrowed by his siblings, who neither paid him money for the machines nor returned them for his own use. Charlie had a remarkably easygoing nature, and he admitted that he enjoyed learning how to repair and maintain snow machines. For this reason, he was – if one was willing to walk the rounds – generally an easy person to find in the evenings, which he spent either at his uncle's learning how to repair snow machines (his uncle worked as the hamlet mechanic), at the hockey arena playing hockey, or, in the summer, fishing with a rod and reel at any of the locally accessible lakes.

At the time Charlie was a sporadic and unproductive hunter, and one might be tempted to think his hunting activities were entirely recreational. In the summertime, he spent most of his free time out on the land fishing with a rod and reel, while during the winter he rarely left town. In the fall, he shot a few rabbits during one afternoon's drive, and he made two day trips for muskoxen. His big activity for the year was a one-week trip to camp at Fish Lake, where he essentially checked nets for some of his relatives. Upon his return from that trip, he remarked that checking nets was hard work but he enjoyed his time there. He returned with fifty fish, and, typical for a man his age, nearly all of them went to his parents. The same was true of virtually all the country food he took that year: most of it went to his parents, and he kept very little for himself.

Also typical of a bachelor of his age, he took almost all of his meals at his parents' house. His own apartment (he lived in a fourplex public housing unit) was used primarily as a place to smoke marijuana and sleep. This changed somewhat after his girlfriend moved in with him late in 1992, but the two of them and their young daughter (then six months old), continued to take meals with either his parents or in-laws; they spent little time at their own apartment.

When asked specifically about hunting, Charlie was adamant that it was simply a matter of motivation. Many members of his own cohort would never amount to anything, he said, because they would never be able to learn the important knowledge with the elders aging and passing away. He said that too many of his generation enjoyed living in town too much, and at their age they would be unable to change their ways and make a decided commitment to being a productive hunter.

By 1997, Charlie had changed jobs several times, but always with an eye toward improving his salary. He had settled on a position with the Housing Corporation as a housing maintainer. The position was similar to Amos's, a job that required significant training and licensing, and over the next two or three years Charlie could be expected to spend several six-week periods attending training courses in Fort Smith. He was bracing for the hardship of attending those courses: while he was training he would receive no pay, and he worried about his girlfriend's ability to meet the rent and pay for groceries. Nevertheless, he was committed and acknowledged that this route was the best way for getting everything he needed. At the time, Charlie noted that he still was not yet an adult but he was "getting there." He and his girlfriend had a second child, and they were planning on getting their own house. Indeed, it had arrived on the annual barge that summer, and they were waiting for it to be finished by the contractors. With his new job, Charlie said, rent on his public housing unit was astronomically high, and it would be far more cost efficient to take out a mortgage and own his own house through the Access Program. He was happy with this arrangement, because he felt his house was in a good spot: it had a good view across Queen's Bay and was also close to his parents' house.

Despite these arrangements, Charlie and his girlfriend, Susie, were not always on the best of terms, and in any given week she might be staying with her parents because of some disagreement. Nevertheless, they were intent on marrying and were hoping to set a date sometime in the spring of 1998, when the hamlet vacation travel allowance (VTA) would provide a large chunk of cash to cover the costs of a brief honeymoon. Charlie was well aware of the advantages of the VTA paid annually to full-time employees at the hamlet. Such a payment, a large sum of money based on the size of the family, allowed for the purchase of big-ticket items such as snowmobiles, boats and motors, and household goods.

It appeared that Charlie had not changed otherwise, except that he was very conscious of his commitment to employment and career at the expense of hunting. He continued to be a very busy person, even if no one knew where he was. He continued to take meals with his parents or in-laws, and much of the produce of his hunting (fish, ducks, and several muskoxen during the year) went to his parents' house. His parents, in poor health in 1992, continued to be in poor health in 1997, and his father was recently diagnosed with Parkinson's disease. Although the medication helped, it prevented him from doing anything associated with hunting or travelling.

Also at this time, Charlie was becoming more active in community life. During the next year, he would sit on the Hamlet Council, the Hunters and Trappers Committee, and the Holman Community Corporation.

By 2001, Charlie has seemingly settled into an adult pattern. He had risen quickly through the ranks at Housing Corporation and was now the foreman. The position was a mixed blessing as far as he was concerned: the salary was marvellous, but the responsibilities that went with it were great. He was responsible for supervising his peers, report-ing to his superiors at the hamlet, and dealing with community issues. Rarely did a weekend go by without someone calling him for emer-gency repairs on a furnace or stove. Even private homeowners – and by 2001 there were forty private units in the community – would call him in an emergency even though he was not obligated to perform such work and was not in private business himself.

The biggest issue in the community in 2001 was the imposition of the new firearms restrictions placed on community members. People like Charlie were required to have a Firearms Acquisition Certificate (FAC) not only for the purchase of a firearm but also for the purchase of ammunition. Since Charlie, like most young Inuit, had neglected to acquire the appropriate licence, he could not legally purchase ammu-nition and was dependent upon his mother, Alice, to do it for him. Alice acquired a licence right away by claiming an exemption as a sub-sistence hunter.

Charlie's biggest complaint was that his job responsibilities kept him from hunting and fishing as much as he would like. By this time he had acquired, at age thirty-four, nearly all of the equipment and material characteristic of a dedicated hunter. The land around his house showed it: several old snow machines were piled on top of each other, he had built two shacks for storing his travelling gear, and he had built several structures dedicated to drying fish and muskox meat. Two food boxes sat on his cold porch; most of his food stayed at his house, now distrib-uted directly to people in town rather than indirectly through his par-ents, as before. And, indeed, during my fieldwork in 2001, Charlie was so conscientious as a provider that he made sure I had plenty of meat and fish during my stay, stopping by every few days with enough meat for a few meals. Nevertheless, he noted that the costs of his housing mortgage ($1,200 per month) and the cost of raising two children kept his effective income quite tight, and it was difficult to scrape together money to keep the ATV and the snowmobile filled with gasoline. In August of that year, he was distraught that his job would prevent him from taking the two weeks necessary to travel to Prince Albert Sound to hunt caribou.

By 2007, fifteen years after I first met him, Charlie was hardly recognizable as the hockey addict who tore down machines for fun. He was still the foreman and had been for nearly eight years, a long time and a testament to his demeanour and political abilities. Most in that position end up quitting after a few years because of the stress involved in bossing people around and the resentment generated because of it. Charlie was still as busy as ever, but fully committed as a hunter within the confines of his job. As the oldest son in his family, he was the primary provider for his own household and those of his parents and his two siblings. One brother did not hunt at all, and neither did a brother-in-law, so both depended largely on Charlie's production for country food. He also supplemented the larder of his father-in-law who, though still active, was slowing down and could not keep up with his own children's needs for country food. During 2007, Charlie was far and away the most productive hunter in his age group, going out nearly every weekend to fish or hunt muskoxen, and using his limited vacation time for several summer caribou hunting trips into Prince Albert Sound.

Consequently, Charlie was home late in the evenings, usually completing paperwork from the day's work, the television turned on to a late hockey game, his wife sleeping on the sofa beside him, wrapped in a blanket. The work kept him busy, but it paid his considerable bills. The hunting, tiring as it was, was a big relief for him, especially as he was now training his youngest daughter to travel on the land, since his son, already a teenager, was spending more time with Charlie's father-in-law. During a conversation one evening, Charlie reflected on where he was, and echoed words from ten years previously, when I asked him what it was like, looking back over a decade, whether it was good to be a real person:

"I hope so. There's good and bad things. The good thing is I have some direction in my life, and I realize what I want and how to go about doing it and how to achieve it. And what *it* is. For everybody it's different. I guess there's no more wondering about who I am going to be with tomorrow. Or, I guess things are more stable, seeing your family, raising a family, passing on knowledge to your kids, and being with them as they grow up."

7

Expensive Women and Unbalanced Lives

BABIES

It is late November, and I am once again sitting on Isaac's sofa. We are drinking tea and watching television. Normally, I would see Isaac at the end of the evening; my usual schedule is to go out to collect my interviews, and stop to see Isaac later, perhaps around midnight. But I have not seen him for several days, and I am a bit ahead on my interviewing. Tonight is a night off from waving around harvest forms.

Isaac's two oldest children are out and about: Ronald, his son, is playing out this evening with some other boys; I am unsure where Amy, now ten, is. Isaac's youngest daughter is a mere eight months old, a baby that he and Ida adopted only a month ago, the child of one of Ida's nieces. She is a happy baby, with a pleasant demeanor. While Isaac and I watch television, she is completely occupied by a pair of socks. He is happy to keep her, and he periodically smiles at her and lapses into baby talk. "Hi, there, Kate! What's up? A-buh. A-buh. Ah?" He sticks his lower jaw out slightly as he makes these utterances, shaking and nodding his head. But this is the extent of his involvement with her.

Ida is out for the evening, visiting one of Isaac's sisters. The weather tonight is unpleasant, blowing snow. It is not quite a blizzard but windy enough for the stronger gusts to shake the house. Because it is uncomfortable to be outside walking, Ida has taken the snowmobile. It has been an unusual autumn. The settlement has been covered in snow since mid-September.

Isaac and I are on our second cup of tea, and the only conversation has been Isaac's baby-babbling at Kate. I am used to the silence. When I arrived this evening, Isaac and Ida greeted my arrival with concern and some guilt: Where had I been? I had not been over in so long, was something wrong? But once Ida left, the conversation stopped. When I first arrived in Ulukhaktok, sitting quietly for long stretches without talking made me very uncomfortable, but I have adapted to it, coming to understand that sociality does not necessarily mean constant talking. We watch the television in a silence broken periodically by the sounds of sipping hot tea – until Kate rips one into her diaper. It is a real bun-flapper, impossible to ignore. The colourless mushroom cloud follows, billowing throughout the room, the smell of toxic diaper. I pull the collar of my shirt over my nose to try to avoid the smell. It does not work. Isaac, though, does not acknowledge it. He hardly moves, his face impassive.

At this point I am still single, and I have never changed a diaper. But I am quite sure that this one is a mess, and I think that the longer Kate sits in it, the worse it will become. Isaac ignores it, even as the smell intensifies. My anthropological curiosity is piqued. How long will it be before he cracks?

A full ten minutes later, Isaac stirs. "Gee, that kid really stinks," he says, seemingly to himself. He rises from the sofa and walks toward her. Finally. Kate sees him coming, and she rocks slightly, smiling. She thinks he is going to pick her up. Isaac ignores her and reaches for the telephone right above her. He dials. Silence, then a muffled voice on the other end.

"Ida there?" More silence from the other end. The Other End is presumably calling Ida to the phone.

"You gotta come change this kid. She really stinks." Isaac hangs up, and he returns to the sofa. Kate wiggles her bottom around on the rug. I wonder if the diaper is leaking yet.

A few minutes later, I hear a snow machine approaching, the engine coming to a dead stop outside the window. Heavy steps on the stairs, followed by the creaking of the porch door, which rattles in the wind. The front door opens. Ida appears, kicking off her Pac boots and unzipping her parka. Kate smiles when she sees her. Ida sweeps her up and marches her to a back room. Five minutes later, Ida is back, and she plops Kate down on the rug, freshly cleaned. Kate discovers a pair of socks to play with. Ida is clearly angry with her husband, called away from a social visit to change a diaper. In silence, she puts her boots back on, zips up her parka, and turns to go – but not before a withering statement: "Gee. You could have called Amy. She's just across the street at Granny and Grandpa's."

I am not sure whether I should be appalled that Isaac could not bring himself to change a diaper or if I should admire him. Upon reflection, though, Isaac was not actively avoiding baby care. It just never occurred to him to do it. There is no New Age fatherhood in Ulukhaktok, at least not in the sense that men and women evenly split the household tasks or that men routinely take care of small children. This is not to say that men are isolated from children. On numerous occasions I have had the pleasure of witnessing normally stoic, quiet, and reserved men reduced to idiocy in the presence of toddlers, *ah-buh*ing, holding small hands and clapping them together, tickling, playing peek-a-boo, and threatening to sniff hiutiks. Sniffing hiutiks was Isaac's favourite game with Kate, who very quickly learned to cover her ears with her hands, giggling madly.

Some four years later, in 1997, I sat with Elizabeth Qulliq, who had agreed to work as an interpreter for my research on the Inuit life course. Although most of my informants could speak English quite well, we felt that it would be useful to have an interpreter present for those who wanted to shift between English and Inuinnaqtun. Elizabeth had also worked for a time as the community health worker, the liaison between the nurses and the community, her primary responsibilities arranging home visits with elders and interpreting at the health centre. Given that she would be working with Maya and me on the interviews, we felt it was important that she also be interviewed herself.

I told Elizabeth I thought we should generate a list of terms that people used to describe the life course. "It would help me if I had some idea of what kinds of terms people here use to talk about different phases of life. I don't know if it is better to start where you consider yourself to be, or if we should start at the beginning." I would have preferred to try to generate the terminology myself, but my attempts at using card sorts to generate life stages had ended in complete failure.

"I'd rather start at the beginning." Elizabeth is very comfortable. Most of my informants, I would find, were less comfortable with the age interview, because I asked for information that few of them actively thought about. Elizabeth, though, is quite sure that she is the expert in this domain.

"Okay, then. So, when a kid is born, what do people call that?"

"*Mirraq.* Even sometimes *ilumiutaq*, which means 'fetus.' Mirraq means 'baby.'"

"How long would you call somebody mirraq?"

"We would call them that for probably about six months."

"And when they stop being mirraq, then what do they become?"

"They become *nutaraq*. But there are so many terms based on what the child can do. We have *kakpangulihaq*, when it has just started crawling, for example."

"So they are all descriptive?" I'm trying to tease out what are general terms for a particular life stage, and what are just descriptions of abilities or physical milestones. I also sense that Elizabeth wants to show off her knowledge, to demonstrate her mastery of Inuinnaqtun.

"Uh-huh. Since I work with children, I have learned a lot of these terms, and there are quite a bit. It is a good thing you are asking me these things. You should make sure to ask other women, too. Men won't be so good at this, because they are incapable of taking care of children."

I was not entirely surprised to hear this, but it was a shock to hear her say it so baldly, to assert that men were genetically deficient when it came to childcare. I was especially uncomfortable given that Maya and I were in Ulukhaktok with our (then) infant daughter, and I was doing my share of the child-care duties, taking my turn to change Sarah's diaper, run her bath, and shove vegetable paste into the moving target of her mouth. Although Maya had, with help, made an *amaun*, a parka specifically for packing a baby, my own travelling parka was large enough that I could, and did, pack Sarah without too much difficulty.

To help ease the transition to Ulukhaktok, Maya was getting out and around town as much as she could, going visiting herself and taking

Sarah with her, or going out to organized sewing nights. Plenty of women brought their babies with them, but Maya did not have an extra set of relatives to help care for Sarah, and she was a rank beginner when it came to sewing skins. So, I kept Sarah with me, reflecting upon the very "Inuit male" nature of the activity: home alone, watching a baby play with a pair of socks while one's spouse was out doing something else for the evening. It was a common experience on my evening rounds of visiting, drinking tea, and watching television with Joseph, Amos, or Edward, a sleeping baby or toddler crashed out on the floor on a foam mattress. The only difference for me was that I was not watching television at my house. Because I wanted to try and get some work done, though, Maya and I agreed that at nine I would go to drop Sarah off at the community hall; then I could go out and get an interview or two that evening. On occasion, Maya would take Sarah with her, and I would arrive later to pick her up and take her away.

My first night up at the community hall was a memorable one. I marched into the hall, a lone male in a hall full of women. I was ignored at first, until some of the women realized that I was packing an eight-month-old baby, at which point there were a few catcalls and whistles, and one audible, telling statement: "Wow. I didn't know you could train them to do that!" The women seemed to feel that Maya had scored a point, though a dubious one. Some of the women were concerned about my ability to pack Sarah properly. There are some (however miniscule) risks to packing a baby in a heavy parka. It does get warm back there, and I have been told it is possible to suffocate a child. This is perhaps why many women packing a baby flap their arms up and down like chickens, promoting the circulation of fresh air.

My discomfort at being at the community hall, either to pick Sarah up or drop her off, never quite wore off. There were always comments, though never malicious: "So, you come here to learn to sew?" usually followed by laughter and other remarks.

The community hall is spacious and large, with women spread out over the entire floor, some leaning along the walls as they sew, others sitting on the low stage, scraping skins, preparing to sew them into kamiks. It is a welcome event for many of the women, young and old, a chance to work on their projects and get some relief from constant childcare. Maya quickly discovered that sewing night was about much more than making handicrafts or clothing. It was a clearing-house for gossip and a chance for real conversation with other women.

There is no comparable outlet for men, whose sociality is different. Men are much more reserved, less social. When men travel on the land, they do so either alone or with one or two other men. Sociality in the settlement is fleeting, occurring either in settings that are overtly competitive, as is the case with hockey or basketball games, or in very mechanistic and brief transactions: the transfer of information, parts or equipment, or drugs. Men rarely gather in large groups to work together or engage in conversation. Even at community-wide events such as Christmas, Easter, or Kingalik Jamboree feasts, the men typically sit with their wives and do not engage each other beyond a handshake and a brief hello.

I was self-conscious about going to the hall for or with Sarah at first, but I soon became aware that other men packed their babies too. Eddie Agluaq was among them, and I often saw him departing as I was arriving, a sheepish look on his face at having been teased. Although it was not usual, it appeared to be something some men were willing to do.

Despite Elizabeth's assertion that Inuit men are incapable of childcare, Eddie's packing his young children suggests that the role distinctions, at least in Ulukhaktok, may not be absolutely rigid. Elizabeth might also be focusing more on what the capabilities of men and women are, rather than on what men and women substantively are. I have caught Amos Tuktu coming back from changing the baby's diaper. While Elizabeth could assert that men are incapable of engaging in certain kinds of child care, it is possible for men to be trained, though in reality the "training" may have more to do with the individual's disposition rather than any sense of inherent maleness.

Indeed, Inuit tend to have difficulty with lumping people into broad categories, which I discovered when trying to understand age terminology. When Maya and I pursued age interviews with a larger sample, we were frequently told that we would have to ask each individual what it was like to be old, because each individual's experience is unique. In this sense, the experience of maleness may be recognized as somewhat idiosyncratic too. Men like Isaac generally do not change diapers, but they can and do engage children, based on their individual preferences. Likewise, while the important and defining feature of manhood is hunting and provisioning, women can and do hunt to the degree their interest dictates. Agnes Kaaktuq, for example, favours a 16-gauge shotgun. I can say from watching her shoot that she is highly proficient. The culture values flexibility, resourcefulness, and creativity, which allow different solutions to the problem of masculinity.

It is important here to note that *inummarik* translates as "genuine person," not "genuine man." The process is about becoming a *person*, and there are (potentially) multiple paths to get there. Because men's hunting is a solitary activity, and because men now find it difficult to be on the land until later in life, they may not train their sons in the way they were trained in their own youth. The difference between Ronald and David Kaaktuq seems to be that, though they are the same age, William has made a concerted effort to teach David. David showed interest; and so William took him out to the land, trained him, taught him, and encouraged him. Ronald was never taken to the land in the same way. Isaac was bound for much of the year to work obligations, and his own son not only did not show much interest, he was protected by his mother and actively discouraged. Consequently, Ronald is beginning the process in his young adulthood, and it may be too late to develop the expertise to be anything but a part-time, "boutique" hunter.

There are alternate pathways. One may not be a fully productive hunter and provider but may still attain those ideals through other means – among them, pursuing wage labour and contributing to the financial well-being of the extended family, or engaging in actions that benefit the entire community. Even so, Elizabeth's statements about men and their capabilities hint at a particular problem, namely, how men and women relate to each other in the contemporary settlement.

EXPENSIVE WOMEN

Through the window I can see Simon Iqaluk and Charlie Hanayi out on the Queen's Bay ice, golfing. They have been at it for some time. It is late April and getting close to twenty-four-hour daylight; the sun is still bright several hours after dinner. The two are just hitting balls around, picking spots to aim for, walking to retrieve the ball, then aiming for another target, the bright orange balls easily spotted against the ice and packed snow. Joseph Qalviaq sits next to me on his sofa. We have an eye on the television too, as the Canucks are playing. Joseph is not a real Canucks fan, but it is a hockey game, and it is the playoffs.

As Simon and Charlie bang golf balls around outside, a snow machine periodically drives up to them, stops, then leaves, only to return a few minutes later. I cannot help asking, "So, what's going on with those two?" I am referring to Simon and to Molly, who is driving the machine. I knew that they were periodically going together, but I was never sure what the story was.

"She's one of the reasons that he's been drinking so much lately, and missing work. She's screwing around with his head so much. Simon's getting so sick of having to deal with her that he was thinking about going to Kugluktuk for a while to get away from all the hassles. But he knows that going to Kugluktuk never solves any problems, so he just stays here."

"How's she screwing around with his head?"

"He says that sometimes she wants to shack up, then she doesn't. Plus, she drives his machine around until she breaks it. He was telling me the other day about it. He tells her to stop, but she can't listen."

Joseph's wife, Rose, who is working on a parka at the kitchen table, chips in, "That one is always drinking too. And she likes to go with other men."

We watch the hockey game in silence, occasionally peering out at the ice. After a while, Joseph speaks up. "I went and closed the traps up last Wednesday."

"Did you have anything?"

"I hadn't been out there for a couple of weeks. I had a dead fox in one trap, and another one that was still alive. That one was missing fur on its tail and back legs, so I killed it and left it out on the land. I'm glad I didn't get any good ones, I didn't feel like skinning any of them. I'm tired of the work."

"How did you do for the season?" I am conducting an interview now, even though I do not have the interview form out.

"I got sixty-two foxes this year. I think I made $1,200 from selling them at the Northern and Co-op, and I am going to get another $1,200 as a subsidy payment next fall sometime." Because prices have been low, the government provides a subsidy of $20 for each fur sold, paid out sometime before the beginning of the next trapping season.

Rose chimes in again. "The trapping really helped us out this winter. The money really helped at Christmastime." Joseph probably could have earned more than the $1,200 he made by selling to the Co-op and Northern. DNR offers a service, bagging and tagging furs and shipping them to a fur auction in Winnipeg, where the prices are usually better. Shipping to Winnipeg delays the return on the fur prices, so Joseph sold them for less in Ulukhaktok but in return received cash right away, when he needed it. He and Rose are struggling a bit financially. Most trappers pursue a dual strategy, shipping their best furs to Winnipeg to get the best price, but selling the substandard ones locally to generate immediate cash and also register another fur eligible for the subsidy.

"It really helped pay the Christmas bills," Joseph adds. "But I don't know if I'll do it next year. It's a lot of work. Maybe if prices are good." He has done all the work himself too, just as he promised earlier in the year. Rose may like the income, but she does not like the work involved, or the mess.

Rose is in a good mood. Normally, when I am visiting she is quiet while Joseph and I talk, or she takes the opportunity to go out and visit with her own family. The parka she is working on is an older one she is tailoring so she can pack her youngest. The weather is very good now, nearly perfect for spring ice fishing, and she would like to go. She combs the fur on the sleeves, and notes that it is worn.

"I should buy new fur for these sleeves, they're really old." I am not sure if Rose is talking to me and Joseph, or just thinking out loud. "My sister was over before, and she was telling me that I must be a really expensive woman, always buying things for myself."

I glance at Joseph, who is nodding in silent, perhaps even pained agreement.

"My sister says she wishes she could be an expensive woman, too. But that Roy, he just sits around, doing nothing."

I watch as Molly once again drives away, leaving Simon and Charlie to hit golf balls some more.

There is some cognitive dissonance in Rose's statement about being an expensive woman. She is quite happy to have the extra income from trapping, but only, it seems, because she was relieved of the responsibility of doing the skins. Foxes are, as Joseph has said, a fair bit of work. Setting and running the trapline is itself a significant time commitment, as he made clear during the season. There were times when he had little interest in going to check his line, because work and weather were actively discouraging him. He was running a very short line, too, one that he could check in a few hours' time. Then there is the actual processing of the foxes, which requires skinning them, then stretching and drying them. When he started in the fall, he knew that Rose would not participate, but he persisted and did almost all of the work himself. Rose had grown up doing foxes – her father was, and still is, a very productive and dedicated trapper. But she had no intention of going back to doing them – she knew how much work they were.

Most hunters understand intuitively that trapping foxes is likely to be a break-even proposition, with a chance, perhaps, for a small profit. And there is a correlation, too: short lines are better than longer ones in terms of profit margins. As we continue to watch the game, Joseph explains that the trapping made a profit in the sense that it has helped see them through, easily covering the costs of running the line, mostly gasoline and a few replacement parts for the snowmobile. Even so, the main attraction of the activity seems to be the promise of the subsidy cheque in the fall, a lump payment that may be used for the purchase of more expensive items, such as a new snowmobile. Joseph has the new catalogues sitting on his coffee table already.

Rose is not the only woman in this cohort with the goal of being an "expensive woman." Though men in the settlement cohort feel strong pressure to be hunters and providers of country food, it is not clear to me that women receive equal pressure to be hunters' wives. Committing to a hunting lifestyle requires sacrifices on a woman's part, among them acquiescing to a different material standard of living. Instead of a new television or sofa, money must go toward equipment, gasoline, or replacement parts. The kitchen table may become a temporary workbench, the stove a heat-treating oven, the porch a fur-processing station. Rose's recusal from fur processing aside, it is an equal commitment in time: a woman must commit to the labour and effort of processing meat and skins. Additional resources may go toward setting up an outside structure for use as a shop and storage area. One young woman once explained to me that she never wanted to marry a hunter because he would just take all the money and spend it on equipment. Some young women, it seems, would prefer to have a man who does not hunt but rather works and makes money. Dad can always provide the valued country food, after all. And some women seem to take it one step further: why shack up with a man at all? Sperm donors are easy to find. You can avoid the hassle of having to live with one and still get what you need from your parents and brothers.

Joseph is not the only man in this boat, and he really has it fairly easy. While Rose refuses to do foxes, she is committed to subsistence activities in most other respects. Isaac in his household has similar difficulties, albeit in other, more subtle ways. Ida only eats a limited selection of country foods, namely, the highly valued caribou, char, and ducks. She strongly dislikes most other country foods, which limits what Isaac produces for his household. For a young man thinking about the kinds of economic strategies he wants to pursue, his partner's desires are a significant issue, as he must balance the pressure to hunt against the possibility that his partner has little interest in such activities and may actively discourage them. For men keenly interested in becoming a hunter, finding a partner equally disposed can be a significant problem. It is especially so in a small village where overlapping kinship ties further limit potential partners. These two reasons may account for why Simon Iqaluk remains unmarried well into middle age.

The longer-term consequence of these relationship problems – a good spouse is still hard to find – is that the nature of the seasonal round has changed significantly, especially as it relates to women's engagement with the land. The months in which whole families leave the settlement are quite restricted. Late April and May see families travelling together to go ice fishing, with some groups even staying out to camp overnight. In June, some families leave the settlement to set up camps for duck hunting, though most travel to Mashuyak and stay in cabins. Some go together on expedition hunts for caribou in August. By September, though, family travelling has ended.

The central problem here is that a dichotomy between "settlement" and "land" has emerged. One interesting shift has been covered to some degree in the literature, namely, that the woman's role in the household has been under pressure with the shift from camp life to town life. Before settlement, there was a clear demarcation between men's and women's responsibilities. While the tent or iglu was a shared space, it was one in which the woman had complete control, especially over the *qulliq*, the oil lamp that provided heat and light. Contemporary house designs (as Dawson [1995] argues) have upset that domestic balance. Most houses in Ulukhaktok today are arranged so that the first area one enters is the kitchen, formerly the most protected woman's space in the household. Employing the stove as a heat-treating oven, or using the kitchen table for engine repair, is clearly a violation of that space. Dawson argues that imported house designs, along with other factors, have increased gender asymmetry in the contemporary North.

That said, although the structure of the household has changed with the advent of southern-based housing designs, the settlement has become a kind of domesticated sphere in its own right, a largely feminine domain. The hamlet government is effectively run and managed by women. Currently, no man sits in any position of authority in the settlement: the mayor is a woman, as was the previous mayor, who herself served multiple terms. The senior administrative officer of the settlement for the past five years has been a woman, the second to hold the position. Most of the administrative staff in the hamlet office are women, effectively overseeing the activities of the service drivers, bylaw officers, and municipal workers, and making hiring and firing decisions. At the Northern and Co-op stores, the assistant managers, who serve directly under the managers, are women; the Northern's assistant manager has been in her position for nearly twenty years. In Ulukhaktok the community is effectively run by either outsiders – RCMP officers, nurses, teachers, store managers – or women. Even in the Community Corporation and the hamlet council, women are ably represented and occupy important roles.

Consequently, the settlement itself has become something like the domain of women, who manage their households while they manage their community. Men, especially men in the settlement cohort, view the land as the masculine domain and strive to engage in activities that take them there directly or support the means to get there.

In the spirit of engaging in activities that would get me onto the land, one of the first things I set about to do when Maya and I arrived in 1997 was to acquire some equipment. Although it was February, the coldest month of the year, I knew that the daylight would increase dramatically over the next several months. Come April, spring fishing season would begin in earnest. It would be better to have everything ready far ahead of time. Many Inuit regard the spring fishing season as the best time of the year. By late April, and continuing through May, the sun rapidly moves toward twenty-four-hour daylight. Temperatures are warm enough so that, though it remains below freezing, it is quite pleasant outside, yet there is enough snow cover to make travel by snowmobile relatively easy. Maya still marvels at jigging for lake trout at 2 AM, the sun just above the horizon, while Sarah slept soundly in the tent, warm and comfortable under the blankets.

That fieldwork year was marked by what most southerners would consider difficult living conditions. The house in which we were staying was a clear challenge, and though I helped Amos install a water system, it required constant tinkering. The water tank was an open, sixty-gallon metal tub. Most water tanks in the settlement are closed units constructed of plastic, with an access pipe running through the wall of the house, exposed to the outside. The delivery driver pulls up to the house, climbs a small ladder, and inserts the hose into the pipe, turns on the pump, and shuts if off when water flows from the overflow pipe.

In the mission house, there was no such arrangement. To deliver water to us, the driver was required to back the truck to the house as close as he could, so the hose could reach my tank. He would then drag the hose up the stairs, onto the porch, into the house, and then into the utility room. Then he would go back and turn on the pump and wait for me to holler madly to turn it off. Water deliveries, then, were by special arrangement, with Jack Tigliktuq usually making plans ahead of time with me to stop at the house and deliver water. It was extra work for him, of course, but I think he enjoyed it, at least a little. It was a break from the monotony, and it was a chance to talk with somebody during the day.

We soon fell into a predictable but friendly conversation, talking about the weather and what significant subsistence activities were fast approaching. Jack commented immediately on my purchase of a snow-mobile, a third-hand machine, still in good shape, that I acquired from a teacher. It was important that I get started now on making sure it was in good shape, he said, as the weather would soon be good for travel-ling. He had some repairs to do on his machine too, so that he could go fishing in the spring.

Over the course of the year, though, Jack did not make much prog-ress. He never quite got his machine running for spring fishing, nor for the eagerly anticipated duck season. He never quite got his boat and motor going for caribou season, either. Indeed, he always seemed to need to do *something* to get everything together. There was always a repair that still needed to be made, a part that was on order but had not arrived, an unfortunate event that prevented the work from being done.

I picked up on the seductive problem of talking about what needed to be done but not doing it quickly, so I immediately made a move to con-struct a set of sleds. My first fieldwork had been memorable because of all of the travel on the land, and I hoped to recapture that experience. I wanted to make sure that Maya could have that opportunity too.

I spent several days acquiring materials: pine boards and steel runners from the hamlet for my sled boards, several old pallets for napus (the hardwood of the pallets being lighter and stronger than pine 2 × 4s), chain and line from the Co-op, and some sheet metal (for stabilizing the boards, to prevent splits) from old ductwork, acquired by foraging at the dump.

I had never built my own sleds before (in 1992, Richard built our sleds while I went out and collected data), so I required some help and advice. Stephen Hakagiak had plenty of advice, but also a warning. People built sleds differently in Ulukhaktok now than they did even thirty years ago. Before the advent of the powerful snowmobile, Inuit were very attentive to sled design, because of the scarcity of materials and the lesser power of their machines. The angle of the bow of the sled, the relief at the stern, how the boards themselves were reinforced – all of these elements were important. Joseph Qalviaq, for example, had built his own sleds some five years previously, with minimal input from his father. He constructed them specifically for a very long trip above Minto Inlet, and they were decent enough that his father would borrow them on occasion. They were not perfect. Joseph was well aware, after his father pointed it out, that the bow was cut too sharply, making the sleds difficult to turn.

Joseph never fixed them, figuring they were "good enough," which is the way that most sleds are constructed – "good enough." Sleds are now over-engineered, with quarter-inch plywood and a million nails tacked into the boards to keep them from splitting on a rock. The extra plywood is effective, of course, but it adds considerable weight. With a 550 engine, though, the additional weight becomes moot. In fact, the plywood might be better. With a 550 engine, the driver is not out for a slow Sunday cruise. The plywood becomes necessary to hold the sleds together as they fly through the air and bounce off rocks at high speed, as men hurry home from a hunting trip, to beat bad weather or to catch Don Cherry's latest rant on *Hockey Night in Canada*.

However, just as in 1992, I have a comparatively underpowered machine. Even if I had a more powerful machine, I still would not be travelling fast enough to warrant the over-engineering. So, with that and a dose of Stephen Hakagiak's advice, I sit outside the mission house, materials scattered on the ground, ready to begin. I have already sketched out on the boards the shape I wish to cut, and the saw is ready to go. Unfortunately, the mission house is nearly in the centre of town, and I am outside, looking at a pile of stuff. It is inevitable that I will attract a crowd.

The first one out is Robert Takputtuq, who lives nearly next door. Robert, an elder, is both curious and helpful, and, it seems, intent on providing assistance. And, being older, it is his right to co-opt the work, to show me how to do it. After some pleasantries and a brief discussion of the weather (though a frigid February day, it is sunny and the air is calm), Robert takes the saw and begins making the cut for me. I hold my breath. I wanted to cut the boards in a very specific way, as I was instructed, but Robert ignores my pencil line. He appears to be cutting freehand. It then occurs to me that maybe Robert cannot see the line. He is nearly blind, after all, trying to see through jam-jar glasses scratched beyond belief.

Robert is not the only helper on these sleds. Isaac Kaaktuq provides significant assistance, though we have a disagreement about reinforcing the sled boards. He favours driving six-inch spikes into them to help prevent splitting, not trusting my sheet-metal sheathing. I think I've won that battle, but I turn out to be wrong. I wake up two days later to the sound of Isaac pounding spikes into my sleds. The way he sees it, he's my older brother. He is responsible for me, to make sure I do not make mistakes. He also has a vested interest in the sleds – after all, he expects to inherit them once I depart in November.

Simon and Amos also have advice, some of it counter to my desires. Many, many more are concerned about my ability to construct a decent set of sleds, and the worksite is a regular stop on the way to the Co-op as Inuit check my progress. In the end, the only part of the sleds I actually do myself is the sheet metal sheathing, which I wrap around the boards and tack into place, and the steel runners, which I nail into the boards. I'm also allowed to build a plywood box. Despite all the assistance, the perception is that they are "my" sleds, which I built myself, for better or worse.

In the end, it is difficult to know whether that communal construction was good or bad. The sleds did last the entire fieldwork period, and Isaac later noted that they lasted for several more years without problems. I did learn from the experience, though, that few if any younger men actually built their own sleds. Most young men – men my age – instead depended upon others to supply or build sleds for them. I already knew from previous experience that many younger hunters acquired their sled from other sources, but I was not aware how deeply the aversion to sled construction went.

I first learned the nature of sled construction and "borrowing" from others during my first year of fieldwork. Toward the end of that year, I began to take an interest in sled design and construction. I was curious that so few men actually had their own sleds, so I started to ask about it. Few men would admit to the real reason for not building their own sleds. Most claimed they knew *how* to build sleds, but they just never did it. At the time, I assumed that resources must be the issue, in that they lacked the cash to acquire the materials. Possibly it was their age – why build sleds when an older relative might just "borrow" them? It turned out that it was quite the other way around, that younger men "borrowed" their older brother's or father's sleds.

Charlie Hanayi was the most forthcoming with the explanation. "I built all three sets by myself without any help from anybody, and I made sure that I did them right. But lots of guys ask their dad to build them, because they're too lazy to do it. But there are two other good reasons. One of them is because they don't know how to build them right, and the second reason is tied to the first reason. When the sleds aren't built right, they slide all over the place, and the wife complains about the rough ride. When a man has his dad build the sleds, then he has an excuse. 'Don't look at me, I didn't build these sleds! Go and complain to someone else.'"

PLANNING A TRIP INTO SAFETY CHANNEL

It is late July, close to midnight, and I am sitting in Don Johnson's little kitchen, sipping tea and talking. Don has been here for a good month already. He is running a field school this summer for undergraduate students from Colorado College, and he's secured a duplex normally reserved for schoolteachers. Teachers usually leave Ulukhaktok with their household intact, and they continue to pay their rent while they go south for their summer break. But there will be a nearly complete turnover this year, so, until the new teachers arrive – in two weeks – Don has his own apartment, and the students are packed into a second unit. These duplexes are in good condition, but they are almost completely stripped bare, save for leftover furniture and some kitchen equipment. They are built right along what used to be the airstrip many years ago but is now just a wide road, the settlement's main street. Almost directly across it is the hamlet building; the fire hall is next door, the Health Centre just beyond.

The settlement has been abuzz with excitement, the college students an instant attraction for the teenagers and young men, the older ones in particular showing off for the young women, trying to catch their eye. The makeshift dormitory where the students are staying – a dozen of them in a three-bedroom apartment – is also an important resource at mealtimes. Some of the local teens are helping themselves to the students' food, and the students have no idea how to say no. These hangers-on create an uncomfortable conflict, as the students are already on short and unusual rations. A steady diet of ramen and macaroni and cheese might be suitable for graduate students, but these ones seem to be used to more refined fare. They are, after all, wealthy undergraduate students. More than a few have been reluctant to try native foods, some because of a commitment to vegetarianism, others because of declared food allergies. To help alleviate at least the problem of overcrowding, I have set my tent up behind my duplex, and some of the students have moved into it.

Don pours himself another mug of hot water. "I am thinking about getting another trip together, so that I can get the students out on the land for a bit, to see something beyond the immediate area around town. We're thinking of going farther down into Prince Albert Sound, maybe to Anialik. Would you like to come?" Don clearly would like the company and feels that I, as an anthropologist, would be an asset, a resource for the students. I do not envy his position, though. Organizing an overnight field trip for a group of students is not undertaking I'd want to take on, as I lack the patience. I would not mind tagging along on another trip, however. I already accompanied the field school on a day trip two weeks ago, which was quite successful, especially since I had no responsibilities.

Don is an archaeologist, working on data collection for what will become his PhD thesis, focusing on ethnoarchaeology and the early contact period. He is in his third summer of work here. Like most graduate students, he has been forced to fund his research by hook and crook, and one of the ways he has done so is by arranging to teach this summer field school, which is focused on contemporary culture and the environment. It pays his airfare – a substantial cost – while providing him with a small salary to offset some of his research expenses. Once the month-long field school is over, he will take off for Walker Bay for the month of August, conducting some field surveys. In the meantime, he has managed to use me in my capacity as an academic and slowly drawn me into the school as a kind of free consultant.

I agree to go, but I'm not sure of the details. With a dozen students, any boat trip will require a good deal of coordination. The previous one was a success, but it was a day trip, and we did not go far from the settlement. An overnight trip will require more planning, and, I think, more boats. "Sure, I'd love to go," I say. "I haven't been down as far as Anialik in a long time."

As we begin to discuss some of the details, we hear footsteps on the porch, and Edward Kuniluk comes into the house. His jeans are dirty, and his hands are greasy. "Hi, Pete!" He goes right to the sink to wash his hands. "Been working on that 25 horse, trying to get it going again. Maybe we could use my sixteen-footer as a hauler?" It is a question to Don. "Pete, you could drive it, too." I hope he is not serious.

"What's wrong with the 25 horse?" I ask. It was running fine last month. Edward, I know, had an eighteen-foot boat, and he had just completed work on an older 60 horse motor for it.

"Someone put paint in the gas can, and it got sucked into the carbs. I gotta take the whole thing apart."

"Who would do that?"

"Dunno." Edward says it in a way that suggests he has a pretty good idea who the culprit is. He has indicated that he's had trouble with a rival family intent on causing him both material and spiritual harm. "If I get it going, we could use it." It is a sensible idea, but I think Don is also on a limited budget, so he cannot be extravagant. We are also nearing the end of the field school. He might be running to the end of his funds.

"Let's see about it. I'm going to talk with William tomorrow and see what he thinks."

"Okay," says Edward. "But William is going to be expensive. Always after money, that guy. He's going to want extra gas so that he can go caribou hunting later. You heard about last summer?"

I nod. I have heard the story, though I do not think Don has. Edward continues. "He took a bunch of kids out for youth camp, but he mixed up all the gas with oil. When the kids burned up all the naphtha right away for heating the tent, there was none left they could use. William did that so they couldn't burn the gas, and he could just keep it for boating later." Although Coleman stoves are designed to burn Coleman fuel and its relatives – all called "naphtha" in Ulukhaktok – it is possible to burn regular gasoline in them. Unless, of course, the gasoline is premixed with oil, as many Inuit prefer to do, not trusting the oil injectors in their boat motors.

"But it taught those kids a lesson, though, right?" I did hear that the camp had plenty of naphtha, more than they should have needed for a summer camp.

"Yuh. They did. But William was sure happy he got all that extra gas, too."

Next day Edward is back at my place after lunch, stopping for a cup of coffee and a brief visit to talk about the upcoming trip. We are each smoking a cigar, courtesy of Edward. He continues discussing his recent problems, which he hinted at the night before.

"Remember that old man, Nuyuaqtuyuq?" Edward asks between puffs on the cigar. "He used to live in the old matchbox below the old hotel. I remember one time I had to go check on him because his power bill was so high. He was heating the house with his oven. Had to try to explain to him not to do that." Nuyuaqtuyuq has been dead for a few years now, his house towed out to the dump and used by the fire department for practice. He was originally from somewhere in the East and had been exiled here by the RCMP for unspecified crimes. One RCMP officer, upon looking at the file, suggested Nuyuaqtuyuq was "set up," and the RCMP, rather than send him to prison, sent him to Ulukhaktok. Even when granted the opportunity, Nuyuaqtuyuq never wanted to go back to his home community. I was told that, before his death, he specified that he wanted to be buried here too.

"He was one of the first people I ever met here," I tell Edward. "I went for a walk out to Ukpillik and met this guy, old and all hunched over, walking back from the lake. He had a fishing spear, a *kakivak*, on his packsack. He started talking at me and pointing, and I had no idea what he was saying. I remember thinking to myself, 'This might be a long year.'"

Edward smiles. "Toward the end no one knew what he was saying. He was really old, that guy. Already talking to the spirits – he was halfway there anyways."

We puff on our cigars. Edward continues. "He wanted to apprentice me as an angatkuq when I was ten or eleven. My dad said it was okay."

"Did you go?" I never knew this about Edward.

"No. I didn't want to go, so I didn't. But that old man sure had power all right. One time I was bringing him some seal meat, and he was waiting for me at the door, and he had a new harpoon head for me. How did he know I broke mine when I was getting that seal? And one time I went with my cousin from Fish Lake down Kuujjua to go to Minto. We went the direct way, cutting across, but that old man was already there ahead of us."

"Did he leave after you, from the same place?"

"Yuh. I figure he could fly when he wanted to."

"Were there any other people like him?" I know the answer to this already – quite a few people in recent memory, now deceased, were known angatkut.

"Oh yeah, and some of them are still hurting people every day, even if they're dead. I get sharp pains, like needles, that I feel in my arms and in my back, like someone is trying to hurt me. But my grandpa says that I don't have to worry, he's protecting me."

The conversation ends when we spot Don heading to William's house. Don is planning the trip this morning. Edward drains his coffee. "Got to work on that motor. Lucky the paint never got sucked into the pistons." He slides into his runners, zips up his windbreaker, and heads out.

I clean up and go out too, thinking to get to the store and see about the mail. I meet Don leaving William's house just as I am passing by. "I think I have everything lined up so that we can make our trip, maybe in a few days," he says happily. "I've got four drivers and boats lined up, so all I need to do is buy the gas and get some supplies, and we should be good. Are you going to bring your tent? That would help."

"My tent is good to go. But do you think four boats will be enough?" My sense is that, with equipment included, we will be overloaded. I also know something that, maybe, Don does not know. If William is driving, he is not the only one likely to be going along in his boat. We will have more than a dozen students, drivers, and instructors on this trip. We have not accounted for associated relatives who will be going, too.

"William said he thought it was good enough."

I leave it at that, but I am a bit nervous about it. Richard Condon died in a boating accident under similar conditions. I am trying to figure out how I can decline to go. I would rather not be in an over-loaded boat. I leave Don at his place and continue my walk to the store. I do not get very far, however, when an AT V pulls up alongside me. It is Shirley Aquti, Albert's wife. She pulls off her helmet. "I heard that Don's only going to take those students in four boats. I don't think that's very safe."

That was pretty quick, I think to myself, maybe five minutes for the news to spread around. "He says William said it was good enough to take four boats." I am wondering if William might have been stalling. I am also wondering if Agnes was on the phone before Don even left the house. Something similar happened to me some years ago, when William offered to lend me a machine to fetch my broken-down Ski-doo, which I had left on the land. He directed me to use one that was parked a kilometre away, which gave Agnes plenty of time to roust Isaac off the couch to accompany me.

"Eddie could drive," Shirley says, referring to Eddie Agluaq, her cousin. "Eddie's boat is good, he's got a new motor on it. That's too many people for four boats, and all that gear, too. It could get scary."

"I agree. Do you want me to tell Eddie?"

"No. I'll go talk to Bessie." Bessie is Eddie's wife. Shirley puts her helmet back on and drives off. It occurs to me that my role here was only as a source of information for the researcher. I have the same con-versation with Elizabeth Qulliq not ten minutes later outside of the Northern Store. It seems as if a decision has been made. The women are organizing the trip for Don. He may be nominally in charge, but he really does not stand a chance.

On my way back from the Co-op, an hour later, Eddie Agluaq comes out of Don's duplex and hops on his AT V. I watch as he circles around the duplex and heads up the road – not to his house but the gas station. He has four gas cans in a homemade AT V trailer.

Don motions from his window, so I go inside. There is hot water waiting for tea.

"I think I am going to go with five boats, not four," he tells me. "I just hired Eddie to drive and gave him some money to buy gas. William said that four boats was good enough, but I think five might be safer." It sounds like it's Don's idea, but really it's a decision that was made collectively and organized by the women. Eddie was almost certainly sent to see Don to offer his services and to do so in such a way that Don could not refuse.

It turns out to be a good idea to have the additional boat. The drivers are widely scattered in age: besides Eddie, William, and Edward, Simon Iqaluk and Paul Tigliktuq are also driving, and none of them is going alone. Simon has his sister's two teenage sons with him. Edward has his two younger brothers. William is accompanied by Agnes and their granddaughter, Helen. People do not travel alone if they can help it, though there is an interesting pattern here. The old men, Paul and William, travel with their wives – the customary pattern, it seems, for the older generation. Husbands and wives travel together on the land when they can. Agnes, for example, goes to Fish Lake with William in autumn and accompanies him on caribou hunting trips during the summer. The only time William goes travelling on the land without her is for day trips for muskoxen, or when he is hauling materials and supplies to a camp. They complement each other; they both draw pleasure from being on the land, and they each see their individual contributions as necessary for comfortable and proper living. And for Agnes, being on the land is like being at home, much more than the house she lives in is home. Like William, she grew up there, not in the settlement.

For the younger men, however, the land and travelling on it seem to be an exclusively masculine domain. The younger drivers are travelling with cousins, brothers, or nephews – not wives and girlfriends. The reasons may be as practical as they are philosophical. Edward's three kids are grade-school age or younger. Were his wife to come, the kids would too, and Edward would no longer be hauling students and their equipment. Even so, generally when men like Edward or Eddie travel, their wives remain in town.

For the younger men, travelling on the land appears to be an activity designed for production, for male bonding, for teaching their junior kin about the land, and for healing. In my experience, the "family trip on the land" for men of my cohort and younger appears to occur during the spring, in ice-fishing season, where trips are rarely of the overnight variety. The summer caribou expedition hunt is another occasion, when a family may go by boat into Prince Albert Sound, camp for a week, and perhaps take a few caribou. But young men and their wives are not inseparable partners on the land in the way that Agnes and William are. The preference may be mutual: women may lack the interest. After all, it *is* bumpy on the sleds.

However, while there may be practical reasons for leaving the wife behind, or gendered reasons why the younger men do not travel with their wives, the corollary is that it takes longer these days for children to be exposed to the land. Camping close to town during duck season or spending a week at Kuuk in summer is minimal exposure, and seasonal. Unless a man is willing to make a concerted effort to take his sons out when they are very young, they may not be immersed in the land until their teenage years or later. Summer youth camps, where a large number of teenagers spend a week supervised by someone like William, cannot take their place. It is telling that Edward is taking with him his two younger brothers – both in their late twenties – and not his two sons.

I have decided to stick with William. He is the oldest, most experienced driver, and the boat is comfortably loaded and properly trimmed. There are six of us in the boat and, because it is flat calm, we aren't pounding the heck out of our behinds and lower backs. Even so, the two students in the boat are learning the hard way that sitting in the stern is poor choice. Though the water is calm, they are still being hit with some spray, too far back for the windshield to provide protection. Even though it is summer, we are all in winter clothing – insulated waders, travelling parkas, wind pants, and, at least for me, long underwear. It is cold on the water.

We have been in the boat for some time, well into Safety Channel, the water mostly calm, when Agnes turns to me. "I used to live there, when I was young," she tells me. "My parents used to stay there long ago. I grew up around here." Though she is quite proficient in English, she rarely speaks it. She looks at William, who turns slightly to speak to me.

"That's where I met her the first time." They are both talking loudly so they can be heard over the sound of the motor, but still I think I am the only one who can hear them.

While William tells me the details of meeting Agnes, she leans over to the grub box and pulls out the thermos. She carefully pours the tea, already sweetened with sugar. William takes the tea in hand, though Agnes doesn't quite remove hers. For a moment, their hands touch, gently, and their eyes briefly meet. They are both recalling the moment, so long ago and fleeting, but equally etched in the basalt that walls the little bay. The land is like that, not merely a geographic location but a storage locker of experience and memory. William begins humming a tune I cannot quite make out, perhaps "Come Thou Font of Every Blessing." Agnes returns the thermos to the box, and the cliffs slowly glide by. The students in the stern have no clue, hearing none of the conversation, though one of them later confides to me that William and Agnes make a handsome couple. Which is true.

A LIFE OUT OF BALANCE

It is the first of October, and I have settled into the routine of living in the little cabin much better than I expected. The daily high temperatures have dropped below freezing, but the cabin retains its heat at night even in the stiff wind we've had for the past few days. It might be a bit chilly in the morning – my thermometer registered nine degrees when I got up – but it heats up quickly when I light the Coleman stove to make coffee, supplemented by a bowl of oatmeal. I am into my second cup when I hear an ATV drive up and stop just outside. Amos Tuktu knocks and enters. He knows I am awake just by the steady hiss of my stove, which is still running.

"I didn't know if you were up yet or not." It is just after nine o'clock. Although school and work have started, there's no reason for me to be really going yet. Amos, who makes his living these days doing odd jobs, is on his own time. He will head over to one of the public houses after seeing me, to finish painting the interior for Housing. "I got your buckets."

I pour a coffee for him as he goes back out to his ATV, which is towing a trailer. Though there is some snow on the ground now, he is still using the ATV. It is not yet too cold to run it, and it is far better on gas than the snowmobile. Last night Amos took two of my water pails to fill them up for me. I could do it myself – there are at least four people within walking distance who would let me fill up, but Amos insisted that he do it, properly noting that water directly from the lake was far better than the treated water in the tanks.

He sets the five-gallon pails down on my floor, sliding one underneath the table where I work and using the other one for a chair. "You heard about last night?"

"No. What happened?" Amos is normally not one to gossip, so it must be serious. I wonder if somebody died.

"The cops went down and picked up Edward last night for beating up Sarah. Guess she went to the store yesterday before it closed, went to spend the SA money on groceries, and she had a pretty good black eye. My wife saw it. He must've hit her early in the morning or around lunchtime. Someone went to the RCMP, and then they came and picked up Edward. It was around suppertime it happened."

The last time I saw Edward was two days ago. "Where's he now?"

"Still in the clink, I heard. But his Honda's at his mum's, so maybe he's there now."

"But maybe one of his brothers took the Honda. What's going to happen now?"

"Nauna. I hear that Sarah and the kids are going to go to Inuvik tomorrow, to the safe house."

"But Sarah's from Kugluktuk. Why doesn't she go back there?" There are a handful of women from Kugluktuk who have married men from Ulukhaktok, Sarah being one of them. It is very common for these women to periodically go back to Kugluktuk to see kin and maybe get out of the Ulukhaktok fishbowl for a bit. And, when marriages are in trouble, of course, it is an important safety valve. Except, apparently, for Sarah.

"She won't go back there. Elsie says that she won't go back because her family treats her worse than Edward does."

I wonder, too, whether there was some pressure from social services to have Sarah go to Inuvik, to check on the children. Their oldest is now in her teens, but they have two still in grade school, and there is the baby, now a toddler, to think about.

"They were supposed to be getting Anguhuqtuq's old house. Genius" – Amos is referring to the Housing liaison, the sarcasm dripping from his voice – "seemed to think that Edward's needed a bigger place than the one they were in, with four kids and only three bedrooms. But he's $4,000 in arrears to Housing, so I can't figure that one out."

All summer Edward was threatened with eviction for being so far behind on his rent, the result of a massive spike in his income for working as a polar bear guide. The case even went to the courts in August, and the rumour was that they were *really* going to be evicted this time. My understanding was that the entire crew would have to move in with Edward's mother, who lives alone in a larger unit. But that never happened, and there seems to be a rule, or even a law, that Housing cannot evict a tenant from their unit once summer is over, because it is too cold. I do not understand the ins and outs of that provision. I am aware that individuals who have been convicted of drug dealing are not allowed to stay in public housing, which accounts for two other cabins, like mine, that sit behind public housing units, power cords running to them.

I am not terribly surprised by the news of a fight. When I saw Edward two days ago, he was complaining that Sarah was being really grumpy, that he was visiting me partly to get away from her. Marijuana was rather scarce at the moment, and regular users were suffering accordingly. While people do not get violent or angry when they are smoking up, they get cranky when their supply vanishes. Sarah and Edward had both been smoking up quite a bit in the past few weeks. It seems that this is an annual pattern for them, their relationship relatively calm and stable during the spring and the summer, when the weather is good, Edward is working and hunting, and they are both active. Once the weather starts to turn toward the winter, though, they spiral into increasingly heavy marijuana use, which then spirals into violence. This time Edward is likely to face charges, and he may be sentenced to serve time in Yellowknife Correctional.

As I go around town during the day, the story begins to move and change. By evening, the accepted tale, highly embellished, is that Sarah and Edward got into a fight early in the morning, so violent that Edward knocked her out and left her lying on the floor while he sat and waited for her to recover consciousness. When she stirred, he asked if she was ready for Round 2, and then he began to hit her again. The actual events are likely to never be known, but it was also clear that there was no alcohol involved, which makes the crime that much more severe.

The following day is a plane day, and Sarah and her children are at the airport, off to Inuvik for an unspecified time, booked to stay in a shelter for battered women and children. Edward, who is staying with his mother, arrives to wish them goodbye. It is a tearful parting. Once the plane leaves, Edward simply moves back into his old house.

Two days after the incident, just after supper, Edward knocks on the cabin door and comes in. I make coffee.

"How's it going?" I ask. I'm not sure if Edward will acknowledge his current problem.

"It's going okay." A pause while he sits on the water pail, shifting his weight to get comfortable. He takes off his motorbiking gloves. "Still warm?" He is smiling. I say I'm very comfortable, and he acknowledges the plywood I have installed on the ceiling. It is not tongue and groove cedar, but it looks better than the blue insulation and spray-in foam it now covers.

"I'm almost done with your machine," he says. "Got that track on without too much of a problem. I found the proper sprocket shaft at the dump, and it's all together. All I got left is to fix the headlight, and it should be good to go. But maybe you should think about the shocks – they're kind of stiff."

Edward is really asking for the money for his labour, and I will pay up after we have the coffee. I suspect that he might be prolonging the work in hopes of getting a little more money out of me. I decline the offer of new shocks. I can get by with the machine the way it is now. Besides, there is snow on the ground, enough to travel on the land. People are getting ready to go to Fish Lake. "What you going to do now?" I ask him. It is a question about immediate activities, not about the damn mess Edward's life is right now.

"Some guys are going to play poker later, so I can turn the money into more. You should try it." He knows I do not gamble.

Aha. The reason for the work, and the need for the money, appears. "No, I suck at poker. I could never figure it out." Which is true. Poker has always been popular, games of chance (which is what poker effectively is in Ulukhaktok) having a special place in Inuit hearts. William and other old men tell stories of players losing everything – dog teams, tents, stoves, their entire toolkit – in a single night of gambling, even in a single hand.

"It's not that hard. I always sit and watch for a while, figure out which is the winning seat, and then take that one when I get chance."

We sit in silence for a while longer, until it is time to go. I give Edward his money, he finishes his coffee, and makes his way out, presumably to play poker.

Two things strike me about the assault, the first of them being my role in all of this. As the anthropologist, I am committed both to studying human behaviour and to, in some vague, unspecified way, helping the people who are kind and generous enough to share their lives with me, tolerating my intrusive and silly questions. But how should I help? I have long been reluctant to simply give money to people in serious need of it, which was certainly the case with Edward. He was trying to run a household with six people based only on seasonal labour, guiding for sports hunters, and, I'm sure, selling marijuana on occasion. And, although his life is a mess at the moment, what has always resonated with me is that he is always trying, trying to keep his equipment running, trying to hunt and provide for his family, trying to find some temporary work or other to keep money coming in. It was one of the reasons I was willing to engage in a kind of reciprocal arrangement with him, hiring him to work on my equipment, and paying him for his time. I am not naïve enough to think that I could make a transformational difference, but I hoped it might be enough to keep him from running into the kind of trouble in which he finds himself. Though I am, as I have written earlier, "one-down" socially in my role as anthropologist, I am certainly "one-up" in other ways, one of them being my relative wealth, and the fact that my existence in an eight foot by twelve foot cabin is merely temporary suffering. I am also likely to be further "one-up": my research feeds directly into my own career advancement.

For me, the fact that Edward keeps trying is important, and it is something that resonates with other Inuit too. Of course Edward is not the only one struggling with money or in a difficult relationship with his partner. But there is a significant difference between Edward and

Isaac Kaaktuq's son-in-law, Sam, who has shown no interest in either working or hunting. Sam, it seems, spends most of his days on the sofa, watching TV and smoking up. Some of the old men note that it is the difference between being a "doer" and a "no-doer;" the no-doers are not worth the trouble or the investment of physical or emotional energy. As William or Harry Tamaryak would likely declare, "I don't care about them." Edward keeps trying, though, and this fact makes him worth the effort in the eyes of his male peers and elders.

Inuit are quite resourceful in their own right, and the community and its members are organized and talented enough to solve their own problems without my butting in. Providing individual assistance, though, is something within my power, and I have tried it to effect in some small way. But what if Edward does not really want help? What if the help that I can offer is not what is wanted or even needed? Is it even help? For Edward, we are in a reciprocal relationship; I am "helping" only in the way that everyone else who engages in such relationships "helps." It is accepted, welcomed, and understood but not necessarily seen as anything potentially transformative. Perhaps that is not surprising, as I have never engaged him any way that could be seen as transformative, hoping he might keep his act together but never admonishing him to do so or treading on his own autonomy.

The second issue that strikes me is that I am driven to help Edward, and perhaps failing at it, is because I perceive that he is trying, and failing, to live up to the expectations of manhood. Of all of the characters portrayed here, Edward is for me the most difficult to fathom. He can be a charming man, friendly and outgoing, easygoing in casual conversation. He is generous with his time when people ask favours of him. He is also, it seems, what southerners would expect in a modern "traditional Inuk." He is a keenly talented drum dancer and has shown a deep commitment to Inuit tradition and values, to a hunting lifestyle and to providing for others. When he goes caribou hunting and comes back with meat, that meat is distributed widely, with special attention paid to elders who can no longer hunt. He may be the most generous hunter in the settlement in that regard. He is constantly thinking and planning his next trip out of town. Inuit and southerners alike recognize these qualities in him. He remains a likable and engaging person, even as his behaviour toward his family is, at least to me, completely mystifying, if not outright reprehensible.

However, it is equally clear that he has some serious issues in his life that he has yet to overcome. Perhaps he never will. Perhaps, like David Kaaktuq, twenty years his junior, Edward has not yet understood that becoming a real person, a real man, an inummarik, goes beyond providing for others: it extends to finding balance. David, as we saw earlier, has yet to figure out that providing for others' well-being extends beyond food. Edward, however, has a more complicated problem. Without balance, he cannot find or develop the proper relationships with others, with the land, or with himself. He seems to want nothing more than to be a provider and a hunter. For part of the year, he succeeds. Being a hunter, however, requires finding a balance that includes tolerating the presence of the Canadian state and its rules, regulations, and demands. Being a provider by necessity requires learning how to negotiate these hurdles. In a sense, Edward has internalized the Inuit life course *too* well. In his desire to adhere to Inuit values, he ignores the southern ones almost completely, and so runs into difficulty with housing, employers, and, ultimately, his family. Amos Tuktu referenced the problem earlier as one of "being in the middle," and it seems an apt assessment. Edward has no desire to be in the middle, and he cannot understand that doing what he wants requires doing what he must.

Others in the settlement clearly recognize these problems. Amos, in his assessment of Edward's predicament, has noted that the problems with his family were some time in coming, that Edward's life in general was unbalanced. Not three weeks previously, Amos suggested that I not travel with Edward on the land. I asked why, for I have known Edward to be very skilled and would have no concerns about my safety travelling with him.

"It's because he doesn't take care of the land. That's why he's a bad person to travel with. This summer I was coming back from caribou hunting with my cousins, and we stopped at places where Edward had been staying. The first one, there was an *ugyuk*, rotting on the beach, with only the intestines removed. And at the next camp, there was a big mess left behind. He's going to get shit from DNR for it.

"And he went across before, got too many caribou to bring back, and he left them there, and they spoiled." Amos was referring to an early summer caribou hunting trip, going across Prince Albert Sound to the south shore. "It's bad to travel with people like that. It gives you bad luck."

Three weeks after Edward is charged, I see him down at his house in the evening. We have been talking about making a trip to Fish Lake, to set some nets and try and get some fish. I've never been sure if Edward is serious or not, though he did mention that part of the reason he wants to make the trip is to get out of town and clear his head. Though my machine is set to go, his isn't. He says he's going to work on his machine once the wind of the past few days dies down, and then we'll just buy gas and grub and go.

But now it is not looking likely to happen. Edward is sitting on the sofa in a pair of old gym shorts and a ripped T-shirt. The television is on, and he is flipping between channels. "Don't think I'm going to go. Got an eviction notice today." He points at an official-looking letter on the table. "I'm gonna lose the house if I don't pay up." He sounds neither happy nor sad about it.

I am still unsure if he can be evicted once the temperatures go below freezing. I suspect that if Sarah and the kids were living here, eviction would be delayed. Sarah, however, will be in Inuvik for at least another month.

"But, Edward, isn't the problem with your arrears due to reporting and not to your actual income?" I recall that the issue was that he was paid a huge lump sum of money for guiding, and he simply failed to complete the proper paperwork. "Couldn't you talk to Housing to work out a way to pay off what you owe? The money you got for guiding wasn't salary – you had to pay your expenses out of that, so shouldn't it be less? Couldn't you claim some deductions?"

"Nauna." I don't think Edward has any interest in pursuing those issues.

"Well, if you're going to sell the machine, you might as well use it to go to Fish Lake and get some fish, right?"

"Yuh." Edward flashes his eyebrows in agreement. He lifts the TV remote and changes the channel. We never do make the trip.

8

Sometimes I Can Feel Heavy

BINGO

Late winter to early spring is a difficult time for many Inuit. Christmas has long since faded into the distance, and even though March is marked by the return of a normal photoperiod, there is not much to do around town. Easter is some weeks away, and the weather is not ideal for most Inuit to consider going out on the land. It is still far too early for spring fishing, as the fish are not ready to bite, and standing over a fishing hole is merely an exercise in getting cold. A few of the more determined hunters make day trips for muskoxen or spend an afternoon out at the crack, shooting at seals, but most are content to remain snugly in town, looking forward to springtime. The only real activity is around the sports hunters. These arrive around the middle of March and keep the guides busy for another six or seven weeks. Still, the most that Inuit do is pay attention to news from the sports hunters and talk about the upcoming spring, when the weather warms up and ice-fishing season starts.

With people sitting around in town, it is an ideal time to visit and catch up with data collection, so I stop by Joseph Qalviaq's house on a Thursday night. Joseph is normally a very busy person, difficult to get in a slow moment between meetings, looking after his parents, or going out for a quick trip on the land. He is, in fact, like Charlie Hanayi in this regard, nearly always up to something. Joseph is rarely in a food coma after dinner.

Joseph, his wife, Rose, and their daughter Mary are sitting at the table when I arrive, staring at pieces of newsprint, each holding an ink bottle in one hand. Joseph looks up as I knock and enter.

"Hi. Come in. There's hot water for tea." Joseph points at the kitchen counter and then motions to the sofa. There are only three chairs around the kitchen table, but the sofa is positioned so that I can sit close to Joseph and pretend to visit. Shit – I forgot it was bingo night.

The radio hisses behind him, "Forty-eight, forty-eight." The signal is crackly over the air, and it sounds like there is a jet engine firing in the background. I can barely make out the number being called.

All three begin stamping their newsprint sheets. Each piece of paper has nine grids. Rose has five sheets, Mary four, and Joseph three. Thup thup thup thup go the ink bottles, blotting out the proper squares. Every player has his or her own style. Mary is a fast blotter, trying to cover the squares as quickly as possible. Joseph is more deliberate, trying to cover each square perfectly with ink.

"What one's this one again, hon?" Joseph asks his wife.

"Picture Frame," she replies. On the winning sheet, the outer strip of squares will have been blotted out.

"Twenty-three, twenty-three." Again, I can barely make out the words. Thup thup thup thup.

In the background of the radio broadcast, the phone rings. Amidst the hissing and crackling, I am reminded of the HF camp radios, the portable transceivers that Inuit on the land use to communicate with people in town. Joseph has one, bright orange and now turned off, its two antenna wires strung through a window and arranged outside for best reception. The presence in the home of one of these radios is a marker of a commitment to hunting; Inuit can spend entire evenings listening and talking to people not only at Fish Lake or in Prince Albert Sound but across the Western Arctic. Anyone using these radios regularly, however, must have developed a special skill for deciphering what people are saying. Even when the communication is in English, I can barely make out what is being said.

The caller at the station has paused to take the phone call. Mary speaks up over the radio's hissing and spitting. "There can't be a winner yet. We're only ten numbers in."

The voice hisses over the radio, as if in response, "Okay, somebody called to say we're going too fast, so we'll repeat the numbers. Last five we called was fourteen, thirty-seven, forty-seven, forty-eight, twenty-three." He says them deliberately, overemphasizing each number, sounding annoyed at the complaint.

There is another pause. All we can hear is the sound of the jet engine – really the bingo machine with the numbers inside, turning over and over – and the crackle of the radio. The game is being carried on the low-power transmitter used for local radio broadcasts. During the afternoons, Inuit use the radio to make public announcements, host an impromptu show or two, and play music. On Thursday nights, it is bingo.

Bingo is the latest fundraiser and diversion. People purchase sheets beforehand for $15 apiece, and for different rounds, with the requirements for winning (a picture frame, completion of an entire square, half a square, an x, or some other pattern) changing from game to game, and the jackpot changing also. The final jackpot of the night can range between $800 and $3,000, depending on how many buy in and which organization is running the bingo. Bingo is very competitive and players take it seriously.

Once the first bingo game starts and the numbers are initially called, the phone begins to ring at the community hall. One ring at a time, and no one at the hall answers: people are setting their phones so they can hit the redial button in case they win. Being first does not matter, however. Once a winner calls in, others who have completed their cards at the same time can also call. Winners then bring their cards to the hall to be confirmed, which provides a twenty-minute or so break between games.

I drink my tea as another ten numbers are called, slowly this time. The phone rings on-air again, and there is another pause.

"Okay, Lena says we're going too slow now, so we'll speed it up. Seventy-five. The next number is seventy-five."

Joseph's tongue is sticking out of the corner of his mouth. Thup thup thup.

There is not much conversation to be had, except my questions about how all of this goes down. It used to be that fundraisers were bake sales or fast-food sales, held at the gym. In the case of fast-food sales, the fundraising organization would place a large order for McDonald's hamburgers or Kentucky Fried Chicken at the respective restaurants in Yellowknife. First Air would fly the order in and it would be picked up at the airport by the fundraising organization. At the community hall or the school, the limp, just-warm food would be sold at a profit.

But bingo is the latest rage, and Joseph remarks between numbers that nearly everyone plays; he is surprised at how much money people in town have at their disposal. Even people without jobs seem to have cash on hand to buy cards. Though Joseph considers Rose's five sheets borderline obsessive, other people manage twice that many and more for a single game.

Bingo will continue for another ninety minutes – there are three more games to call – and they seem to get longer as the evening wears on, simply because a winner has to complete a larger percentage of a sheet. Joseph looks at me sheepishly while this game finishes. There are three more to go, but he hands his remaining cards to Mary to play. He pours more tea and comes to sit on the sofa. The phone rings again at the hall.

"Okay, someone says we're going too fast, so we're going to call the next game slower." The speaker then breaks into song, belting out Johnny Cash's "Ring of Fire." I realize that it is Matthew Aqiaruq calling the numbers.

Some Inuit would ignore a guest while they play bingo, but Joseph would rather visit than play. "I never win those things," he says. "It's just something to do. But some people really think they're going to get rich playing bingo. My parents say it is just stupid."

"How is your dad, by the way?" Over the years, Joseph has had to manage his relationship with his parents. Forty-seven now, he spent the formative part of his childhood on the land, living in sealing and fishing camps during the summer, often down in Prince Albert Sound, and running a trapline with his father during the winter with his two younger brothers. Looking back, he says that his parents were like taskmasters, demanding perfection out on the land. "If you set the trap up even the slightest wrong way, boy, you could really hear about it. It really made you not want to make mistakes in front of him."

Joseph gives the report on his father. "Well, he's okay. The winter has been hard for him, he's really slowing down. My mum said she's been worrying about him, he gets tired so easy now." Joseph's father, in his early seventies, has been suffering from a heart condition that has slowly grown worse over the past few years. Joseph says his father is not a good patient and does not want to accept that he cannot hunt and travel the way he used to. The real problem is that, after a winter of sitting around the house, it becomes more difficult to get the body moving again in the spring and summer. "It's like he's seizing up, like an old engine."

Conversation soon turns to equipment. Joseph is thinking about replacing his ATV or, rather, purchasing a second one. With several teenagers in the house, he is weighing the costs and benefits of a new ATV, which would allow him to take his boys out in the summer and get both him and Rose to and from camp and around town. It would mean he always had use of a machine. I'm not sure whether he is talking himself into a new machine, or whether he is calculating that his current ATV is nearing middle age, a time when one can expect constant breakdowns and repairs and the cost of replacement parts can get out of control. Joseph has some money, enough for a new machine, but he recently quit his job at hamlet. The old ATV, he reasons, could be a "town machine." He figures it is better to purchase new equipment and sell the old before it reaches the stage of constant repair. However, without a job, he is not sure he can afford a new machine.

"I can't stay at hamlet, though, it was killing me. The money is good, but it's like I'm stuck in town all the time, and I gotta get out there and hunt more, and get my boys out there too."

As I leave the house, I find myself amused at the conversation. Fifteen years ago, Joseph and I might have had the same discussion about equipment, but the conversation would have been wistful, and the catalogue would have been for hockey gear. Joseph, I muse, is beginning to sound like some elders I know when he talks about equipment, wanting to hunt more, and the futility of playing games.

Figuring that nearly everyone will be playing bingo for the next hour, I decide to go to William Kaaktuq's. I know he will be home. And he is, sitting alone on the sofa, flipping television channels as I walk in. The volume is off, however. To my surprise, I can hear the hiss and pop of the radio in the background.

"Anybody home?" I call from the porch as I stamp the snow off my kamiks and peek around the corner.

"There's nobody here. Nobody's home." William is pretending that I am not here by looking straight at the television.

"But I see your kamiks and your parka. Somebody must be home." This is a regular routine now, with minor variations.

"No, there's nobody here. Not for you. You're dreaming, it must be."

"Then who is making all this noise?"

"Uh … nobody, I guess." William laughs, his unique rapid-fire machine gun laugh, followed by a sigh and a fit of coughing.

I walk in and sit down on the other sofa. Agnes is out visiting, and William's daughters have since gone to their own homes to play bingo. If William and Agnes were a younger couple, I would not make a note of Agnes's absence. Younger couples, like Joseph and Rose Qalviaq, or William's son Isaac and his partner, Ida, spend much of their time apart. After dinner, the women usually go out visiting or to sewing club, while the men stay home. Agnes and William, though, spend very little time apart. Like many elder couples, they have grown together over the course of their lives and are usually only apart when Agnes attends meetings (William long ago gave up on meetings) or one of them is running errands around town. They even travel on the land together, the only exception being day trips (Agnes goes spring fishing, William muskox hunting) or when William gets a tag for a polar bear.

William reaches over and turns off the HF radio on the end-table next to him, the wire antenna snaking through the closed window and outside. William is not listening to bingo at all. He is listening for news of Isaac, who is out on the ice with a sports hunter, looking for bears. William reports that they are in camp now, that they saw some tracks today but they were old. Donald Aiviq, who is helping Isaac on this hunt, is having trouble with his engine.

"How come you're not playing bingo?" I already know why, and it is why I decided to visit him. William has no tolerance for these kinds of things.

"I don't care about bingo, it's just wasting money."

"But you could win $1,000 playing bingo! C'mon, you should play, you could get really rich, you could be a big shot."

We have had this conversation many times. William is an intensely practical person, and as he sees it, the problem with bingo is that there is nothing useful about it. One sits at home, often alone, fixated on a piece of newsprint, an ink bottle, and a poor-quality radio broadcast. There is no social value to the activity. Even if other people are there, they are not engaging with each other. The money makes no sense to him, either. Fifteen dollars for a piece of paper? Two pieces of paper is nearly the equivalent of five gallons of gasoline, meaning that he could travel halfway to Fish Lake and back, doing something useful, like hunting.

Not that he has $15 to spend. He and Agnes have an arrangement about finances. She controls the money in the household, and he asks her for some. She balances the bankbooks, keeps track of income and expenses, and determines when William can make purchases and what he can buy. He acknowledges that she is the sensible one in the relationship. He knows he would spend all the money on hunting equipment, regardless of real need. Still, he tries. Only a month ago he was thumbing through a catalogue and asked Agnes if he could buy a new .243. Her response? *Don't you already have a .243? Yes. Is there something wrong with it? No. Then why do you need a new one?* William had to admit he could make do with what he had.

He is grateful for the restraint. He has been very clear over the years on the importance of money management, often expressing his views in terms that economists would easily recognize. For William, living as a hunter is a matter of trying to stay just ahead of what he calls "the line." A good hunter purchases new equipment just a little too early rather than too late, plans for contingencies in the event of emergency needs, and always works the social networks to know where parts and help can be located quickly. Once a hunter gets behind the line, William says, it is difficult to catch up. Forces seem to conspire to push one further and further behind, until it is nearly impossible to dig out of the hole. It takes more and more money to try to get back to the line, which is moving further and further away as equipment, fuel, parts, and supplies all become more expensive.

"The line" is something of which William has always been aware, but it is especially true now that he is in physical decline. He turned responsibility for his dogs over to Isaac. Since William no longer guides sports hunters himself, he has lost a significant source of income. Neither he nor his wife has ever had wage work. They always preferred a more traditional lifestyle based on hunting, fur sales, arts and crafts sales, and casual labour. William no longer traps, either, and so their income now is limited mostly to their old age pensions.

It is more and more difficult for him to even hunt. Although he managed to recover from a terrible case of arthritis through sheer force of will, it never went away, and it has had pronounced effects on his body. One knee no longer seems to bend, so he walks with a limp, a normal step followed by his hip swinging the damaged leg forward with a thunk.

The pain of his gait is apparent as he turns off the mute television and hobbles to the kitchen to make tea. Rather than coming back to the sofa, he moves into the room on the other side of the kitchen and sits at the table. I follow. When I visit many younger Inuit in their homes, the television tends to remain on, and everyone watches, often in silence punctuated by occasional conversation. William simply turns the TV off. As I sit, he has an old photo album on the table. He opens it, and we look at the pictures.

I suppose he was spurred to get out the album by a visit I made last week. I had managed to collect some digital copies of old photographs taken by Father Henri Tardy, an Oblate priest who lived in Ulukhaktok for thirty-five years before retiring in the early 1980s. Father Tardy's old photos had been in limited circulation for some time, but William had not seen them. Only a month ago, I arranged to borrow the CD and copied the set onto my laptop. I had shown them to William and Agnes, who were keenly interested. They were featured in some of those photos, when they were considerably younger. As William says tongue-in-cheek, he was very handsome, the best-looking Inuk in the Western Arctic.

William was pretty good at identifying the people in the photos, but not nearly as good as he was at identifying what he felt were the important things. He was deadly accurate in identifying the location of specific photos and at identifying the firearms the people were holding. A true hunter.

We sip our tea and look at an old photograph of his mother and father, both smiling into the camera, taken shortly before William was born. He tells me about his father, himself a traveller. He had been as far as Iqaluit in his youth, says William: he used to go all over. Agnes walks in while William tells the story. As he speaks and moves on to another photo, she makes herself some tea and sits down to offer her own commentary. I am engrossed by the stories and their personal histories, but I have no interest in trying to record them. I am simply listening, asking an occasional question to clarify when I lose track of the people or places involved. They relate very personal narratives of their lives: the first time they met, William's favourite bear dog, coming to Ulukhaktok for Easter. Were I to whip out a recorder (which, thankfully, I do not have with me), it would ruin the moment and offend them in the process. And, truly, William and Agnes are telling these stories not to me but to each other, reminding themselves of the events of their marriage and own lives, recalling friends and relatives long passed away, and reliving old jokes. It is an honour that they share such things with me, a mere part-timer in the community.

We are well into a second cup of tea and tales of near death in a Twin Otter when there are footsteps on the porch, steps with a purpose. The door opens, and Lucy pokes her head in. She is their great-granddaughter, now thirteen, a vibrant girl nearly always with a wry smile on her face. I would be hard-pressed to say where she lives. With her mother? Grandmother? Great-grandparents? She has no home, or multiple homes, depending on how one looks at things. She seems to flit from household to household, from her mother's to an auntie's to William and Agnes's, depending on whim and circumstance. Every evening there are phone calls to determine where she will be for the night. She is not here to stay, however, as she is standing in the porch, keeping her shoes on.

"Granny, I want some junk, and the store is open tonight."

She is referring to Eli's snack shop. Eli, a young Inuk trying to make a space for himself in the local economy, is filling a niche. In the evenings, when both the Co-op and Northern are closed, there is a real market for soda, beef jerky, and candy. Eli started by purchasing in bulk from the Northern and Co-op and then reselling at a significant markup, producing a tidy profit. With the early proceeds, he acquired a lot in town and built a 12 × 16 structure that he uses as both a store and a warehouse.

Eventually the Northern and Co-op caught on to his strategy, but rather than squash him like a bug by opening their own after-hours snack shops and underselling him, they simply refused to sell to him in bulk. So Eli turned elsewhere and now makes bulk orders from a wholesaler in

Edmonton, paying air freight to have it shipped to Ulukhaktok. He says that buying from the wholesaler and shipping via First Air is less expensive than if he bought from the Northern, so the profits are even better. He has also discovered another advantage of ordering directly from a wholesaler: the selection is better. He can offer candy that kids cannot buy at either of the stores. He is angling for a barge order this summer, which would drastically reduce his shipping costs.

Part of the reason for the Co-op and Northern not aggressively dealing with Eli as competition is due to social connections. The Co-op, for example, is run by the manager in consultation with a local executive board, which makes basic decisions about the direction of the business. While the board does not have much power, they can direct the manager not to compete with someone like Eli. Inuit villages are not necessarily sites of unbridled capitalism, and the Inuit on the board recognize that someone like Eli should be allowed to try to make it – even if there is harm to the Co-op's bottom line. The other reason Eli continues to operate is, I think, because both managers underestimate Inuit. They seem to assume that because he is young and native, Eli lacks the ability or intelligence to make a business like his work.

From my interaction with him, however, I sense he is a real entrepreneur. He tracks his sales, test-markets new products with his customers, and adjusts his prices based on supply and demand. Moreover, he seems to do these things more efficiently and intuitively than the managers at the Northern or the Co-op do. Both stores have shelves full of product that Inuit will simply not purchase, even at steep discounts. Most importantly, Eli is making a decent living with his business, though time will tell if he can continue his success.

The store hours are somewhat irregular lately: Eli has a new baby and cannot always trust others to work the store for him. A few of his employees have walked away with inventory. He also must be sensitive to others in the settlement. The Anglican Auxiliary, for example, runs an after-hours snack shop as a fundraiser once a week, so Eli does not open for business until they close. There have been attempts to rob his store too, kids trying to break in after hours. But, as Eli says, he was young once. He knows all their tricks.

When Lucy says she wants junk, she is referring to one of the major food groups in Ulukhaktok. "Junk" is a category of food that encompasses gum, candy of various kinds, chips, and pop. I am unclear whether beef jerky counts as junk. It seems to be in a class by itself, perhaps the highest-volume product at any of the stores, the combination of dried meat, salt, and nitrates a powerful lure for Inuit taste buds. Jerky closely resembles mipku, the dried meats that are already an important part of the Inuit diet, though mipku cannot compete with the salt, sugar, and chemical content of jerky.

"I have no money," Agnes tells Lucy says sadly.

Lucy looks to William, who shrugs. He begins to jingle his pockets. He is wearing loose-fitting carpenter's pants with multiple pockets, but there are only keys in them. Agnes gets up and heads to her bedroom.

William reaches into his wallet, and shows Lucy the inside of it. Empty. He holds it upside down and shakes it out.

"Gee." Lucy is disappointed. "I really want to have junk tonight."

Agnes glides back into the room, a handful of coins clinking in her palm. Lucy's demeanour instantly changes, and she smiles again. Agnes hands her three loonies and two toonies: $7 total. It seems that she rummaged through couch cushions for the change. "Bring me back a ginger ale, ah?" It is half question, half directive.

"Yes, Granny. Thanks!" And she is gone, bounding off the porch into the street, skipping the stairs. She will return, in about thirty minutes, with a ginger ale. She knows how much Agnes enjoys ginger ale.

William opens his wallet again, revealing $200 in crisp twenties. He was hiding them in the wallet's divider. He smiles. We go back to the photos, Agnes giggling at William. A few minutes later, more footsteps outside, a crunch and squeak on the cold snow, and the hinges of the outside door creak. Young Margaret peeks around the corner.

"Hi, Granny. The snack shack is open. I want money for junk!" She places the emphasis on *junk*.

A script: William fiddles in his pockets while Agnes revisits her coin stash. William prefers Orange Crush.

HIKUHUILAQ

For once I am ready to go before my travelling partner is. My sleds are properly loaded, the box and tarp tied down, the machine fuelled. I am waiting for Albert to gas up. Though it is 9 A M, the sun is already high in the sky. The calendar is turning toward late April, and we are well on our way to twenty-four-hour daylight. It is still cold, however, and the east wind is blowing hard enough to chill. The flags at the school and the hamlet are stiff but not snapping violently. The wind is hard enough to keep any half-hearted hunters in town, but Albert is determined to go.

"The weather can't get worse." The forecast is calling for moderate wind but not much else. Albert knows the weather report to follow is the one from Sachs Harbour, which is a strong predictor of the next winds for Ulukhaktok. "Besides, sometimes you just gotta get out there. Can't wait for perfect conditions, or you'll never go anywhere."

He makes a last check of his sleds. Though I have a plywood box attached to my sleds, which makes packing a bit easier, Albert prefers to travel without a box, wrapping everything in a heavy canvas tarp instead. He tugs the line one last time and, satisfied, starts the engine. Normally he would be at work this morning and would wait for the weekend to go hunting. The drawback of weekend hunting, however, is that the weather does not always cooperate. He has been stuck in town for the last four weekends because of howling winds and whiteout conditions. Work has been slow at the shop, so he has taken the remainder of the week off to get out on the land. Usually he makes the day trip for muskoxen on his own, but he has invited me to come along today. And, though the wind is a bit of a problem, I trust his judgment that conditions will not grow worse.

I follow him out of town, along the main drag of the settlement, past the Housing shop and garage, where we drop off the airport road and onto the snowmobile trail that parallels it. We cross the turn-off to Ukpillik Lake and Air Force Lake, pass the dump, and finally leave the airport road behind at the bridge. Dropping down and crossing the river, we find ourselves on the Fish Lake trail. Soon we pass Ukpillik Lake on our right and begin a gentle, steady climb away from the shore, heading inland.

Albert does not intend to travel all the way to Fish Lake, though we will go much further than most hunters in our search for muskoxen. "Close to town, they know about machines. People just chase them, and they get tough. Further out, we can get some that are better." Albert has become something of a snob about muskox meat.

Hunters of all ages tend to resort to chasing the animals, which has conditioned them to run from the mere sound of a snowmobile. Indeed, the first sight of a herd of muskoxen is usually of them running over the far hill, after which the hunt becomes a roundup. There are reasons for running them: once the animals are exhausted, they stop and can be shot from close range. If they can be driven to a flat, dry spot for easy butchering, so much the better.

I have participated in many of these roundup hunts. The previous summer, Edward and I engaged in a roundup hunt on ATVs. Edward got his animal, but the rest of the exhausted herd just stood gazing at their fallen colleague, too tired to care. Edward and I resorted to throwing rocks at them until they wandered off and allowed us to approach the downed animal.

Albert wants to avoid running animals, though his reasons are purely practical. Chasing down muskoxen is a bit like running over rabbits, hard on both machine and body. Albert says animals that have not been run taste better. "The meat is softer" is how he puts it. He is willing to put in a bit of extra time and effort for better-tasting meat, though he is unusual in this regard. A decade into muskox becoming an important (perhaps the most important) meat for many families, some Inuit still say that they do not like it. Albert thinks the general dislike of muskoxen is more due to lazy hunting and tough meat than anything else.

I think, also, that Albert has internalized a lesson he has acquired from his elders. *Mustn't be lazy* is how he would say it, referring to the importance of doing the job properly, of avoiding taking the easy way out. Normally, such a lesson would refer to hunting in general, and life more broadly, but Albert seems to have narrowed this philosophy to particular hunting strategies.

We are moving along at a good clip, though I cannot tell how fast. As on most snowmobiles here, my speedometer has long since broken. I think Albert would normally travel even faster; he is going a bit slower for my sake. But there is plenty of snow on the land, so the road is good and makes for a smooth ride. Albert occasionally looks back to check on me, but I have no trouble keeping up, even with my less powerful engine.

After what seems like an hour of driving – I did not bring a watch – we stop at a lake after a good, steady climb, the line of sheer cliffs and jumbled rocks well off on our right. Albert produces a thermos of hot coffee laced with copious amounts of sugar and evaporated milk. We snack on pieces of mipku, dried caribou, shipped in from a relative in Kugluktuk a few weeks ago. Albert is scanning the snow on the lake, making a broad circle around the machine.

"Harry Tamaryak shot a couple of muskox here the other day. There could be more around. This is Akaluataq, by the way." Albert senses I do not know where I am, and he is right. I am about ten or fifteen kilometres outside my comfort zone on the land. "Which way to town?" he asks me as I look around.

It is a question frequently asked of children, part of their training. I fail, pointing back down the trail at the last bluff that we came around. "We go that way to get back to town." I always make this mistake, pointing to the route I would take to get home, not the direct line.

"Nope. Town is that way." He points toward Ulukhaktok, some forty kilometres as the raven flies. It is an important skill, being able to keep one's bearings regardless of where the trail goes.

Sheepishly, I walk in the opposite direction, making my own broad circle around the machines, coming upon a set of small tracks in the snow. I shout to Albert and he makes his way over. When I call out that the tracks are small, he walks more quickly. "Caribou?" Even I know these are not caribou tracks.

They are muskoxen, so he is disappointed. "Old, though. But maybe we could see caribou, too." It is wishful thinking. Caribou are rarely seen this close to town these days.

"Can you shoot caribou around here? I thought caribou hunting was banned this close to town."

Albert swills the last of his coffee. "You could shoot them, all right. The ban is for north of Kuujjua. If you shoot them here, it's good. That's what I heard, anyway."

I have heard this, and many other opinions too, about the ban, which was instituted in 1993. Not even the Fish and Wildlife officer seems to know what the current regulation is, or what the punishment for violators should be. Is the regulation merely voluntary, an advisory issued by Hunters and Trappers, without teeth? Is it a hamlet bylaw? Is it a Wildlife regulation backed by territorial and federal law? Knowing Albert, he does not particularly care. If he sees a caribou, he will shoot first and worry about the consequences later. If the animal is offered, he feels compelled to take it. We start the machines and move on.

We cross several sets of tracks over the next hour or so, but each time the tracks head into rocky hills, so we do not pursue them. As we drive, I think about the local perception of abundance. Inuit constantly talk about how there are muskoxen "all over the place," but we have driven quite a few kilometres and have yet to see a single one, only a few old tracks.

I leave the tracking to Albert and enjoy the remarkable scenery. We seem to be heading ever so slightly down now, into a new drainage, entering a wide valley with broken hills and low but sheer cliffs on our right, gently rolling hills on our left. The sun sparkles on the pure white snow, and I am grateful for my sunglasses. I have no idea where we are, though I am aware Albert is going a bit faster and that he is following a set of tracks down this drainage. I can see tracks alongside the trail that his snowmobile makes in the snow.

After some time, he changes course up the northwest side of the wide valley and stops his machine. I pull alongside and kill my engine too. Through binoculars, he can see the dark shapes of a small herd of muskoxen moving slowly over a rise. They are perhaps a little more than a kilometre away, though it is difficult for me to judge distance across such open spaces. Albert hands me the binoculars. "There's some good-sized ones in there. We'll go around and try and come at them the other way." I think he wants to change course a little, taking a more direct route to where he thinks the herd is going while approaching the animals from the west, downwind. He takes his .243 out of its case and inserts the loaded magazine, leaving the chamber empty for the time being. He has seen too many accidents with firearms to leave the firing chamber loaded, and he does not trust the safety. He once nearly drowned when his cousin accidentally fired his shotgun through the bottom of his boat. A friend nearly died when the friend's gun went off after hitting a bump in the trail. There will be enough time to load the chamber later. He slings the rifle over his shoulder and starts the engine.

We find the herd right where Albert thought they would be. They are against a low cliff, perhaps twenty feet high, protected from the wind and standing in a field of large rocks that have broken from the cliff. They do not run, perhaps because they have yet to be aware of us, or perhaps because they feel safe in the field of rocks. I stay back as Albert stops the engine, dismounts, and quickly raises the rifle. He shoots a medium-sized animal twice, hitting the head both times, from a distance of perhaps 125 metres. The animal staggers forward for a few steps and lies down. It does not rise, and even at this distance I can see blood pouring from its nose. Before the other animals panic, Albert turns his attention to a second one. It is slightly larger, and beginning to move, showing us its flank. Albert fires three times in succession, hitting the shoulder each time. The animal sways unsteadily for a moment before also going down, either from a broken shoulder or because Albert hit the heart. The remainder of the herd, now nervous, begins to trot off to the north.

Albert starts the engine of his machine and drives over to the dying muskoxen. The sound of the engine and the speed of the snowmobile send the other animals into a run, and they disappear over the rise. Albert pulls up as close as he can, some twenty metres from the animals, and again stops the machine. He checks the rifle, opening the bolt to eject the last, empty shell. Removing the magazine, he tucks it into his parka pocket. He puts the rifle into its case and retrieves his skinning knife. I do the same.

"Where are we?" I ask, partly curious and partly because people will ask me where I went on my trip.

Albert looks around. "Hikuhuilaq is just over that way, maybe five or six miles." He points in the direction we have been travelling so far. "There's a lake just over that way, a funny one, it's like it empties out in the winter, the ice all smashes in on it."

Sheltered from the wind and working in the bright sunshine, we remove our parkas as we warm up. Skinning muskoxen is not an easy task. The knives quickly dull, and we periodically stop and sharpen them with a small file. A file is much quicker for touching up the edge than a stone or honing rod.

Sometime later, when we have finished skinning and cutting the animals, we load the meat onto the sleds. I drag the meat from the kill spot to Albert's sleds while he loads, but I notice that Albert has put quite a bit of meat in my box. When I look closely, it is the entirety of the smaller animal. There are, I think, two reasons for this. Albert shot the second animal mostly for me, knowing that I cannot legally shoot muskoxen. In a sense, he is working from the assumption that, if I could, I would have shot one. At the same time he is also operating under the directive that travelling partners share their catch, so that each returns to town with a somewhat equal load. A hunting trip during which one hunter shoots three caribou and the other gets a skunk typically results in the skunked hunter coming home with one caribou on his sled, both a measure of generosity and the recognition that good fortune plays a significant role in hunting success.

Strictly speaking, though, it is illegal even for me to accept the meat as a gift. Joshua Qulliq, the Wildlife officer, reminded me of this regulation when I applied for my bunny licence earlier in the year. "You know the rules on hunting, but they're written here on the paper. You should read them again," he said as he handed me the NWT hunting guidelines. "I also got to tell you that you can't take meat from people in town. That's against the law too."

Joshua looked stern when he said this, his demeanour no doubt exacerbated by his official uniform. I was taken aback. "It is? I didn't know it was illegal to accept meat. How come?"

"Too many Qablunaat are doing stuff like trading for meat, or giving money to people and getting meat in return, claiming that it is a gift. We're trying to crack down on that."

I could see his point. In Ulukhaktok a steady traffic of outsiders come through. Many of them, especially during the summer, are construction workers. As a group they have developed a reputation for supplying residents with alcohol or drugs in exchange for meat or sex. Many Inuit my own age date the arrival of marijuana to the construction of the Health Centre in the mid-1980s, for example.

At the same time, though, what was I going to do? I regularly received meat from a few friends. Even if I tried to decline, I am sure they would not let me say no. I certainly did not want to have to rely on meat from the store. During my first winter in Ulukhaktok, I had been violently ill from eating tainted meat. I tried to avoid store meat, remarkably overpriced, low quality, and usually freezer-burned, as much as I could.

I thought about this new problem while Joshua completed the paperwork and processed my cheque. As he handed me the licence and I rose to leave, he asked, "By the way, how are you doing on food? Do you have enough?"

In Joshua's mind, of course, the only real food is meat, and the only real meat is from the land. Was he trying to trap me?

"No, I only got here last week. I have nothing."

It was not quite true. The day I arrived, Matthew Aqiaruq called me over as I walked by his house, handing me the rear quarter of a muskox as a welcome back. I threw it over my shoulder and carried it home, all the way across town. Since I was now apparently in violation of the law, I could not admit that to Joshua, though perhaps he had seen me and already knew I had meat.

"Hmm." He looked thoughtful. "I've got some muskox steaks from one I shot last week. I'll bring some by for you. That was a good one."

I tell Albert, "I don't need this much. You should take half of this." It is true: half a muskox will be plenty of meat for me. I have some in the freezer already, and I have enough char, ducks, and trout too. I also know that Albert, as the eldest son in his family, hunts for at least five households: his own and those of his sister-in-law (who is unmarried and with two children), his younger sister (who has a husband, but he is, as Albert says, "useless"), his parents (who travel only in the summer because of poor health), and his in-laws (who are elderly and do not hunt at all). Whenever I ask him about food sharing, he just shrugs. "People come and get food. When the box is empty, I fill it up again. I try to make sure it is never empty."

For a moment we engage in a brief stare-down. My goal was to travel with Albert, not claim a share of his catch. He is trying to follow etiquette. Eventually, we reach a compromise. "Just carry it home on your sleds," he says, "I'll come by tomorrow and take whatever you leave in the sled box."

He looks at his watch. "Four o'clock. If we hurry, we could get home for the hockey." Then he pauses. Like me, he has realized that we have not eaten since mid-morning. We both spontaneously dig into our grub boxes and emerge with a very late lunch of caribou mipku, char quaq, bannock, a can of frozen sardines, and several slabs of frozen Klik. Albert has another thermos, this one with hot water, and we chase our meal with tea. As we eat, I am struck by the absolute silence of the land here, disturbed only by the breeze rippling over the tarps and the sounds of our eating. I try to chew more quietly.

It is just past seven when we roll into town, splitting up just before the main drag. Albert heads down the hill and along the shore to his house, I down the main drag to mine. I note as I pass the hamlet building that the flag is at half-staff, as is the school flag. I wonder at this for a moment but then put it from my mind. Albert's wife, Shirley, who works at hamlet, told me some time ago that the hamlet flies the flag at half-staff in high winds. It doesn't occur to me that the winds are now quite light, the flag nearly limp.

I walk into the house for a quick meal of leftover muskox stew and a shower. The house is uncomfortably warm. My face feels hot, and it has become something of a negative raccoon, deeply tanned save for a white strip around my eyes from my sunglasses. Though I am tired from the travelling and feel sleepy in the warm house, it is only eight. Too early for bed, so I decide to go visiting. Perhaps I too can watch the hockey playoffs on TV.

The settlement is quiet this evening. Normally, there is a meeting somewhere, marked by the parked snowmobiles outside the building. The hamlet building, the Community Corporation offices, and the Community Hall all appear to be empty. There are no meetings tonight? It is very odd.

I stop by to see Amos Tuktu, whom I have not seen for over a week, but he is not at home and the house is dark. His machine is parked in front of the house, though, nearly always a sign that he is home. Perplexed, I meander down the road and stop three houses down, to see Charlie Hanayi. He is home alone, watching the hockey game. As I walk in, he offers tea, so I help myself and sit by him on the sofa. He seems subdued, not his usual talkative self. I wonder if he and his wife,

Susie, have been fighting, as they occasionally do. Perhaps she has moved out, as also happens perhaps once a year. Sensing that this might not be a good time to visit, I resolve to finish my tea and not stay long.

After several more minutes, though, Charlie breaks the ice. "Boy, it was a really terrible tragedy today."

"Tragedy? Why? What happened? I only just got back an hour ago."

"You never heard? Jonathan shot himself this morning."

Uh, oh. Charlie's youngest brother is named Jonathan, though there are others who share his name.

"Which Jonathan?" I ask hesitantly. I am hoping it is not Charlie's brother. I am not sure what I could say or do if it is.

"Aullaq." Not Charlie's brother. "He and Emily were drinking last night. I heard they got into a fight and he shot himself this morning. Susie is over at her parents' now." Emily and Susie are cousins, and I presume that, since Emily's parents have passed away, Emily is there, too.

This is a shock. Though Jonathan seemed to be always struggling economically and socially – he and Emily always seemed to be "having trouble," as others put it – he seemed to have his life on track. He had a steady job as a truck driver for hamlet, and he seemed to be making an effort to hunt more than he used to. He had at least taken to net fishing in recent years. That he would kill himself does not make much sense to me.

Charlie seems aware that I am dazed by the news. "Sometimes it's like that. That guy's life must not have been turning out the way that he wanted." Charlie has had far too much experience coping with suicide. Since 1992, there have been something like a dozen suicides, perhaps more. I have lost count. Charlie's older brother was one of them.

We sit in silence, not really watching the game, and I recall that this is the first suicide in several years. There seems to be a kind of self-aggrandizement behind a suicide. Following the victim's death, he – for the victim is nearly always male – becomes elevated in stature, fondly remembered for being a wonderful father, magnificent hunter, supportive brother, even if none of these things were true. The blame for his death is placed squarely on his wife or girlfriend. For this reason, it has always seemed to me as if suicide is used as a threat or a punishment more than anything else. *If you don't do what I want, I will kill myself, and then you'll be really sorry* seems to be the logic behind some of these deaths, though alcohol and mental illness surely play a role. And, indeed, I was to learn in the following days that Jonathan's suicide was no different: Emily bore quite a burden. Few details about the death emerged, but various "facts" about Jonathan and Emily's relationship did. Emily was too hard on poor Jonathan. She had too many rules in the house. She kept all the money and never let him have any of his own to spend. Roy Kudlak was quick to point out that Jonathan only owned three pairs of pants and a single pair of snow pants.

These observations, used to justify why a man might kill himself, seem a stretch. I only own three pairs of pants in Ulukhaktok myself. Why would anyone need more? Fashion? In Ulukhaktok? A couple of pairs of jeans are good enough for around town, and good wool pants are essential for travelling. Add snow pants or wind pants for travelling, and you have all you need. Would only owning three pairs of pants be enough to send someone over the edge? As for money, it was never apparent to me that either Jonathan or Emily had much of it, despite his steady job. Furthermore, Jonathan was not known to be violent or abusive, or to be much of a drinker, for that matter.

Nevertheless, despite the blame cast at Emily, and despite Jonathan's canonization as a wonderful father, dedicated hunter, and all-around good person, I become aware of a counter-reaction to the suicide, evidence that perhaps the spate of suicides in the recent past has become wearying. A number of men, some of them elders, others like Charlie, do not attend the funeral, shrugging their shoulders at yet another senseless death. Harry Tamaryak, who has lost two grandchildren to suicide, openly declares that he has had enough of going to funerals for people who kill themselves, so he is not going anymore. "I'm tired of it," he states matter-of-factly. "Young people, they're too easy to give up, always expect someone else to fix things for them." He does not attend Jonathan's funeral.

The funeral is Sunday, four days after Jonathan's death. The space between is filled by some of the men working on the arrangements. His brothers purchase the plywood and lumber from the hamlet for the coffin, and others track down the location of the working jackhammer and dig the grave in the permafrost, out at the cemetery. Relatives stay with Emily, a steady stream of women coming into the house to offer condolences, be with the family, and grieve with her. The support will continue for weeks afterward. Emily will have plenty of visitors, and in the evenings there will be music, people coming to pray, sing, and grieve, belting out gospel classics, "I Am a Pilgrim" and the Inuinnaqtun version of "Amazing Grace" among them.

The funeral service is held in the school gym, a sorrowful affair full of tears and keening. The coffin is open, Jonathan bundled in a blanket wrapped over his body and around his head in an attempt to hide the gunshot wound. After the service, the coffin is sealed and taken by truck to the cemetery. Another brief ceremony follows, the coffin put in the grave, followed by the task of filling the hole with dirt and gravel. A wooden cross, painted white, is placed at the head, among other members of Jonathan's family. His parents are close by. Some of the graves still have plastic flowers over them, secured by clear plastic with rocks along the edges.

Meanwhile, as Charlie and I discuss Jonathan's life, and how people are coping, Charlie switches gears on me and asks about my trip with his uncle. After I describe the day, he says, "Boy, it must be really nice to be able to go out like that whenever you want. It's such a great way to relax, to get out of town and just travel on the land."

I agree. "It's always something when it's so quiet too. It feels really calm when the only noise is me."

"The silence and calm is probably why so many old people refuse to give up travelling," Charlie says.

I COULD SEE GOOD ENOUGH

I am sitting with Mark Pihuktuq in the kitchen of the Roman Catholic Mission house, the "RC Mission." My wife and I are renting the house from the diocese for the year. It is largely due to Mark, the mission's caretaker, that we are staying here. Because I am on dissertation funding, my research budget is limited – not much more than what a family entirely dependent upon Social Assistance might make in a year. What little housing that is available would be far too expensive for us, so Mark pulled a few strings with the diocese to allow us to stay.

Mark looks after two buildings, one a Quonset hut – a residence and meeting hall that will soon be sold to the hamlet and converted into a women's shelter and community centre. The building we are in is the original mission house, constructed in 1937, one of the oldest buildings in the settlement. It is showing its age. Mark, at seventy-six, lacks the energy to maintain it properly. The exterior needs paint, some of the roof shingles have blown off, and a few windows have been smashed and boarded up. When Maya and I arrived, we found that the pipes that formed the rudimentary plumbing system had burst, and the furnace wasn't working. For all we knew, the insulation in the building might be original.

Not all of these issues are Mark's fault, of course. The diocese has little money in its budget for maintaining a house last occupied full time over a decade ago. The closest priest is in Kugluktuk, and he only travels to Ulukhaktok for Christmas, Easter, and weddings. This year he will skip Easter altogether.

Nevertheless, I am grateful to Mark for arranging this, though he does worry about my family and me. He is a dear friend, one of the first Inuit I met in Ulukhaktok, and we grew close during my first stay in 1992. We travelled together frequently during the autumn and spring and saw each other nearly every day.

Usually Mark comes to visit me, especially this year, when he can no longer travel on the land because of his health. He is drawn, I think, by the need to get out of his own house for a while. He is also drawn by coffee. He especially likes coffee brewed in a French press, a habit that both he and I picked up from Rick Condon, who was rather fanatical about having a supply of "good" coffee from Yellowknife. I have followed suit, and Mark is grateful.

I also think Mark feels a certain sense of responsibility for me. He seems worried that the house is not suitable, and constantly asks if everything is going well. He also insists on supplying us with country food, a significant gesture, since he himself depends on others for his own food, as he no longer hunts.

This afternoon I have convinced Mark to answer some questions about his health. He is sceptical, especially after an interview earlier in the summer when I asked him about life stages. He seems to think that what he knows or has to say might not be of value, or that he might not be eloquent enough to say what he wants to say. My sense is that his hesitation is partly because of the novel nature of my interviewing and partly because he has not been interviewed often. Usually when researchers come into the settlement to interview elders, they stick to a group of "usual suspects," Inuit known for being willing to talk, for their charisma and their media savvy. Mark is not one of those people, at least to outsiders. Still, he agrees to let me interview him, perhaps for the potential entertainment value.

One reason I want to interview Mark about his health is because it is, in my estimation, rather poor. Lately he is having difficulty getting around. He has a bad hip. Though he is not using a cane or a walker, carefully placed chairs and tables in his house enable him to move from room to room and keep him steady on his feet. Maya and I have done the same thing in our house, leaving a chair or two, disguised as places for putting on kamiks and hanging mittens and hats to dry, so Mark can move easily from the doorway into the kitchen.

His hip is not his only problem. Some years ago, he became lost in a blizzard. He often travelled alone when he was younger, partly by preference and partly because, as a notoriously early riser, he simply could not wait around for potential companions to get their lazy bones out of bed. Even in old age, he is still an early riser, and when I travelled with him in 1992, I learned to be up early and ready to go. I was usually not early enough. I would still be dressing and eating when Mark came by to see that I was reasonably far along, and then he would simply head out of town, trusting that I would drive fast enough to catch up to him.

On this particular trip, Mark was returning alone from Fish Lake in poor weather that kicked up into a full-blown blizzard. On the numerous occasions Mark has told me this story, he has said he was not worried about the weather as he was navigating from both memory and the snowdrifts. Since drifts typically lie in the direction of the prevailing winds, he knew that he was on course and would eventually run right into the settlement, or into the coast, which he could then follow home. Everything was fine until he ran low on gasoline.

Running low on gas is a common problem – snow machines pulling loads simply drink the stuff, and travellers carry cans of fuel with them on their sleds. All hunters have an intimate knowledge of how much gas their machine will take to reach a certain point, and they carry accordingly, often with an additional five-gallon can or two for good measure. Mark was no different, and he had plenty of fuel to get home. He simply walked back to his sled to retrieve a full can.

The sled was not there. At some point the towrope on the sled snapped. Entirely focused on staying on course, He had stopped paying attention to his sled. With no gas in his tank, he could not retrace his trail to find it. Stuck in a blizzard with no sled – and so no tent, stove, snow knife, or other survival gear – he went in a heartbeat from the minor inconvenience of travelling in bad weather to a serious threat to his life.

He realized he had no choice but to walk for it, to keep moving, though he had only a rough sense of how far he was from the settlement. He thought he was twenty to twenty-five kilometres from Ulukhaktok, so off he went, knowing that stopping meant he would freeze. To make matters worse, he ended up going slightly off course into a narrow valley that led east of the settlement. Though it sheltered him somewhat from the storm, the valley has such steep walls that climbing out is very difficult, and pointless in any case: climbing up onto the plateau and walking west toward the settlement (not a long walk in a direct line), one is confronted by the cliffs overlooking King's Bay. It is possible to find a path down but not wise to try in the middle of a blizzard.

Mark kept walking south, making it to Mashuyak. Once there, he sheltered in an empty cabin, found a little food, and rested. He also realized that his feet were frozen. Once sufficiently recovered, he walked the final ten kilometres back to Ulukhaktok and the bottle of whisky he kept under the bed. He eventually recovered, though he lost several toes and his feet were never quite right afterward – "easy to get numb," according to him.

Mark was also, in his old age, legally blind. He had been blind in one eye from the time he was a child, the damage done by an uncle who unwittingly brained him with a shovel, damage compounded by what Mark described as having "medicine" – my guess was an iodine mixture of some variety, though Mark was never clear on this – poured into his eye to make it better. Because of the injury and failed attempt at a cure, he was evacuated from his parents' camp and sent to Aklavik, where he lived for several years before returning home. He went through adulthood with a "spoiled eye," as he called it, but in later life his other eye developed cataracts. He eventually had surgery for these, but, because of difficulty with the interpreter, who spoke a different dialect from Mark, he did not comply properly with his post-surgery instructions.

Nevertheless, he has continued to drive his ATV around the settlement, much to the alarm of many Inuit, who are afraid he might run over a child or crash into a building. Mark, however, only has a few routes he travels – to my house, the Co-op, the Northern, and a few friends, routes he knows by memory. Everyone seems to know when he's coming and give him a wide berth. He drives his machine slower than most people walk.

"Okay, Mark," I begin, "I'm going to ask you some questions about your health. If you could, answer each question on a scale of one to five. If something is really good, the best, you give it a one, eh? If it is really bad, a five. You got that?" Like many old men, Mark is hard of hearing too. It is why I wear earplugs when I drive a snowmobile.

"Right. Go ahead." As is his custom, Mark has his head askew, keeping his one reasonably useful eye trained on me.

"Okay, I'd like you to rate your hearing. Compared to other people your own age, how would you say your hearing is?"

"Well, it's good enough. I'd say a three."

I move on. "How about your eyes. How are your eyes?"

"Well, they're no more good, you know. My one eye is spoiled, I'm telling you that story. Five."

We move on again, working through his digestion, teeth, bones and muscles, memory. For each, his scores vary between three and five. Mark seems to agree he's not in good shape.

"Okay, how would you rate your overall health?"

"Oh, it's good enough, I guess. I'd say two. Pretty good, you know."

Well, that is news, and it surprises me. I let it pass for the time being, and move on to some questions about activities of daily living. Activities

of Daily Living (ADL) and its companion, Instrumental Activities of
Daily Living (IADL), are assessments used in geriatrics and gerontology to determine the well-being and functionality of the aged. I am
trying to adapt these assessments to Ulukhaktok, to get a sense of how
functional the elderly in Ulukhaktok actually are. To do so, however,
requires a different set of questions than those that normally appear on
the standardized ADL or IADL, because the social context in
Ulukhaktok is so different. I begin by asking a number of standard
questions: Can you dress yourself? Can you go shopping at the store?
Some of these are a bit confusing – Mark rarely shops at the store, for
example, so the question is difficult for him to answer – but he says he
does not have too many problems, though he might be humouring me
at this point.

"How well can you walk around town?"

"Well, I can't walk too good, you know. Must be a five, pretty bad. I
have to drive everywhere." Aside from his general assessment of his
health as "pretty good," Mark seems to have an unflinching acceptance
of his poor health and his physical limitations.

"How well can you drive an ATV?"

He pauses for a moment. "Oh, I guess it's good enough. Must be a
two."

I cannot let this one pass, so I decide to probe a bit. As I noted earlier,
Mark is well known in town, people scattering when they see him
coming. "Mark, you need to explain something to me. You say that
you're pretty well blind and you can't see, but you're telling me that you
can drive an ATV just fine. I don't understand."

Mark looks at me out of his better eye for a moment. "Well, it's good
enough, you know. I know how to get everywhere in town. I can tell
from the shapes of the buildings."

So he's navigating around town through a combination of memory
and trust: trust that people he might not see will just get out of his way.
Yikes. "But what about camp? How do you get out there?" Mark still
spends time out at his fishing camp out in the suburbs. Indeed, he
spends most of his summer out there.

"My wife tells me where to turn. You just get the tires into the ruts of
the trail, and the Honda steers itself. She tells me when to stop."

Mark's definition of his health is partly based on what he can still do, even if doing that activity is acutely impaired. I imagine that most non-natives would not try anything near like this, though I do recall my grandfather taking out the car for a spin now and then, just to prove he still could. My grandmother knew about it, but their children only learned about it several years later, when he finally caused an accident.

I am beginning to get a sense of Mark's general worldview in this matter of health. As we age, he seems to say, what is important is not that we maintain our good health – though it would certainly be nice – but rather that we maintain a proper attitude. We are doomed to increasing limitations. What is important is that we manage these limitations and carry on in spite of them. Furthermore, Mark, like many elders, seems to apply this philosophy to his entire life. It might explain an observation made by many nurses I have known over the years: Inuit seem to live with conditions that would cripple a Qablunaaq, remaining functional and even economically productive despite limitations that would put a southerner in a wheelchair.

"Okay, let's go back. Tell me about your overall health. You're telling me that your eyes are no good, it's hard to walk, and your bones and muscles are weak. How come you say that your health is pretty good?

As Mark again thinks, I can hear the slight rattle of air as it moves in and out of his lungs. His lip is starting to quiver. "Well, it's I'm still alive, isn't it? Most everybody my own age is dead, eh?" His chest shakes and rattles and he smiles at me, a silent yet clear laugh, as if to say that a sense of humour is important too.

SAFETY CHANNEL

"It is good to be back." Don Johnson, here for the summer working on his dissertation, is helping fund his own archeology work with a summer field school. The gaggle of undergraduate students will be in the settlement for the month, studying Arctic ecology and culture. They have been here a few days and seem to be settling in without too much difficulty, though they are suffering at least some culture shock, and all the attention must be a bit unnerving for them. They are a novelty here. When they go out, a herd of children follows them around, peppering them with questions. "What's your name? You're from States, ah? From where you get your jacket?"

The younger children, though, will eventually grow tired of the students when they realize there is little in the way of excitement going on in the duplex. The older teens and young adults present a subtly different problem, and they will hang around for the entirety of the course.

Dennis Iqiahuuyuq is one of the young men who is hanging around. Smitten by the young women, he has been doing his best impression of a traditional Inuk, happily providing information and advice about Inuit culture, hunting, and living on the land. Paul Tigliktuq tells me outright that Dennis is an "Eskimo for a week," playing up his heritage in front of the students even though he knows next to nothing about being an Inuk. "All that guy does is watch TV and smoke up," says Paul. "He only sees animals on the TV. Never goes out on the land" – which is not entirely true. I know Dennis was at Fish Lake once when he was twelve, with his grandfather.

Don has made coffee, and he and I are discussing the state of my fieldwork, his plans for the summer after the students leave (he is going to Walker Bay to do some site surveying), and how the summer course is shaping up. His immediate priority is getting the students out on the land, and he is planning a trip into Safety Channel to see some of the archaeological sites down there. A Thule-era house, long since abandoned but reasonably close, is worth a trip. Ten years ago such a field trip might have been impossible. In 1992, for example, the ice in Queen's Bay did not break up and clear until mid-July. In recent years, however, break-up has arrived much earlier. This year, 2007, Inuit were hunting ducks by boat because the ice broke up so early. This apparent change over the past fifteen years has pushed some Inuit to reconsider their equipment strategies. With a longer open-water season, some are prioritizing boats rather than snowmobiles.

"How's it going?" I know Don has already put wheels in motion, trying to strike while the weather is good.

"Oh, really great, really great. We're finalizing plans to make the boating trip. I've got drivers and boats lined up, got the gas, bought some food. We're going to try and go tomorrow morning. I've just been talking with William Kaaktuq about squaring everything away. Could you come? It would be really good to have you along. You could talk with the students about subsistence and local history." Unlike the second trip we will make in a few weeks, which will take us further into the Sound and require an overnight on the land, this is a mere day trip, very close to town.

I agree to go, but my energies are best devoted to a formal presentation during one of their class sessions, after the trip. There will be plenty of Inuit going, and the students will be better served interacting with them – the boat drivers and assorted brothers, cousins, or children that tag along.

The following morning, the students are dressed and ready to go, but there is one problem. Overnight the wind shifted to the south, and Queen's Bay is plugged with ice. There are small pieces of floating ice in the bay itself, but what is truly problematic is a large sheet right at the entrance to the bay, clear across it. It appears that the trip will not happen today. The students are unhappy – like most southerners, they are accustomed to making plans and sticking with them, the weather never really a consideration. The reality of the North is a bit different: you travel when conditions permit. William shrugs his shoulders. "There's no road. Can't do anything about it. Maybe by tonight it will be better." Don, who understands these limitations, simply tells the students to hang out, and we will go when William says we can go. In the meantime, we will have tea. There is always time for tea.

Weather is, of course, a significant problem for Inuit who are dedicated to hunting but committed to working a job for wages. The weather can and does change suddenly, and it is one reason that working and hunting are, for the most part, mutually exclusive. Some, like Albert Aquti, resort to taking a day off from work to hunt or fish when the weather is reasonably good. Others plan their entire year around a few specific trips, taking all of their holidays for three weeks of an expedition hunt for caribou, and hunting only when "weekend" and "good conditions" coincide.

The wind, however, is playing tricks on us today and shifts earlier than William expected. By late afternoon we can get out of the bay and make our way down to Mashuyak. Whether we can get past Mashuyak, or even past Karukut, is unclear yet, but we can try. William is worried about the winds down around Karukut. "Lots of currents down there, it can be dangerous. And if the wind is strong, we're not going to get past Karukut. I'm not that crazy to try it anyway," he says.

I have scouted all the available boats, and for my money I am sticking with William. Matthew Aqiaruq's boat is already full, and of the other drivers, William is the oldest and most skilled. I stake my claim by placing my pack in the bow. Edward Kuniluk nudges me as the students are loading in. "William is going to get there first. You watch. These old guys are really into getting there first."

And, indeed, William's boat, last into the water and last through the ice field, races by the other boats once he opens the throttle of his 75-horse in open water. Edward only runs a 60, as does Matthew, Tigliktuq runs an old 55, and Simon is running a 40. They have no chance to keep up, though Edward notes later that you pay for the horsepower, and a 75 practically drinks gasoline.

Happily, the wind is down, so the boat at full throttle is planing easily. In even a light wind, though, the chop can be severe, the aluminum boat pounding on the water. It can be as painful on the spine and bum as a snowmobile going over rough ground, but a snowmobile at least has a suspension. Though aluminum boats can last for many years, their longevity is due more to the limited season for open water than anything else. Like other equipment, the environment takes its toll. The pounding on the water loosens rivets. Every summer, boat owners can be found at some point hammering loose rivets or replacing them, resorting to caulk or other creative means to seal leaks in an attempt to extend a boat's life. A new boat and motor can cost twice the price of a snowmobile.

Eventually we pull up on the beach at Mahsuyak, our first pit stop. Mark Anguhuqtuq is camped here for the summer, taking seals and setting nets for fish. Don wants the students to talk with him about his work here. Though living at Mashuyak during the summer has been part of Mark's routine for many years, the Department of Fisheries and Oceans makes much of it possible. Part of his summer is spent collecting samples from the seals he takes. For each seal he shoots, he removes the reproductive organs and the teeth, part of a long-term project monitoring contaminants under the DFO's direction.

I have heard what Mark has to say about this before, so my attention turns to the three young teens at the end of the point. They are behind a blind, in a shallow dugout in the gravel, rifles trained on the little channel between Mashuyak and Holman Island. Clearly, they are looking for something, scanning the water between the floating ice chunks. These are three of Mark's grandchildren, out here for most of the summer. The kids are genuinely interested in being here, but the feeling is mutual. Mark and Irene want them here partly for the help they can provide in the camp and partly to get them out of town, where there are too many distractions. Here, these young teenagers have an opportunity to acquire some important skills from their grandparents.

I see it long before the teens do – the tiny head sticking out between the floating ice. I point, and hear Edward utter, "Yup." He saw it before I did. The three hunters in the blind have yet to spot it.

After another half minute, one of them sees the young seal and shouts. All three are soon on it, trying to stabilize their rifles for a clean shot. The report from their rifles echoes across the narrow channel. The seal dives.

"Damn scope," one of the teens yells. It is Charlie Hanayi's son, Zachary. He pulls out a coin, and adjusts the telescope on his rifle.

We sit quietly for a few more minutes, watching and waiting. Edward, who has years of experience with ringed seals, seems to already know where it will come up, and he directs me to the spot with a nudge. "Current goes this way through here," he says, motioning with his arm, though I can see that already from the drifting ice.

Sure enough, right around where Edward points, the seal emerges. Because it is young, and because it dove suddenly, it did not get a complete breath. It needs air.

The boys again see the seal late and shoot high and wide. It was less than fifty metres away. Zachary swears as he misses and it dives. "That fucking scope!" He fiddles with the settings again and tries to sight in on a piece of floating ice some sixty metres away. He again misses.

Edward shakes his head. "It's not the scope, son. You can't blame the scope." He smiles, and we walk back to Mark, who is holding court with the students. "Slow to learn, my nephew. But he'll figure it out."

He might, if he gets enough practice, which is the entire point of having him here. Because the DFO funds Mark's work, Mark has plenty of ammunition at his disposal, and these kids will need to shoot nearly all of it to develop a proficiency with their rifles. Shooting is not like Hollywood, where the good guy simply points his gun at the bad guy and the bad guy falls down. There are far too many variables involved, especially in the Arctic. Stocks warp, barrels expand and contract in the cold, and bouncing around in sleds does not help things. It also does not help that the rifles these boys have are low-quality firearms, likely the least expensive in the catalogues from which Inuit order. The ammunition that the Northern and Co-op stock is of equally low quality. So are the telescopes. Despite Edward's observation, it could well be the scopes, though I suspect that Mark checked them before letting the boys use them.

The more experienced hunters have a keen sense of all these potential problems, and, more importantly, how to solve them. Consequently, the teens have to learn not only how to judge distance and wind direction but also to adjust for the limitations of their equipment. Over the rest of the summer, their grandfather will provide some guidance, allowing the boys the luxury of trial and error mixed with some direct instruction. Most importantly, they will watch Mark as he hunts.

Once Mark has finished his lecture, we reload the boats and hit the water again, travelling down around Karukut and into Safety Channel, to our next stopping place. The wind, happily, has remained light, so we have no problems. It is long past dinnertime in Ulukhaktok when we pull into the little bay, and none of us has eaten in some time. We make our way up the beach to Albert Aquti's cabin. We are on a beach, in a little protected bay, and there are several cabins here. Albert and his wife, Shirley, are setting nets for fish, getting away from the settlement for a little vacation. They deliberately chose to come to this place, thinking it unlikely they would see anybody from town. This time of the year, most people are travelling by ATV up and down the coast, north and west of the settlement. There is no way to get down here by ATV, and few boaters are coming this way yet. Even if they were, they would likely be headed further into Prince Albert Sound to hunt caribou and would not stop in.

Albert did not reckon on a field school, however, and we have descended upon him, five boatloads of college students, a couple of anthropologists, and a handful of Inuit. Albert is a bit taken aback, but he is pleased that he does not have to feed us. He could not, in any case. Though he has been setting nets for char, he has not been catching many fish, perhaps five a day, enough to feed him, his wife, and the two grandchildren who are camping with them.

We are well supplied with tea, coffee, piffi, mipku, and the standard store supplies for travelling. The students make hot chocolate and eat the cookies they've brought, while the rest of us go for the traditional grub.

After a snack, the students take a nature walk along the beach with Don, focusing on plants and geology. Don plans next to head over to the Thule house on the other side of the bay. Most of the Inuit sit down to chat with Albert, drink tea, and enjoy the weather, which is beautiful for this time of year. Agnes Kaaktuq, who has come with William in the boat, has produced two whole char picked earlier today from her son Isaac's nets. She begins splitting them open, removing the guts, and cutting them into steaks. The Coleman stove hisses as the water heats. When it boils, she drops in the fish. William claims the heads. "I'm the oldest," he says.

Paul Tigliktuq, who is also driving, makes his own claim. "There's two heads. I'm next oldest, so I get one."

William responds. "No. Both for me. My wife is cook."

There's laughter all around, but I am not sure William is joking. The head is the prized part of the fish. I particularly like the cheeks, but I know Isaac prefers the eyes. He says they pop nicely in the mouth when crunched.

Albert is getting the news from town. He is trying to avoid going back, but he knows he has plenty of work waiting for him. Multiple building lots need new gravel pads, and there is plenty of other work for the loader. Albert only works casual now, having officially retired from his job at the hamlet several years ago, at age forty-eight. But he is needed, and he feels obligated. There are others who can drive the loader, but most people seem to prefer Albert. A second limitation is Shirley. She also works, full-time, and her vacation is nearly up.

As for me, I came to explore the area, and I want to walk around. I grab my rifle, a lightweight .22, and make to climb the hill behind the camp. Simon sees me and volunteers to come along. Soon we are over the crest of the hill, out of sight and mind of the others below. I load the .22 and, as we walk, I periodically plunk at the many rocks sticking out of the ground. It is a bit of a pastime when I walk, a weak attempt to try to develop a skill of particular importance to Inuit, the ability to put the sights or scope onto a target and fire quickly. Eventually, if they keep at it, those boys at Mashuyak will develop that ability, to spot the seal, raise the rifle, and fire at the target the first time they have the crosshairs on it. Their biggest problem today was trying to hold the scope on the seal's head to make the perfect shot. As Edward says, though, "The perfect shot is the one that makes it dead."

"That's a nice rifle. But you should shoot something with it." The rifle, a .22 semi-automatic, fascinates Simon. It breaks into two pieces, nice for carrying in a backpack. And, given that it is a semi-auto, it makes for decent protection from the biggest problem around the settlement: wolves. They are an increasing nuisance, and, despite what some people say, quite willing to go after humans. William had a close call a few years ago down at Kuuk. While he was relieving himself, two wolves approached him. Throwing rocks at the pair saved him, keeping them at distance as he hobbled back to the campsite. Mark Anguhuqtuq discovered wolves terrorizing his dogs last winter. The wolves were taking the food off of the line and, in a stroke of wolf genius, leaving the dogs so there would be another feeding.

"I *am* shooting something with it. I'm practising my shooting on all these little rocks."

I know what is coming next. Simon is having fun with me, and testing me too. We have hunted and fished together enough to be comfortable with each other. "You know what I mean. You should kill something. You'll feel better."

There is nothing around but rocks and rather a lot of birds, mostly snow buntings, flitting from rock to rock, chirping loudly. Aside from them, there is nothing to kill. So I ignore Simon and plink a few more rocks. "I feel fine now."

Simon is not going to let me off the hook. "C'mon, you really should shoot something. Like one of the birdies."

I am uncomfortable shooting something for what seems to me to be no reason. "Are you going to eat it if I shoot it?"

Simon, like most men our age, has eaten birds like these before. He has told me before about catching little "brown birds" as a child – longspurs and horned larks that his grandmother made into soup. "No, I haven't eaten those since I was a kid. But you should shoot one."

Simon is, I think, making two points here. The first is that he wants to see how I am at shooting, so I acquiesce. If I do, he might leave me alone. "All right. Which one?"

He waves at a little snow bunting, black and white, sitting on a rock some forty metres away. I raise the rifle, put the scope on the target, and fire, all in a swift motion. We will see if the practice has paid off.

The bunting vanishes in a puff of feathers. "Oooh, nice shot! That's a really nice rifle." Inuit sometimes attribute successful marksmanship to the rifle rather than the shooter. Given the state of the rifles around here, it makes sense, but I would like a little credit. I have improved since our first hunting trip together years ago.

Simon having made his point, we continue our walk. "My parents have a cabin just over that way." He points down the hill, further into the bay. "We used to stay there when I was a kid. Spent whole summers down here, just hunting seals and fishing. The whole family."

Being on the land tends to bring more reminiscences out of people than just being in town. Particular places seem to hold memories, and Simon is no exception. He did not just spend a summer or two here: he practically grew up in this area. His parents were some of the last to pursue a seasonal subsistence round spent mostly out of town, trapping foxes in winter and spring, hunting seals in spring and summer. It was not until Simon's teens, when the seal market collapsed, that his parents gave up and stayed in town more and more.

"You don't come down here much now, do you?"

Simon ponders. "Not really. No one really hunts seals anymore, not for the skins anyway. My parents still use the cabin, though. They come down here when they've been having trouble. Sometimes they drink too much and get into trouble with each other. That's when they come down here, to get away from the problems of town, and get themselves right. Sure wouldn't mind to live down here again, but it would be kind of hard to go without television. Back when I was a kid, boy, I wanted nothing more than to be in town, I hated being down here all the time. The other kids used to make fun of me and my brother, because we never knew about T V, or hockey, or things like that. Now I know better. It's like life was easier then, there was less to worry about."

We walk in a large circle, over a ridge and around a low hill, before we return to camp. We have staved off our hunger by chewing the flowers and stalks of the sorrel growing along the ground, sweet with a hint of sour. We know the pot of fish will be long gone. All that will be left will be piffi and mipku.

We get back to the camp a short time after the students, who are again eating cookies. They form their own group, and we sidle back up to the Inuit table, where there is hot water for tea. Simon cannot hold it in. "Pete shot a little birdie." He's feeling mischievous again. Though he says it in front of the Inuit drivers, Don also hears me. Thankfully, the students are out of earshot.

"Did I hear that right?" Don asks. "Did you shoot a bird?"

I decide to have a little fun with him, so I channel Harry Tamaryuk. "Yup." A pause. "A little snow bunting." I lower my voice, put an edge on it like Harry would. "I blew it away!"

Don looks horrified at the thought of shooting an innocent songbird. Edward, thinking of his uncle, chuckles. William simply nods. The other point Simon was making was that this is a malevolent world. Unlike the wealthy society of the South, which insulates us from unpleasant things, survival here requires killing animals and doing so without hesitation. They are all gifts. If the animal is offered, one is obliged to take it, and one is neither happy nor sad to have done so. Death, whether in the form of a butchered muskox, a blown-away little bird, or a cousin's suicide, is omnipresent. It cannot be compartmentalized or isolated from daily affairs.

While Don seemingly contemplates whether I am an evil person, Edward examines the rifle. "What kind of bullets are these?" He has opened the chamber and is inspecting the ammunition. He has not seen the ammunition I am using before in this calibre – high-velocity loads with hard points. Most .22 shells available here are soft points. With my permission, he fires a few rounds at some floating ice. He is impressed by the rifle's accuracy even at 140 to 150 metres. It is a quality firearm, which hides the fact that I am, by comparison, a relatively lousy marksman. I still wish Simon would at least acknowledge that I have some ability, though.

Dennis Iqiahuuyuq, who has wandered over from the students – the cookies are gone –speaks up. "That's a cute rifle. Nice toy." Like most of the young men in town, he seems to think that a .22 is a child's rifle. Paul glares at him.

Edward shrugs. "Old Agnes took out a bear with a .22, long ago. You should ask Mark about it sometime. He was just a kid. With the right ammunition, you could take practically anything." He turns back to me. "Can I have some of these bullets? From where you get them?"

We break camp, reload the boats, and leave Albert in peace as we move across the bay to investigate the Thule site. Everyone is fascinated, of course, even the younger boat drivers. Edward and Simon both did some work on this house when it was excavated, when they were teenagers themselves. Once we return from inspecting the old house site, Agnes brings out the second course. In addition to the fish, she has brought a very young seal, a *natiaq*. It was found this morning, she says, in Isaac's nets with the fish. She hypothesizes that the animal, very small and not very fat, lost its mother and was starving. It tried to eat the fish in the nets, became entangled, and drowned.

She lays the carcass out on the gravel beach and begins to flense it, cutting the skin and blubber, removing it in one piece. She then opens the body cavity, removing the internal organs one by one. The liver she lays out on a rock.

Dennis's eyes light up. "That's my favourite, seal liver. I haven't had some in a long time, too, and I am really hungry." He seems to be encouraging the students to try some. I see a chance for payback. He insulted my rifle, after all. Perhaps I am channelling Simon's mischievousness, or Paul's assessment of Dennis's manhood.

Dennis slices off a bit of the liver and begins to eat. Edward, Simon, Paul, and I do the same, and a few of the braver students slice off small chunks, giving it a try. It is very rich. To me it tastes like very rare steak.

"Oh, I love seal liver, boy. It's one of my favourite things. And it's really good for you, too." Dennis waxes rhapsodic, playing up his heritage.

I pounce. "Yup. It is really good for you. If you don't get a tapeworm. Seals have those. Liver flukes, too, I think. Oh, and lungworm. Seals can get that too. Can people get lungworms from seals? Seals also carry distemper, and I think they can get rabies, can't they?" I look at Simon and Edward. The students put down their knives, deciding they are no longer willing to risk it.

Dennis's chewing slows down, and he finishes his bite. "I guess I'm pretty full after all that fish before. Maybe I'll go see what Don's up to." He walks off.

Simon smiles. "Great thinking. More for us!" Paul chuckles, his laugh echoing off the rocks of the little bay.

Edward cuts another chunk and pops it into his mouth. "There doesn't look like there's anything wrong with this one. Agnes wouldn't let us eat it if it looked funny."

I CAN FEEL HEAVY

When William Kaaktuq said that he was really only the driver now, he meant it. He's in his early seventies, and the years have taken their toll on his body – not only the arthritis but the numerous injuries from snowmobile crashes, the labour of driving dogs, the constant exposure to the elements. His body has been ravaged internally too. Shortly after the boating trip into Safety Channel, I stop in to see him one evening and find Agnes alone on the sofa, sewing and sitting by the telephone.

I am surprised William is not at home, especially with Agnes there. In the evenings, if she is not at sewing club or at the Anglican clubhouse, she and William are nearly inseparable. And in summer, William tends to stay indoors. The dust in the air really bothers him.

"He had a doctor's appointment," Agnes tells me. "He went to Inuvik." This is news to me. I see William frequently: surely he would have let it slip that he was going for a scheduled trip to Inuvik for a medical? I go over to see Isaac. He is home, having just returned from running his dogs. He has a new crop of pups this spring and is quite pleased with them. He lets them off the line, and they chase the ATV around, working up their stamina in the process.

I sit and have tea with Isaac. The television is on, *Survivorman* again. Normally Isaac enjoys pointing out all of the mistakes that the Survivorman makes. On this night, however, we sit in silence until the show ends.

"We went up to the nursing station today." A simple statement of fact.

"Why did you go there? Was anybody sick?"

"No, we just had X-rays taken. I can't believe that Matthew, though. He was taking the X-rays, and he stayed right in the room and didn't put on an apron or anything. That guy is sure lazy."

This is odd, that Isaac would have an X-ray taken, but the topic shifts to Matthew Aqiaruq, Isaac's neighbour at the end of the street. Slightly younger than Isaac, he is also a hunter – indeed, the two men often travel together – but according to Isaac, Matthew never cleans up his camps, he drinks too much, and his equipment is in poor condition. Years ago, before Isaac took over his dad's dogs full time, he ran into an ethical dilemma. At the time, he was feeding his dad's dogs and training the pups, all of them chained on a line slightly out of town, close to a small pond, so that the dogs could access water. Matthew kept his dogs nearby. Isaac had been out to feed his dogs and told me, "Boy, that Matthew, his dogs are so poor. They're really starving out there. I don't know the last time he's been out to feed them."

I wasn't sure whether this was a general complaint, the bellyaching that is common in small communities where people can build up a lifetime of real and imagined slights. Dogs only work during the late winter and early spring, after all. "Why feed them well in the summer?" I asked Isaac.

"You gotta treat them right in the summer too," he said, "so they can be strong for pulling." Duh. Over the years I have provided Isaac with more than enough evidence to convict me of being an imbecile.

However, over the course of several days he kept saying that Matthew's dogs were in bad shape – the ground they were on was increasingly muddy and wet, the dogs were filthy, and they were not being fed. They appeared to be dying. Isaac was torn: he had a genuine concern for the dogs, but they were, after all, Matthew's, and Isaac was loath to impinge on Matthew's affairs and personal autonomy.

Finally, after ten days, Isaac decided to confront Matthew, but to do so in a way that he felt was indirect. He would simply tell Matthew that his dogs looked in poor shape. One had died, and Isaac, under the guise of concern that the rotting corpse might spread disease, thought he would simply notify Matthew. "I went and told him he had a dead dog on his line," Isaac reported to me later that evening. "He told me that I was wrong: he had two dead dogs on his line."

That episode convinced Isaac that Matthew was irredeemable. Our discussion of Matthew's latest offences, however, threatened to obscure the real issue: why was Isaac having an X-ray taken? I puzzle this out in my head while we talk, and it slowly dawns on me what has happened. William has nearly always had a pretty good cough going, something that has grown worse over the years, until by 2007 it was full bore. William would periodically be overcome by fits of coughing, mostly dry hacking, loud and unpleasant. In the name of trying to help him, I ordered a small HEPA filter for him and told him to put it in his bedroom and keep the door shut. With all of the dust and other particulate matter in the air, especially during the summer months, William was not the only person to have difficulty with his sinuses and lungs. Other elders who suffered from sinus or lung issues had HEPA filters in their bedrooms and reported significant improvement in their breathing, a few going so far as to reclaim some of their sense of smell.

I gave it to Agnes, with the instructions: put it in the bedroom, run it all the time, keep the door shut. William's breathing should improve some in a few nights. Agnes nodded. A week later, I asked William how it was, and he responded. "Really works good. Really helps" – before he broke into another hacking cough.

He soon discontinued its use. It made the air smell funny, he said. Rather than hurt my feelings and return the gift, he passed the filter onto another friend, one who already had a HEPA filter, who informed me that the "funny smell" was simply William's sense of smell returning. The filter was returned to me, and I ran it in my bedroom instead.

"So, who got X-rays taken?" I ask Isaac.

"Just me, Ida, and Sonny. We went up this afternoon." Isaac fishes around on the shelf for the cards and the crib board, not looking at me.

"What about your mum? Did she have X-rays, too?" I shift into data collection mode.

Isaac is still not looking in my direction. "Ah, she went up in the morning to have hers done."

"And when is your dad coming back? On the next plane?" The next flight from Inuvik is two days away.

Isaac is looking uncomfortable now, about to crack. "I'm not sure. We're not supposed to say anything about it. The nurses want us to keep it quiet."

"Why? What does William have? Did he test positive for TB?"

TB is precisely what William has had, active tuberculosis, for who knows how long, and thus the X-rays taken of all of the family members. Luckily, no one else has tested positive. But William is in quarantine and will remain there until he has completed his initial regimen of medication and is declared cured. Given the damage that tuberculosis caused in the Arctic, even well into the 1970s, the medical people are taking no chances.

Over the next few weeks, the discussion around the settlement is about William and TB. Despite attempts to "keep it quiet," nearly everyone knows within a day that William is in quarantine. Among the hunters, the concern is whether this will finish William. Given his physical condition, will he be fit enough to travel during the autumn?

I recall an interview I did with William some ten years ago, in which he clearly laid out the central concerns of being old and the necessity to keep fighting, believing that one's force of will could overcome nearly anything.

"William, what are the major worries or concerns for people who are *angut* or *nuliangituq*?" These are not life stages but rather descriptors, the first meaning literally, "man," or "father," the second a descriptor meaning "has a wife." More generally, these are terms for adult men. William's response clarified his worldview.

"I don't know what to call it. People don't, they're worrying about money. They don't ... it's not the same, eh? Like me, I think lots about money because I don't work, I don't make money by a job. I try to make lots of money by hunting, trapping, carving. But some people don't.

They're just waiting from government, that's all. That money is so easy, getting money from the government, like welfare. Some people never try anything, like Abraham Kayuqtuq, that kind of people, who never do anything. They never worry about getting money or about hunting because the government spoils them, so these people, they're waiting for the money to finish so they can get welfare. Not like my age. When I was that age we try, try, try, because there's no government. Government spoils the people. It's really easy now. Now people they stay in the houses all the time where it's really warm. Long ago we used to play outside all the time, even in winter. Makes people tougher."

"What is the best part about being in this age group?" I have found that these "best part" and "worst part" questions effective. Simple, yet direct, and they let the interviewee then direct the conversation.

William paused for a moment. "I don't know. I never think of that." Another pause. "I'm alive is the best. From about fifteen to forty years old, my life is really good. I like that life. If I want to go anywhere, I can. After about forty, it gets different. I can feel heavy. I like that life before, it's not lazy. Feel light all the time. Travel lots, to Sachs Harbour, Kuujjua, Umingmagiuk, De Salis Bay, we could go anywhere. We were really ready to go anywhere. Sometimes we stay in Sachs, sometimes Umingmagiuk, sometimes Kuujjua, we never stay in Ulukhaktok. Then the government brings houses, school, power, and we move here, and everybody comes here. But even at that time, when people started coming here, it was really good, too. No problem. Everybody had a good life. There were lots of games, people were hunting together, everybody was friendly with each other. But then the funny life started coming. People started arguing, started fighting, and then there was lots of trouble. In 1969, we got the first sports hunters. The first ones never brought liquor with them. From 1970, 1980, they start to bring liquor. Some people, they learned to drink from the sports hunters. They liked to take sports hunters out because they could get liquor from them. It got worse after 1980."

I asked, "What is the worst thing about being in this age group, about being adult?" Ideally, I would have liked William to talk about what it was like to be an adult today, but, like many Inuit, he was comfortable referencing only his own experiences.

"It's just like there was no worst thing from those times. Sometimes it was really hard to get animals, but we never worry about anything. Our life was like that."

Some common themes stood out in his response, among them the repeated mentions of worry, concern, and the difference between "heavy" and "light." Nearly all of the old people I spoke with made this distinction, between the dangers of worrying, which leads to feeling heavy, both negative conditions that are likely local conceptions of depression. For many of the old people, living in the settlement is full of heaviness, especially when contrasted with the independence and freedom that corresponded with those remembered good times.

The important distinction that emerges, however, is not simply a sense that the old days were good just because they were the old days. William, and even Isaac, Albert, and many men my age, can easily list the negatives of town life and set them off against the positives of pre-settlement life. As William noted, in those old days, what made people "light" was the sense of true community, people helping each other, meaningful social interaction, and general friendliness, all things that Inuit perceive are gone today. The modern settlement is characterized by the heaviness of fighting and drinking and, in William's eyes at least, the presence of a government safety net that makes everything too easy for people. At the same time, however, I have never heard any Inuk long for the days of living in a damp, poorly lit iglu, nor have I heard anyone wax poetic about going without food for days or weeks during certain times of the year.

We moved on to the next life stage. "What are the major worries or concerns for people who are *inirnikhaq*? William, like many others, identified this stage as what southerners might call middle age – no longer a fully healthy adult, inirniq, in possession of a fully developed body, but rather one who was becoming something else. Sixty-three at the time of the interview, William was to my mind on the edge of this distinction, but because of his physical health and his activity, he still considered himself in this category of being inirnikhaq, rather than *inutquaq*, old.

"I'm an old man. Well, not really old, but not really young. I don't know. I never worry about anything. Sometimes I worry about some things, like when I'm making dog food. I get worried about my dogs in winter, when it is too cold and I'm not using them much. But I never worry about anything else.

"What is the best thing about being in this age group? What's best about being inirnikhaq?"

William paused to think. "Like I'm not really a good life right now, you know, because I can't run. No more best times, but I never worry about best times anymore, because my life is heavy. It's not young anymore. One of my friends from Tuk [Tuktoyuktuk], I saw him last fall. He's just like me. He told me he got no more best times because he is not lively anymore. But it's a good life, though. If you got everything, it's good enough."

"What is the worst thing about being in this age group?"

"Nothing. Two to three years ago was my worst things. Really, really worse, really bad. Can't even lift five gallons of gas, can't even lift it up, not even to my Ski-doo. I had to tie rope to move cans to my Ski-doo. Because of arthritis. For three months I sit like that. Right there," he said, hitting the sofa. "I eat, eat, eat. Never go anywhere. Really bad arthritis. My wife start telling me, 'You should get up and walk around, go somewhere. You're not sick.' She had arthritis once and fight it and get better. I said, 'Nah. I don't feel like it. My sinews are sore.'

"Tom Smith," he says, referring to a biologist and close friend who has worked in Ulukhaktok since the late 1960s, "he came, and he ask me, 'William, you like hunting?' 'Yes,' I said, 'yes, I like hunting.' Tom said, 'If you like hunting, you should walk around for a while. Walk really far. If you sit like that, you aren't going to shoot anymore.' So I go out and walk up the bluff three times a day. I walk all around. Every day I exercise for a half hour. Half an hour is a really long time to exercise. I get hot and really sweat. Time goes so slow. That's how I can carry two jerry cans now. My life has come back to normal. That's why some people are sitting around. They can't go anywhere anymore. Boy, half hour is a really long time. I don't exercise now. My life is back to normal. I got no more sore sinews, that's why I don't exercise anymore. I get so much arthritis one time, I can't even lift my cup. Can't even use the axe. Now I can do anything. I could push my boat by myself. I can put my Honda in the boat by myself. I feel really good."

I had heard this story before the interview, of course, and I was expecting it to emerge. The event was an important one in William's life, his recovery from arthritis through sheer force of will. For William, as for Mark Pihuktuq, moving from a healthy adulthood into old age is not so much about the grace of having good health but rather the ability to manage poor health effectively. One has to keep trying, refuse to give up in the face of increased limitations.

"What are the major worries or concerns for people who are *inutquaq* and *aaquaq*?" These are the next stages, literally "old man" and "old woman," distinct from inirnikhaq because of, I think, activity levels.

William's response was quick. "For them life is really easy. They feel lazy, they don't feel for to do anything. Even they could do anything, but they don't feel like they'd like to. Because they're old. Not young anymore."

"What is the best thing about being in this age group?"

"Sitting around, I guess."

"What is the worst thing about being in this age group?"

"No worst things. Just sitting around, they have a really good time just sitting around. They never go visiting anymore. Got no worse things, just sitting around until they die. My father-in-law was like that at the end – just sitting around. Don't go to church, don't go to gym. Just sitting around until they die. My father-in-law was really old. After he died, I told my wife that if I get really old, I go tell the cop to come down and shoot me. It's getting really old and people could suffer."

I knew Agnes's father, if only briefly, for he passed away in 1992. One of the last to recall meeting Stefansson when he was a young boy, Hakugiktuq, a powerful man in his youth, was in his early nineties. At the end he required oxygen and had difficulty moving around, to the point where there was discussion about whether he should be in a nursing facility in Yellowknife. The family refused to send him away, of course, and the nurse, who had long years of experience in Ulukhaktok, concurred, providing everything in the Health Centre's arsenal to keep him at home and comfortable until he passed away.

"How does someone become inutquaq?"

"If I get old, I'm just going to sit there. Never hunting polar bear, trapping, travelling, fishing, never look for seal holes, never feed the dogs, never have dogs. I'm going to just want to sit around. Old people is like that anyway, I know."

"You said that people who are inutquaq just sit around and wait to die, but you put Harry Tamaryak into this category. How come?" So, is one truly old when one hits a certain age? Or does being old have more to do with one's physical condition? William's own preference for considering himself "middle aged" at sixty-three suggests that physical condition is the primary concern.

"They never stop. Well, really, when it's a really good life. Life is strong, that's why. Everything is good. Leg is good, arm is good, that's why they never stay home. Still trapping, hunting seals. It's only eyes, the eyes get funny a little bit, they get blind a little bit, then you can't do anything."

"So when do people start to sit around?"

"Body is no good. No good for anything. No good to go out. All they can do is sit there, sit there all the time by themselves. That's all they have to do."

"What group would you most like to be?"

"I don't know. I don't even know how I'm going to answer that. But I'll never forget between fifteen and forty years. I'll never forget that time. I'd wish to be that old right now. Good dogs, hunting, enjoying the people, visiting around lots, go anywhere. That life is good."

It Feels Good to Give That Much

IHUMA, INUMMARIIT, AND UYARAKTUQ

As I have reflected upon the various experiences I have had in Ulukhaktok, it has become increasingly clear to me that the important lesson Inuit men learn as they mature is that becoming a person is more about cognitive development than material development. That is, regardless of social and economic contexts, manhood is largely about achieving an ideal model of what it means to be a person. Other societies, including those in of the United States and Canada, typically view transitions from one life stage to the next as based on observable markers such as changes in household structure, physical growth and decay, and economics – something documented by Keith, Fry, and colleagues (1994). Movement into adulthood is marked by the dual events of getting married (familial) and starting a career (primarily economic). My undergraduate students frequently suggest that the transition from adulthood to middle age and then to old age is marked by the appearance of grandchildren – another familial transition.

For Inuit, there is some indication that social, domestic, or physical changes in one's life can mark movement through the life course and establish new social roles, just as they do in southern society. However, for Inuit, the markers of maturity and aging are to a much greater extent based in how one thinks and, by extension, behaves.

In many contexts, the term Inuit use for this stage of maturity is *inummarik*, which means, literally, "genuine person." The plural form, *inummariit*, is often used to refer to the concept, which has been discussed at length elsewhere, most notably in Hugh Brody's *The People's Land* (1975), where he notes that living as a genuine person – *inummariititut*, literally, "in the manner of a real person" – is something that one eats, sleeps, or works, an ideal that permeates every aspect of an individual's existence. John O'Neil (1983) employed the same concept in his study of teenage and young adult men in the Central Arctic, demonstrating how the concept of and desire to become a genuine person was the organizing framework these men used in transitioning to adulthood in a contemporary community. Other scholars, among them Stairs (Stairs 1992, Stairs and Wenzel 1992), Searles (2001), and Fienup-Riordan (1986), have addressed inummariit as a lifelong process of proper behaviour and attitudes towards other people, towards animals, and towards oneself. In particular, the central theme that emerges from these discussions is that, regardless of the contemporary social context, one continues to strive to be a genuine person, regardless of what is happening around oneself. Despite a belief that settlement life represents a falling away from tradition and that Inuit culture is dying, as Isaac and Helen both noted in the second chapter, it is important for an inummarik to continue to try to live in a proper manner.

A companion concept to inummariit is *ihuma*. Different scholars have translated ihuma in different ways, though the most common is a reference to the capacity for reason or the possession of wisdom. Ihuma, like inummariit, is a developmental process that continues throughout the life course. Gubser (1965, 211–13), for example, reported that ihuma generally appears at age four or five and then grows as the individual develops the capacity to solve problems. Ulukhaktomiut recognize a similar process and denote that the development of ihuma corresponds to an increased awareness. This is often referred to as "waking up": *When I first started waking up, I began to see that what I was doing was wrong* is one way a person might look back upon a wayward youth. Briggs (1970, 358–63) mentions that the possession of ihuma specifically defines adultness in ways largely independent of physiological development. In Ulukhaktok, the term is most often translated as meaning "thinking" or "mind."

Together, however, these two concepts, ihuma and inummariit, are the underpinnings of how an individual moves from a life stage that Condon called adolescence through the physical maturation of adulthood and then into middle age. An Inuk's progress is marked not by career or family development or physical maturation but rather by the demonstration that he or she has developed the capacity for reason, wisdom, and knowledge. These achievements are coupled by a demonstration of being able to use those abilities to live properly, a genuine Inuk, committed to his or her own well-being and that of others. No two developmental paths are identical, nor does it seem there is a single way to demonstrate mastery of these lessons. As William and Mark highlighted in the previous chapter, one of these lessons is the importance of continuing to strive in the face of difficulty, to comprehend that, despite feeling heavy, one persists. To paraphrase Brody (1975, 126), one of these lessons is to patiently resist hardship in difficult circumstances, or, as William says, to always "try, try, try."

Riding along in sleds is not really an enjoyable experience, even in the best conditions, though I doubt many Inuit would consider it a true hardship. Sleds have no suspension, so they bounce up and down, landing on the hard snow or ice with a thud when they hit even the smallest bump. They also slide back and forth across the ice, jerking to a sudden course adjustment, as when Simon Iqaluk speeds up his machine or the sliding sled hits a rock. My knees are sore from the bouncing despite the padding we have put in the box. My arms are sore from holding onto the sides.

We are moving along at a pretty good clip, heading to Uyaraktuq for an early attempt at fishing. Simon is something of a nut for fishing, especially when Uyaraktuq is involved. Just as he developed grand plans for tracking an entire hockey season many years ago, so too is he fixated on catching a Big One from Uyaraktuq. The lake is known for containing very large trout, and could, I think, be a candidate for producing the NWT record. Perhaps it has already done so. Several years ago, Simon's sister-in-law caught a remarkably large one, chopping at the hole to enlarge it and eventually land the monster. Alas, it was never weighed.

"It tasted very good," according to Simon's brother, who was there. "We ate it that night. Fed ten people for two meals. We were all really full." The bones in the head were huge.

Simon is convinced, however, that even larger fish can be found in the lakes down in Prince Albert Sound. "One time I was in a helicopter with the mining company, coming back to town," he says. "Saw a big one in Tahiryuak. Like a submarine, just floating on the surface before it went down. The helicopter pilot was almost scared."

Uyaraktuq, however, is much closer than those lakes. In a straight line from Ulukhaktok, it is only twelve kilometres away, but access from town is difficult because of the cliffs just west of the settlement along King's Bay. In summer there is no road for ATVs, unless one is willing to drive the long way around, making for a hundred-kilometre round trip. A large lake running north-south for some fifteen kilometers, Uyaraktuq is lined by the cliffs that give it its name, further limiting ATV access to the north end. One can get to it in summer by boat, making it close to Simon's parents' camp, but again access is difficult from anywhere but the south end.

However, Uyaraktuq is a popular spot for spring fishing for some families, partly because of those very large fish. Simon says there are char in Uyaraktuq too, that they can travel up the short river that empties the lake into Safety Channel.

Very Large Fish is the reason Simon and I are here. In fact, Simon is really all about fish. Inuit in general seem to develop certain affinities with animals over the course of their lives. This is certainly true for many of today's elders. George Putdjugiaq is widely recognized as being particularly talented at setting nets – he always seems to catch fish, even when others nearby get nothing. Harry Tamaryak occasionally talks about a fellow in Bay Chimo who, he knew, was "really good at wolves." Even my daughter Sarah, who was only in Ulukhaktok for a summer in 2005, began to develop a reputation for catching (and eating) *uugaq*, Arctic cod, impressing a few Inuit that she had an affinity for a food that typically flies under the radar of most Qablunaat.

For Simon, fishing is the thing. Though he usually fishes only with rod and reel or by jigging, he catches a prodigious amount. He seems to know intuitively the best place to cut a hole in the ice, the right spot for casting a line, or the right bait to employ. It is part of the subsistence strategy he has developed over the course of his adulthood.

Albert Aquti, by contrast, is best described as an expedition hunter, someone who drives his machine miles and miles to get food, coming back with the sled loaded – as he did on the trip on which I accompanied him (though that was a short trip for him). An adult muskox has an edible weight on the order of seventy kilos, nearly twice that of the caribou that people take here, according to Usher (2000). In the summer Albert makes a long boating trip into Prince Albert Sound for caribou and fish, returning with a laden boat while caching excess meat down at the end of the Sound. During the winter, once the ice is in, he will travel by snowmobile to retrieve it.

There are also times when Albert catches nothing, though, and then expedition hunting becomes an expensive failure. Caribou hunting by boat in Prince Albert Sound, for example, carries risks, among them poor weather that hinders travel, or, perhaps worse, no caribou. A failed expedition can be up to $800 sunk costs for gasoline and supplies, not to mention the wear and tear on equipment. Despite the risk of failure, though, Albert feeds multiple households. An additional advantage of the expedition hunter is that people see him coming and going, and they see the results of his activities.

Simon pursues a far different strategy. Because he works multiple part-time jobs to stay afloat economically, he focuses his activities locally, taking the occasional muskox in the winter but not travelling far from town. In summer it is all about fish, short trips to local lakes. He rarely comes home empty-handed and produces nearly as much food by weight as Albert. For Simon, however, it is about fish, seals, and birds, with the occasional muskox. For Albert, it is primarily muskox and caribou.

I should say, however, that Simon rarely returns to town empty-handed, but he did six months ago.

In the sled with me is the gas auger, the long-handled ice tuuq, a grub box full of food, a couple of rifles, jigging sticks, our emergency bags, and a gas can. We are close enough to town that we could walk home if we had to, so Simon has not brought much more than a basic toolbox. We pull up on the lake underneath the cliffs on the west side. Simon hops off the machine. As always, he has much more energy when he is on the land than when he is in town.

"This is a good spot to fish, we'll get lots here. There's a shallow ledge that comes off from shore. Then it drops off very deep. You always get fish right at the drop-off." The auger comes out, and Simon checks it over before trying to start it. "My dad's one. Just got it out yesterday. It's practically new." His father purchased it just over a year ago, he says, in anticipation of last spring's ice fishing season. I can tell he dug it out recently: there's snow crusted on it in various places.

Twenty minutes later, Simon abandons the auger. Though it started fine last night, it sure is not starting now. It appears to be completely dead, and Simon suspects the spark plug. We did not bring a replacement. "Piece of shit," he says with disgust, though his anger is short-lived.

"We could use the tuuq, though. Can't give up," he says cheerfully. He pulls out the chisel, removes the cover from the very sharp blade, selects a spot, and begins chopping into the ice.

I happen to have my watch with me, so I note the time. How long does it take to chop a hole in lake ice, one wide enough for fishing? Taking turns with the tuuq, we finish the job in twenty-five minutes, though we note that the ice is only six feet thick.

Simon is both happy and concerned about this development. Happy, because we have finished chopping, but concerned at the thinness of the ice. "Usually, the ice is thicker, like seven or even eight feet. But it's been a warm winter." The last few winters have all been warm.

There could worse problems than thin ice. One spring Simon and I went fishing after a cold winter and found that Simon's "best" spot for fishing was frozen right to the bottom, which we discovered when the auger began kicking up sand and gravel. The advantage of the auger, of course, was that we could quickly drill a new hole and look back with humour on the error.

Simon grabs a jigging stick from the sled, an old hockey stick docked to about a foot in length and notched at either end to accept a winding of fishing line. He unwinds a good seven feet of line, letting the hook drop further and further down the hole. His first goal is to find where the bottom of the lake is, to get a sense of how much space there is between the bottom of the hole and the bottom of the lake. He does not unwind much before he frowns. He pulls up the line.

"What's wrong?" I am not quite sure what the trouble can be. The ice is not as thick as we thought. We should be fine, especially if there is a steep drop-off here.

"Ooooh. We're still on the ledge. We didn't go out from shore far enough. There's only about six inches under the ice." Simon laughs, maintaining his sense of humor.

We are going to have to cut another hole. On the bright side, my arms and back are not as stiff as they were after the bumpy ride.

The second hole takes forty minutes, but now we are confronted by another problem. With an auger, we could very quickly drill two holes so both of us could fish. With the tuuq, neither of us is inspired to chop another hole. It is, however, not that important. We take turns jigging, holding the stick and gently and rhythmically moving the lure up and down in the water. The other takes the opportunity to eat, the usual camping food, a mixture of canned meat and fish – this time we have the luxury of real Spam with our sardines – and mipku and pilot biscuits with peanut butter and butter.

The real limitation of the useless auger is that this hole is it for fishing. Inuit do not spend much time at a single lake, or even a single hole, unless it quickly produces fish. On most trips, Inuit drill several holes and fish for only a few minutes, perhaps ten at most. If the fish do not strike, then it is off to another part of the lake, or another lake entirely. When I was first in Ulukhaktok, I thought this behaviour was indicative of some kind of strange Inuit short attention span, until I was with a group when we hit the right lake.

Before, I would ask people about their fishing trips, and Inuit would remark that they "went fishing" and returned with "seventy fish," and add that "Boy, they were really biting. It's like you put your hook down, and you got another fish." I thought these were mere fish stories until this happened to me. The fifth lake was the charm on that trip, and we returned with forty-five trout. Spring fishing is only recreational and fun when the activity produces food, and plenty of it.

After some time, Simon and I have had no luck. He rationalizes that it is still too early in the year to fish Uyaraktuq. The best time to fish the lake, he adds, is when the snow on the ice is gone and the ice is beginning to retreat from the shore. That time, unfortunately, is still six weeks away.

"Not done yet, though. I need to bring something home," he says, again optimistically.

He starts the machine, I hop into the box, and we head a little east and north, into the little narrow valley full of the "skinny long lakes" that Mark Pihuktuq walked across in a blizzard so many years ago. We are going to head back to Ulukhaktok a different way, driving through this valley, across Piringilik, and then down to Ukpillik Lake and home past the golf course. Simon is not saying, but I suspect that he wants to find a muskox to shoot.

We stop at one lake to investigate some tracks. There are muskox tracks in the snow, quite recent, and also some wolf scat and tracks. But both are going into the rocks, up on the plateau the overlooks Ulukhaktok itself. "Muskox like to go up there. They use it like a road to get down into Prince Albert Sound. But we can't drive up there."

We drive in the long circle and back into town without seeing a single muskox. As Simon and others would say, they only thing we have caught is a skunk. Over tea at his house later, he ruminates on the problem. "Boy, I've been really unlucky lately. It's like I can't catch anything, not since before Christmas. I tried for muskox last weekend and didn't see any then, either."

"How do you make it better?" I am wondering if there is a metaphysical explanation for Simon's string of hard luck.

"*Ayurnarman.* It can't be helped. I just have to keep trying."

PAIYUQTUGGING AROUND

"Okay, Joseph, I'd like to ask you some questions about the people that you share with. This is called an ego net interview. What I'm going to do is generate a list of the people that you share with, ask you to evaluate how often you share with them, and then ask you how the people that you named share with each other."

We are sitting at Joseph Qalviaq's kitchen table. He is between jobs, so there is plenty of time to do an interview. Rose is out for the afternoon, and the kids are at school.

"Right."

"So, who would you say that you share with? People that you give things to, and people that you get things from?"

"You mean, like country food?"

Joseph is not quite sure how this will play out. It is the first time I have done any interviewing using a laptop. Because this will be a lengthy interview, it is far easier to input the data directly into the software. I will be asking about Joseph's alters – the people with whom he shares – which could generate a long set of questions and answers. If Joseph names twenty-five sharing partners, then I will ultimately be asking him to assess how well alter number 1 shares with each of the others. There is the potential for an incredible number of questions and the additional difficulty of keeping track of all the alter-alter relations. The software makes it far easier. I can also generate a diagram immediately afterward and show it to him, and in turn generate more data when he talks about the diagram.

It all looks very impressive, so much so that Fred Ukalliq remarked after I interviewed him and showed him his network, "This looks like it could be really useful. Not like most research around here." I think it was a compliment.

"Yes, country food," I reply, "but also money, people you eat with, people that you give parts to, that sort of thing."

Joseph looks more comfortable. This is the easy part. "Well, I give food to my parents, and my in-laws, and there's my brothers and sisters."

"Which ones?" I type as he names the kin connections. "All of them, or only some?"

"Well, there's John, and Jack's, and Douglas." The last is his sister-in-law's husband. He's counting on his fingers, keeping track of his siblings. "Oh, what about out of town? Them, too?"

"Yes, anyone you share with."

"Anthony sent me some geese last week, snow geese they got from Sachs." It is, indeed, that time of year. In Sachs Harbour, there is a large migration of snow geese, and people there hunt them and send some to their relatives in Ulukhaktok. It is part of a multi-community network of sharing. In return, Ulukhaktomiut later in the year will send foods not as available in Sachs Harbour – eider ducks or Arctic char. Similarly, relatives in Kugluktuk send caribou meat to their kin in Ulukhaktok when they have none available. Beluga muktuk comes in from Inuvik, in the Mackenzie delta.

Eventually, with some probing, Joseph generates a list of thirty-one households with which he shares. It takes some time to get there. The first part of the list is easy, those named early in it being those with whom Joseph commonly shares. After about ten, however, it becomes more difficult. Teasing out the remainder is partly because Joseph, like most informants, is trying to minimize his effort, providing, he thinks, just enough information to satisfy me. The other factor is that food sharing is second nature to Inuit, a cultural behaviour that people do not always pay attention to. When Joseph finally confesses that he shared a chunk of muskox meat with his second cousin two months ago, is the lapse in his memory because he simply forgot about it, or because he was reluctant to mention it?

In most cases, I am prepared to think he simply forgot about it, that the gift simply did not register, that only after probing did he recall the incident. Sharing is such a common occurrence that most Inuit simply do not actively think about it. Yet giving is such an important source of esteem that maximizing those with whom one shares is critical. It is an opportunity to demonstrate, if only to the anthropologist, that one is adhering to important cultural values.

We finally have the list, so it is time to move onto the next section of the interview. "Okay, now that we have the list of people that you share with, I'm going to ask you some questions about each of these people. We'll start at the top of your list. You named your parents first, so that takes care of the first question. On to the next. How often do you share country food with them? Often, like every week? Less often, like, say every month? Or less than that?

"Often. All the time. I'm over there every day. I've got the key to their freezer, too."

Joseph is referring to the community freezer, which sits on the ridge between Queen's Bay and Jack's Bay. The freezer is a very large walk-in building, divided into lockers of various sizes. The older people in town tend to have the largest lockers, and they store excess country food there.

Typically, the parents hold the key, but one son also has a copy, and he will store his catch there too. Such arrangements make an assessment of sharing much more difficult. If Joseph goes caribou hunting and returns with several animals, he will give some of his catch away himself and store the remainder in his parents' freezer. From there, his parents will take some of that meat and give it away to others. Joseph will not necessarily know who is getting that meat. Is he then sharing with those other people, even if he does not know about it?

By the end of 2007, the pattern had changed regarding freezers. Because of a budget crunch at the hamlet, it was rumoured to be going bankrupt during that summer, and the hamlet SAO lost his job. The writing, or, more accurately, mold, was on the wall for some time, however. As a common property resource, the community freezer suffered from some abuse. There were complaints about theft from lockers, cases where hunters laid out fish to freeze on the floor, straight and rigid, so that they could be stacked later in the locker, like cordwood; some of these fish disappeared, and accusations began to circulate.

Eventually, the hamlet pulled the plug, literally, because of the cost of operating and maintaining the unit. By 2007, supplemental programs run through Hunters and Trappers had provided nearly everyone with top-loading freezers that were more energy efficient and in any case transferred the costs of running freezers to individual residents. The fact that Joseph has the key to his dad's freezer space is largely symbolic.

"What about store food? How often would you say you share store food with your parents?"

Clearly, Joseph has never considered this question before. Is sharing store food really sharing? He thinks a moment. "I would say only sometimes. Like when the store is closed and Mum runs out of sugar, she might call me up and ask if I have any. Or if they are out at the cabin and need tea, they might ask me to pick some up at the store and bring it out. But it's not like I'm going over there and my parents are saying 'Here, take some hamburger home' or anything like that. People don't go to the Northern and buy steaks and say, 'Hey, let's give some to so-and-so.'"

I expected that answer. Store food lacks the same power as country food, at least in the kind of sharing I'm asking about. And, as we move through the list of alters, it becomes increasingly clear that while store food does circulate between parents and adult children, it does not circulate otherwise, except on rare occasions.

"How about eating? How often would you say you eat with your parents?"

"Often. Really lots. It's like I'm over there every day. I'm always checking up on them anyway, you know, my dad's health is not so good. But I eat over there all the time. The kids too."

"How about money? Do you share money with them?"

Joseph again pauses. I am not sure if that is because he does not want to say, or because he is trying to recall whether he does share money with them, and how much. He finally responds. "Do you mean, do I just give them cash? Or they give me cash?"

So that is the problem: he is not sure how to answer the question. "You decide. How do you give them money?"

"Does giving money to my kids count? Because they're always over there, bugging Granny for money so they can get junk food at the store. And what about things like gas? Like the other day Dad said he needed gas for the boat, so I went and took his gas cans and bought gas at the gas station for him."

"Both count. Do your parents ever give you money directly?"

"No, I haven't got any money from them in a long time now. I would feel bad asking. I don't need it. But my brother gets money from them, I know."

We move down the list, and Joseph discovers that this is going to be a tedious process, especially as we get past those with whom he shares the most. When we come to his sister-in-law, however, we run into a stumbling block.

"How about her? Are the answers the same for your other in-laws? Some, None, Some, None?" We've fallen into a kind of pattern. Joseph knows the four questions and their order, and he can call out, quickly, his answers.

He pauses here. "Stacy's different. I'd say that it's some, some, some, some. But I'm not sure."

He is at least taking the evaluation seriously. Some of my informants, once they discover the tedium of the interview, try to take the easy route and just give the same response repeatedly. I have to vary the order of the questions, or the order of the alters, to keep them on their toes. Not that I blame them.

"Why are you not sure?"

"We used to give her money, but now we don't." Sister-in-law Stacy is a special case, a young woman with two children. She and her partner separated a few years ago, and he has since moved out of the community. It is a not uncommon occurrence, and single women can do quite well for themselves in town. They can rely on their own parents and siblings for access to country food, with the added advantage of not having to live with a man in their own house. One woman commented years ago that the problem with men is that they take the money and spend it on gas and equipment. They make a mess of the kitchen when they skin foxes on the floor or repair the engine on the table. They are, simply put, too much trouble, trouble that becomes worse if the man is violent and abusive.

"How come you don't give her money?"

"She came to us about a year ago and said she needed money for food and Pampers for the kids, so we gave her some. She did that a couple of times, and then we found out she was taking the money and just going to buy hoot with it, or to buy a bottle from a bootlegger. That made Rose really mad, because Stacy said she needed it for the kids. So we finally sat down with her and told her that if she needed things for the kids, we would take her to the store and buy groceries right there for her."

"And how often do you do that? Buy food at the store for her?"

"We only did it once. She hasn't asked us since."

Joseph and I finally complete the interview, which has taken quite a bit of time, well over an hour to complete this section. Normally, I would take my leave, but Joseph insists I stay for coffee, as it is nearly coffee break time anyway. He still has the ATV catalogue on the coffee table, and he picks it up and looks at it again. I can tell he is still trying to talk himself into it.

"I'm not quite sure where the money is going to come from, though. Not until I find another job anyway."

"Are you okay on money? Isn't the mortgage killing you, like it is everybody else?" I am still puzzled that he would quit a hamlet job that paid so well, though I understand the social reasons for his doing so. Joseph's position was one in which he had to, as he says, boss people around, something many Inuit try to avoid.

"No, we're okay for now. The mortgage isn't too bad, I refinanced it last year, and that's down to about $300 a month now. I'll have that paid off in three years." He says this somewhat proudly. He knows that many of his age-mates have tried to buy their own houses under various ownership plans, but many are having difficulty keeping up.

"It's the food bills that are a big problem. Or maybe it's having teenagers. Heating fuel, too, that's been getting expensive. Lucky that winter is over soon. No, we're going good on money these days, Rose's job is paying the bills, and I started carving again. The Co-op is paying pretty good. But I might try for the Fish and Wildlife job. I hear Joshua has had enough and is going to quit."

I am not sure that Joseph will do better in a new job. He would just be trading old problems for new ones. If he did not like bossing people around at hamlet, he is sure not going to like bossing people around in the community. Though, come to think of it, Joseph's style might work at Fish and Wildlife. Rather than confront people, in uniform, he is far more likely to visit them in the evening over tea to address a problem. The anxiety at the Fish and Wildlife job will likely be with his Qablunaat superiors.

"Let me see your list." He changes the subject somewhat abruptly. Though we just did an interview using the laptop to collect ego net data, one we will finish in few days, I also did my bi-weekly sharing interview with him. Indeed, it is one of the reasons we are talking about mortgages, money, jobs, and hunting. The interview might be officially over, but the questions primed the pump for our conversation. Joseph is merely returning to the same issues again.

I pull out the paper, which lists the answers to the questions. *Did you go hunting in the last two weeks? Where? Did you give anybody any food? What? Who?* Joseph takes the paper and looks at the list. Over the last two weeks, he went hunting several times with his sons, bringing back three muskoxen. He also went fishing with his wife over the weekend and came back with several dozen lake trout. Together, it was far more food than he would have produced had he been working.

"Let's see," he says, as he looks down the list of people to whom he has given food. Quietly, he reads off the names: "Mum and Dad's, Rose's parents, Granny, Granny Margaret, Harry's, William's." It is somewhat unusual: he has given muskox or fish to over a dozen different households. Actually, he has not taken the food himself. Rather, he directed his sons to take meat to specific households, something that his parents made him do when he was a teenager. "Paiyuqtugging around" is what Joseph calls it, a curious anglicization of an Inuinnaqtun word, *paiyuqtuqtuq*, meaning "to carry," and referring to the movement of meat from one household to the next.

He hands the paper back to me. "It sure feels good to give to that many people. Makes you feel like somebody."

BEING ON THE LAND

"How was the caribou hunting?" It is early September 2007, and I am back in town after a month away. I am almost literally just off the plane. Willie, driving the taxi, has dropped me off, and my bags are sitting outside by the stairs to the house. Isaac had coffee waiting, and we are catching up.

"It was a good trip." Isaac and his son Ronald went two weeks ago; they were planning their boating trip in early August, just as I was leaving. They were waiting to find out what the weather would be, the combination of reports on ice conditions in Prince Albert Sound and wind forecasts. The advent of Internet has been a tremendous boon for hunters. Environment Canada maintains several webpages with the latest forecasts, and, while these are important for hunters, many have long known that the forecasts are iffy at best. Weather can and does change quickly in and around Ulukhaktok, and different places can and do have slightly different weather patterns. Most Inuit long ago learned that the best way to know what the weather will be is to listen to CBC Radio for the forecast from Sachs Harbour, which nearly always predicts what the next weather will be here. Unfortunately, CBC North out of Inuvik recently decided to change their reporting. They now provide only temperatures and precipitation for the communities, two of the least useful pieces of information for travellers. Wind direction and barometric pressure are far more important.

Luckily, that information is accessible via the Internet. Environment Canada also posts the latest satellite imagery, which provides clues on ice conditions in places like Prince Albert Sound. Rather than make the boat trip down into the sound, burn gas, and then have to turn around, hunters can check the ice maps and see for themselves what conditions look like, saving time and money.

Isaac does not own a boat, however, so he must borrow his father's, and that delayed him too. William went down with Agnes and David to hunt caribou. "I'm just the driver," says William yet again, having long turned over most responsibilities to David, though, truth be told, he should not even be driving at all, according to the nurses. He has only just recovered from a case of tuberculosis. He is supposed to be taking it easy.

William continues to drive, though, because of a desire to do *something* productive. He can and does shoot when the opportunity presents itself, but his days of walking on the land for caribou are long past. By driving, he still has the opportunity to talk to his grandson. David will benefit from watching William handle the boat, read weather and ice conditions, and select campsites, and from listening to him talk about past experiences. It was a successful hunting trip; they returned with six caribou.

Once the boat returned, Isaac and Ronald took their turn. Could they have all gone together? I suppose so, but then there would be no room in the boat for their catch, and, early August is still too early to hope to cache any meat. Some families take August for hunting caribou, a couple taking their children to camp out on the land for a week or so. In one sense, it is a vacation, although an expensive one, at roughly $400 for grub, $100 or more for gasoline, and no guarantee of catching anything. Amos Tuktu had done that very thing with his kids, caught two caribou in a week and figured that, form a purely economic standpoint, two caribou cost him about $12 per kilogram, more expensive than meat one would purchase out of the store.

The family trip has significant advantages, however. The kids are out of town and on the land, away from the distractions of the settlement. Parents and children have the opportunity to interact solely with each other. It is a place where real cultural transmission can and does occur. The kids are connecting with their parents and their heritage in ways that go far beyond just "being on the land."

Amos solved the "problem" of $12 per kilo caribou in a rather common and practical manner. Once he and the family returned from their vacation, he turned right around with Eddie Agluaq and Joshua Qulliq, loaded up Eddie's boat – Eddie had the biggest motor – and went back into Prince Albert Sound. They travelled down the shoreline, past Safety Channel and along the shore, hunting caribou the entire time. They were gone for 36 hours, they did not sleep, and they returned with a dozen caribou, the boat in the water nearly to the gunwales. The price for the animals in terms of gasoline and supplies? $1 per kilogram. "That's much better," said Amos after we figured out his costs. "But it sure is tiring, doing it that way."

When William returned, Isaac took Ronald out, and they went caribou hunting themselves. "It was a good trip. No ice in the way, which really helped." As usual, Isaac provides me with the report very slowly, between sips of tea.

The moving ice is a significant problem. One runs the risk of getting to a camp, bagging caribou, and then getting stuck by wind or ice. There is no way to store the catch, save by drying it, and drying up four or five caribou is a significant effort that may or may not pay off. If the weather is warm and wet, hunters can lose a whole trip's worth of food. I think about this as we sit in silence. We listen to the water truck pulling up, then hear the clunk of the hose into the tank. After another minute, we can hear water hitting the sides of the tank in the utility room.

"Sonny got four caribou," Isaac adds.

"Oh. So you're just the driver now?" I am giving Isaac a hard time. His oldest daughter has two children, so he is a grandfather multiple times over. "Getting to be inutquaq, eh?"

Isaac flashes his eyebrows and smiles, running his hands over his close-cropped hair, flecked with much more grey than when I first met him.

Isaac and Ronald really could not have taken many more animals. The caribou they were hunting down in Prince Albert Sound are, strictly speaking, Peary caribou, the caribou of the High Arctic Islands. They are quite small, more the size of large dogs. The herd that Ulukhaktomiut hunt, however, migrates between Ulukhaktok and Cambridge Bay, on the other side of the island, and those animals tend to be a bit larger than prototypical Peary caribou. Probably there has been some mixing with barren ground animals, which have been migrating to Victoria Island across the ice from the mainland, something that has been happening for about fifteen years. "Those bigger caribou, they taste like the land. But our caribou are really *mammaq*. Delicious," says Isaac. "But we got all big ones. Still, it's good enough."

Ten caribou between two porch freezers is a lot, and both William's and Isaac's were packed full. It is not yet cold enough, and will not be for at least another month, to just store food in a plywood box on the porch.

"Who did you come back with?" I ask, knowing that boaters rarely travel alone.

"Edward was down there with his brother. They got three."

I finish my coffee and go out, dragging my stuff to the cabin where I will be staying for the next three months. Because I was caught up in data collection before I left, the shack is only partially habitable. I will need to spend the rest of the afternoon and evening opening up, cleaning out the junk, and making a space for sleeping. I had hoped that something else might become available, but there is no housing whatsoever.

As I haul my bags to the cabin. Paul Tigliktuq, my old and new neighbour, is out having a smoke and comes by to say hello. He has also brought his drill, a battery-powered model, which will be very useful for opening the cabin. He hands it to me, along with some bits. Finishing his smoke, he leaves me to my work moving in.

It is not long, however, before Edward Kuniluk drives by on his AT V. He has a package on the back, suggesting he has just come from the post office. "Heard you were back," he says. "Someone said you were staying here. Going to rough it, eh? Live like we did long ago?" There is a big smile on his face. I dig out the stove and coffee pot and make coffee, even though coffee break is long past. It is, in fact, closer to dinnertime, judging by the increased AT V traffic, everyone going to and from the stores before they close.

"Heard you went caribou hunting a couple weeks ago," I say. In a small town, news travels fast. "How was the trip? You were with Isaac's?"

"Yup. I got three. Went with my little brother, but he never got any. He kept bragging and bragging that he was a really good hunter, that he was going to get a lot of caribou, but when he went out from camp, he never even saw any. He sure learned his lesson. You never talk about the animals like that before you hunt them. They can hear you."

"I heard Isaac never shot any. I was giving him a hard time about being old."

Edward laughs. "Isaac could've shot all right. He had lots of chances to. I think he was letting Ronald do it, trying to get him right again. His girlfriend broke up with him, and he hit the bottle last month. I heard he was trying to kill himself. Being on the land always helps people get over their problems. For a while at least." He sips at his coffee.

"How's the boat?" I ask. It was beginning to leak pretty badly when we were down in Safety Channel last month. Edward didn't know how old the boat was. He had lost track of its history after counting four previous owners.

"I think it's finished. The 25-horse seized up, too." He is referring to a smaller motor, which is on a smaller, sixteen-foot boat. "So I'm going to take the 60 and put it on the sixteen-footer. That boat will really fly. Going to work on that later. If the weather could get good, I might make another trip."

He finishes the coffee, and I look at my watch. If I hurry, I might have enough time to get to the store and get a little grub. I left coffee, sugar, and a few dry goods in the cabin when I left, but there is not enough for dinner, or for breakfast tomorrow, for that matter. Edward, reading my mind, pre-empts me. "Come by after. We're going to have a late supper tonight. You don't have time to get to the store anyway."

So, a few hours later, I see Edward was serious about working on the boat. He has it hauled up next to the house, and his tools are on the benches inside. I make the trip up the stairs, my footsteps alerting the occupants. Before I can even knock, I hear Edward yelling at me to come in.

The air is heavy with marijuana smoke, and a quick glance at the kitchen counter confirms it: a saucer, the top end of a twenty-ounce soda bottle, and a pair of tarnished butter knives sit next to the stove. Edward's eyes are bloodshot. "Hey, Pete. Come in." He's on the sofa, shirt off, flipping channels. It is warm in the house, even though the kitchen window is open wide.

"Must have been a shipment today, eh?" I suspected as much when I saw the box.

"Oh, yeah, there's really lots in town now. You heard about Darren and Bobby?"

"I heard they got busted. Wilma was complaining about them before, said they were dealing."

Edward only raises his eyebrows in agreement. In the absence of a comment, I decide to ask, since it is relatively rare for anyone to be busted for drugs, even when *everyone* knows who is dealing. "How do the cops ever catch anybody?"

"Got to have someone rat them out, and then the cops have to catch them with it. One time I was selling around town, going house to house, eh? The cops were kind of following me around, so I went into Willie's, sold him a couple of joints, told him he could have an extra couple if he kept my stuff for a few minutes. Went back out, and the cops stopped me and asked if I was dealing, and searched me."

"What did you do?"

"Got all mad at them, yelled at them for accusing me without proof. They went away right then, and I went back in to get my stuff from Willie. Boy, my hands were really shaking, I needed a joint right then just to relax."

"So Darren and Bobby were ratted out while they had stuff?"

"Heard they were picked up out at the airport, probably waiting for a box to come in on the plane. Someone probably pissed because they got less than they thought they should last time. Probably went back to them to complain, got nothing, found out they had more coming, and so turned them in."

"There's coffee," Edward's wife, Sarah, calls from the kitchen. Edward's house dates from the mid-1970s and has been rehabilitated at least three times since. Unlike William's house, it is small: a single room with a kitchen on one side and a living area on the other, and three tiny bedrooms leading off of it. Edward and Sarah have split the main room into the kitchen and a TV area by using the television shelf as a kind of divider. This arrangement of furniture is only about a month old, however. Because the houses are so tiny, and the house plans nearly identical, residents frequently rearrange the furniture to mix things up a bit.

It seems to be the analog to moving camp, which Inuit sometimes did simply so they could change the view.

Edward and I collect our mugs, add sugar and creamer. This is my fourth cup of coffee in about four hours. We sit in silence, watching the television, turned to CNN. Sarah is making dinner. It looks like we will be eating at about nine – a bit late for supper, but it's still very much summer, and Edward and Sarah are still backwards. After all the coffee, I will soon be too.

"So, you going to go back out for caribou?" I ask. I know that Edward has not been making money, at least legally, since early in the summer, when he spent some time working for the mining crews above Minto.

"Going to try to, if I can get the boat fixed up, and see if I can get some money from somewhere. I'm just about out of gas. Bought a couple of barrels in June, finally finishing it up. Boy, it was a great summer, I tell you. Set nets for fishing and got really lots of char, big fat ones for quaq, small ones for piffi. Went boating and started shooting natiaqs again, I hadn't done that in a long time. I got one a couple weeks ago, brought it to my mum, and she said, 'Bring it to John Takuyuq's,' so I did, and they were ever happy. Margaret said that no one ever brings them natiaqs, they hadn't had any in such a long time. Their son doesn't hunt, eh?"

I nod at this. Their lone son living in the settlement neither works nor hunts. Indeed, I rarely see him around town.

Edward continues, "I shot a couple of muskox on the ATV, got some caribou. Really good to hunt. Nice to have a full freezer." He remembers my question. "Why? You want to come caribou hunting?" It is a genuine invitation, but there is an edge there. His first statement, that he is using up his gas, is also an invitation. I would be purchasing at least half the gasoline.

"We should see how the weather does, eh?" I respond. "Might be getting a little late. The east wind is really giving her now." The wind has come up this afternoon, and, this time of year an east wind can blow for days, if not weeks. We can hear the porch door creaking a little, with gentle thump as it bangs on the jamb.

"Yuh." Edward raises his eyebrows at this. It is best not to talk about it unless it actually happens.

"Supper." Sarah has already served herself – chicken and Rice-A-Roni, accompanied by bannock and grape Kool-Aid. We get up and help ourselves. After dinner, we will have yet another cup of coffee.

GIVING THANKS

It is Thanksgiving night in Ulukhaktok, the first weekend in October. Today is a municipal holiday, and everyone celebrates. I have never been quite sure of the meaning of Canadian Thanksgiving for Inuit, although it is an occasion for extended family eating and visitation. Everyone seems to have a turkey, donated, I am told, by the IRC, usually a ten-kilogram frozen bird. The fact that every household receives a turkey means there is a remarkable excess. As all of the adult children eat with their parents, their turkeys go unused. Some of those extra birds end up at the community hall or gym for community feasts at Christmas and Easter. The remainders sit in the freezer, used at some other point during the year.

Stephen Hakagiak recalls returning to his house to find a turkey on his porch, part of the Christmas distribution of birds. "What am I going to do with a ten-kilo turkey?" he asks me. "I live alone. My oven can't cook such a big bird. The thing was frozen solid."

"What did you do?"

"Chopped it up with an axe, and boiled the pieces one at a time. Fed me for weeks. Got really tired of turkey."

At Thanksgiving, the transient Qablunaat who have not lived long-term in the settlement tend to celebrate Thanksgiving together, often assembling a potluck meal that resembles something close to a Thanksgiving done down South. It is typically the only holiday celebration that the Qablunaat have in Ulukhaktok. At Christmas, the teachers and nurses tend to flee south if they can, and at least one of the regular RCMP officers will do so. The same used to be true for Easter.

In my time living in the settlement, I have not had occasion to celebrate Thanksgiving in town, for I have always been camping at Fish Lake. This Thanksgiving, however, I am in town. I have avoided the invitations of the Qablunaat, so I am uncommitted for the day, and my plan has been to sit and relax, take a day off from tracking down victims for interviews. The weather has been crummy. The daylight is receding quickly: the radio reports that Ulukhaktok loses fifteen minutes of sunlight each day, and in the past week the weather has turned stormy, winds shifting from east to west and then back again, bringing precipitation with them.

Isaac and William have been planning a trip to Fish Lake for over a week now, but the travelling has been postponed for this weekend. The ice is not yet in on the lakes, according to the reports, and there is little in the way of snow up on the land. Having driven over bare ground on a snowmobile, I do not care to repeat the experience. Isaac has been thinking of trying his ATV for the trip, provided the temperatures do not dip too low. The advantage of ATVs is that they are much better on fuel efficiency, and they can do quite well in the autumn, provided there is not too much snow. However, they do not like the cold, and they seem to break down easily when temperatures dip below about –15°C.

So, we are waiting for weather. I am trying to cobble together a sled for the trip. I have several small sleds, but not one big enough for a lengthy camping trip. I am also trying to keep my decrepit snow machine running. As the weather has turned, it is becoming cranky again. The headlight is out, the newly installed track now seems to be having trouble with the bearings in the wheels. I am not sure it will hold up for a 160-kilometre trip. In truth, I am not sure I want to go to Fish Lake this year. I am already camping out in my cabin. I do not need to go to Fish Lake to camp.

I am not the only one with machine issues. William is trying to get his second snowmobile going. David has been out every evening this past week working on it. I have had the privilege of watching some of his effort and listening to the remainder, the sounds of the engine starting up, idling for a moment, then sputtering and dying, followed by David cursing alternately in English and Inuinnaqtun. I am learning some new words.

Others are also at their machines. The Rangers are coming to town immediately after Thanksgiving, holding training exercises at Fish Lake. The Rangers are something like the National Guard for the Arctic, formed in 1947 as a kind of local military force in the event of a Soviet military invasion over the Pole. Most Inuit males join in young adulthood. In the old days, enrolling was practically a no-brainer: each Ranger received a set of gear, including a Lee-Enfield .303 rifle and 200 rounds ammunition each year, plus a spiffy red sweatshirt. Training occurred annually, the military representatives arriving in the settlement to take the active Rangers out on the land for manoeuvres. "Mostly, those guys just got cold. They couldn't deal with our weather here, they just stayed in the tents," one former Ranger summarized.

Some years, however, did result in actual training, and this year there are plans for such at Fish Lake. Although Inuit are expected to devote their time solely to military activities, many will take nets along to set in the lake, collecting fish while they practise shooting.

In anticipation of the trip, many of the young men are in the uncomfortable position of repairing their machines. David is not the only one swearing into the darkness and wind. There is nothing worse than working on a snowmobile in –20°C temperatures and thirty kilometre winds in the dark of an October night. Some of these men are looking at their machines for the first time since last June, when they took them water skimming on Jack's Bay. A summer's worth of salt, water, and dust has taken a toll on the engine, the wheel bearings, and the body, and they are settling in with the realization that they have a lot more work to do than they seemed to remember.

Indeed, working conditions will get worse. Wednesday after Thanksgiving, the night before the departure, a nasty storm will blow in that will drop power lines around town. There will be quite a few men sitting on their porch stairs in the dull orange glow of a string of cigarettes, waiting for the power to return.

All that is still a few days away, however. I am sitting in my cabin, tiny but cozy, writing field notes and listening to the CBC and the sound of my snowmobile cover flapping in the wind. As the weather has grown colder, I have discovered that the cabin has stayed reasonably warm. I declined the use of Edward's tent heater in favour of an electric space heater that William provided. At its lowest setting, it keeps the cabin more than comfortable. Now that October is here, I find that I have to leave it on almost constantly – I have electronics – but it isn't costing me much to run it. Aside from the heater, I am only running a lamp, an alarm clock-radio, and my laptop. When I pay William's electric bill at the end of the month, my usage will count for very little against the 650 kilowatt hours he shows on his bill. The bigger problem is digging out the extension cord I am running to his house. By late November, it will be buried under a five-foot deep snowdrift.

Although the winds have picked up, the cabin is in the lee of the community freezer, well protected from the east winds tearing at the houses on the other side of town. A sudden knock on the door, however, jolts me slightly. Because of the wind, I did not hear the visitor approaching. In typical Inuit fashion, the knock occurs just as the door is wrenched open. Cold air and blowing snow enter the cabin. It is Sadie.

"Gee, Pete, what are you doing? Dinner was served ten minutes ago. You're late!"

It is a tone of, I think, both affection and exasperation, as in *It is Thanksgiving dinner, and we are eating, and here you are sitting out here by yourself when you should be with family. What is wrong with you!*

"I didn't realize it was dinnertime. I don't want to intrude on Thanksgiving dinner, though."

Sadie just looks at me, more confirmation that Qablunaat are just plain weird. "Whatever. Come eat." It is an order. I can no longer refuse, nor would I want to. I throw on my runners and march over to the house with her.

The house is full. Most of William's children are there save Isaac, who is eating with Uncle Putdjugiaq and will arrive later. The meal has already been served. Agnes points at the plates on the counter and simply says, "Have food." I know the routine. I grab a plate and kneel on the floor, where the cooked meats sit in their pots. In addition to the roasted turkey, there is a leg of boiled muskox. Some mipku also sits on the cardboard, a large knife next to the pile, for trimming big pieces down to manageable sizes. On the table behind is a Jell-o salad, a salad of mixed greens, a bowl of stove-top stuffing, and some cooked mixed vegetables. Several pies have already been cut into by the practical ones who do not wish to waste time getting up again or those who worry they won't get any if they wait. There are multiple teenagers at dinner. They tend to begin with dessert and work backwards.

"You'd better hurry up. I'm ready for seconds. My name means 'hungry,' you know." William chuckles again at the joke he has used a million times.

Sadie rolls her eyes. "Oh, Dad."

There are not nearly enough chairs or table space in the room. William is in one chair. I do not think he could sit on the floor if he had to, or, at least, he would have difficulty standing back up. Agnes has the other. The rest of us sit along the floor, backs against the walls, cups of juice at an elbow, plates in laps. We are in a house, for sure, but otherwise this is no different than if we were in a cabin or tent on the land.

"Pass the salt and pepper, please and thank you." There is not much else in the way of conversation while we eat. Eating is serious business. We work our way through the meal, many returning for seconds on the turkey or the muskox. Unlike in the South, the turkey is not carved according to Emily Post or Miss Manners: chunks have been hacked off with the knife, legs torn out of their joints. There is plenty for everyone, though the side dishes get far less attention than the meat. Bones are nibbled and gnawed. Meat is followed by the imiraq from the muskox, the liquid flavoured with Lipton's instant onion soup and beef broth.

Following dinner, the bowl of hot water and a bar of soap follows, and we take turns washing up, cleaning our hands and wiping our greasy mouths. Next come tea and cookies, despite the pie many of us have already had.

"Where's David?" He has not yet made an appearance.

"He's over at Qulliqs," says his mother, Sadie. "He wanted to see about a part for the Ski-doo. He might make it after."

Indeed, David does make it in a few minutes later. "Just talked with Joshua. He says he has the part for that Ski-doo, wants to know if we have a couple of bearings for it." He is speaking to William now, who nods. "Go ahead."

"Great, I'll go to him after. Should get that machine going. When we going to go?"

"When the weather could get good." Even at Thanksgiving, they are still thinking about the next trip.

"Have food." Agnes nods at the cardboard in the corner. David flashes his eyebrows, takes a plate from Sarah, who has started to wash up, and helps himself.

"I had some at Qulliqs', but I could eat more all right," he says, taking a chunk of turkey.

There are no arguments here, no discussions of politics, merely family members sitting and eating together, falling easily into long-accepted roles, discussing equipment, parts, weather, and how others in the settlement are faring.

The Rangers did eventually make it out of town to Fish Lake, just as William and Isaac did. From their reports, I am glad I didn't go. William and Isaac have been back for four days, but I have not seen much of Isaac yet.

"I heard Isaac's got some hunters coming in," Simon says as he and I are having tea and watching a hockey game on television.

"Yes, they've been here for a few days," I reply. "Grumpy about the weather."

The past few days have been poor, windy and blowing, with some snow. All fall it has been nothing but wind. The hunters have been cooped up in the hotel or at Isaac's, waiting to go on the land. Like most tourist hunters, they are anxious to get out and kill something, and they feel urgency because of the money they've paid for the privilege of hunting muskoxen and the vacation time they've used to come here. "They're driving Isaac nuts. He was barely unpacked from Fish Lake, wasn't sure he'd make it to town before they got here. They went out today, though." Indeed, I saw them leaving earlier.

"Sports hunters are like that. Couple of years ago Tigliktuq had one that just complained all the time. We're out on the ice and the weather is bad, really almost whiteout, and the hunter thinks we can go. Finally, Paul harnessed up the dogs and took him out. Just went in a big circle around the camp, made the hunter cold. Then he shut up.

"That hunt was no good, though. I was helper, and that hunter got a bear, but when Tiglik skinned it out, we left most of the carcass on the ice. Weather got really bad when we were coming home because we never covered the carcass." It is tradition to cover the body with snow. "By the time we got to Mashuyak, it was really terrible, I tell you, cold, blowing, couldn't see. I said to Tigliktuq, 'You covered the body, didn't you?' He never answer me. He's older than me, too. He should've known better."

It is just past ten when I walk by Isaac's. The porch light illuminates the narrow alley between Isaac's house and that of his neighbour. He and Phillip, his helper, are finishing processing two muskoxen. The two hunters got their animals. Isaac and Phillip are packaging them up for shipment out tomorrow. Isaac is finishing the task, chopping the boss and horns off the head, and wrapping that, and a bit of the meat, with the skin. He finishes by wrapping the whole package with a tarp, which he then compresses with an entire roll of duct tape.

"Where are the hunters?" I ask.

"Back at the hotel. They got cold, had to go in to warm up." Sports hunting is usually an exercise in bouncing around on the back of a sled or ATV and then pulling the trigger. Not much more is involved save for writing the cheque. The guide does nearly everything.

Isaac finishes and invites me in for tea, leaving Phillip to deliver the packages to the hotel. We sit, and Isaac starts calculating his costs and his profit, about $3,000 for a day of work and two days of babysitting. "Not too bad," he says.

I take a look at his reckoning sheet. In addition to Phillip, he hired Matthew Aqiaruq as a second helper and rented two machines for the sports hunters, the rentals costing Isaac an additional $300 once gas was included.

"Isaac, how come you hired Matthew too? And how come you rented those extra machines?" It is most unusual. Normally, an HTC-sponsored sports hunt includes a guide and a helper for each hunter. The sports hunter gets to suffer on the sled. It seems to me that Isaac could have hired just Phillip and hauled the two hunters on their sleds. That way Isaac would have made an extra $1,500.

He thinks a moment. "Those hunters said they wanted to Ski-doo themselves, so I figured I could let them try. And I have to spread the money around, eh? Isn't that the right thing to do?"

I take my leave of Isaac and make my way over to visit Amos. I haven't seen him since the Rangers trip. They returned two days ago, and I'm curious about how things turned out. I know he'll be up and about, even at midnight. Like me, he is backwards now.

We sit on the porch and look up at the Aurora while he smokes a cigarette. I distinctly remember our talk those years ago down at

Mashuyak, when he insisted he would have "everything" by the time he was forty. He seems to have accomplished that.

"How was the trip?"

"Long. Took us six hours to get to Fish Lake. There's hardly any snow on the land. The wind has blown it all away up there, except for big drifts of really soft snow. So we tried to stay on the lakes, but everybody just kept spinning out on the ice. Some of them guys don't know how to drive."

"Did you go fishing up there?" Before leaving, Amos suggested that he would bring nets, to make the trip at least somewhat worthwhile.

"Yup. Me, Eddie, Joshua, and James brought nets, we were the only ones. James got some fish, I know. Eddie got none. Well, he got lots of lake trout, but he didn't want those, so he put them back. I got ten char but no red-bellies. But one of them was a giant, almost forty inches." Amos exhales, cigarette smoke swirling around him. "And it was funny – right when we were coming back to the cabins, we got lost. I was following Joshua coming back. He asked me if I had my GPS, but I didn't, so Joshua started leading. But he's got no headlight, so I'm following him, trying to light up the trail for him so we don't hit a bump or anything."

"How come you were following? Shouldn't you have been leading?"

"I guess, but Joshua's older. I should've never listened to him. We kept going, and we weren't going the straight way to camp, he kept turning a little east, then a little east, then a little east, and pretty soon we're back at the nets. So he tried again. Joshua tried to make a wrong turn a second time, but we wouldn't let him."

Amos finishes his smoke, and we head in, sit on the sofa to drink our tea, helping ourselves to a bowl of pretzels and chips. The television is tuned to APTN, which is showing one of the old Netsilik films from the 1960s. The scene is of a fellow drilling a hole with a bow drill so that he can place a rivet or nail through a piece of bone.

"Boy, that was sure hard to do back then," says Amos. "It was better once we got guns. Then we could just shoot something to make a hole." It is, indeed, something Inuit did regularly, a .222 making a perfect hole through a ski or sled runner – a very handy trick for repairs on the trail.

"But before metal, it must have been really hard to get along."

Amos thinks. "Well, I saw my dad make a blade out of a caribou antler one time. It was really sharp. It just didn't stay sharp as long as a metal knife did."

Amos's wife, Stephanie, who has been watching quietly, changes the subject. "Hon, did you remember to bring fish to Margaret? Your mum said before that Margaret had nothing." Stephanie was at her in-laws for supper earlier.

"Yeah, I'll do it after."

"Do you have fish?" I ask. "What did you do with the Fish Lake fish?"

"Well, I kept the really big one. Most of the rest are gone now. I gave some to Joshua before we were coming home, and I put half of the rest in my parents' porch. The last one I'll bring to Margaret later."

LISTEN

Joseph and I are having tea at his house. Everyone else has gone out. It is late July, high summer and going on toward 9 PM. Rose has gone to her parents' for an evening visit. Mary, the oldest daughter, has come and gone, stopping by for a shower. Her apartment is out of water, and, having learned the value of money, she refuses to pay for a call-out from the water truck, an additional $25 charge on top of the cost of the water pumped into her tank. William Kaaktuq has declared that "young people" have little comprehension of the value of money, and its scarcity, because the government makes it too easy for them, but Joseph's children seem to be belie that assessment. With five children of his own, and two more that he and Rose have adopted, he knows the value of a limited resource. Ten years ago, when Brandon and Mary were in their early teens, Joseph declared that, once they turned eighteen, they were expected to pay room and board if they wanted to stay in the house. "They thought I was joking, until I gave Brandon the first bill. He moved out the next week. It's good. They have to get out there and make their own way. It's the only way they'll learn."

Mary moved out a week after she turned eighteen, getting on the public housing waiting list but moving in with two cousins in the interim.

"Brandon took some more pictures from up there," says Joseph, referring to the mining camp about Minto. "There's more funny stuff going on with those guys."

Joseph has cause for concern. Although the interest in mineral exploration in the area goes back to the early days of the settlement, the last decade has seen a growing resurgence in exploration, likely an outgrowth of the mineral boom in the Northwest Territories in general. Platinum and nickel seem to be the targets, but everyone is looking for diamonds too. The exploration companies themselves have not conducted their business in a particularly above-board manner, choosing, it seems, to buy their way into a community rather than win people over legitimately.

Joseph has become particularly opposed to mining exploration. During the summer of 2004, I witnessed the first of these mining companies travelling to Ulukhaktok for a community consultation and environmental assessment of a plan to do some drilling and exploration down in the Prince Albert Sound area. The fellow representing the exploration company had requested a community meeting so he could present his plan. On the evening of the presentation, the room was fairly well packed with Inuit of all ages.

The representative began by stating the usual business about the potential for job creation, the ways in which the company would care for the land, and the respect they would show to the people. I looked at the proposal as he belched this string of platitudes. It was nothing more than a list of coordinates where they apparently planned to drill cores. Otherwise, there was no information about their plans. The package of data seemed to have been designed to do nothing but confuse readers in a manner that would keep them silent.

Inuit themselves were not convinced about the plan, but their concerns were based on the location of the drilling. The company proposed to drill in an area important to Inuit as a summer caribou hunting ground – the end of Prince Albert Sound. Several Inuit, including Joseph, spent several minutes questioning the representative about the potential problems working in the middle of a caribou herd.

As Joseph spoke, it occurred to me that he looked rather like a professor grilling an especially unprepared graduate student. "We have serious concerns about how your proposed project will affect the caribou that live down there during the summer. We really depend on those animals for our food, and we worry that your activity down there will scare them off." Well into his questioning, he was becoming more serious.

"Well, there is no indication anywhere that mining activities have any effect on caribou populations," replied the agent. "We aren't doing anything that will affect the population." People in Paulatuk had been very pleased with the steps the company took to mitigate the problems of working in an important hunting area, he said.

Joseph grew indignant. "That's not what people in Paulatuk say. Ever since they started down there, there are no caribou. That's not good enough. And what about bears? We have concerns about bears, and what will happen if your teams come across bears? You have nothing in here" – he thumped the paper on the table – "about what you will do about bears."

The agent seemed relieved to leave the subject of caribou behind. "We are very concerned about the safety of our workers, so our crews will always have someone with both bear spray and a firearm for protection." He said it smugly, a pat answer to a soft-ball question.

"I don't think you understand," Joseph said, echoing the sentiments of many in the room. "We're worried about the bears, not about your safety. We want to make sure no harm comes to the bears."

This went on for some time, with many of the younger Inuit in the room, like Joseph, familiar with bureaucratic wrangling and the ways of Qablunaat, becoming increasingly hostile to the representative's presentation and demeanour. After some time, however, a few of the elders began to speak. They had been sitting silently, taking in the conversation and measuring the room's mood. Detecting the emotions of the younger people, one by one they began expressing their displeasure with the proposal. Once the old people had spoken, that was effectively the end of the meeting. A vote was taken, and the proposal was denied.

Unfortunately, that was not the end. The mining company appealed to the federal government and went ahead and drilled anyway, using Cambridge Bay, on the other side of the island, as their supply base. Joseph, like many others, was livid.

That meeting, Joseph says, was a real eye-opener for him. "It's like I finally woke up and saw what I needed to be doing. It's like the elders don't know about things like mining companies these days, so we have to help them. Before, I was on HTC and them committees, but it was mostly for the money. Now, it's like I have to do it to try and protect something for my kids."

The current outfit exploring did not make the same mistake as the first company. Knowing that success near the old Muskox Mines site required a community buy-in, the organizer spent plenty of time in the settlement, established relationships, and grossly overpaid for housing and labour. He had no trouble getting permission to do his work. Joseph is still sceptical. "It's not like they want to hire Inuit for real jobs. They hire what the IRC makes them hire, and they try and get young guys they can push around."

Joseph also knows why the company had so much success receiving community approval for their work. "It's because no one goes up there anymore. Ever since the caribou there went down, we don't go there. But my parents say that we'll need to hunt there again, we need to take care of that place."

Joseph and I sip our tea and look out the window. He was at his parents' camp this afternoon, checking on things. The mention of his parents turns the conversation. "Mum and Dad wanted the kids out there with them yesterday and today, they all slept out there. I just went out to check on them."

"How were they?"

"Well, you know my kids. At that age they can be really tiring, and it's so easy for my dad to get tired these days, I don't want to wear them out. I think I made Mum and Dad mad at me, though."

"How did you do that?" Joseph's mother is known for having a bit of a temper, especially with her own children. Perhaps it is not a temper so much as what Sam Ihumayuq called being "very stern." The first year I was in Ulukhaktok, Joseph was a very serious hockey player. At one point, he was injured by a slapshot that went astray and hit him in the collarbone, nearly breaking it. His mother was not shy in expressing her opinion that he was wasting his time, that he was going to hurt himself doing nothing.

"I think Mum was mad that I didn't trust them to look after the kids, that I should just stay away for a while," he says. "She told me to go home and stop worrying. She says that they're really well behaved out there, not bouncing off the walls like they are in the house."

Another sip. "Then I made Dad mad too. He was trying to get his nets ready to set, and I tried to help. He just said no, he could do it. So I came back here."

I know that voice, a "no" uttered tersely, and clipped, a glottal stop ending the word. It is a quick and simple expression of annoyance, the kind that conveys displeasure simply and subtly. There are other ways of expressing the same sentiment. "Up to you" uttered in response to a request can mean exactly the same thing: you can do this if you want to, but it will make me angry. Joseph, in this case, was immediately aware he had overstepped the bounds of autonomy, that his father, while perhaps appreciating the sentiment, really did need to perform the task himself, even if it would take far longer. For men, and old men especially, remaining productive is critical to their sense of self-worth. Joseph's offer of assistance, as well-intentioned as it was, was a blow to his father's self-esteem. To Joseph's credit, he recognized the error immediately.

"So, what you going to do now?"

"I don't know. It's really quiet here without the kids. I'm thinking to go for a drive after. Mum said that the freezer is getting low, and Tikligtuq says there's a herd of muskox on the other side of Hanigayuq. His son Jack got one there yesterday. But maybe I'll work on the boat too. Getting to be time to go for caribou, and Dad's going to want to go when the weather could get good."

I finish my tea, and make to head out. "What are you going to do?" Joseph asks.

"I don't know. I guess I have to think about putting my stuff away. I'm going back next week. So I have to put my stuff in the shack, close it up. I have to get my last round of interviews before I go, and see people too."

"There's always something to do, isn't there? It never stops," says Joseph, as we put on our runners and head out the door.

10

Real Northern Men

"We should go out hunting once more before you have to leave. You should go out on the land one more time," Charlie Hanayi says. As usual, we are sitting in his apartment in the fourplex, drinking coffee and playing cribbage. His girlfriend, who moved in during midwinter, is at her parents' house for the evening. They are in town briefly to re-supply before going back down to Mashuyak, where they will remain through break-up. There's a solid sheet of fast ice between town and Mashuyak, but it has been warm, and cracks are opening and getting wider. This will be their last trip into town until mid-July.

Charlie's apartment, then, at least for the evening, is back to being a bachelor pad. We have played several games of cribbage and consumed a fair amount of coffee. Charlie has just skunked me, and in the process he revealed his secret for beating me at cards. When we play at the kitchen table, he says, he makes sure his back is to the television, which distracts me but not him. I ponder Charlie's cleverness and promise myself never to sit facing the television again.

Once he makes the invitation to go hunting, it hits me. It is June 1993. My fieldwork time is nearly over, and I'm departing soon. I may never come back. It's not until now that I even think about it. Charlie continues, discussing how we can get out on the land and where we might go. His ATV needs work. By the time I leave, we've made nebulous plans for "Friday" and "after work."

That's on Tuesday, and though we haven't spoken about it or made concrete plans in the meantime, we both know we'll be going out Friday evening. And so, after supper, we're preparing to go hunt muskox.

Charlie's small food box is empty, but, more importantly, so is his parents'. Charlie did not catch much food this year, but when he did, nearly all of it went to his parents. Another hunter has reported a herd of muskox some fifteen kilometres up the coast, so we have our destination. Although there's a wedding reception in town that evening, we decide instead to go out on the land. Charlie says something about priorities when he stops by after work. "Plus, I haven't been muskox hunting since we went last fall," he says as additional justification.

We're not going alone. Matthew Aqiaruq has decided to come along, and he's taking his fourteen-year-old son, Robert. Robert will ride on the back of Matthew's AT V. Charlie and I each have our own machine. Charlie owns his, of course, a Frankenstein-like machine put together from three older, broken ones he collected, but mine has been borrowed from a schoolteacher now on summer holidays. Teachers rarely go out on the land, so the AT V has been lightly used and is in good shape, nearly new. If we have a breakdown, I'm pretty sure it won't be on my account. Even so, my pack includes the standard toolkit that comes with the AT V and my own small bag of tools. I also have a pump and plugs for tires.

Still, I'm a bit nervous as we head out. This is the first time I have been on an AT V since last summer. I am unsure about how these things handle. At least the one I'm driving is a Honda without a clutch. Last summer I tried to drive a three-wheeler, and I had to contend with the terrain, the instability of three wheels on that terrain, and my lack of coordination in engaging the clutch with my hand and shifting with my foot. With the AT V all I need to do is shift with my foot and take my thumb off the accelerator for a moment. The four wheels make for a more stable machine too.

The weather is beautiful this evening, temperatures hovering between 5 and 7°C, with very light winds. By nine we're ready to go. The June sun is above the horizon, so we are in no hurry to get home before dark. We start our bikes and head down the airport road, crossing the bridge over Ukpillik River and immediately turning off onto the AT V trail toward the beach. We follow the trail down to the cabins along the beach, passing below the airport runway, and then down the coast. We zoom by the summer camps that dot the raised gravel beach, waving at the few people out here for the weekend. Most of these are elders, preparing their camps for next month's runs of Arctic char.

We leave the last of the camps behind, climb to a higher, raised beach, and cross Hanigayuq's River. The water is very high now and flowing quickly, draining the melting snow and lake ice off the land. Charlie and Matthew cross without hesitation, and I follow suit, a little nervous when the ATV begins to float.

I make it across without incident, however, and we pick our way carefully through the rocks and the low-lying, marshy areas, trying to find the easiest road while keeping an eye out for muskox. It's a very bumpy and wet ride. My legs are muddy from the knees down, and I understand why Charlie insisted I wear wind pants and waders. Still, I struggle to keep up. Charlie and Matthew are much more comfortable with ATV riding, and I am stunned by the landscape too. I have travelled this route multiple times, most recently three weeks ago, and I thought I knew the land around Ulukhaktok. Hanigayuq's River is only seven kilometres or so from the settlement. However, I feel like I am in a completely different part of the Arctic. Without its blanket of snow, the tundra looks foreign, the browns and faint greens much different from the bright, unchanging whites of snow and ice.

We continue along the coast, mudding our way through marshy areas and then cruising along drier, gravel-covered, exposed patches. After about forty-five minutes, we stop for a short rest, largely because Robert needs a break. Riding on the ATV is bumpy for the driver, but he at least has a padded seat and footrests to brace against. Robert is sitting on the rear cargo rack, hanging on for dear life and bouncing on the metal bars, with only a chunk of carpet foam as a cushion. His arms and behind will be sore tomorrow. While he stretches, Matthew pulls out a thermos of hot, sweet tea. We stand on the small hillock, looking out over the Beaufort Sea, listening to the steady chirps of unseen songbirds. A patch of landfast ice clings to the shore. I pull out my binoculars to get a better look at dark shapes on the ice. In focus, they are ringed seals, basking in the evening sun. A few look warily in our direction, though I doubt they can see us. I am told that seals have poor vision, and we are several hundred metres away. Matthew, for his part, pulls out something more serious than binoculars. He has his

.303, and he is looking down the sights. He fires, the retort piercing the relative quiet.

"Missed," he mutters, and returns the rifle to its case. He will not get another chance at the seals. All of the dark dots went into the water at the sound of the gunshot. We finish our tea, stow the mugs and thermos, and start out again.

Charlie and I soon split from Matthew and Robert, taking a slightly different route. We make our way up and along a higher ridge, away from the beach. We can still see Matthew, perhaps a kilometre away and below us, moving along the beach line. Charlie wants to be on higher ground for the view. Still, we parallel Matthew until I signal a need to stop. One of my tires has gone flat – so much for me not being the one to break down. From the perspective of a Qablunaaq, it is one of the infuriating problems of Arctic travel that newer, better-maintained machines seem to break down just as frequently as those like Charlie's old Frankenbeater. It is one reason why Inuit spend little time worrying about maintenance and more about developing the flexibility to address uncertainty and to improvise repairs.

Still, this is not a serious problem. I have a repair kit. The real trouble is finding the source of the leak, though even this is thankfully a simple task. A particularly sharp rock has penetrated the tire. We spend ten minutes plugging the hole and pumping the tire.

We expected that Matthew would be out of sight by now, but we can see that he too has stopped – some distance away, but we can make out the bright red of his machine against the dull background of the beach. As we work on the tire, Charlie looks to see what Matthew might be up to. We hear the report of the .303 and realize he has shot something. In the binoculars, it looks light brown and small. Charlie decides Matthew has shot a caribou, and we are both excited. Caribou have not been seen this close to Ulukhaktok for at least five years.

We soon realize that was wishful thinking. Matthew has shot a young muskox. By the time we reach him, he and Robert have nearly finished skinning it. In the distance, we see three other animals walking north slowly, away from us. Charlie takes his rifle out of the case, loads it, leaving the chamber empty for the time being, and drives after them. I follow, my camera loaded and ready.

In the dead of winter, muskoxen are beautiful, stately animals, perhaps more so because they appear to live by eating only snow. By June, however, they are rapidly shedding their *qiviut*, the soft, thick hair that insulates them against wind and cold during the winter months. Clumps of qiviut hang from the long guard hairs, dragging along the ground. Wet from running through the muskeg, fleeing Matthew's ATV, the animals now look like giant wet rats of the Arctic tundra. They do not run from us but huddle together on the gravel, backs to the sea. They have already run once today. We stop. Charlie selects the medium-sized male and shoots it.

The animal drops immediately, but the remaining two refuse to move. Five minutes pass, but they continue to stand over their fallen comrade. Charlie and I resolve to drive them off. We throw rocks, make loud noises, sing songs, and finally rev up our ATV engines. The two simply stare at us, unimpressed.

After thirty minutes, they have moved all of ten feet away from the carcass. Charlie decides this is enough room and directs me to drive up to the fallen animal. He hops off my machine, quickly ties the animal and hooks the line to the ATV, telling me to drive off with the carcass in tow. This all happens fast. Charlie is worried that one of the remaining animals may charge. Success: I stop in a soft patch of short grass. Charlie unhooks the line, and we pull out our skinning knives and get to work. The two remaining muskoxen stare on, but as we make our first incisions into the hide, we hear them shuffling off.

When I first went hunting with Charlie back in October, I had no idea how to butcher a muskox. Eight months and several hunts later, I have a pretty good idea how this should go. Charlie and I make fairly quick work of the animal, stopping periodically to sharpen our knives with the file. As I remove the front leg from the carcass, I realize that Charlie has stopped to watch me work. "Gee, Pete, you're turning into a real northern man." He says it with a smile. I take it as a compliment.

We continue to work on the animal, and I feel the glow of being competent at something. "That's great. But what *is* a 'real northern man'?"

We laugh. A few minutes later, though, Charlie has a response to clarify his initial compliment. "Well, a northern man means you have to do two things. If you come to live in the North and you want to be a real man, you have to go out hunting. Then, you can't be lazy."

We return to skinning the animal, removing each of the legs to a plastic tarp. This will keep gravel and dirt from getting into the meat. We will wrap the tarp around the pieces and then tie the entire bundle to the back of Charlie's ATV. Once the legs are off, Charlie guts the animal, removing the massive stomach and intestines, setting them aside on the ground. He then removes the heart, kidneys, and liver and cuts out a section of an artery running along the back of the body cavity. He holds it up to show me.

"This stuff is great for chewing. When we were kids, we used to chew it like gum. My kids really like it." He places it in his packsack. The organs go into a separate, larger bag, with the meat from the back of the animal. These we load onto the back of the Honda, along with the legs. Everything is wrapped in the same plastic tarp and tied down.

We wash our hands in a small meltwater pond just behind the beach and sit down for coffee from Charlie's thermos, already laced with sugar and evaporated milk. Susie's bannock and some mipku make the rest of our snack. We munch in silence for a few moments, listening to the chirps of the birds behind us, and I ponder Charlie's assessment of what makes a northern man. For this entire year of fieldwork I have been following men like Charlie around, assessing their commitment to hunting, trapping, and fishing – the kinds of activities that, apparently, characterize northern men.

"Charlie, are there any real northern men living in Holman?"

He swallows a mouthful of mipku. "No, I don't think so. There aren't many real northern men in Holman anymore."

We sit for a while longer, taking in the continued birdsong, and I change the subject. All this year I have been trying – without much success – to learn Inuinnaqtun. I quickly found out that men of my generation do not readily speak the language. Most of the young men I worked with indicated that they were too embarrassed to try to speak Inuinnaqtun, citing the numerous mistakes they make with their grammar and all the vocabulary they do not know. Not that they did not understand the language, for their parents often spoke to them in it, but they would usually respond in English.

Charlie, however, is one of the few who knows the language reasonably well, and he is not embarrassed to speak it publicly. So, I figure, now is as good a time as any to ask.

"Charlie, what are all these birds called?" I know from a casual interest in birding that the songbirds making the most noise are, in English, Lapland longspurs and horned larks. They are ubiquitous. Around the meltwater ponds are other species, ruddy turnstones and various small plovers. Most of these I have seen just outside town. But there is one, sitting twenty yards away, light brown on top, a black stripe through its face and along its sides, pale below. It is striking, and I do not know what it is – in either English or Inuinnaqtun.

"You mean in Eskimo? I got no idea. We just always called them 'brownbirds.' We used to catch them when I was small. My granny would give me and my brother the .22, and we'd share that and go out and try and catch them. Sometimes I'd use a slingshot."

I point at the different bird, brown, tan, and buff, sitting there, not far away. It's a good thing there are no eight-year-olds with slingshots here. They might kill it to find out what it is. "What's that one called?"

"That one? We used to call it a 'toolit toolit.'"

The name sounds very un-Inuinnaq to me, but before I can ask why it is called that, the answer comes to me. *Toolit toolit!* sings the bird, and flies away.

Charlie looks at me and nods. Now I have my answer. I later consult my bird book and discover it to be a lesser golden plover.

What is a real northern man? I pondered that question during the ATV ride back to town, and I have pondered it since. The question is a principal reason for writing this book. To this point, though, I have presented a series of ethnographic episodes that for me capture important components of what it means to be a "real northern man," as Charlie phrased it. My intent has been to present the narrative with limited theorizing or speculation – avoiding, as Inuit might conceive of it, telling the reader what to think, and instead encouraging reflection on the multiple meanings of these stories. For the remainder of this concluding chapter, however, I return to some of the theoretical issues raised in chapters 2 and 3. In particular, I focus on several issues that are pertinent to my understanding of the process of becoming a real northern man. I dig into the personal nature of ethnographic fieldwork, focusing on the discovery of cultural processes and the choice of research strategies that researchers and communities make. I address the nature of knowledge transmission and what makes for legitimacy from an Inuit perspective, integrating Inuit conceptions of the life course, personhood, and the meaning of successful aging.

THE PERSONAL NATURE OF ETHNOGRAPHY

The muskox hunt with Charlie and Matthew occurred in June 1993, at the tail-end of my first fieldwork in Ulukhaktok. I left several weeks later. During that fieldwork year, which I outlined in chapter 3, both Richard Condon and I were recording the activities of this cohort of men, Richard being primarily interested in the various barriers and hurdles that made it very difficult for young men – many of them adolescents during the research that led to his *Inuit Youth* (1987) – to fully participate in the "traditional" subsistence economy. During that year, it was evident that the men in our study sample were not very active hunters, a state of affairs that we attributed both to the high costs of mechanized foraging from the settlement and to the more pernicious effects of the economic and political climate in which these men were raised. As I have noted earlier in this book, they were educated in schools rather than hunting camps, they socialized primarily with each other, and they were exposed to a set of values seemingly incompatible with those held by their parents and grandparents. All of these factors, we felt, effectively prevented the transmission of the knowledge necessary to hunt adequately, although, and perhaps more importantly, there was a decided lack of practice too. When men like Charlie were in their teens, the market for sealskins collapsed, and many families simply gave up seal hunting and began staying in town even during the summer months.

Hence, structural conditions stunted their growth as hunters. In the 1993 sample, only one of the men I interviewed was hunting in a manner that resembled the style of the older generation. This outlier was particularly instructive. Although he was young enough to be in our study sample, he was socially much older. He travelled with the older men and pursued the same strategies as they did. Indeed, he stated several times during the year that, even as a young boy, he knew that the only thing he ever wanted to do was to hunt. The rest of the guys were much less active, only up to making a few day trips for muskoxen, as Charlie and I were doing. A few took longer overnight trips, but these men still produced food quite differently from the way their parents did. Looking back, anything else would have been startling, given their childhood experiences and backgrounds.

William Kemp argued in 1971 that one of the primary drivers of the adoption of the snowmobile was the fact of settlement life. The snowmobile allowed a hunter to get quickly from the settlement to a hunting area, hunt, and then return to town with the meat. The snow machine satisfied two important needs: acquiring food *and* remaining in proximity to kin. As an example of different production, the younger guys in the settlement cohort took these needs – snow machine and proximity to kin – to another level. The young men were increasingly enamoured of the more powerful, liquid-cooled engines that began appearing in the early 1990s, because, in addition to being loud and equipped with amenities like hand and feet warmers and coming in cool colours, they could go faster and pull a heavier load. These men found that they could travel further, take more with them, and still get back to town in time for dinner and *Hockey Night in Canada*.

There were trade-offs. For example, those machines were prone to overheating in warmer weather. Likewise, they required a different kind of sled design to take the stresses of the speed and the load. Consequently, young guys' sleds were very different from those of their parents; they were reinforced with plywood and used heavier crosspieces; plywood boxes were used to hold gear. The sleds of their parents were lighter and minimally reinforced with a piece of sheet metal here and there and lighter crosspieces. Older hunters did not use heavy plywood boxes, and their sleds showed greater concern for the angles of the sled boards and the overall length of the sled. Many older men had multiple sleds designed for different conditions, some for sea ice travel, others for travel on the land.

I discovered these issues accidentally during my own attempts to make sleds in 1997. The older men directed and advised me to construct my sleds along the more traditional lines, leaving me open to some serious criticism from my peers, who insisted that the sleds I was building were too fragile to survive. Isaac, who expected to inherit them when I left, was particularly concerned, enough so that I woke up one morning to the sound of him "improving" my sleds for me by driving metal spikes into the boards.

And none of the men in the 1992–93 sample, with the exception of that single outlier, were producing food in the same manner as their parents either. Most of the young guys' activities tended to revolve around shooting a muskox here or there, helping Dad with the summer fishing, and maybe taking a summer trip for caribou down in Prince Albert Sound – also with Dad, and usually with his equipment. Part of this battery of activities reflected knowledge limitations and concern for safety. Most guys my age had limited experience with travel on the sea ice and its constantly changing conditions. Remaining on land, hunting muskoxen close to town, was a far safer strategy.

These men were not producing much food. Some hunted hardly at all, their activities better understood as "driving around" rather than hunting, or else they limited their activities to the few weeks of June duck hunting. They *talked* about hunting, but they did not *do* much of it. Or so it seemed to me.

It was all very depressing, a way of life going away, and difficult for me to process. I had, like most young anthropologists, a romantic sense of tradition. Apparently the young guys were simply doomed to become town-dwellers. Charlie's comment about the decline of real northern men certainly indicated that he, at least, believed it. I believed it too, falling into the trap of allowing my pre-existing values to colour my interpretations. These were values I cultivated first by reading the academic literature and then from living in the settlement. The acculturation perspective that ran through the literature, which I outline in some detail in chapter 2, viewed Inuit culture and modernity as a process by which Inuit were becoming more and more like southerners, becoming townspeople, but beset by numerous problems, among them alcohol, suicide, culture loss, and domestic violence. *Things are really changing around here.* Qablunaat who insisted on playing Local Expert likely arrived at the same conclusions independently of the academic literature. They replicated many of the same themes, focusing on the numerous social problems, the perceived dim prospects for young men who lacked interest in school, and the increasing dependence upon social assistance.

Inuit, in turn, likewise replicated this belief that things were changing for the worse, that Inuit culture was dying, or at least changing into
some lesser form. I heard numerous variants of "We are losing our elders and traditions" during my first year in the field. What turned me
away from this received wisdom was my return to Ulukhaktok in 1997
and the subsequent validation I gained because my wife and baby
daughter were with me.

Ethnography and its principal strategy, participant observation, require a serious and intense commitment on the part of both ethnographer and those under study. Unlike the case with survey research, there
is very little buffer between the researcher and the researched. In
Ulukhaktok, the survey researcher is in the community only for a brief
period, typically staying in the hotel. Interaction with informants occurs under conditions controlled tightly by both Inuit and researcher
as if by mutual agreement. Little emotional investment is involved for
either side. Participant observation, on the other hand, is much riskier
for both parties.

Doing ethnography encompasses a number of different styles and
strategies, of course, from complete participation and immersion to
complete, detached observation, each with different kinds of risks and
rewards. In my case, I was following a strategy somewhere between
Gold's (1958) definitions of "participant-as-observer" and "complete
participant," living with and alongside Inuit as much as possible, eating
the same food, participating in the same activities, living under the
same (or slightly worse) housing conditions. I was not entirely a "complete participant" – impossible, given that it was well known that I was
"doing interviews" – but I was an engaged participant observer. There
are, of course, numerous advantages to pursuing this strategy of immersion. Hammersley (1992), among others (Brewer 2000, 56–63,
Davies 2008, 77–87, Wolcott 1999, Hammersley and Atkinson 1983,
Miller and Russell 2005), notes that the goal of the ethnographic enterprise is to comprehend the cultural scene. Ethnography is about discovering the natural world, understanding social processes, and
making sense of the complexities that underlie those processes. It is
inherently an exploratory endeavour, designed to comprehend the
meanings behind cultural behaviour. The strategy of participating and

observing allows the ethnographer to develop at least some sense of what it is like to be a cultural insider.

But ethnography is also intensely personal. The men I have profiled here were more than informants: they were friends, which could and did make for uncomfortable situations when it came to boundaries and loyalties. On one occasion I made the mistake of arriving at Joseph Qalviaq's house and, after an hour spent drinking tea and playing cribbage, asked to interview him. His response was chilling: "Gee, and I thought you just came to visit. As a friend." There can be tremendous pressure to remain the detached observer in the name of science. As the student of the culture, the ethnographer is always on call and feels a continual urge to try to take everything in, to record everything, no matter how minute, to answer the door for every visitor because of the potential for discovering new insights. Everything is fair game for observation and analysis, which could make it difficult when enmeshed in sensitive situations. Such was the case during my first Inuit funeral, and I struggled with the choice between grieving participant and detached observer.

It is impossible to truly go native, of course, because of the ethnographer's pre-existing cultural baggage, and there were certainly moments when being in the scene became too stressful, when I preferred to just lock the door and not entertain visitors, when I wanted chicken nuggets rather than yet another meal of boiled duck. During 1997, on more than a few evenings Maya and I wished that the school principal and his wife would invite us over for a scotch or a coffee and some intellectual conversation.

On another level, the personal nature of ethnography emerges more clearly in the way I present the guys. I was studying men of my age, participating in the same activities, living in a similar manner. As an American graduate student, I began to see parallels between my life and theirs, especially in the domain of the life course and becoming an adult. Graduate school is much like a prolonged adolescence, a lifestyle revolving around limited resources, substandard living conditions, flexible and unpredictable social schedules, and uncertainty about the future. When would I be recognized as a *real* adult? My return to Ulukhaktok in 1997 drove the point home precisely because I arrived with Maya and Sarah. Being married and a father validated me socially, and in ways that were quite different than in the South. I was the only one in my graduate cohort to have a child; indeed, only one other graduate student was even married. As graduate students, Maya and I were socially off-time. As academics in training, we were far too young to be married, let alone to have a child. In Ulukhaktok, the opposite was true. We were very much considered on-time. Furthermore, in Ulukhaktok we discovered a social support network that did not exist in State College, Pennsylvania, where were had been living. In Pennsylvania, the closest grandparents were a seven-hour drive away. When Sarah was born, we had little idea what to do with her. She did not come with a user's manual, and our only significant and readily available cultural resource on child rearing was the rather alarmist *What to Expect When You're Expecting* series, books that lead new parents to believe that a common cold is probably encephalitis, or worse.

My purpose here is to highlight that the discovery process of the ethnography is very much influenced by the value-driven background of my own cultural baggage and my discovery that some of my research objectives resonated with, and were driven by, my own life circumstances. Hence, one reason for the eyewitness accounts I present here is partly because these episodes were instructive, providing insights into the struggles and processes behind becoming an adult in communities like Ulukhaktok.

From a research perspective, the problem is balance. At one level, there is potential risk in pursuing a line of inquiry that is close to one's own personal circumstances. Perhaps I went too far in my role as fieldworker, becoming a complete participant rather than a participant observer? Hammersley and Atkinson (1983, 90–104), who discuss some of the inherent problems with the different roles that ethnographers adopt in the field, pay particular attention to these issues. Becoming a complete participant is a risky strategy precisely because it limits lines of inquiry, constrains behaviour, and creates dilemmas about loyalties. However, although there is ample discussion of the reflexive nature of research, social relations themselves underlie research on social relations (Crang and Cook 2007, 9; see also Davies 2008, Hertz 1997, Brewer 2000, 128–33, Hammersley and Atkinson 1983, 14–16). Strategies and roles are also dictated by the studied, and in Ulukhaktok the roles I assumed were not entirely my choice. After three months in Ulukhaktok, in 1992, there seemed to be some sentiment that I become more of a complete participant in the cultural scene. For me the first such indicator occurred at the hockey arena, when two pre-teen girls approached me, apparently sent by someone else, and asked if I "had a honey." I later realized this was an inquiry into my potential availability as a romantic partner. The arrival of Isaac's sister-in-law over Christmas – a matchmaking attempt by his wife – was another attempt to draw me further into the social relations of the community. My identity with the guys was as much driven by Inuit as it was by my own position and pre-existing cultural baggage. The fact that the children of some of my informants and friends began calling me "uncle" further reinforced my role as something more than a researcher or generic Qablunaaq.

KNOWLEDGE, PERSONHOOD, AND THE INUIT LIFE COURSE

The other, less discussed risk in treading into complete participant territory is the threat that the study becomes an exercise in self-aggrandizement rather than ethnography. The personal nature of the ethnographic experience is one reason why I situated myself at the centre of the narrative. The ethnography here is about what I observed, events that were particularly instructive about men's lives, lessons learned while in the field. There is a second and equally important reason for keeping the narrative focused as much as possible on events in which I was a direct participant. For Inuit, legitimate knowledge is acquired through direct experience supplemented by guidance from recognized, and frequently older, experts.

Examples abound. Aporta and Higgs (2005) describe training methods in precisely this manner, as the development of skills based on experience, scaffolded by older men, who impart their wisdom in knowledge at the conclusion of the activity. Briggs (1991) discusses the multiple ways in which children observe others and practise the skills and abilities they seek to acquire. Once a child demonstrates some competence, adults test them, sometimes harshly, as Joseph discovered when he lost track of his traps. Albert Aquti's question "Which way is town?" is an extraordinarily common example of such testing. Other methods of instruction are subtler. During one spring trip, Isaac felt the need to teach me about behaviour in the natural world. We were out fishing, without much success, and Isaac took a moment to point at two gulls flying overhead. He nudged me, raised his rifle and shot one. It fell to the ice with a thud, and the second gull – apparently its mate – descended, crying loudly. When it landed next to the corpse, it walked slowly around the dead bird, still crying, poking at the body. Isaac looked at me, and he said, "See? They do that." The lessons, I suppose, were many. Gulls are like people in that they form relationships and grieve. The world is a malevolent place. Death can come at any moment. Isaac turned back to jigging.

Consequently, Inuit learning depends on attention to detail, observing social interaction, listening to conversations and, once ready, demonstrating social and physical competence and developing experience. These markers signal to the older and more experienced that the learner is capable of and ready for further engagement. Crago's examination of child socialization practices documents these processes in clear detail. Kawagley (1995, 18), in his discussion of Yupiaq worldviews and knowledge, is more explicit: indigenous learning is at its core participant observation, an exercise through which the individual discovers his or her place in the social, physical, and spiritual worlds. Annahatak (1994) likewise highlights the important ways that her parents' guidance led her to use and apply her experience and developing skills in ways that fit properly within the context of Inuit values. In comparing her early experiences with those of the southern-based educational system, she observes that the apparent disconnect between elders and juniors today is due to the changing nature of social interaction and inherent conflicts in philosophy. School-based education proceeds from a top-down approach – teachers assess when a student is ready to learn. In the Inuit way, the learner directs the process. The central problem, as Annahatak sees it, is that both sides – children and elders – are waiting for the other to make the first move. Elders wait for children to take the initiative and demonstrate their readiness. Children wait for their elders to initiate the process, waiting for tasks to be set out for them.

Throughout this book I have made the case that the settlement cohort of men were born and came of age during a critical time in Inuit history. Their lives are quite different from those of their parents and grandparents, not only because of the changes that have profoundly affected Inuit communities but also because of the timing of those changes. This is hardly a novel idea: as I noted earlier, Glen Elder and colleagues have made this very case for other contexts of significant change, among them the important influence of the Depression upon the lives of members of different age cohorts.

Nevertheless, the construction of lives is not a random process, and, as anthropologists Christine Fry and Jennie Keith have argued (1982), the life course is a cultural unit that, though itself flexible, guides individual lives and connects individuals to the cultural collective. Life stages, and their associated roles, provide reference points for the individual and family. What life stage should one be in? When should one enter and exit that stage? What are the normative behaviours for people in that life stage? Condon's interests in adolescence as a new life stage in the settlement cohort led me to an initial interest in this literature. When do these Inuit men leave adolescence and become adults? My dissertation fieldwork in 1997 (Collings 2000, 2001) was very much focused on this question. To that point, there had been no academic attention paid to the structure of the Inuit life course.

Because of my prior experience in Ulukhaktok, I approached the study of the Inuit life course with an expectation that the members of the settlement cohort would have quite a different view of how their lives should be constructed and structured. I had good reasons for hypothesizing that such was the case, based on the numerous and visually obvious changes in Arctic communities, supplemented by academic and local perspectives about culture change. In particular, it seemed plausible that experience with schooling, apparent language loss, and lifestyle changes would all lead to a different construction of the life course. A novel construction was of course possible, but I half expected that the Inuit life course was becoming more like a southern Canadian and American one.

And there were differences. When I set out to do the interviews with my informants, I found that few of my younger informants knew the

Inuinnaqtun terms for different life stages. When they did, they possessed only a rudimentary knowledge of the meanings of the terms. Many of my younger informants – among them the men portrayed here – stated that terms like inuuhuktuq and inuhaat meant "teenager," as if teenager were a literal translation. The nuances of the meanings of the words appeared to have been lost. My elder informants could name the Inuinnaqtun terms and describe their meanings in nuanced detail, but they also had a greater arsenal of terms at their disposal. They frequently noted that the life stage terms were rather crude means for identifying people. Consistent with Inuit notions of integrity, individuals defy categorization, as each person is an entity with a unique history, characteristics, and circumstances. I certainly discovered this when I set out to elicit the terms using card sorts with hand-drawn pictures of people at different stages of their lives.

One of my first victims was Roy Kudlak, a recently retired hamlet truck driver. He was at home, waiting for coffee break, and with nothing better to do, he was game to see what kind of silly activity I had come up with. I was rather proud that my cards looked like people and not simple stick figures.

"Okay, Roy, I've got these cards here, and I'd like you to look at each picture and put the pictures that go together in the same pile." Once he had the piles, I planned to ask him what he called the people in each pile, and thus generate the age terminology without leading him along. It should be simple. After generating the terms, I could ask him some questions about the common experiences for people in each category.

"Okay." He picked up the first card, an image of an old man, slightly bent, leaning on a cane. "Hmm." Roy thought hard for a minute, going so far as to lift his glasses up so he could more closely examine the picture.

"This one looks like Ephraim. So, I'll put in this pile." He snapped the card down on the table. He picked up the next card. It was of two figures, each holding the hand of a much smaller figure, young parents holding the hand of a toddler.

Roy thought for another minute. "This looks like Brenda and Jimmy with Mary." He was referring to his daughter, her husband, and his granddaughter, Mary. "I'll put them right here." He snapped the card down next to Ephraim, in a separate pile.

The next card was a young woman packing a baby. "This one looks like Kathy." He declared it quickly. Kathy is another daughter, unmarried, with a new baby. He put that card down on the table, apart from the other two.

Seventeen cards later, there were twenty individual piles, each with their own set of attendant names. Roy did not organize anything. I asked, "Roy, don't you think that Brenda and Kathy might go together at all? Are they the same in any way?"

"No, one is Kathy and one is Brenda. They're different. Brenda is shacked up, and Mary is older. Kathy's one," referring to the baby, "is new."

"Okay, then." I had to salvage something of value out of this exercise. "Let me ask you some questions about the cards. I'm interested in how people experience getting old, what their lives are like."

"Right."

"So, this one here." I picked up the picture of the old man with the cane, whom Roy identified as Ephraim. "What would you call a person who was like this?" I was hoping I could generate the term this way.

He looked at me funny. "I'd call him Ephraim. That's what he looks like. Ephraim, you know, he walks around with a cane and everything. Doesn't go out much, you know. He's old, that's why."

"Okay, but is there an Inuinnaq word to describe him? You said he was old. Is there a word for that in Inuinnaqtun?"

"A word? Oh, yes, we'd call him inutquaq. That's old. Like Ephraim is."

Finally I was getting somewhere. I already knew that word, but I wanted Roy to say it, for the sake of good social science. "Okay, then. Let me ask you another question. What is life like for people who are inutquaq? What's it like to be in that part of life?"

"I don't know. Nauna." Roy was almost chuckling as he answered, the emphasis, a slight rise in tone, on *know*. He pushed his glasses back up his nose and looked at me. "You'd have to ask Ephraim what it's like to be Ephraim."

As the fieldwork progressed, it became apparent that the real differences in perceptions about the life course were not based on age. That is, young people and old people were in general agreement about the nature of the Inuit life course, in how the life course is constructed, what the specific life stages are, and what should characterize those life stages. Differences, when they appeared, were based upon gender. Women tended to construct the life course a bit differently from the way the men did. Men, for example, focused more on economic and domestic themes as important markers of life course transitions. That such should be the case is sensible, as men answered "How do you know you will be an adult?" with responses that included being able to provide for a family, having a house, or marriage. Women, for their part, focused more on social relationships and the assumption of community responsibilities.

A second exploration of the Inuit life course focused on the concept of "successful aging," paying attention to Inuit notions of what constitutes a "good old age." Inuit identified two particular areas that essentially defined what it means to age successfully. Mark Pihuktuq (I include an excerpt of his interviews in chapters 6 and 8) hit upon two major themes of aging successfully. Having a good old age, he said, depends upon remaining active and productive in the face of increasing limitations, but equally important is maintaining a proper attitude. Nearly all my informants stated that having good health in old age is unrealistic. Hence, an old person considered to be aging well is one who maintains a good outlook and persists in the face of declining physical abilities. Though Inuit were clearly worried that Mark continued to operate an AT V – he was legally blind – they admired him because he kept going. He refused to give up. The importance of this attitude is not limited to managing physical health. Simon maintained the importance of continuing to try despite his unexplained lack of hunting success. Joseph noted the need to "keep going." He knew precisely why his father resisted help in setting nets, and knew that he made a mistake by offering to help.

The other component of successful aging focused more on psychological issues. In addition to having a proper attitude about health, my informants included having a proper social attitude. Critical to aging well was engagement with young people – children and grandchildren – commonly referred to as "those coming up behind." This relationship is commonly referred to as "talking to" young people (or, conversely, being talked to), the means by which elders impart their accumulated knowledge and experience and advise about proper behaviour. My Inuit informants were quite clear that those who were aging poorly did none of those things. They did not engage with their juniors, they were grumpy and moody, and they were stingy.

Two noteworthy items are worth discussing here. The first is that the importance of these psychological features and definitions of managing old age made Inuit notions of life course transitions and successful aging quite different from those in other societies in which these topics have been explored (see especially Ikels et al. 1992, and Keith et al. 1994). In other societies where successful aging has been investigated, having good health was an important component of aging well, followed by economic and familial factors. For Inuit, the expectation seems to be that being old generally implies declining health, and the primary determinant of aging well is one's attitude. Economic and familial issues appear to be of lesser importance, perhaps because having a proper attitude in old age virtually assures one of economic and social support.

The second item of discussion here is that my study of successful aging focused largely on "old age," though it is quite apparent that some of the themes implied in a successful old age also apply to aging across the life span. This fact exposes a major limitation of the life course perspective. While it can generate insights about structural processes, it cannot, as Katherine Newman (1996) argues, illuminate the meaning of generational experience. Inuit life stages are helpful in guiding lives and providing structure for individuals as they age, but they do not provide insights into the meaning of aging in a particular context. Inuit life course structure has been a reference point for the men I profile here, something that these men have used to help them make the transition from an idle teenagerhood toward a productive and meaningful adulthood. And now, many are beginning to transition into middle age and elderhood. Some of these men are now grandparents, and some are, in the eyes of the IRC at least, elders. In this sense, social structure plays a critically important role in how lives are constructed.

By themselves, these stages are merely guideposts. They do not impart meaning to either the Inuit who reference them or to the anthropologist who documents them. The stages – nutaraq/child, inuhaat/ teenager, inirngniq/adult, inirnikhaq/middle age, inutquaq-aaquaq/old man-old woman – are physical and social descriptors that alert individuals to their position and appropriate role expectations. As Guemple (1983) points out, however, there is a great deal of flexibility even in reference to these signposts, as Inuit manipulate their position through various means, among them adopting grandchildren or changing activity patterns.

What, then, about the meaning of aging? At various points in the book I have highlighted the importance of two concepts, ihuma and inummariit, that organize Inuit human development. Life stages may be only guideposts, but they alert individuals to where they should be in reference to these concepts. Ihuma – the development of knowledge and wisdom – and inummarik – the genuine person – are the guiding themes of passage through life. Successful aging is not merely about old age and maintaining a proper attitude and remaining engaged with others: it is a feature of the entire life course. A successful adulthood is predicated upon developing ihuma and developing and demonstrating the characteristics of an inummarik.

I have emphasized the importance of recognizing the autonomous nature of the individual and of respecting integrity. For the outsider lacking cultural competence, asking questions and making demands are extraordinarily rude behaviours, tolerated only from children. Restraint, indirectness, subtlety, and the avoidance of conflict are all critical to getting along in society. The essential lessons are: stay out of other people's business, let others manage their own affairs, withhold judgment about others' character, and respect others' space. It is one reason, as I noted earlier, that I have not investigated sensitive, private, and potentially painful domains like suicide, domestic violence, or alcohol use.

It may seem, based on these discussions, that Inuit view the person as a bounded, discrete entity. Perhaps paradoxically, the Inuit notion of the *person* is in many ways exactly the opposite: the person is the sum total of the individual's place in society. The importance of ihuma and inummarik is their recognition that the individual is neither isolated nor bounded. The complete, genuine person is one who is defined by his or her relationships and actions toward others. As Stairs (1992; Stairs and Wenzel 1992) makes clear, the genuine person is one who recognizes and understands the balance of group interdependency within the context of self-sufficiency. Brody (1975) discusses the ways in which these ideals appear, paying particular attention to how sharing food and eating together are an essential definition of what it means to be inummarik, that sharing uniquely binds people together, points also made by Graburn (1972) and Fienup-Riordan (1983). In this context, Briggs (1991) argues that the real value of ihuma is that one who has it recognizes the boundaries of what should be individual and private and protected within the context of community needs. Genuine persons are those who are precisely in balance in behaviour with the people around them and the physical environment in which they live.

Despite the seismic changes marked by settlement and the collapse of the fur economies, the Inuit life course structure remains present and largely the same. Adulthood, inirngniq, in the meaning of "fully developed body," means the same thing today as it did in 1955. Likewise, the concepts of ihuma and inummariit are also unchanged. They remain ideals to which individuals aspire. Rather, the essential problem is that two parallel processes – markers of belonging to a particular life stage, on the one hand, and markers of genuine personhood, on the other – no longer occur alongside each other. Self-sufficiency for settlement cohort men is extraordinarily difficult to achieve before middle age. The men in the settlement cohort, as I hope I have demonstrated here, have been forced to depend more heavily on parents and in-laws for economic support, well into adulthood. Indeed, from this ethnographic perspective, it appears that, for many of these men, developing the balance characteristic of inummariit has taken rather longer to develop. Isaac Kaaktuq appears to have developed that sense by his early forties, assuming the responsibilities for his father's dog team, instructing (or, at least, trying to instruct) his nephew in proper consideration of others' needs, and acting in ways that maximize community benefit, "spreading around" the money generated from a sports hunt, rather than maximizing his own profit.

Joseph Qalviaq has likewise developed these same principles as he has approached middle age, contributing to community well-being through involvement in governance, discovering the limits of assistance to others, becoming enmeshed in community sharing networks. More importantly, Joseph could hardly be called an active hunter; although he has a genuine interest in hunting, his activities are largely limited to a single summer expedition hunt for caribou and an occasional muskox at other times during the year. Being an active hunter, let alone an expert one, is not a prerequisite for being inummarik. A proper attitude, however, is.

SAFETY CHANNEL

Stephen Hakagiak and I have been on the water for nearly twelve hours, a boating trip down into Prince Albert Sound. Stephen is a long-time resident of Ulukhaktok, in his early sixties; he moved here some time ago from points south and decided to settle permanently. He has, over the years, been a steady friend, a font of information and assistance. In many ways, he epitomizes inummarik. The primary purpose of our trip today, however, has been to get out of the settlement. It is high summer and too hot and dusty to stay in town. My trip to Ulukhaktok has been almost entirely for pleasure, anyway: I am here for a few weeks to visit with friends. So, today, we are sightseeing, stopping at points of archaeological or cultural interest along the shore.

Ulukhaktomiut once lived the entirety of their lives outside the confines of a settlement, and the shoreline is riddled with evidence of current and previous occupation. The time spans range from modern cabins to tenting sites littered with rusting cans and bleached bones, to Thule-era whalebone houses, and even to the remnants of Dorset-era longhouses.

That said, travelling with Stephen means travelling in a manner similar to the "old days" of the contact-traditional era. The boat is loaded with survival gear: a tent, poles, stove, extra fuel, several rifles, a fish net. The food we have with us is also contact-traditional: several piffis and boxes of pilot biscuits – called *hikulaaqs*, because they fracture and shatter when chewed. We also have two pounds of butter, and plenty of teabags. If we are stranded, we will not starve. Plenty of other people are out and about, too; the ice is long gone, the winds are down, and many boats are making their way into Prince Albert Sound, in search of caribou. We are hardly alone out here.

Even so, given that it is high summer and a warm day, between 15 and 20°C, it is still cold on the water. I'm wearing my insulated waders, long underwear, a heavy sweater, and my winter pullover. By the end of the day, we are both feeling chilled. Piffi is nutritious, but it is trout piffi and very low in fat, and we have been sitting in the boat, inactive.

Much of our trip is spent in silence. Hakagiak travels slowly, with a much lower horsepower motor than most Inuit use, and he runs it at a lower speed. If we go too fast, the choppiness of the water bothers his back, damages the boat, and uses far too much fuel for his liking. So, it is a slow cruise, with the added advantage of allowing for a scan of the water. If we see a natiaq within range – if it is offered, in other words – he will take it.

Unfortunately, while we see plenty of seals, apparently interested in the different sound of our slow-moving motor, they are not young enough or close enough for him to shoot. Instead, we watch the shoreline as it passes by. Stephen marvels at the colour of the land.

"It didn't used to be this green. Even a few years ago, it wasn't this green. Now the summer comes a month early, and the land gets green faster. Didn't used to be this way."

We ponder this as we approach the entrance, or, in this case, exit, of Safety Channel. This opening on Amundsen Gulf, Caution Channel on the maps, is guarded by a small island. The outer islands of Safety Channel lie to the south, beyond which is Prince Albert Sound. That Qablunaat should call it Safety Channel makes perfect sense, as the outer islands protect boaters from the swells and rougher waters that can roll in from Amundsen Gulf and the Beaufort Sea. Victoria Island and the entrance to Shoal Bay lie to the north. I can clearly see from here the ridge where Simon encouraged me to blow away a snow bunting. To the south, I can see the island where we hunted Bugs Bunnies and I shot at my first seal. I understand why being on the land is so important for Inuit: the places themselves hold memories that span the generations.

Though we are both chilled and sore from sitting for hours, we are still not moving fast. It is not far to Mashuyak, and we will stop to visit with Mark and his family. They are camped there, as they are every summer, and we will likely have a meal.

The gunshot, however, calls to us. It comes from the little island, and Stephen changes course toward the sound. Even at this distance, we can see the boat pulled up onto the beach, in a small, protected little gravel turn, and we can make out a figure standing on a rock, rifle in hand. We have been asked to stop.

When we pull in, Edward Kuniluk guides our bow onto the beach, slowing it slightly to reduce wear and tear on the hull. He grabs the bowline, securing it to a large boulder. I hop out and pull the boat higher on the beach.

"What you guys up to? Just boating around?" Edward has a big smile on his face. He of course knew we were down here today. He saw us leaving Ulukhaktok some twelve hours ago, as he was heading off to bed.

Off the water, it is quite warm, and Edward is stripped down to a ripped and faded t-shirt; his sweater and parka lie on a rock. As we get out and stretch, he pulls a battered plywood box – his grub box – from his boat and places it on the beach. He reaches in for a wrapped package, dirty white, almost yellow, and hands it to Stephen, who grabs it before I can make a move. Declaring, laughing, "Me first – I'm older, you know," he pulls out his pocket knife and hacks off slices, popping them into his mouth.

It looks something like cheese, but it is *tunnuq* – caribou fat, hard fat, something like lard, rendered down and formed into a block. I wait patiently, and, when it is finally my turn, devour several slices. In a few minutes I feel better, the fat already generating heat in my body. The chill subsides.

"There's coffee in the thermos. Hot water for tea soon." Edward points at the pot and the kettle, sitting atop the stove, hissing away.

Edward is not alone. Two of his nephews are with him, young men in their late teens. Both sit on a rock close to the stove. One has a package quite different from Edward's tunnuq, a box of Kraft dinner. The other is pouring Kool-Aid mix into a plastic bottle and mixing in water. We say hello.

"How's it going?" I ask, turning to Edward.

"Oh, pretty good. Going across." He waves his arm toward the south shore of Prince Albert Sound. About a forty-kilometre crossing from here, it is potentially dangerous in small boats like those we are using, especially since there is not one bit of ice in the water to reduce the swells, and no protection out on the open water. There is something of a tradition of "going across" by boat early in the summer. One reason is the caribou there, but before a series of early break-ups over the past decade, pack ice frequently drifted into Prince Albert Sound, preventing boat travel into the end of the Sound. Edward is adhering to an old pattern. Luckily, conditions are near perfect, about as flat calm as one could hope for, so it is unlikely to be dangerous. That could change quickly.

"Weather is good for it. Taking these young boys with me too, my sister wanted me to take them. We're stopping here to check everything. Going to have our supper too, we never eat yet." I know already that Edward's oldest son, about the same age as these two, is with his in-laws down in Halahaqvik.

Edward's trip, like many boating trips, is something of an expedition hunt. Edward could stay out at least a week, perhaps longer if he rationed his fuel. He hopes, however, for a quick trip. I know he wants to shoot multiple caribou and come right back with as many as his boat can handle. The weather is one reason for a quick trip. There are few protected areas on the south shore of the Sound. If bad weather comes, they could be stranded for some time. Also, it has been so warm that, should they take any animals, they need to get them back to town quickly and into the freezer.

"Got to teach these boys, get them out on the land." We are at a distance from the teens. They are still sitting on their rock, tending the stove and boiling the noodles for their dinner. Stephen has wandered off down the beach. I pour myself coffee from the thermos. It is just the thing to melt the tunnuq now in my stomach. "Feeling better?" Edward asks.

"Oh, yes. That hit the spot. I forgot that Stephen doesn't travel with much in the way of food."

Edward laughs. "Yuh. He's an old-timer, that one. But native food, fills you up, makes you strong. These two," he says, looking over at his nephews "they'll learn pretty soon." In a lower tone he says, a smile on his face, "That's the only juice I brought. Got lots of dry meat and piffi, though, and biscuits and butter."

"Store food" apparently does not include Klik, sardines, pilot biscuits, tea, sugar, or butter, all of which Edward includes as traditional staples.

"Aren't they going to complain?" Amos Tuktu told me several years ago that being out with the family could be a trial. Once the junk food is gone, the complaining begins. Sugar withdrawal can last for days.

"No. They know better than to bitch around me. Mustn't complain."

Stephen returns, and we sit together on the beach for forty-five minutes or so. We have moved on to dry meat – mipku made from caribou Edward shot last week. This is his second trip for caribou this summer. We eat, drink coffee and tea, and look out at the water. The sun is behind us, low on the northwestern horizon. Edward, thinking about some of the potential problems of hunting on the other side of Prince Albert Sound, talks about a previous trip many years ago, when he was a teenager himself.

"Once, we were down there a little late in the year, farther down." He waves toward the east. "When it gets cold the caribous don't come down to the water like when it's hot. We couldn't just drive along the shore to find them. Water really rough too, boy. So, we camped down by a little river, out of the wind, and had to walk inland to get them, me and my dad and my brother. Like the old days. We got three that one time. Must have walked ten or fifteen miles a day to get them, really had to walk. Mine, we came over a little hill and saw one, about a thousand yards away, in a wet place. I didn't know how to go to it, but my dad, he said to hold up our arms like we had antlers, and walk to it. Every time that one lifted its head, we put ours down like we were getting something to eat. Got to about forty yards before I shot it. After, my dad said he learned that from his dad."

The teens finish their Kraft dinner and Kool-Aid and, without being told, pack up the gear and reload the boat. Edward puts his parka on and pushes the boat out. One nephew unties the line and holds the bow, just touching the gravel of the beach. The other nephew drops the propeller into the water, and Edward starts the engine and lights a cigarette. As his nephew pushes off and hops in, Edward engages the motor, backs around, and slowly turns the bow south, heading for the narrow passage between two islands. He puts the boat on a plane, and they disappear behind the rocks of the far island, heading across for caribou. Stephen and I load our boat, push it into the water, and head our own way back toward Mashuyak and Ulukhaktok beyond.

Glossary of Inuinnaqtun Terms

aaquaq An old woman.

amaun A woman's parka, designed for packing a baby.

angatkuq The Inuinnaqtun word for *shaman*, a reference to the possession or use of spiritual power. Plural is *angatkut*.

arnaruhiq A teenage girl.

audluak A common word meaning to camp or to travel. Often anglicized today as *audluaking*, the proper Inuinnaqtun form is *aullaaqtuq*, "is travelling" or *aulaqtuq*, "has departed."

ayurnarman "It can't be helped," or "You can't do nothing." A phrase used to express that something is beyond an individual's control.

higaaq Cigarette, but commonly referring to marijuana. *Higaaq* is a loan word, from English *cigar*.

hikulaaq Pilot biscuits, hardtack, or ship's biscuits. The term apparently references the propensity of the biscuit to fracture and break, like thin ice, when bitten.

hiun An ear. Dual form is *hiutik*.

iglu House, but usually in reference to a snowhouse.

ihuma Literally, thinking, but generally accepted to mean wisdom or knowledge.

ilumiutaq Fetus.

imiraq The broth in a pot of boiled meat. By custom, Inuit eat the meat out of the pot, then finish the meal by drinking a bowl of the *imiraq*.

inirnikhaq A term corresponding to Canadian and American notions of middle age.

inirniq A life course reference that most closely corresponds to western notions of adulthood.

inuhaat Commonly used today to mean teenagers or young people. Singular form is *inuhaaq*.

Inuinnait People, used in reference to speakers of Inuinnaqtun, often referred to by outsiders as Copper Eskimos or Copper Inuit. Singular is *inuinnaq*.

Inuinnaqtun An indigenous Inuit language, related very closely to Inuktitut.

inummarik A real, or genuine, person. A reference to someone who understands his or her place within the community and the environment and behaves in a manner that maintains a proper balance between them. The plural form of inummarik is *inummariit*.

inutquaq An old man.

inuuhuktuq A teenaged boy.

Inuvialuit People, or Real People, a term used to identify Western Arctic Inuit, but also employed to reference all members of the Western Arctic land claim settlement, who live in the Inuvialuit Settlement Region.

ivitaaruq Spawning char, known as red bellies, because of the colour of their skin. They are prized for their rich taste and high fat content.

kakivak A three-pronged spear, or leister, used for catching fish.

kamiks Skin boots, usually constructed with moosehide soles, the uppers made of seal or caribou skin. Kamiks intended for travelling may also be constructed of canvas uppers. The insides are usually lined with polar fleece or some other fake fur, with the addition of woollen duffel socks. Sheepskin is sometimes employed for sole inserts.

Kangiryuarmiut Literally, People of the Big Sound, a band of Inuinnait who lived and travelled around Prince Albert Sound prior to contact. By the mid-1960s, almost all of these people had relocated to Ulukhaktok. The suffix –*miut* means *people of* and is usually a reference to residence in a particular place.

Kanghiryuatjagmiut The people of Minto Inlet, Inuinnait who lived and travelled around Minto Inlet, northwestern Victoria Island, and southern Banks Island.

kuvyiqtuq A wooden device with a pivoting arm attached to a line, used for setting a net underneath the ice.

mamaq Delicious.

mipku Dried meat. By default, *mipku* refers to dried caribou meat. Ulukhaktomiut also make *mipku* out of muskoxen but refer to it always as *muskox mipku*.

mirraq Baby.

muktuk The skin and blubber of a whale. In Ulukhaktok, *muktuk* is from beluga whales. It is usually eaten raw or boiled, or, less commonly, slightly stinky. Common accompaniments include soy sauce and hot sauce.

naammaktunga "I am well," "I am fine."

napu Crosspieces on a sled, usually made of recycled 2 × 4s or pallet wood.

nattiaq A young ringed seal.

nauna "I don't know."

nauyaat Literally, seagulls, but also a reference to places where seagulls roost, usually cliffs along the ocean.

nukatpihaat Teenagers, though not all Ulukhaktomiut use this term.

nutaraq Child; plural is *nutaqqat*.

paiyuqtuqtuq To carry, in reference to bringing country food to other households in the settlement. Frequently anglicized as "paiyuqtuqing around."

panik Daughter. In Ulukhaktok, often used as a term of address for the eldest daughter in the family.

piffi Dried fish, made by filleting the fish but leaving the fillets attached to the tail, then hanging them over a line or pole to dry.

Puivlingmiut A band of Inuinnait whose original territory was the southern portion of Victoria Island. Many traded at the Hudson's Bay Company post at Read Island. When that post closed, some of this band relocated to Ulukaktok.

Qablunaaq A reference to non-natives, historically believed to be descended from dogs. The Inuinnaqtun plural is *Qablunaat*, but in everyday discourse, the plural is *Qablunaaqs*.

Qanuripit "How are you?" A common greeting in Ulukhaktok.

qingak A hole cut into the wall of a tent or cabin to allow air exchange, supplying fresh air and preventing suffocation.

qingalik King eider duck. Plural, *qingaliit*, though more commonly anglicized to *qingaliks*.

qiviut The soft underhair of a muskox.

quaq Frozen raw meat, usually eaten in small chunks accompanied by tea. The most commonly eaten *quaq* is char and caribou, though some Ulukhaktomiut eat muskoxen as *quaq*.

qulliq The traditional stone lamp used for burning seal oil.

tunnuq Caribou fat, rendered and hardened into a block.

tuuq An ice chisel, a large tool usually made from the leaf spring of a truck suspension and attached to a long wooden handle.

ugyuk A bearded seal.

ulu A traditional semilunar knife, typically used by women. The name Ulukhaktok, "the place where ulu blades are found," refers to the large bluff between Queen's and Jack's Bays, from which stone for making ulus was taken. Once made of stone, today ulus are constructed locally of carbon steel blades with a bone or wooden handle.

uugaq Arctic cod.

Bibliography

Agar, Michael H. 1996. *The Professional Stranger.* 2nd ed. San Diego: Academic Press.

Akiyama, H., T. Antonucci, and R. Campbell. 1990. "Exchange and Reciprocity among Two Generations of Japanese and American Women." In *The Cultural Context of Aging: Worldwide Perspectives,* edited by J. Sokolovsky, 127–42. New York: Bergin & Garvey.

Ames, R., D. Axford, P.J. Usher, E. Weick, and G. Wenzel. 1988. *Keeping on the Land: A Study of the Feasibility of a Comprehensive Wildlife Support Programme in the Northwest Territories.* Ottawa: Canadian Arctic Resources Committee.

Annahatak, Betsy. 1994. "Quality Education for Inuit Today? Cultural Strengths, New Things, and Working Out the Unknowns: A Story by an Inuk." *Peabody Journal of Education* 69, no. 2: 12–18.

Aporta, Claudio, and Eric Higgs. 2005. "Satellite Culture: Global Positioning Systems, Inuit Wayfinding, and the Need for a New Account of Technology." *Current Anthropology* 46, no. 5: 729–53.

Balikci, Asen. 1964. *Development of Basic Socioeconomic Units in Two Eskimo Communities.* Bulletin 202. Ottawa: National Museum of Canada.

– 1970. *The Netsilik Eskimo.* Garden City, NY: Natural History Press.

– 1989. "Ethnography and Theory in the Canadian Arctic." *Etudes/Inuit/Studies* 13, no. 2: 103–11.

Benedict, Ruth. 1934. *Patterns of Culture.* New York: Houghton Mifflin.

Berger, Thomas R. 1977. *Northern Frontier, Northern Homeland: The Report of the Mackenzie Valley Pipeline Inquiry.* 2 vols. Ottawa: Supply and Services Canada.

Berkes, Fikret. 2008. *Sacred Ecology.* 2nd ed. New York: Routledge.

Biesele, Megan. 1997. "The Ju/'hoan Bushmen under Two States: Impacts of the South West African Administration and the Government of the Republic of Namibia." In *Hunters and Gatherers in the Modern World: Conflict, Resistance and Self-Determination,* edited by M. Biesele, R. Hitchcock, and P. Schweitzer, 305–26. Providence, RI: Berghahn Books.

Billson, Janet Mancini. 1990. "Opportunity or Tragedy: The Impact of Canadian Resettlement Policy on Inuit Families." *American Review of Canadian Studies* 20, no. 2: 187–218.

– 2006. "Shifting Gender Regimes: The Complexities of Domestic Violence among Canada's Inuit." *Etudes/Inuit/Studies* 30, no. 1: 69–88.

Billson, Janet Mancini, and Kyra Mancini. 2007. *Inuit Women: Their Powerful Spirit in a Century of Change.* Lanham, MD: Rowman & Littlefield.

Blackman, Margaret B. 1989. *Sadie Brower Neakok: An Inupiaq Woman.* Washington: Douglas & McIntyre.

Bodenhorn, Barbara. 1990. "'I'm Not the Great Hunter, My Wife Is:' Inupiat and Anthropological Models of Gender." *Etudes/Inuit/Studies* 14, nos. 1–2: 55–74.

– 1993. "Gendered Spaces, Public Places: Public and Private Revisited on the North Slope of Alaska." In *Landscape: Politics and Perspectives,* edited by Barbara Bender, 169–203. Providence, RI: Berg.

Bodley, John H., ed. 1987. *Tribal Peoples and Development Issues: A Global Overview.* Mountain View, CA: Mayfield Publishing.

– 2008. *Victims of Progress.* 5th ed. New York: Altamira Press.

Borre, Kristen. 1990. "A Bio-Cultural Model of Dietary Decision Making among North Baffin Island Inuit: Explaining the Ecology of Food Consumption by Native Canadians." PhD thesis, Department of Anthropology, University of North Carolina.

Bosk, Charles L., and Raymond G. de Vries. 2004. "Bureaucracies of Mass Deception: Institutional Review Boards and the Ethics of Ethnographic Research." *Annals of the American Academy of Political and Social Science* 595: 249–63.

Brewer, John D. 2000. *Ethnography.* Philadelphia: Open University Press.

Briggs, Charles. 1986. *Learning How to Ask: A Sociolinguistic Appraisal of the Role of the Interview in Social Science Research.* Cambridge: Cambridge University Press.

Briggs, Jean. 1970. *Never in Anger: Portrait of an Eskimo Family.* Boston: Harvard University Press.

– 1991. "Expecting the Unexpected: Canadian Inuit Training for an Experimental Lifestyle." *Ethos* 19, no. 3: 259–87.

Brody, Hugh. 1975. *The People's Land: Eskimos and Whites in the Eastern Arctic*. New York: Penguin.

Buijs, Cunera. 1993. "The Disappearance of Traditional Meat-Sharing Systems among Some Inuit Groups of Canada and Greenland." In *Continuity and Discontinuity in Arctic Cultures*, edited by Cunera Buijs, 108–35. Leiden: National Museum of Ethnology.

Bumpass, Larry L. 1990. "What's Happening to the Family? Interaction between Demographic and Institutional Change." *Demography* 27, no. 4: 483–98.

Burch, Ernest S. 1975. *Eskimo Kinsmen: Changing Family Relationships in Northwest Alaska*. St Paul, MN: West Publishing.

– 1985. *Subsistence Production in Kivalina, Alaska: A Twenty Year Retrospective*. Technical Paper Series, no. 128. Juneau: Alaska Department of Fish and Game.

– 1994. "The Future of Hunter-Gatherer Research." In *Key Issues in Hunter-Gatherer Research*, edited by E.S. Burch, and L.J. Ellana, 441–55. Oxford: Berg Press.

Burton, Linda M. 1990. "Teenage Childbearing as an Alternative Life-Course Strategy in Multigeneration Black Families." *Human Nature* 1, no. 2: 123–43.

– 1996. "Age Norms, the Timing of Family Role Transitions, and Intergenerational Caregiving among Aging African American Women." *The Gerontologist* 36, no. 2: 199–208.

Burton, Linda M., Peggye Dilworth-Anderson, and Cynthia Merriwether de-Vries. 1995. "Context and Surrogate Parenting among Contemporary Grandparents." *Marriage and Family Review* 20, nos. 3–4: 349–66.

Cesa, Yohann. 2002. "Échange commercial et usages monétaires non-marchands dans le cadre du programme d'aide aux chasseurs du Nunavik." *Etudes/Inuit/Studies* 26, no. 2: 175–86.

Chance, Norman A. 1966. *The Eskimo of North Alaska*. New York: Holt, Rinehart & Winston.

Collier, Richard. 1998. *Masculinities, Crime, and Criminology: Men, Heterosexuality, and the Criminal(ised) Other*. London: Sage.

Collignon, Beatrice. 2006. *Knowing Places: The Inuinnait, Landscapes, and the Environment*. Edmonton: CCI Press.

Collings, Peter. 2000. "Aging and Life Course Development in an Inuit Community." *Arctic Anthropology* 37, no. 2: 111–25.

– 2001. "'If You Got Everything, It's Good Enough': Perspectives on Successful Aging in a Canadian Inuit Community." *Journal of Cross-Cultural Gerontology* 16, no. 2: 127–15.

– 2005. "Housing Policy, Aging, and Life Course Construction in a Canadian Inuit Community." *Arctic Anthropology* 42, no. 2: 50–65.

– 2009a. "Participant Observation and Phased Assertion as Research Strategies in the Canadian Arctic." *Field Methods* 21, no. 2: 133–53.

– 2009b. "Birth Order, Age, and Hunting Success in the Canadian Arctic." *Human Nature* 20, no. 4: 254–74.

– 2011. "Economic Strategies, Community, and Food Networks in Ulukhaktok, NT, Canada. *Arctic* 64, no. 2: 207–19.

Condon, Richard G. 1987. *Inuit Youth: Growth and Change in the Canadian Arctic*. New Brunswick, NJ: Rutgers University Press.

– 1990a. "Adolescence and Changing Family Relations in the Central Canadian Arctic." *Arctic Medical Research* 49: 81–92.

– 1990b. "The Rise of Adolescence: Social Change and Life Stage Dilemmas in the Central Canadian Arctic." *Human Organization* 49, no. 3: 266–79.

– 1992. "Changing Patterns of Conflict Management and Aggression among Inuit Youth in the Canadian Arctic: Longitudinal Ethnographic Observations." *Native Studies Review* 8, no. 2: 35–49.

– 1994. "East Meets West: Fort Collinson, the Fur Trade, and the Economic Acculturation of the Northern Copper Inuit, 1928–1939." *Etudes/Inuit/Studies* 18, nos. 1–2: 109–35.

– 1995. "The Rise of the Leisure Class: Adolescence and Recreational Acculturation in the Canadian Arctic." *Ethos* 23, no. 1: 47–68.

– 1996. *The Northern Copper Inuit: A History*. Norman: University of Oklahoma Press 1996.

Condon, Richard G., and Pamela R. Stern. 1993. "Gender Role Preference, Gender Identity, and Gender Socialization among Contemporary Inuit Youth." *Ethos* 21, no. 4: 384–416.

Condon, Richard G., Peter Collings, and George Wenzel. 1995. "The Best Part of Life: Subsistence Hunting, Ethnicity, and Economic Adaptation among Young Adult Inuit Males." *Arctic* 48, no. 1: 31–46.

Crago, Martha. 1992. "Communicative Interaction and Second Language Acquisition: An Inuit Example." *TESOL Quarterly* 26, no. 3: 487–505.

Crago, Martha, Betsy Annahatak, and Lizzie Ningiuruvik. 1993. "Changing Patterns of Language Socialization in Inuit Homes." *Anthropology and Education Quarterly* 24, no. 3: 205–23.

Crang, Mike, and Ian Cook. 2007. *Doing Ethnographies*. Thousand Oaks, CA: Sage.

Critical Research on Men in Europe (CROME). 2005. "Men, Masculinities, and 'Europe.'" In *Handbook of Studies on Men and Masculinities*, edited by M.S. Kimmel, J. Hearn and R.W. Connell, 141–62. Thousand Oaks, CA: Sage.

Dahl, Jens. 1989. "The Integrative and Cultural Role of Hunting and Subsistence in Greenland." *Etudes/Inuit/Studies* 13, no. 1: 23–42.

– 2003. *Saqqaq*. Toronto: University of Toronto Press.

Damas, David. 1969a. "Characteristics of Central Eskimo Band Structure." In *Contributions to Anthropology: Band Societies*, edited by D. Damas, 116–34. Ottawa: National Museum of Canada Bulletin no. 228.

– 1969b. "Environment, History, and Central Eskimo Society." In *Contributions to Anthropology: Ecological Essays*, edited by D. Damas, 40–64. Ottawa: National Museum of Canada Bulletin 230.

– 1972. "The Copper Eskimo." In *Hunters and Gatherers Today*, edited by M.G. Bicchieri, 3–50. New York: Holt, Reinhart, and Winston.

– 2002. *Arctic Migrants/Arctic Villagers: The Transformation of Inuit Settlement in the Central Arctic*. Montreal and Kingston: McGill-Queen's University Press.

Davies, Charlotte Aull. 2008. *Reflexive Ethnography: A Guide to Researching Selves and Others*. 2nd ed. New York: Routledge.

Dawson, Peter C. 1995. "Unsympathetic Users: An Ethnoarchaeological Examination of Inuit Responses to the Changing Nature of the Built Environment." *Arctic* 48, no. 1: 71–80.

Dorais, Louis-Jacques. 2010. *The Language of the Inuit: Syntax, Semantics, and Society in the Arctic*. Montreal and Kingston: McGill-Queen's University Press.

Dyck, Noel, ed. 1985. *Indigenous Peoples and the Nation-State: 'Fourth World' Politics in Canada, Australia, and Norway*. Social and Economic Papers no. 14. St John's: Memorial University of Newfoundland, Institute of Social and Economic Research.

Elder, Glen H. 1974. *Children of the Great Depression*. Chicago: Chicago University Press.

– 1978. "Family History and the Life Course." In *Transitions: The Family and the Life Course in Historical Perspective*, edited by Tamara K. Harevan, 17–64. New York: Academic Press.

Elder, Glen H., and Susan Bailey. 1988. "The Timing of Military Service in Men's Lives." In *Social Stress and Family Development*, edited by J. Aldais and D.R. Klein, 157–74. New York: Guilford Press.

Elder, Glen H., Jeffrey K. Liker, and Bernard J. Jaworski. 1984. "Hardship in Lives: Depression Influences from the 1930s to Old Age in Postwar America." In *Life Span Developmental Psychology: Historical and Generational Effects*, edited by K.A. McCluskey and H.W. Reese, 161–201. New York: Academic Press.

Fall, James. 1990. "The Division of Subsistence of the Alaska Department of Fish and Game: An Overview of Its Research Program and Findings: 1980–1990." *Arctic Anthropology* 27, no. 2: 68–92.

Fienup-Riordan, Ann. 1983. *The Nelson Island Eskimo: Social Structure and Ritual Distribution*. Anchorage: Alaska Pacific University Press.

– 1986. "The Real People: The Concept of Personhood among the Yupik Eskimos of Western Alaska." *Etudes/Inuit/Studies* 10, no. 1–2: 261–70.

– 1998. "Yup'ik Elders in Museums: Fieldwork Turned on Its Head." *Arctic Anthropology* 35, no. 1: 49–58.

– 2001. "'We Talk to You Because We Love You': Learning from Elders at Culture Camp." *Anthropology and Humanism* 26, no. 2: 173–87.

Flaherty, Martha. 1997. "Inuit Women and Violence." In *Women and the Canadian State*, edited by C. Andrew and S. Rogers, 180–4. Montreal and Kingston: McGill-Queen's University Press.

Fleras, Augie, and Jean Leonard Elliot. 1992. *The Nations Within: Aboriginal-State Relations in Canada, the United States, and New Zealand*. Toronto: Oxford University Press.

Fogel-Chance, Nancy. 1993. "Living in Both Worlds: 'Modernity' and 'Tradition' among North Slope Inupiat Women in Anchorage." *Arctic Anthropology* 30, no. 1: 94–108.

Friedl, Ernestine. 1978. "Society and Sex Roles." *Human Nature* 1, no. 4: 68–75.

Fry, Christine. 1996. "Age, Aging, and Culture." In *Handbook of Aging and the Social Sciences*, 4th ed., edited by R.H. Binstock and L.K. George, 117–36. San Diego: Academic Press.

Fry, Christine, and Jennie Keith. 1982. "The Life Course as a Cultural Unit." In *Aging and Society*, edited by M.W. Wiley, M. Johnson, and A. Foner, 51–71. New York: Russell Sage Foundation.

Gerami, Shahin. 2005. "Islamist Masculinity and Muslim Masculinities." In *Handbook of Studies on Men and Masculinities*, edited by M.S. Kimmel, J. Hearn, and R.W. Connell, 448–57. Thousand Oaks, CA: Sage Publications.

Gold, Raymond L. 1958. "Roles in Sociological Field Observations." *Social Forces* 36, no. 3: 217–23.

Gordon, Elisa J. 2003. "Trials and Tribulations of Navigating IRBs: Anthropological and Biomedical Perspectives of 'Risk' in Conducting Human Subjects Research." *Anthropological Quarterly* 76, no. 2: 299–320.

Graburn, Nelson. 1969. *Eskimos without Igloos: Social and Economic Development in Sugluk*. Boston: Little, Brown.

– 1972. *Eskimos of Northern Canada*. New Haven, CT: HRAF Books.

Grant, Shelagh. 2005. *Arctic Justice: On Trial for Murder, Pond Inlet, 1923*. Montreal and Kingston: McGill-Queen's University Press.

Gubser, N.J. 1965. *The Nunamiut Eskimo: Hunters of Caribou*. New Haven: Yale University Press.

Guemple, Lee. 1983. "Growing Old in Inuit Society. In *Growing Old in Different Societies: Cross-Cultural Perspectives*, edited by Jay Sokolovsky, 24–8. Belmont, CA: Sage.

– 1995. "Gender in Inuit Society." In *Women and Power in Native North America*, edited by Laura F. Klein, and Lillian A. Ackerman, 17–27. Norman: University of Oklahoma Press.

Gurven, Michael, Hillard Kaplan, and Maguin Gutierrez. 2006. "How Long Does It Take to Become a Proficient Hunter? Implications for the Evolution of Extended Development and Long Life Span." *Journal of Human Evolution* 51: 454–70.

Gutmann, Matthew C. 1997. "Trafficking in Men: The Anthropology of Masculinity." *Annual Review of Anthropology* 26: 385–409

Gutmann, Matthew C., and Mara Viveros Vigoya. 2005. "Masculinities in Latin America." In *Handbook of Studies on Men and Masculinities*, edited by M.S. Kimmel, J. Hearn, and R.W. Connell, 114–28. Thousand Oaks, CA: Sage.

Hagestad, Gunhild. 1985. "Age and the Life Course." In *Handbook of Aging and the Social Sciences*, edited by R.H. Binstock and E. Shanas, 35–61. New York: Van Nostrand Reinhold.

– 1990. "Social Perspectives on the Life Course." In *Handbook of Aging and the Social Sciences*, 3rd ed., edited by R.H. Binstock and L.K. George, 151–68. San Diego: Academic Press.

Hammersley, Martyn. 1992. *What's Wrong with Ethnography?* New York: Routledge.

Hammersley, Martyn, and Paul Atkinson. 1983. *Ethnography: Principles in Practice*. New York: Routledge.

Harper, Kenn. 2000. "Inuit Writing Systems in Nunavut." In *Nunavut: Inuit Regain Control of Their Lands and Their Lives*, edited by J. Dahl, J. Hicks, and P. Jull, 154–68. Copenhagen: IWGIA.

Hashimoto, Akiko. 1996. *The Gift of Generations: Japanese and American Perspectives on Aging and the Social Contract*. Cambridge: Cambridge University Press.

Healey, Gwen K., and Lynn M. Meadows. 2007. "Inuit Women's Health in Nunavut, Canada: A Review of the Literature." *International Journal of Circumpolar Health* 66, no. 3: 199–214.

Hearn, Jeff, Keith Pringle, Ursula Müller, et al. 2002. "Critical Studies on Men in Ten European Countries: (1) The State of Academic Research." *Men and Masculinities* 4, no. 4: 380–408.

Hensel, Chase. 1996. *Telling Ourselves: Ethnicity and Discourse in Southwestern Alaska*. Oxford: Oxford University Press.

Herdt, Gilbert H. 1987. *The Sambia: Ritual and Gender in New Guinea*. Fort Worth, TX: Holt, Reinhart, & Winston.

– 1994. *Guardians of the Flutes: Idioms of Masculinity*. Chicago: University of Chicago Press.

Hertz, Rosanna. 1997. *Reflexivity and Voice*. London: Sage.

Hogan, Dennis, and Takashi Mochizuki. 1988. "Demographic Transitions and the Life Course: Lessons from Japanese and American Comparisons." *Journal of Family History* 13, no. 3: 291–305.

Honigmann, John J., and Irma Honigmann. 1965. *Eskimo Townsmen*. Ottawa: St Paul University, Canadian Research Centre for Anthropology.

– 1970. *Arctic Townsmen: Ethnic Backgrounds and Modernization*. Ottawa: St Paul University, Canadian Research Centre for Anthropology.

Hughes, Charles Campbell. 1965. "Under Four Flags: Recent Culture Change among the Eskimos." *Current Anthropology* 6, no. 1: 3–69.

Hungerford, T.L. 2001. "The Economic Consequences of Widowhood on Elderly Women in the United States and Germany." *The Gerontologist* 41, no. 1: 103–10.

Huntingdon, Henry P. 1992. *Wildlife Management and Subsistence Hunting in Alaska*. Seattle: University of Washington Press.

Ikels, Charlotte, Jennie Keith, Jeanette Dickerson-Putnam, et al. 1992. "Perceptions of the Adult Life Course: A Cross-Cultural Analysis." *Ageing and Society* 12, no. 1: 49–84.

Jaimes, Annette, ed. 1992. *The State of Native America: Genocide, Colonization, and Resistance*. Boston: South End Press.

Jenness, Diamond. 1922. *The Life of the Copper Eskimos*. Ottawa: F.A. Acland.

Kamo, Y. 1988. A Note on Elderly Living Arrangements in Japan and the United States. *Research on Aging* 10, no. 2: 297–305.

Kawagley, A. Oscar. 1995. *A Yupiaq Worldview: A Pathway to Ecology and Spirit*. Prospect Heights, IL: Waveland.

Keith, Jennie, Christine L. Fry, Anthony P. Glascock, et al. 1994. *The Aging Experience: Diversity and Commonality across Cultures*. Thousand Oaks, CA: Sage.

Kemp, William B. 1971. "The Flow of Energy in a Hunting Society." *Scientific American* 223, no. 3: 105–15.

Kimmel, Michael S., Jeff Hearn, and R.W. Connell, eds. 2005. *Handbook of Studies on Men and Masculinities*. Thousand Oaks, CA: Sage.

Kohli, Martin. 1986a. "Social Structure and Social Construction of Life Stages." *Human Development* 29: 145–80.

– 1986b. "Social Organization and the Subjective Construction of the Life Course." In *Human Development and the Life Course: Multidisciplinary Perspectives*, edited by A.B. Sorenson, F.E. Weinert, and L.R. Sherrod, 271–92. Hilldale, NJ: Lawrence Erlbaum.

Kruse, Jack. 1986. "Subsistence and the North Slope Inupiat: The Effects of Energy Development." In *Contemporary Alaskan Native Economies*, edited by S.J. Langdon, 121–52. Maryland: University Press of America.

Kruse, John A. 1991. "Alaska Inupiat Subsistence and Wage Employment Patterns: Understanding Individual Choice." *Human Organization* 50, no. 4: 317–26.

Langdon, Steven J. 1991. "The Integration of Cash and Subsistence in Southwest Alaskan Yup'ik Eskimo Traditions." In *Cash, Commoditisation and Changing Foragers*, edited by Nicolas Peterson, and Toshio Matsuyama, 269–91. Osaka: National Museum of Ethnology.

Laugrand, Frederic B., and Jarich G. Oosten. 2010. *Inuit Shamanism and Christianity: Transitions and Transformations in the Twentieth Century*. Montreal and Kingston: McGill-Queen's University Press.

Levine, Martin P. 1998. *Gay Macho: The Life and Death of the Homosexual Clone*. New York: N Y U Press.

Lonner, Thomas D. 1980. *Subsistence as an Economic System in Alaska: Theoretical and Policy Implications*. Technical Paper no. 67. Anchorage: Alaska Department of Fish and Game Division of Subsistence.

Lowe, Ronald. 1983. *Kangiryuarmiut Uqauhingita Numiktittidjutingit: Basic Kargiryuarmiut Eskimo Dictionary*. Inuvik: Committee for Original Peoples Entitlement.

– 1985. *Kangiryuarmiut Uqauhingita Ilihautdjutikhangit: Basic Kargiryuarmiut Eskimo Grammar*. Inuvik: Committee for Original Peoples Entitlement.

Malinowski, Bronislaw. 1929. *The Sexual Life of Savages in North-Western Melanesia: An Ethnographic Account of Courtship, Marriage, and Family Life among the Natives of Trobriand Islands, British New Guinea*. New York: Halcyon House.

Marcus, Alan Rudolph. 1995. *Relocating Eden: The Image and Politics of Inuit Exile in the Canadian Arctic*. Hanover, NH: University Press of New England.

Masquelier, Adeline. 2005. "The Scorpion's Sting: Youth, Marriage, and the Struggle for Social Maturity in Niger." *Journal of the Royal Anthropological Institute* 11, no. 1: 59–83.

Mayer, Karl Ullrich, and W. Müller. 1986. The State and the Structure of the Life Course. In *Human Development and the Life Course: Multidisciplinary Perspectives*, edited by A.B. Sorenson, F.E. Weinert, and L.R. Sherod, 217–45. Hillsdale, N J : Lawrence Erlbaum.

Mayer, Karl Ullrich, and Urs Schoepflin. 1989. "The State and the Life Course." *Annual Review of Sociology* 15: 187–209.

McDonald, Leander R., Richard Ludtke, and Kyle J. Muus. 2005. "Chronic Disease and Functional Limitations among American Indian and Alaska Native Elders." *Journal of Native Aging and Health* 1, no. 1: 7–14.

– 2006. "Health Risk Factors among American Indian and Alaska Native Elders." *Journal of Native Aging and Health* 1, no. 2: 17–24.

McElroy, Ann. 1975. "Canadian Arctic Modernization and Change in Female Inuit Role Identification." *American Ethnologist* 2, no. 4: 662–86.

– 1978. "The Negotiation of Sex-Role Identity in Eastern Arctic Culture Change." *Western Canadian Journal of Anthropology* 6: 184–200.

McNabb, Steven. 1991. "Elders, Iñupiat Ilitqusiat, and Culture Goals in Northwest Alaska." *Arctic Anthropology* 28, no. 2: 63–76.

Mead, Margaret. 1963. *Sex and Temperament in Three Primitive Societies.* New York: Morrow.

Messerschmidt, James W. 1993. *Masculinities and Crime: Critique and Reconceptualization of Theory.* Lanham, MD: Rowman & Littlefield.

Miller, Henry, and Lisa Russell. 2005. "The Personal, Professional, and Political in Comparative Ethnographic Educational Research." *Methodological Issues and Practices in Ethnography* 11: 57–72.

Mitchell, Marybelle. 1996. *From Talking Chiefs to a Native Corporate Elite: The Birth of Class and Nationalism among Canadian Inuit.* Montreal and Kingston: McGill-Queen's University Press.

Morrell, Robert, and Sandra Swart. 2005. "Men in the Third World: Postcolonial Perspectives on Masculinity." In *Handbook of Studies on Men and Masculinities*, edited by M.S. Kimmel, J. Hearn, and R.W. Connell, 90–113. Thousand Oaks, CA: Sage.

Morrow, Phyllis. 1996. "Yup'ik Eskimo Agents and American Legal Agencies: Perspectives on Compliance and Resistance." *Journal of the Royal Anthropological Institute* 2, no. 3: 405–23.

Müller-Wille, Ludger. 1978. "Cost Analysis of Modern Hunting among Inuit of the Canadian Central Arctic." *Polar Gerography* 2, no. 2: 100–14.

Murchison, Julian. 2010. *Ethnography Essentials: Designing, Conducting, and Presenting Your Research.* New York: Wiley.

Myers, Heather. 2000. "Options for Appropriate Development in Nunavut Communities." *Etudes/Inuit/Studies* 24, no. 1: 25–40.

Myers, Heather, and Scott Forrest. 2000. "Making Change: Economic Development in Pond Inlet, 1987 to 1997." *Arctic* 53, no. 2: 134–45.

Nadasdy, Paul. 2003. *Hunters and Bureaucrats: Power, Knowledge, and Aboriginal-State Relations in the Southwest Yukon.* Vancouver: UBC Press.

Nardi, Peter M., ed. 2000. *Gay Masculinities.* Thousand Oaks, CA: Sage.

Nelson, Richard K. 1969. *Hunters of the Northern Ice*. Chicago: University of Chicago Press.

Newman, Katherine. 1996. "Ethnography, Biology, and Cultural History: Generational Paradigms in Human Development." In *Ethnography and Human Development: Context and Meaning in Social Inquiry*, edited by R. Jessor, A. Colby, and R.A. Shweder, 371–93. Chicago: University of Chicago Press.

Nowak, Michael. 1977. "The Economics of Native Subsistence Activities." *Arctic* 30, no. 4: 225–33.

Nuttall, Mark. 1992. *Arctic Homeland: Kinship, Community, and Development in Northwest Greenland*. Toronto: University of Toronto Press.

O'Neil, John. 1983. "Is It Cool to Be an Eskimo? A Study of Stress, Identity, Coping, and Health among Canadian Inuit Young Adult Men." PhD thesis, Department of Anthropology, University of California San Francisco.

– 1986. "Colonial Stress in the Canadian Arctic: An Ethnography of Young Adults Changing." In *Anthropology and Epidemiology: Interdisciplinary Approaches to the Study of Health and Disease*, edited by C.R. Janes, R. Stall, and S.M. Gifford. Dordrecht: Reidel.

Paine, R. 1996. Saami Reindeer Pastoralism and the Norwegian State, 1960s–1990s. *Nomadic Peoples* 38: 125–36.

Perry, Richard J. 1996. *From Time Immemorial: Indigenous Peoples and State Societies*. Austin: University of Texas Press.

Peterson, Nicolas. 1991. "Cash, Commoditisation and Authenticity: When Do Aboriginal People Stop Being Hunter-Gatherers?" In *Cash, Commodification, and Changing Foragers*, edited by N. Peterson and T. Matsuyama, 67–90. Senri Ethnological Series 30. Osaka: National Museum of Ethnology.

Plattner, Stuart. 2003. "Human Subjects Protection and Cultural Anthropology." *Anthropological Quarterly* 76, no. 2: 287–97.

Popenoe, David. 1988. *Disturbing the Nest: Family Change and Decline in Modern Societies*. New York: Aldine Transaction

Quigley, N.C., and N.J. McBride. 1987. "Structure of an Arctic Microeconomy: The Traditional Sector in Community Economic Development." *Arctic* 40, no. 3: 204–210.

Rasing, W.C.E. 1994. *Too Many People: Order and Nonconformity in Iglulingmiut Social Process*. Nijmegen: Recht and Samenleving.

Reimer, Gwen. 1993. "'Community-Based' as a Culturally Appropriate Concept of Development: A Case Study from Pangnirtung, NT." *Culture* 13, no. 2: 67–74.

Riches, David. 1990. "The Force of Tradition in Eskimology." In *Localizing Strategies: Regional Traditions in Ethnographic Writing*, edited by R. Fardon, 71–89. Edinburgh: Scottish Academic Press.

Riley, Matilda White. 1986. "The Dynamisms of Life Stages: Roles, People, and Age." *Human Development* 29, no. 3: 150–6.

Saladin d'Anglure, Bernard. 1986. "Du foetus au chamane, la construction d'un 'troisieme sexe Inuit.'" *Etudes/Inuit/Studies* 10, no. 1–2: 25–113.

– 1992. "Le Troisieme sexe." *La Recherche* 23, no. 245: 836–44.

– 2007. "Troisieme sexe social, atomie familial et meditations chamaniques: Pour une anthropologie holiste." *Anthropologie et Societes* 31, no. 3: 165–84.

Scheper Hughes, Nancy. 1983. *Saints, Scholars, Schizophrenics: Mental Illness in Rural Ireland*. Berkeley: University of California Press.

Searles, Edmund. 2000. "Why Do You Ask So Many Questions? Learning How Not to Ask in a Canadian Inuit Society." *Journal for the Anthropological Study of Human Movement* 11, no. 1: 247–64.

– 2001. "Fashioning Selves and Tradition: Case Studies on Personhood and Experience in Nunavut." *American Review of Canadian Studies* (Spring/Summer): 121–36.

Smith, Eric Alden. 1991. *Inujjuamiut Foraging Strategies*. New York: Aldine de Gruyter.

Smith, Janell, Penelope Easton, Brian L. Saylor, and the Elders from the Alaska Villages of Buckland and Deering. 2009a. "Inupiaq Elders Study: Aspects of Aging among Male and Female Elders." *International Journal of Circumpolar Health* 68, no. 2: 182–96.

Smith, Janell, Penelope Easton, Brian L. Saylor, Dennis Wiedman, and Jim LaBelle, Sr. 2009b. "Harvested Food Customs and Their Influences on Valuable Functioning of Alaska Native Elders." *Alaska Journal of Anthropology* 7, no. 1: 101–21.

Smith, Jannell, Valerie A. George, and Penelope S. Easton. 2001. "Home-Grown Television: A Way to Promote Better Nutrition in a Native Alaskan Community." *Journal of Nutrition Education* 33, no. 1: 59–60.

Smith, Janell, Brian L. Saylor, Penelope Easton, Dennis Wiedman, and the Elders from the Alaska Villages of Buckland and Deering. 2009. "Measurable Benefits of Traditional Food Customs in the Lives of Rural and Urban Alaska Inupiaq Elders." *Alaska Journal of Anthropology* 7, no. 1: 89–99.

Smith, Thomas G., and Harold Wright. 1989. "Economic Status and Role of Hunters in a Modern Inuit Village." *Polar Record* 25, no. 153: 93–8.

Stairs, Arlene. 1992. "Self-Image, World-Image: Speculations on Identity from Experiences with Inuit." *Ethos* 20, no. 1: 116–26.

Stairs, Arlene, and George Wenzel. 1992. "'I am I and the Environment': Inuit Hunting, Community, and Identity." *Journal of Indigenous Studies* 3, no. 1: 2–12.

Stern, Pamela R. 2000. "Subsistence: Work and Leisure." *Etudes/Inuit/Studies* 24, no. 1: 9–24.

Stern, Pamela R., and Richard G. Condon. 1995. "Puberty, Pregnancy, and Menopause: Lifestyle Acculturation in a Copper Inuit Community." *Arctic Medical Research* 54, no. 1: 21–31.

Street, Deborah, and J. Quadagno. 1993. "The State, The Elderly, and the Intergenerational Contract: Toward a New Political Economy of Aging." In *Societal Impact on Aging: Historical Perspectives*, edited by K.W. Schiae and W.A. Achenbaum, 130–50. New York: Springer Publishing.

Stuart, Mary, and E.B. Hansen. 2009. "Danish Home Care Policy and the Family: Implications for the United States." In *Cultural Context of Aging: Worldwide Perspectives*, 3rd ed., edited by J. Sokolovsky, 266–76. Westport, CT: Praeger.

Taga, Futoshi. 2005. "East Asian Masculinities." In *Handbook of Studies on Men and Masculinities*, edited by M.S. Kimmel, J. Hearn, and R.W. Connell, 129–40. Thousand Oaks, CA: Sage.

Tester, Frank, and Peter Kulchyski. 1994. *Tamarniit (Mistakes): Inuit Relocation in the Eastern Arctic, 1939–1963*. Vancouver: UBC Press.

Townsend, Peter. 1981. "Structured Dependency of the Elderly: A Creation of Social Policy in the Twentieth Century." *Ageing and Society* 1, no. 1: 5–28.

Usher, Peter J. 1965. *Economic Basis and Resource Use of the Coppermine-Holman Region, N.W.T.* Ottawa: Department of Northern Affairs and National Resources, Northern Co-ordination and Research Centre.

– 1971. *The Bankslanders: Economy and Ecology of a Frontier Trapping Community*. Vol. 3, *The Community*. NSRG 71-3. Ottawa: Northern Science Research Group, Department of Indian and Northern Affairs and Northern Development.

– 1972. "The Use of Snowmobiles in Trapping on Banks Island." *Arctic* 25, no. 3: 171–81.

– 1976. "Evaluating Country Food in the Northern Native Economy." *Arctic* 29, no. 2: 105–20.

– 2000. *Standard Edible Weights of Harvested Species in the Inuivialuit Settlement Region*. Ottawa: Northern Contaminants Program, Department of Indian Affairs and Northern Development.

Vallee, Frank G. 1962. *Kabloona and Eskimo in the Central Keewatin.* Ottawa: Department of Northern Affairs and National Resources, Northern Coordination and Research Centre.

– 1967. *Povungnetuk and Its Cooperative: A Case Study in Community Change.* Ottawa: Department of Northern Affairs and National Resources, Northern Coordination and Research Centre.

Wachowich, Nancy. 1999. *Saqiyuq: Stories from the Lives of Three Inuit Women.* Montreal and Kingston: McGill-Queen's University Press.

Waldram, James B. 2004. *Revenge of the Windigo: The Construction of the Mind and Mental Health of North Amercian Aboriginal Peoples.* Toronto: University of Toronto Press.

Walker, Robert, Michael Gurven, Kim Hill, et al. 2002. "Age-Dependency in Hunting Ability among the Ache of Eastern Paraguay." *Journal of Human Evolution* 42: 639–57.

Wenzel, George. 1981. *Clyde Inuit Adaptation and Ecology: The Organization of Subsistence.* Ethnology Service Paper 77, Mercury Series. Ottawa: National Museum of Man.

– 1986. "Canadian Inuit in a Mixed Economy: Thoughts on Seals, Snowmobiles, and Animal Rights." *Native Studies Review* 2, no. 1: 69–82.

– 1987. "'I Was Once Independent': The Southern Seal Protest and Inuit." *Anthropologica* 29, no. 2: 195–210.

– 1989. "Sealing at Clyde River, N W T: A Discussion of Inuit Economy." *Etudes/Inuit/Studies* 13, no. 1: 3–22.

– 2000. "The Social Economy of Sharing: Traditional Economics and Modern Hunter-Gatherers." In *The Social Economy of Sharing: Resource Allocation and Modern Hunter-Gatherers*, edited by G. Wenzel, G. Hovelsrud-Broda, and N. Kishigami, 1–6. Senri Ethnological Series No. 53, 2000. Osaka, Japan: National Museum of Ethnology.

– 2001. "'Nunamiut' or 'Kabloonamiut': Which 'Identity' Best Fits Inuit (and Does It Matter)?" *Etudes/Inuit/Studies* 25, nos. 1–2 (2001): 37–52.

Wenzel, George, G. Hovelsrud-Broda, and N. Kishigami, eds. 2000. *The Social Economy of Sharing: Resource Allocation and Modern Hunter-Gatherers.* Senri Ethnological Series No. 53. Osaka, Japan: National Museum of Ethnology.

Wexler, Lisa. 2006. "Inupiat Youth Suicide and Culture Loss: Changing Community Conversations for Prevention." *Social Science and Medicine* 63, no. 11: 2938–48.

Wexler, Lisa, and Brenda Goodwin. 2006. "Youth and Adult Community Member Beliefs about Inupiat Youth Suicide and Prevention." *International Journal of Circumpolar Health* 65, no. 5: 28–38.

Wexler, Lisa, Ryan Hill, Elizabeth Bertone-Johnson, and Andrea Fenaughty. 2008. "Correlates of Suicide and Suicide Attempts in Northwest Alaska." *Suicide and Life-Threatening Behavior* 38, no. 3: 311–20.

White, Richard. 1983. *The Roots of Dependency: Subsistence, Environment, and Social Change among the Choctaws, Pawnees, and Navajos.* Lincoln: University of Nebraska Press.

Wolcott, Harry F. 1999. *Ethnography: A Way of Seeing.* Walnut Creek, CA: Altamira.

Wolfe, Robert J. 1979. "Food Production in a Western Eskimo Population." PhD thesis, Department of Anthropology, UCLA.

Wolfe, Robert J., and R. Walker. 1987. "Subsistence Economies in Alaska: Productivity, Geography, and Development Impacts." *Arctic Anthropology* 24, no. 2: 56–81.

Index